ZAGAT®

America's Top Restaurants 2008

STAFF EDITORS
Shelley Gallagher and Robert Seixas

Published and distributed by
Zagat Survey, LLC
4 Columbus Circle
New York, NY 10019
T: 212.977.6000
E: americastop@zagat.com
www.zagat.com

ACKNOWLEDGMENTS

We thank Claudia Alarcon, Alicia Arter, Olga Boikess, Amanda Boyd, Nikki Buchanan, Lauren Chapin, Suzi Forbes Chase, Ann Christenson, Elaine Cicora, Bill Citara, Andrea Clurfeld, Gabrielle Cosgriff, Camas Davis, Lorraine Gengo, Jeanette Foster, Rona Gindin, Sharon Gintzler, Meesha Halm, Judith Hausman, Lynn Hazlewood, Edie Jarolim, Lena Katz, Marty Katz, Michael Klein, Rochelle Koff, Gretchen Kurz, Karen Lipson, Sharon Litwin, Lori Midson, Maryanne Muller, David Nelson, Jan Norris, Angela Pettera, Joe and Ann Pollack, Virginia Rainey, Laura Reiley, Mike Riccetti, Heidi Knapp Rinella, Julia Rosenfeld, Shelley Skiles Sawyer, Helen Schwab, Merrill Shindler, Jane Slaughter, Robert Strauss, Ruth Tobias, John Turiano, Alice Van Housen, Carla Waldemar and Kay Winzenried, as well as the following members of our staff: Chris Miragliotta (editorial project manager), Amy Cao (editorial assistant), Caitlin Eichelberger (editorial assistant), Sean Beachell, Maryanne Bertollo, Catherine Bigwood, Sandy Cheng, Reni Chin, Larry Cohn, Bill Corsello, Carol Diuguid, Deirdre Donovan, Alison Flick, Jeff Freier, Curt Gathje, Michelle Golden, Randi Gollin, Caroline Hatchett, Karen Hudes, Roy Jacob, Natalie Lebert, Mike Liao, Christina Livadiotis, Allison Lynn, Dave Makulec, Rachel McConlogue, Andre Pilette, Josh Rogers, Becky Ruthenburg, Troy Segal, Carla Spartos, Kelly Stewart, Kilolo Strobert, Donna Marino Wilkins, Liz Borod Wright, Yoji Yamaguchi, Sharon Yates and Kyle Zolner.

Contents

Ratings & Symbols

Zagat Top Spot	Name	Symbols	Cuisine	Zagat Ratings			
				FOOD	DECOR	SERVICE	COST

Area, Address & Contact	☒ **Tim & Nina's** ◑ *Chinese* ▽ 23 | 9 | 13 | $15
	W 50s | 4 Columbus Circle (8th Ave.) | 212-977-6000 | www.zagat.com

Review, surveyor comments in quotes	"You're the tapas" croon connoisseurs of the "cheap" cart-circulated Chinese-Castilian cuisine at this "cramped" concrete-clad Columbus Circle compound; to the contrary, critics claim Tim and Nina "push the concept too far" with dishes such as sweet-and-sour sardines, Szechuan ceviche and Beijing-Barcelona bouillabaisse, with service that comes from Spain in the '30s and China in the '60s.

Ratings   **Food, Decor** and **Service** are rated on a scale of 0 to 30.

0 – 9	poor to fair
10 – 15	fair to good
16 – 19	good to very good
20 – 25	very good to excellent
26 – 30	extraordinary to perfection
▽	low response | less reliable

Cost reflects our surveyors' average estimate of the price of a dinner with one drink and tip and is a benchmark only. Lunch is usually 25% less.

For **newcomers** or survey **write-ins** listed without ratings, the price range is indicated as follows:

I	$25 and below
M	$26 to $40
E	$41 to $65
VE	$66 or more

Symbols

☒	Zagat Top Spot (highest ratings, popularity and importance)
◑	serves after 11 PM
☒	closed on Sunday
Ⓜ	closed on Monday
⇎	no credit cards accepted

About This Survey

Here are the results of our **2008 America's Top Restaurants Survey,** covering 1,416 places across the country. Like all our guides, it's based on the collective opinions of thousands of savvy local consumers who have been there before you (i.e. it represents the diner's point of view). This guide's coverage of the top restaurants in 42 major markets manifests the fact that dining throughout America just keeps getting better and better.

WHO PARTICIPATED: Input from over 132,000 frequent diners forms the basis for the ratings and reviews in this guide (their comments are shown in quotation marks within the reviews). Of these surveyors, 47% are women, 53% men; the breakdown by age is 9% in their 20s; 26%, 30s; 22%, 40s; 24%, 50s; and 19%, 60s or above. Collectively they bring roughly 23 million annual meals worth of experience to this Survey. We sincerely thank each of these participants – this book is really "theirs."

HELPFUL LISTS: While all the restaurants in this guide were chosen for their high quality, we have prepared two separate lists to facilitate your search: see Top Food Rankings by Area (pages 7-9) and Most Popular by Area (pages 10-12). We've also provided various handy indexes.

OUR TEAM: We especially thank our editors, Shelley Gallagher and Robert Seixas, for their hard work; this is the second edition of this guide that they have collaborated on. Thanks also to the many in-house and local contributors without whom this book would not be possible.

ABOUT ZAGAT: This marks our 29th year reporting on the shared experiences of consumers like you. What started in 1979 as a hobby involving 200 of our friends has come a long way. Today we have well over 300,000 surveyors and now cover dining, entertaining, golf, hotels, movies, music, nightlife, resorts, shopping, spas, theater and tourist attractions worldwide.

SHARE YOUR OPINION: We invite you to join any of our upcoming surveys – just register at **zagat.com,** where you can rate and review establishments year-round. Each participant will receive a free copy of the resulting guide when published.

AVAILABILITY: Zagat guides are available in all major bookstores, by subscription at **zagat.com** and for use on a wide range of Web-enabled mobile devices via **Zagat To Go** or **zagat.mobi.** Either of the latter two products will allow you to contact any restaurant by phone with one click.

FEEDBACK: There is always room for improvement, thus we invite your comments and suggestions about any aspect of our performance. Just contact us at **americastop@zagat.com.**

New York, NY
October 26, 2007

Nina and Tim Zagat

What's New

No question, American diners expect more from the restaurants they visit these days, especially with the average cost of a meal at $33.29 ($72.08 for a meal among the most expensive places), and 67% paying more than they did two years ago. In turn, the industry – particularly the nation's best restaurants – has responded by offering more creativity and better quality.

HEALTH KICK: Healthier, more environmentally conscious food is being incorporated into menus across the country. Good thing, since heart-friendly options are important to 69% of surveyors, and 65% want to see trans fats abolished from restaurants nationwide.

 GOING GREENER: The farm-to-table movement that began with Berkeley's Chez Panisse 36 years ago has spread to the nation's most notable kitchens. It has become almost definitional for a top toque to cultivate relationships with local growers, raise vegetables in a backyard garden or even become a farmer himself (as at Blue Hill at Stone Barns in Pocantico Hills, NY). The fact is great food depends on having the freshest ingredients, and customers can taste the difference: a full 59% say they'd pay more for food that's sustainably procured.

SERVICE CHECKUP: Given that 70% of our surveyors nationwide say service trumps all other irritants when dining out, it's clear that front-of-the-house hospitality remains the industry's weakest link. Nevertheless, tipping has edged upwards over the years, from a national average of around 18% in 2002 to 19% today (just one percentage point shy of the 'Golden 20%' that staffs hope for). Go figure.

NEIGHBORHOOD NOSHING: Representing one of the restaurant industry's greatest areas of expansion, casual eateries can now be found on nearly every corner in every U.S. city. Often run by young culinary grads or chefs from abroad, these unpretentious options receive little press but have much to do with why Americans, on average, eat out or take away 51% of all meals.

DOWNSIZED DISHES: The prevailing mood for a dressed-down experience has helped fuel the rise of small-plates dining. The boon to restaurants is they can market menu flexibility and informality on the correct notion that patrons will order more – and thus pay more.

CHEMICALLY ENHANCED: For the most part, cooking's recent Age of Enlightenment can be traced directly to Spain's El Bulli restaurant, and to its chef, the great Ferran Adrià. His influence in the U.S. is most noticeable in Chicago, at places such as Alinea and Avenues, two exemplars of so-called 'molecular gastronomy.' Although there have been many unsuccessful attempts at this Adrià-ized cooking, a number of American chefs, while eschewing the extreme, are cleverly using a chemical arsenal to make foie gras powder or, say, to gelatinize consommé to replace the pasta in their 'fettuccine carbonara.'

New York, NY
October 26, 2007

Nina and Tim Zagat

Top Food Rankings by Area

ATLANTA
29 Bacchanalia
28 Quinones Room
  Rathbun's
  Ritz/Buckhead Din. Rm.
27 Aria

ATLANTIC CITY
27 SeaBlue
  White House
26 Chef Vola's
  Mia
  Dock's Oyster

AUSTIN
28 Vespaio
  Wink
  Hudson's
27 Jeffrey's
  Musashino Sushi

BALTIMORE/ANNAPOLIS
28 Sushi Sono
  Joss Cafe/Sushi
27 Charleston
  Samos
  Peter's Inn

BOSTON
28 L'Espalier
  Oishii
  Clio/Uni
27 No. 9 Park
  Aujourd'hui

CHARLOTTE
29 Barrington's
28 Volare
27 McIntosh's
  Sullivan's
26 Nikko

CHICAGO
29 Carlos'
28 Les Nomades
  Tru
  Alinea
  Tallgrass

CINCINNATI
29 Jean-Robert at Pigall's
28 Daveed's at 934
27 Boca
  Nicola's
  BonBonerie

CLEVELAND
29 Chez François
28 Downtown 140
27 Three Birds
  Johnny's Bar
  Lola

CONNECTICUT
29 Thomas Henkelmann
28 Cavey's
  Le Petit Cafe
  Ibiza
27 Jean-Louis

DALLAS/FT. WORTH
29 French Room
28 York Street
  Abacus
  Aurora
  Lola

DENVER AREA
28 Mizuna
  Frasca
  Fruition
  Sushi Den
27 Sushi Sasa

DETROIT
28 Lark, The
27 Bacco
  Zingerman's
  Tribute
  Beverly Hills Grill

FT. LAUDERDALE
27 Cafe Maxx
  La Brochette
  Eduardo de San Angel
  Casa D'Angelo
26 Cohiba

HONOLULU
28 Alan Wong's
27 La Mer
26 Hoku's
  Roy's
  Chef Mavro

HOUSTON
28 Mark's American
27 Da Marco
  Brennan's
  Bistro Moderne
  Pappas Bros.

KANSAS CITY

27 Bluestem
26 Oklahoma Joe's
   Le Fou Frog
   Tatsu's
   40 Sardines

LAS VEGAS

28 Rosemary's
   Lotus of Siam
27 Nobu
   Picasso
   Michael Mina

LONG ISLAND

28 Kotobuki
   Maroni Cuisine
27 Kitchen à Bistro
   North Fork Table & Inn
   Jedediah's

LOS ANGELES

28 Mélisse
   Nobu Malibu
   Asanebo
27 Matsuhisa
   Brandywine

MIAMI

28 Michy's
27 Palme d'Or
   Nobu Miami Beach
   Romeo's Cafe
   Prime One Twelve

MILWAUKEE

29 Sanford
26 Eddie Martini's
   Five O'Clock Steak
   Immigrant Room
   Bacchus

MINNEAPOLIS/ST. PAUL

28 La Belle Vie
   112 Eatery
   Alma
   Bayport Cookery
27 Lucia's

NEW JERSEY

29 Nicholas
28 DeLorenzo's
   Chef's Table
   Cafe Panache
   Bay Avenue Trattoria

NEW ORLEANS

28 August
   Brigtsen's
   Bayona
   Stella!
   Alberta

NEW YORK CITY

28 Daniel
   Sushi Yasuda
   Le Bernardin
   Per Se
   Peter Luger

ORANGE COUNTY, CA

28 Basilic
   Stonehill Tavern
27 Tradition by Pascal
   Napa Rose
   Hobbit, The

ORLANDO

27 Le Coq au Vin
   Victoria & Albert's
   Chatham's Place
   Del Frisco's
   Taquitos Jalisco

PALM BEACH

27 Chez Jean-Pierre
   Marcello's La Sirena
   L'Escalier
   Four Seasons
   Little Moirs

PHILADELPHIA

28 Fountain
   Le Bar Lyonnais
   Birchrunville Store
   Le Bec-Fin
   Vetri

PHOENIX/SCOTTSDALE

28 Pizzeria Bianco
   Sea Saw
27 Binkley's
   Barrio Cafe
   T. Cook's

PORTLAND, OR

27 Paley's Place
   Genoa
   Apizza Scholls
26 Higgins
   Heathman

SALT LAKE CITY AREA
27 Takashi
   Mariposa, The
26 Red Iguana
   Shabu
   Mazza

SAN ANTONIO
28 Le Rêve
27 Lodge/Castle Hills
26 Korean B.B.Q. House
   Biga on the Banks
   Bistro Vatel

SAN DIEGO
27 WineSellar & Brasserie
   Sushi Ota
   Pamplemousse Grille
   Arterra
   A.R. Valentien

SAN FRANCISCO AREA
29 Gary Danko
   French Laundry
28 Cyrus
   Erna's Elderberry
   Fleur de Lys

SEATTLE
28 Herbfarm, The
   Nishino
   Lampreia
   Rover's
   Mistral

ST. LOUIS
28 Sidney Street Cafe
   Paul Manno's
27 Tony's
   Trattoria Marcella
   Niche

TAMPA/SARASOTA
28 Cafe Ponte
27 Restaurant B.T.
   Beach Bistro
   SideBern's
26 Mise en Place

TUCSON
28 Dish, The
26 Vivace
   Grill at Hacienda del Sol
   Le Rendez-Vous
   Cafe Poca Cosa

WASHINGTON, DC
29 Inn at Little Washington
28 Makoto
   Citronelle
   Marcel's
27 Eve

WESTCHESTER/HV
29 Xaviar's at Piermont
28 Freelance Café
27 Blue Hill/Stone Barns
   Rest. X/Bully
   Aroma Osteria

Most Popular by Area

ATLANTA
1. Bacchanalia
2. Rathbun's
3. Bone's
4. Chops/Lobster Bar
5. Aria

ATLANTIC CITY
1. P.F. Chang's
2. Chef Vola's
3. Old Homestead
4. White House
5. Dock's Oyster

AUSTIN
1. Chuy's
2. Salt Lick
3. Eddie V's
4. Vespaio
5. Uchi

BALTIMORE/ANNAPOLIS
1. Clyde's
2. Ruth's Chris
3. Prime Rib
4. Charleston
5. McCormick & Schmick's

BOSTON
1. Legal Sea Foods
2. Blue Ginger
3. Hamersley's Bistro
4. L'Espalier
5. No. 9 Park

CHARLOTTE
1. Barrington's
2. Upstream
3. Mickey & Mooch
4. Bonterra
5. Palm

CHICAGO
1. Charlie Trotter's
2. Tru
3. Frontera Grill
4. Wildfire
5. Morton's

CINCINNATI
1. Jean-Robert at Pigall's
2. Montgomery Inn
3. Jeff Ruby's Steak
4. JeanRo
5. Nicola's

CLEVELAND
1. Lola
2. Blue Point
3. fire food & drink
4. Parallax
5. Three Birds

CONNECTICUT
1. Thomas Henkelmann
2. Frank Pepe
3. Barcelona
4. Coromandel
5. Jean-Louis

DALLAS/FT. WORTH
1. Abacus
2. Del Frisco's
3. Mi Cocina
4. Mansion on Turtle Creek
5. Café Pacific

DENVER AREA
1. Frasca
2. Sweet Basil
3. Mizuna
4. rioja
5. Barolo Grill

DETROIT
1. Zingerman's
2. Lark, The
3. Tribute
4. Beverly Hills Grill
5. Common Grill

FT. LAUDERDALE
1. Blue Moon Fish
2. Casa D'Angelo
3. Mark's Las Olas
4. Eduardo de San Angel
5. Greek Islands Taverna

HONOLULU
1. Alan Wong's
2. Roy's
3. Hoku's
4. La Mer
5. Duke's Canoe Club

HOUSTON
1. Mark's American
2. Cafe Annie
3. Carrabba's Italian
4. Pappas Bros.
5. Brennan's

KANSAS CITY
1. Fiorella's Jack Stack
2. Plaza III
3. Lidia's
4. McCormick & Schmick's
5. 40 Sardines

LAS VEGAS
1. Picasso
2. Aureole
3. Delmonico Steak
4. Bellagio Buffet
5. Prime Steak

LONG ISLAND
1. Peter Luger
2. Bryant & Cooper
3. Cheesecake Factory
4. Kotobuki
5. West End Cafe

LOS ANGELES
1. Spago
2. A.O.C.
3. Café Bizou
4. Water Grill
5. Mélisse

MIAMI
1. Joe's Stone Crab
2. Prime One Twelve
3. Nobu Miami Beach
4. Blue Door
5. Barton G.

MILWAUKEE
1. Maggiano's
2. P.F. Chang's
3. Sanford
4. Lake Park Bistro
5. Potbelly Sandwich*

MINNEAPOLIS/ST. PAUL
1. Oceanaire
2. 112 Eatery
3. Manny's
4. La Belle Vie
5. Vincent

NEW JERSEY
1. Nicholas
2. Cheesecake Factory
3. Legal Sea Foods
4. River Palm
5. Amanda's

NEW ORLEANS
1. Galatoire's
2. Bayona
3. NOLA
4. Emeril's
5. Brennan's

NEW YORK CITY
1. Union Square Cafe
2. Gramercy Tavern
3. Le Bernardin
4. Babbo
5. Jean Georges

ORANGE COUNTY, CA
1. Napa Rose
2. French 75
3. Roy's
4. Sage
5. Fleming's Prime

ORLANDO
1. California Grill
2. Emeril's Orlando
3. Seasons 52
4. Victoria & Albert's
5. Wolfgang Puck Café

PALM BEACH
1. Kee Grill
2. Abe & Louie's
3. Café Boulud
4. Chez Jean-Pierre
5. New York Prime

PHILADEPHIA
1. Buddakan
2. Le Bec-Fin
3. Fountain
4. Lacroix/Rittenhouse
5. Brasserie Perrier

PHOENIX/SCOTTSDALE
1. T. Cook's
2. Roy's
3. P.F. Chang's
4. Mary Elaine's
5. Mastro's Steak

PORTLAND, OR
1. Higgins
2. Andina
3. Paley's Place
4. Wildwood
5. Bluehour

SALT LAKE CITY AREA
1. Market Street
2. Red Iguana
3. Bambara
4. Cucina Toscana
5. New Yorker Club

SAN ANTONIO

1. Paesanos
2. Le Rêve
3. Biga on the Banks
4. Boudro's on the Riverwalk
5. P.F. Chang's

SAN DIEGO

1. George's Cal. Modern
2. Pamplemousse Grille
3. Marine Room
4. Roppongi
5. Ruth's Chris

SAN FRANCISCO AREA

1. Gary Danko
2. Boulevard
3. Slanted Door
4. French Laundry
5. Michael Mina

SEATTLE

1. Wild Ginger
2. Dahlia Lounge
3. Metropolitan Grill
4. Canlis
5. Cafe Juanita

ST. LOUIS

1. Sidney Street Cafe
2. Annie Gunn's
3. 1111 Mississippi
4. Trattoria Marcella
5. Tony's

TAMPA/SARASOTA

1. Bern's Steak
2. Columbia
3. Roy's
4. SideBern's
5. Bijou Café

TUCSON

1. Cafe Poca Cosa
2. Grill at Hacienda del Sol
3. Terra Cotta
4. Wildflower
5. Janos

WASHINGTON, DC

1. Kinkead's
2. Citronelle
3. Jaleo
4. Zaytinya
5. TenPenh

WESTCHESTER/HV

1. Blue Hill/Stone Barns
2. Xaviar's at Piermont
3. Crabtree's
4. Harvest on Hudson
5. Rest. X/Bully

RESTAURANT DIRECTORY

Atlanta

	Restaurant	Cuisine
29	Bacchanalia	American
28	Quinones Room	American
	Rathbun's	American
	Ritz/Buckhead Din. Rm.	French/Mediterranean
27	Aria	American
	Bone's	Steak
	Tamarind Seed	Thai
	Park 75	American
	di Paolo	Italian
26	Floataway Cafe	French/Italian
	MF Sushibar	Japanese
	McKendrick's Steak	Steak
	Taka	Japanese
	Nan Thai	Thai
	Chops/Lobster Bar	Seafood/Steak
	JOËL	French
	La Grotta	Italian
	Madras Saravana	Indian/Vegetarian
	New York Prime	Steak
	Restaurant Eugene	American

OTHER NOTEWORTHY PLACES

Antica Posta	Italian
Atlanta Fish Market	Seafood
BluePointe	American
Canoe	American
Ecco	Continental
Eurasia Bistro	Pan-Asian
French American Brasserie	American/French
Georgia Grille	Southwestern
Kyma	Greek/Seafood
Muss & Turner's	American/Deli
ONE. midtown	American
Shaun's	American
Sia's	Asian/Southwestern
Sotto Sotto	Italian
South City Kitchen	Southern
TAP	American
Tierra	Pan-Latin
Trois	French
Watershed	Southern
Woodfire Grill	Californian

	FOOD	DECOR	SERVICE	COST

Antica Posta *Italian*

24 | 20 | 21 | $43

Buckhead | 519 E. Paces Ferry Rd. (Piedmont Rd. NE) | 404-262-7112 | www.anticaposta.com

"Tuscany, here I come" say fans who feel "transported" to the region by this Buckhead Northern Italian where the "expertly prepared" fare is "simplicity at its finest"; though the space is "a bit cramped", the "cozy" atmosphere makes it a "favorite" for a date and the staff will have you feeling "like you're the only one" in the place; to skeptics, though, the service is only "so-so" and the food "doesn't match the price tag"; N.B. it now serves lunch on Saturdays.

☑ Aria ☒ *American*

27 | 25 | 25 | $51

Buckhead | 490 E. Paces Ferry Rd. (Maple Dr.) | 404-233-7673 | www.aria-atl.com

"Gerry Klaskala continues to be at the top of his game" at this Buckhead "beauty" where he creates "amazing" New American cuisine "with a soul", while pastry chef Kathryn King's desserts are some of the "best in town"; the "gorgeous" space (which includes a "cozy" patio) has recently been renovated, and though the scene can get "way too loud" at times, "superb" service makes "you feel like a million bucks"; it's "expensive" too, but "you get what you pay for."

Atlanta Fish Market *Seafood*

23 | 19 | 20 | $38

Buckhead | 265 Pharr Rd. NE (bet. Peachtree St. & Piedmont Rd.) | 404-262-3165 | www.buckheadrestaurants.com

"If it swims, you can get it" at this "seafood lover's paradise" from the Buckhead Life Group, where an "unrivaled selection" of "schools upon schools" of "fabulous fish" flown in fresh three times daily is prepared "any way imaginable"; you can almost "feel the ocean breezes" in the "welcoming" "nautical" setting, though "even with reservations" it can be a "two-glasses-of-wine wait" when it's packed with as "many tourists" as on a "Carnival Cruise"; regulars recommend eating here primarily for "business" or "group" dining.

☑ Bacchanalia ☒ *American*

29 | 25 | 28 | $77

Westside | Westside Mktpl. | 1198 Howell Mill Rd. (bet. 14th St. & Huff Rd.) | 404-365-0410 | www.starprovisions.com

"Any conversation about Atlanta's best" must include this "seamless" Westside New American – voted the city's Most Popular and No. 1 for Food – with a "big-time wow factor" that "could make a rainy Tuesday seem like a special occasion"; "husband-and-wife-team" Anne Quatrano and Clifford Harrison's "focused" cuisine guarantees "gastronomic ecstasy" that's a "bargain despite the price", and though the "refined" warehouse space has a "laid-back" feel, the "sublime" service ("choreographed like a ballet") is evidence of its "top-tier status."

BluePointe *American*

24 | 26 | 21 | $47

Buckhead | 3455 Peachtree Rd. (Lenox Rd.) | 404-237-9070 | www.buckheadrestaurants.com

Everything about this New American "marvel" on the "ground floor of a Buckhead high-rise" is "gorgeous", from the "sleek" and "modern" dining room with a lofty "ceiling in the clouds" to the "pure artistry" of "Asian-inflected", "fish-heavy" cuisine that "hits the right note" to the "electric" lounge scene crackling with "celebrities, VIPs" and "beautiful women"; despite grumbles about servers with "attitude" and "gold diggers" "hoarding the bar", it's still a "shining star" on the city's "glitterati" dining scene.

☑ Bone's Restaurant *Steak*   27 | 22 | 26 | $55
Buckhead | 3130 Piedmont Rd. (Peachtree Rd.) | 404-237-2663 | www.bonesrestaurant.com
"Impeccable" right "down to the bone", this "carnivore central" in Buckhead delivers a "wow experience" "time and again" with "classic" steaks "Fred Flintstone would die for", "generous sides", "big, cold drinks" and a "phone book" of a wine list; "polished" servers and "fabulous bartenders" "take excellent care" of the crowd of "serious business-lunchers", "power players" and others in a "plush red", "old-world" setting that's "drenched in testosterone" as well as "tremendous history and personality" – this "local legend lives on."

Canoe *American*   25 | 26 | 24 | $46
Vinings | Vinings on the River | 4199 Paces Ferry Rd. (Chattahoochee River) | 770-432-2663 | www.canoeatl.com
In a "beautifully landscaped" setting "on the banks of the Chattahoochee River", this Vinings "favorite" has ambiance that "goes on for days" while its "adventuresome" chef Carvel Grant Gould "successfully navigates" the dining scene with "stunning" New American cuisine that's heavy on "Southern hunter's fare"; "impeccable" service adds to an experience so "romantic" that dating doyens declare "if you don't get lucky after going here, then it's time to end the relationship."

☑ Chops/Lobster Bar *Seafood/Steak*   26 | 24 | 24 | $55
Buckhead | Buckhead Plaza | 70 W. Paces Ferry Rd. (Peachtree Rd.) | 404-262-2675 | www.buckheadrestaurants.com
A "bit of heaven on earth" for "carnivores and their fish-loving brethren", this "spectacular" Buckhead Life Group production offers "exemplary" steaks and "unbeatable seafood" plus a "phenomenal wine list" and "pampering" service that "makes you feel like royalty"; there's a bar scene peopled by the "'in' crowd" in the "elegant", "man's man" chophouse upstairs, while the "dungeon of deliciousness" below boasts an "awesome" "Grand Central Station"–inspired look.

di Paolo Ⓜ *Italian*   27 | 21 | 25 | $37
Alpharetta | Rivermont Sq. | 8560 Holcomb Bridge Rd. (Nesbit Ferry Rd.) | 770-587-1051 | www.dipaolorestaurant.com
For its "loyal army of regulars", this "magnificent obsession" is "worth the drive to the end of the earth" (i.e. Alpharetta) for "superb" Northern Italian creations from an open kitchen that'll "knock your socks off" plus "impeccable" service; there's a "surprise with every detail" in the "relaxing" dining room, and though the "old strip-mall location doesn't do it justice", for many it's the "perfect choice for any occasion"; N.B. a post-Survey redo is not reflected in the above Decor score.

Ecco *Continental*   - | - | - | M
Midtown | 40 Seventh St. NE (Cypress St.) | 404-347-9555 | www.ecco-atlanta.com
The Fifth Group (South City Kitchen) offers a fresh take on the neighborhood restaurant with this casual Continental housed in a former fencing club in Midtown; chef Micah Willix's simple, seasonal small

and large plates are served in a Johnson Studio–designed space that combines modern and old world with a blend of marble, leather and dark walnut, and includes several dining areas, an expansive lounge and an outdoor patio.

Eurasia Bistro ⑤ *Pan-Asian* · 25 | 23 | 24 | $30

Decatur | 129 E. Ponce de Leon Ave. (bet. Church St. & Clairmont Ave.) | 404-687-8822 | www.eurasiabistro.net

For a "slice of calm in the middle of Decatur", head to chef/co-owner Wendy Chang's "refined" restaurant where a menu with "no bad options" features "fabulous presentations" of Pan-Asian cuisine (including "fish cooked to perfection"); it's a "pleasure to be waited on" by the "spectacular" staff in a "sophisticated", "romantic" setting that "makes you feel like you're Downtown" with its "upscale" ambiance.

Floataway Cafe ⑤Ⓜ *French/Italian* · 26 | 22 | 24 | $43

Emory | Floataway Bldg. | 1123 Zonolite Rd. NE (bet. Briarcliff & Johnson Rds.) | 404-892-1414 | www.starprovisions.com

Locals "never tire of" this "foodies' delight", the "more informal" sibling of Bacchanalia and Quinones Room that wins praise for "deceptively simple" yet "stunning" French-Italian cuisine emphasizing "local organic produce", an "eclectic" wine list and "gracious" service; nestled in an "oasis of artists' studios" near Emory, the "sleek" space with "ethereal curtains" cultivates an "energetic" vibe – if they could "just get rid of the noise", it "would be the perfect place."

French American Brasserie ⑤ *American/French* · – | – | – | M
(aka F.A.B.)

Downtown | 30 Ivan Allen Jr. Blvd. (W. Peachtree St.) | 404-266-1440 | www.fabatlanta.com

Fans of the late Brasserie Le Coze take note: chef Kaighn Raymond has returned from NYC (where he trained with Le Bernardin's Eric Ripert) to take the kitchen reins at this Downtown restaurant offering an expansive menu of New American and French brasserie fare; cheery tiles, lampposts and columns were resurrected from the original venue, and the expansive multilevel art nouveau space also includes street level and rooftop outdoor dining.

Georgia Grille Ⓜ *Southwestern* · 24 | 18 | 20 | $33

South Buckhead | Peachtree Sq. | 2290 Peachtree Rd. NE (bet. Peachtree Hills Ave. & Peachtree Memorial Dr.) | 404-352-3517 | www.georgiagrille.com

Namesake "Georgia O'Keeffe would have loved" chef-owner Karen Hilliard's "comfy" South Buckhead eatery where you can "always count on" "delightful", "well-thought-out" Southwestern dinner fare, including "to-die-for" lobster enchiladas; a "low turnover in staff" "ensures" "amazing service", and the "cozy" space (graced with works by the eponymous artist) is particularly "good for a date."

JOËL ⑤Ⓜ *French* · 26 | 26 | 24 | $58

Buckhead | The Forum | 3290 Northside Pkwy. NW (W. Paces Ferry Rd.) | 404-233-3500 | www.joelrestaurant.com

Joël Antunes is a "true artist" creating "brilliant" French cuisine in the "lavishly appointed kitchen" of his Buckhead establishment; the food is paired with a "formidable" wine list and service that strikes a few as "snooty" but nevertheless "superb", which may explain why most keep this "standout" "high on their list for special occasions"; still, "perfection" may not be "for the faint of pocketbook"; P.S. an August 2007 redo has transformed the "stunning" interior into an intimate dining room with fewer than 50 seats.

Kyma 🛇 Greek/Seafood   25 | 24 | 23 | $47

Buckhead | 3085 Piedmont Rd. NE (E. Paces Ferry Rd.) | 404-262-0702 | www.buckheadrestaurants.com

"I didn't know Atlanta was on the coast" gush groupies about this "brilliant conceptualization" of an "upscale Greek taverna" from the Buckhead Life Group, where "simple preparations" of the "freshest fish" "allow" the "flavors to shine", and an "amazing wine program" complements "marvelous meze"; plus, a "polished" staff delivers "wonderful" service in a "gorgeous" space, making the "expense-account" experience "worth every penny."

La Grotta 🛇 Italian   26 | 22 | 25 | $49

Buckhead | 2637 Peachtree Rd. NE (bet. Lindbergh Dr. & Wesley Rd.) | 404-231-1368
Dunwoody | Crowne Plaza Ravinia Hotel | 4355 Ashford Dunwoody Rd. (Hammond Dr.) | 770-395-9925
www.lagrottaatlanta.com

"La Grade A" is what aficionados call this "anniversary-worthy" duo where "fabulous" Northern Italian cuisine that "never disappoints" and "exemplary" service from a "professional" staff represent "fine dining at its very best"; an "older, affluent crowd" is unfazed by the Buckhead original's "strange basement location", enjoying a "sense of calm" and "great acoustics" during dinner, while the Dunwoody off-shoot (which also serves lunch) provides an "elegant", "plush" setting overlooking a garden and waterfalls.

Madras Saravana Bhavan Indian/Vegetarian   26 | 10 | 14 | $15

Decatur | North Dekalb Sq. | 2179 Lawrenceville Hwy. (N. Druid Hills Rd.) | 404-636-4400 | www.madrassaravanabhavan.net

Faithful fans wish they had "more arms than Vishnu to shovel in all the wonderful delights" at this "superb vegetarian" Indian in Decatur offering "incredible", "extremely spicy" fare at "affordable prices"; service can be a "crapshoot" and the decor resembles something like "tiki hut meets" the subcontinent, but aficionados just "close their eyes" and "wallow in the smells and tastes" that "take you to India for the price of three coffees from Starbucks."

McKendrick's Steak House Steak   26 | 21 | 25 | $52

Dunwoody | Park Place Shopping Ctr. | 4505 Ashford Dunwoody Rd. NE (bet. Hammond Dr. & Perimeter Ctr.) | 770-512-8888 | www.mckendricks.com

This "high-end" "power" spot in Dunwoody "competes with the best of Buckhead" via "fabulous" steaks that are "worth the cholesterol", "huge", "tasty sides", an "impressive wine list" and "wonderful" "old-fashioned" service that "makes you feel special"; the atmosphere is "vibrant" (and a "little noisy") in "quintessential" steakhouse surroundings of "dark oak" and "white tablecloths" – just be sure to "bring lots of money" because "everything's à la carte."

MF Sushibar *Japanese*

26	23	21	$39

Midtown | 265 Ponce de Leon Ave. (Penn Ave.) | 404-815-8844 |
www.mfsushibar.com

At this Midtown Japanese serving what surveyors call the "best sushi in town", "lovingly prepared" offerings of "amazingly fresh" fish are "literally art" and the "fresh wasabi" is "not to be missed"; located in a "wonderfully renovated section" of Ponce, the "modern" space attracts crowds of "hip", "eye-appealing" types (the "cool factor is high"), so "make reservations" and be prepared to "pay extra" or "forget about eating here."

Muss & Turner's ⊠ *American/Deli*

25	19	23	$17

Smyrna | 1675 Cumberland Pkwy. (S. Atlanta Rd.) | 770-434-1114 |
www.mussandturners.com

"These guys know their stuff" aver admirers of this "gourmet" deli/restaurant in Smyrna; during the day, it dishes out "amazing" (albeit "pricey") sandwiches that "always hit the spot" and has arguably the "coolest takeaway", but it goes full-service in the evenings, when a menu of New American small plates and entrees is offered; "witty" menu descriptions can "make deciding difficult", but the "helpful" "owners and employees love their work" "and it shows."

Nan Thai Fine Dining *Thai*

26	27	24	$41

Midtown | 1350 Spring St. NW (17th St.) | 404-870-9933 |
www.nanfinedining.com

This "smoothly sexy" "high-end" Midtown Thai (and Tamarind Seed sibling) is "like a trip to Bangkok without the airfare" thanks to a "dazzlingly dramatic" Johnson Studio–designed space that simply "gushes Asian sophistication and charm" ("even the restroom is gorgeous"); the cuisine is "art on your plate" that's delivered with "impeccable" grace by a "gorgeous" staff, making it "an experience you don't want to miss" and what some call the "best place" to "impress your friends, clients or in-laws."

New York Prime *Steak*

26	22	24	$57

Buckhead | Monarch Tower | 3424 Peachtree Rd. NE (Lenox Rd.) |
404-846-0644 | www.newyorkprime.com

"Oh yeah, baby" crow carnivores who "rejoice" over this "prime" Buckhead chain link that's "rising in the ranks" with "perfect" steaks that "melt in your mouth", side dishes "to die for" and a "phenomenal" wine list; the "special occasion"– and "expense account"–worthy experience is set in a "masculine" space where there's a staff of "real pros" with "attention to detail" and "a happening happy hour" ("better not mind cigar smoke").

ONE. midtown kitchen *American*

21	25	20	$38

Midtown | 559 Dutch Valley Rd. (Monroe Dr.) | 404-892-4111 |
www.onemidtownkitchen.com

At this Midtown "favorite", New American dishes are paired with a "reasonable" wine list, while an "attentive" staff adds to a "stylish" "see-and-be-seen" "scene" that morphs from "geriatric" to "glitterati" as the evening progresses; plus, the "beautiful" Johnson Studio–designed space includes a recently spruced-up patio; N.B. the post-Survey arrival of chef Tom Harvey is not reflected in the Food score.

Park 75 *American*

27 | 25 | 28 | $60

Midtown | Four Seasons Atlanta | 75 14th St. (bet. Peachtree &
W. Peachtree Sts.) | 404-253-3840 | www.fourseasons.com

The "elegant" Four Seasons "lives up to its image" with this "flawless"
New American showcasing the "extraordinary flavors" of chef Robert
Gerstenecker's "sublime" cuisine, including a "beyond-belief brunch";
the service is "off the charts", mapping "power meals" for "neighborhood lawyers, bankers, headhunters" and other "who's who" guests
who gather in the "handsomely appointed" room; P.S. the "divine"
chef's table in the kitchen is a "fantastic experience."

☑ Quinones Room at Bacchanalia ⑤Ⓜ *American*

28 | 27 | 28 | $122

Westside | Courtyard of Bacchanalia | 1198 Howell Mill Rd. (bet. 14th St. &
Huff Rd.) | 404-365-0410 | www.starprovisions.com

Bacchanalia may have "one-upped" itself with this "truly remarkable"
prix fixe–only "experience" in the same Westside complex, where "every bite" of the New American cuisine offers an "unforgettably superb
taste" and "fantastic wine pairings" "won't disappoint"; "impeccable",
"synchronized" service and a "gorgeous", "intimate" room with "won-
derful linens" add to the "$$$'s no object special-occasion" ambiance
that's "worth every penny" according to fans, who feel it should be on
everyone's "once-before-I-die list."

☑ Rathbun's ⑤ *American*

28 | 25 | 25 | $45

Inman Park | Stove Works | 112 Krog St. NE (bet. Edgewood Ave. &
Irwin St.) | 404-524-8280 | www.rathbunsrestaurant.com

"The raves are true" about this "trendy but not pretentious" New
American in a "refurbished industrial area" of Inman Park: it "leaves
the hip pretenders in the dust" thanks to Kevin Rathbun's "spectacu-
lar", "visually appealing" "creations" that offer "something for every-
one" and "every budget", topped off with "small and perfect"
desserts; daily "hand-scrawled" menus and "homey" "greetings from
the man himself" are part of the "charming" service, and the "beauti-
ful" "rehabbed stove plant" resonates with a "lively" vibe (but "bad
acoustics") that "makes life seem glam and fun."

Restaurant Eugene *American*

26 | 25 | 24 | $56

South Buckhead | The Aramore | 2277 Peachtree Rd.
(Peachtree Memorial Dr.) | 404-355-0321 | www.restauranteugene.com

"Tradition and innovation pat each other on the back" in the kitchen of
this "first-class" New American in South Buckhead, where the
"husband-and-wife duo has got it going on" with a "constantly chang-
ing menu" of "fresh", Southern-accented fare emphasizing "local" in-
gredients and an "impressive boutique wine list"; "impeccable"
service "makes everyone feel welcome" in the "beautiful" "quiet"
room, and satisfied surveyors even say it's "a pleasure to pay the bill."

☑ Ritz-Carlton Buckhead Dining Room ⑤Ⓜ *French/Mediterranean*

28 | 27 | 28 | $82

Buckhead | Ritz-Carlton Buckhead | 3434 Peachtree Rd. NE (Lenox Rd.) |
404-237-2700 | www.ritzcarlton.com

Near "perfect from beginning to end", this "elegant" Buckhead "grande
dame" showcases New French–Med cuisine from chef Arnaud Berthelier

that "holds a universe of remarkable", "simply unforgettable" flavors; the green damask setting with "cozy" booths is another "treat for the senses", but what will really "make you feel like a Rockefeller" is a "kind" and "impeccable" staff, including a "knowledgeable" sommelier who is "helpful" with her "wine novella" and "the best maitre d' in town"; N.B. jackets required.

Shaun's Ⓜ *American*

| | | | M |

Inman Park | 1029 Edgewood Ave. (Hurt St. NE) | 404-577-4358 | www.shaunsrestaurant.com

Foodies have already taken notice of this cozy, creative Inman Park bistro where chef-owner Shaun Doty produces heartfelt but moderately priced New American cuisine; a sense of simplicity pervades the 'lodge-chic' setting (courtesy of the Johnson Studio), a space that's been pared down to painted brick, a rustic communal table and an open kitchen; N.B. closed Mondays and Tuesdays.

Sia's Ⓩ *Asian/Southwestern*

| 26 | 22 | 24 | $45 |

Duluth | 10305 Medlock Bridge Rd. (Wilson Rd.) | 770-497-9727 | www.siasrestaurant.com

For "cutting-edge" cuisine "without the drive to Buckhead", aficionados recommend owner Sia Moshk's "wonderfully inventive" Asian-Southwestern in Duluth, an oasis of "flair and finesse" "in the midst of the big box chains" that delivers a "little spice" to the 'burbs; a "friendly" staff provides "consistent" service in an "attractive" "art deco"–inspired room – in short, they "do it all well."

Sotto Sotto *Italian*

| 26 | 19 | 21 | $37 |

Inman Park | 313 N. Highland Ave. NE (Elizabeth St.) | 404-523-6678 | www.sottosottorestaurant.com

"Riccardo Ullio continues to set the bar" high for "elegant" Northern Italian cuisine with "dazzling performances in the kitchen" of his "super trattoria" that's the "highlight of Inman Park", where "heavenly" dishes are paired with a "well-chosen" wine list and the signature chocolate soup dessert is "divine"; the "courteous" service "seduces with small touches", "acoustical ceiling tiles" have "improved the din" in the "cozy" space and there's also a "nifty little" patio.

South City Kitchen *Southern*

| 24 | 20 | 21 | $35 |

Smyrna | 1675 Cumberland Pkwy. (Atlanta Rd. SE) | 770-435-0700
Midtown | 1144 Crescent Ave. NE (14th St.) | 404-873-7358
www.southcitykitchen.com

"Dixie meets Manhattan" at this "upscale" Midtown venue from the Fifth Group (Ecco), a "long-term member of the can't-miss club" for fans of its "magnificent" "eclectic" Southern cuisine with a "new accent" that's brought to table by a "knowledgeable" staff; the renovated "old house" with a "trendy urban groove" can get "crowded" and "loud", but it's "worth enduring for the food"; N.B. the Smyrna location opened post-Survey.

Taka Ⓩ *Japanese*

| 26 | 14 | 21 | $38 |

Buckhead | 375 Pharr Rd. NE (Grandview Ave.) | 404-869-2802
"Insiders" are tickled by the "hilarious" e-mails they receive from chef-owner Taka Moriuchi, an "absolute delight" who turns out "artistic" sushi and "sashimi that will make your head swim" at his Buckhead

Japanese; even the "waiters are a joy" and "good about making recommendations" in the "small" venue that's "never crowded", making this one of the "best in town – without the attitude."

Tamarind Seed Thai Bistro Thai

| 27 | - | 23 | $32 |

Midtown | Colony Sq. | 400 Colony Sq. (bet. 14th St. & Peachtree St.) | 404-873-4888 | www.tamarindseed.com

"As genuine as the best in Bangkok", this "off-the-charts" Midtown Thai (and elder sibling of Nan) serves "perfect" "beautifully presented" cuisine that's "worth every penny", and an "impeccable staff" delivers "tip-top" service that "leaves an impression"; though it's made a move to a new location down the street, odds are you'll still "see famous golfers", as "it's a favorite of Masters champions."

TAP ● American

| - | - | - | I |

Midtown | Hines Bldg. | 1180 Peachtree St. NE (14th St.) | 404-347-2220 | www.tapat1180.com

The latest from restaurant wizard Bob Amick and his Concentrics group (ONE. midtown kitchen, Trois), this multilevel gastropub is already mobbed with Midtowners eager to pair New American bar fare with a global suds selection; the digs are done up in bright reds and stainless steel, with a glass-enclosed wine and beer vault above the bar and a bustling 1,800-sq.-ft. patio facing out onto Peachtree Street.

Tierra ⊠Ⓜ Pan-Latin

| 25 | 18 | 25 | $34 |

Midtown | 1425B Piedmont Ave. NE (Westminster Dr.) | 404-874-5951 | www.tierrarestaurant.com

Take a "superb" "culinary tour of South America" at this Midtown Pan-Latin where "knowledgeable and passionate owners" Ticha and Dan Krinsky "carefully" craft an "ever-changing seasonal menu" of "superb" dishes "with great integrity" (the signature tres leches cake is "to die for") that's matched with an "intriguing" wine list; the "itty-bitty" space near the Botanical Garden is unimposing from the outside, but the "pleasant bistro atmosphere" and "great" outdoor patio are "conducive to a comfortable evening."

Trois French

| - | - | - | E |

Midtown | 1180 Peachtree St. NE (14th St.) | 404-815-3337 | www.trois3.com

This polished Midtown offering from the Concentrics group (ONE. midtown kitchen, TAP) swings into full Gallic gear with white-clad servers delivering superstar chef Jeremy Lieb's New French cuisine; in keeping with the name, sweeping staircases link three floors: a top-story event space, a mid-tier dining room with artwork suspended from poles and a street-level bar with aluminum flooring that's pierced to let light stream into the room.

Watershed Southern

| 25 | 19 | 21 | $30 |

Decatur | 406 W. Ponce de Leon Ave. (Commerce Dr.) | 404-378-4900 | www.watershedrestaurant.com

"Superb hardly sums up" chef Scott Peacock's "whimsical, chic and nostalgic" "interpretations of Southern fare" at this "asset to Atlanta's dining scene" in Decatur, where cognoscenti caution "stay out of our way" on Tuesday nights, the only time the "best fried chicken in town" is served (topped off by the "best damn chocolate cake ever"); a "great

FOOD DECOR SERVICE COST

staff" serves a "diverse clientele" in the "minimalist" (some say "cold") converted gas station space, and while wags dub the "pricey" affair "'Walletshed'", most agree it "never disappoints."

Woodfire Grill *Californian*

FOOD	DECOR	SERVICE	COST
24	21	22	$41

Cheshire Bridge | 1782 Cheshire Bridge Rd. NE (Piedmont Ave.) | 404-347-9055 | www.woodfiregrill.com

This Cheshire Bridge "altar to fresh food" is a "foodie's paradise" where chef Michael Tuohy's "outstanding" "homage to Californian cuisine", including a "tremendous cheese plate" and a "delectable wine list" that's "half price on Sundays", is served by an "attentive" staff in a "softly lit" space redolent with the "lovely smell of a wood fire"; while some smolder over "expensive" "small portions", most agree this "crowd-pleaser" is "burning up the competition" and its more "casual" cafe is "quite a bargain."

FOOD | DECOR | SERVICE | COST

Atlantic City

TOP FOOD RANKING

	Restaurant	Cuisine
27	SeaBlue	Seafood
	White House	Sandwiches
26	Chef Vola's	Italian
	Mia	Italian
	Dock's Oyster	Seafood

OTHER NOTEWORTHY PLACES

Old Homestead	Steak
Ombra	Italian
P.F. Chang's	Chinese
Specchio	Italian
Wolfgang Puck/Grille	American

Z Chef Vola's M ⌀ *Italian* 26 | 10 | 23 | $49

111 S. Albion Pl. (Pacific Ave.) | 609-345-2022

Although you "take one look and stare in disbelief" at the decor, when the Italian "food comes out you'll understand" why this cash-only, 86-year-old Atlantic City basement BYO is a "cult" classic for so many admirers; true, it may not be the "best-kept secret it once was", but you still have to "know someone" to get a reservation.

Z Dock's Oyster House *Seafood* 26 | 20 | 23 | $49

2405 Atlantic Ave. (Georgia Ave.) | 609-345-0092 | www.docksoysterhouse.com

Since 1897, this "venerable" Atlantic City seafood house has been a picture of "consistency", turning out "fantastic" fin fare that begins with "impeccably fresh" fish and includes the "best" oysters, all in a "wonderful", wood-filled room; P.S. the extensive selection at the raw bar is "everything you could ask for."

Z Mia M *Italian* 26 | 23 | 23 | $58

Caesars on the Boardwalk | 2100 Pacific Ave. (S. Arkansas Ave.) | 609-441-2345 | www.miaac.com

"Georges Perrier has done it again!" with this Caesars Italian where Philly's most celebrated chef has teamed up with protégé Chris Scarduzio to create "unbelievable" fare supported by "tip-top" servers in an airy setting; thanks to who's behind this "great" addition, the "quality is as you'd expect", as perhaps is the "arm-and-a-leg" pricing.

Z Old Homestead *Steak* 25 | 24 | 23 | $68

Borgata Hotel, Casino & Spa | 1 Borgata Way (Atlantic City Expwy., exit 1) | 609-317-1000 | www.theborgata.com

"Heavy eating" is necessary at this Borgata Hotel, Casino & Spa chophouse (a satellite of the NYC legend) that sends out "some of the best slabs of beef you've ever seen" into a "beautiful" space adorned with art deco touches; "hit the jackpot" before arriving, but thanks to "excellent" service, you'll feel "like a high roller" anyway.

Ombra ⓜ Italian
25 | 27 | 22 | $52

Borgata Hotel, Casino & Spa | 1 Borgata Way (Atlantic City Expwy., exit 1) | 866-692-6742 | www.theborgata.com

Capturing the ambiance of a wine cellar, albeit one that's as "beautiful" as it is "comfortable", this Borgata Italian features stone, wood and glass decor, "fantastic" cooking from executive chef Luke Palladino and an "amazing" vino selection sourced from some of Italy's smaller producers; it all goes down well, as long as you're ready for the "pricey" bills; N.B. closed Mondays and Tuesdays.

⚡ P.F. Chang's China Bistro ❶ Chinese
21 | 21 | 19 | $31

The Quarter at the Tropicana | 2801 Pacific Ave. (Iowa Ave.) | 609-348-4600 | www.pfchangs.com

Hordes "go out of their way" to sample the "delicious food" at this somewhat "high-end" (but "loud") Chinese that's AC's Most Popular eatery; there are "long, long waits", but you can always "take advantage of the full-service bar" for "unusual drinks" and "great appetizers"; in short, it's a "formula" but "the formula works."

⚡ SeaBlue Seafood
27 | 25 | 25 | $73

Borgata Hotel, Casino & Spa | 1 Borgata Way (Atlantic City Expwy., exit 1) | 609-317-8220 | www.theborgata.com

Michael Mina, the celebrated chef of the eponymous San Francisco restaurant, has landed in the Borgata with this "clear winner" whose "extremely fresh" and "incredibly" prepared wood-grilled seafood earns it the top rating for Food in AC; a "well-developed" wine list and Adam Tihany's "beautiful" room also help to ensure that this expense-account addition is an undeniable "home run."

Specchio ⚡ⓜ Italian
25 | 25 | 24 | $63

Borgata Hotel, Casino & Spa | 1 Borgata Way (Atlantic City Expwy., exit 1) | 609-317-1000 | www.theborgata.com

An "ethereal" experience awaits at this Borgata Italian where chef Luke Palladino's cuisine is "nothing short of outstanding" (and features "fresh" vegetarian options) and where tables are spaced "far enough apart" to lend a "romantic" ambiance to the "beautiful" room; the consensus: "double down your bet – this one's worth the chips."

⚡ White House ⊟ Sandwiches
27 | 7 | 15 | $13

2301 Arctic Ave. (Mississippi Ave.) | 609-345-1564

"Sub lovers" surrender to the "world's best" hoagies at this all-day South Jersey "legend" (since 1946) where the service is "gruff, the meat ain't tough" and "unreal" bread makes the sandwiches "great"; once you've tasted the goods, you'll understand the "crazed" scene and the "lines down the street."

Wolfgang Puck American Grille American
23 | 23 | 21 | $50

Borgata Hotel, Casino & Spa | 1 Borgata Way (Atlantic City Expwy., exit 1) | 609-317-1000 | www.theborgata.com

"Don't ever leave!" is what enthusiasts demand of Wolfgang Puck, whose arrival at the Borgata brings plaudits for his "oh-so-good" New American lunch and dinner fare; designer Tony Chi has divided the "cool" space into two distinct dining areas: one a "wonderful" tavern and the other for more formal meals; "regardless of where you sit", however, it's a "real winner"; N.B. closed on Tuesdays.

Austin

TOP FOOD RANKING

	Restaurant	Cuisine
28	Vespaio	Italian
	Wink	American
	Hudson's	American
27	Jeffrey's	American
	Musashino Sushi	Japanese
	Aquarelle	French
	Mirabelle	American
	Fonda San Miguel	Mexican
	Driskill Grill	American
26	Uchi	Japanese

OTHER NOTEWORTHY PLACES

Restaurant	Cuisine
Bess	Eclectic
Chuy's	Tex-Mex
Cibo	Italian
Eddie V's	Seafood
Fino	Mediterranean
Jasper's	American
Salt Lick	BBQ
Starlite	American
TRIO	Seafood/Steak
Zoot	American

Aquarelle 🚫Ⓜ *French*   27 | 26 | 26 | $54

Downtown | 606 Rio Grande St. (W. 6th St.) | 512-479-8117 |
www.aquarellerestaurant.com

"Enjoy a leisurely dinner" of "exquisite", "expensive" fare with "layer upon layer of flavor" at this "romantic" "French gem" set in a "beautiful" "old Downtown Austin home"; not only does the "authentic" Classic and Provençal cuisine attain a "wonderful" level of "refinement", but the "attentive", "knowledgeable" staff provides "outstanding service" and "will offer sublime pairing suggestions" from the "excellent wine list", making it "the place to go to celebrate special occasions" – or to "take your future parents-in-law."

Bess *Eclectic*   - | - | - | M

Downtown | 500 W. Sixth St. (San Antonio St.) | 512-477-2377 |
www.bessbistro.com

Set in the basement of a Downtown apartment building, actress Sandra Bullock's casual Eclectic is loaded with historic charm; executive chef Brenton Childs' menu features comfort and bistro standards that are executed with elegant flair and easily paired with one of the bar's signature cocktails or a selection from the ample wine list.

Ⓩ Chuy's *Tex-Mex*   21 | 21 | 19 | $16

Great Hills | 11680 Research Blvd. (Duval Rd.) | 512-342-0011
North Austin | 10520 N. Lamar Blvd. (Meadows Dr. N.) | 512-836-3218

(continued)

Chuy's

Zilker | 1728 Barton Springs Rd. (Lamar Blvd.) | 512-474-4452
Round Rock | 2320 I-35 N. (W. Old Settlers Blvd.) | 512-255-2211
www.chuys.com

"Elvis meets Tex-Mex" – "emphasis on the Tex" – at this chain of "green-chile" meccas rated Most Popular among Austin restaurants; it "always hits the spot" with "young" types who willingly "endure long waits" to revel in its "raucous" atmosphere and "kitschy decor" while downing "delicious margaritas"; speaking of those "strong" libations, it's also "notable" for the "international fame" it achieved when "the Bush twins were busted for underage drinking" at the flagship location in the city's Zilker neighborhood.

Cibo ⊠ *Italian*   – | – | – | E

Downtown | 918 Congress Ave. (10th St.) | 512-478-3663 |
www.ciborestaurant.com

The latest from local chef Will Packwood, this Downtown Italian is housed in a vintage brick space that's been refurbished with a minimalist aesthetic and hung with abstract paintings, resulting in a welcoming, relaxed atmosphere; its ever-changing menu of innovative fare is built around fresh local and seasonal ingredients and backed by an impressive selection of wines from The Boot.

Driskill Grill ⊠Ⓜ *American*   27 | 26 | 26 | $52

Downtown | Driskill Hotel | 604 Brazos St. (6th St.) | 512-391-7162 |
www.driskillgrill.com

Lauders "love everything about" this "upscale classic" nestled in a "Texas landmark", Downtown's "historic Driskill Hotel"; the kitchen "does wonders", "combining beautiful presentations and amazing flavors in every course" of the "exquisite" New American cuisine, which is "impeccably served" by a "top-notch" staff in an "elegant" room "decorated with no-holds-barred Western-luxury style"; sure, it's "expensive, but it's worth it" "to splurge" on a "magnificent experience" that's "sublime from start to end."

⊠ Eddie V's Edgewater Grille *Seafood*   25 | 24 | 24 | $42

Arboretum | 9400 Arboretum Blvd. (N. Capital of Texas Hwy.) |
512-342-2642
Downtown | 301 E. Fifth St. (San Jacinto Blvd.) | 512-472-1860
www.eddiev.com

Though primarily seafood focused, the "extensive menu" of "consistently" "delicious" fare at this pair of "upscale (but not uptight)" "high-end winners" sports "great steaks too"; the Arboretum outpost boasts "great views", while the Downtown location is "dark, jazzy and intimate", but both offer "outstanding service" and an "excellent wine list" – plus one of "the best happy-hour deals in town", including bargain "half-priced appetizers."

Fino ⊠ *Mediterranean*   23 | 25 | 23 | $36

West Campus | 2905 San Gabriel St. (29th St.) | 512-474-2905 |
www.finoaustin.com

"Modern, minimalist decor" that's both "casual and chic" makes for a "welcoming atmosphere" at this "hip" player in the "West Campus cuisine scene"; also "inviting" is the "inventive" Med menu featuring

	FOOD	DECOR	SERVICE	COST

"fresh ingredients" in "simple, flavorful" preparations, which are served with "interesting mixed drinks" and "wonderful" wines by a "personable staff"; P.S. "when the temperature dips below 100 degrees", the "great" outdoor seating is "hard to beat."

Fonda San Miguel *Mexican* | 27 | 27 | 24 | $34

Highland Park | 2330 W. North Loop Blvd. (Hancock Dr.) | 512-459-4121 | www.fondasanmiguel.com

"The huge antique wooden doors signal that you're entering another world" at this "charming", "upscale" Highland Park "landmark" known for "divine" regional cuisine featuring "authentic dishes from all parts of Mexico"; set in "a building resembling a hacienda", with a "lovely bar and inside courtyard", it's a "stunning and dramatic yet festive and relaxed" destination; P.S. though pricey, its "legendary" Sunday brunch makes for "an exceptional end to a visit by out-of-towners."

☑ Hudson's on the Bend *American* | 28 | 23 | 25 | $44

Lakeway | 3509 Ranch Rd. 620 N. (Texas St.) | 512-266-1369 | www.hudsonsonthebend.com

"All of God's creatures have a place on this earth, and if Hudson's had its way, it would be next to the mashed potatoes" claim carnivores crowing about this "upscale" New American in Lakeway (about a 30-minute drive from Austin), a bastion of "inventive" "Hill Country haute cuisine" that's known as the "best destination for wild game" around; "expect excellence" in all aspects, including "a unique setting" with "rustic" decor and a patio that's "a divine place to dine under the Texas sky"; P.S. "bring friends, family and a fat wallet."

Jasper's *American* | - | - | - | E

Northwest Austin | The Domain | 11506 Century Oaks Terr. | 512-834-4111 | www.jaspers-restaurant.com

Located in an upscale Northwest Austin shopping center, this New American addition offers the gourmet backyard cuisine of celebrity chef Kent Rathbun (of Dallas' Abacus) in a modern, comfortable interior; the staff is always ready to offer menu suggestions and wine pairings from an ample list, and patrons can sip signature cocktails as they people-watch on the breezy patio.

☑ Jeffrey's *American* | 27 | 23 | 27 | $51

Clarksville | 1204 W. Lynn St. (12th St.) | 512-477-5584 | www.jeffreysofaustin.com

For "a really special night out", this "cozy culinary haven" in Clarksville is a "perennial" "fine-dining" "favorite", with a "friendly staff" offering "impeccable service"; its "take on Texas cuisine" renders "palate-pleasing presentations" of near-"flawless" New American fare ("the tasting menu is not to be missed"), enhanced by "excellent wine" pairings and a "casual setting" that's both "intimate and romantic."

Mirabelle ☒ *American* | 27 | 21 | 24 | $32

Northwest Hills | 8127 Mesa Dr. (bet. Spicewood Springs Rd. & Steck Ave.) | 512-346-7900 | www.mirabellerestaurant.com

Situated "in a strip mall" in Northwest Hills, this New American is "a true treasure" thanks to "plentiful portions" of "creative" seasonal cuisine and "generous pours" "at reasonable prices", plus "unique pairings" that provide "the average person" a chance to "try new things and learn about wines"; the "cool, arty decor" "defines casual elegance", and the "knowledgeable staff" adds to the "well-crafted dining experience", making it "a great alternative to Downtown."

☑ Musashino Sushi Dokoro Ⓜ *Japanese* — 27 | 18 | 19 | $32

Northwest Hills | 3407 Greystone Dr. (Mo-Pac Expwy.) | 512-795-8593 |
www.musashinosushi.com

"Tucked away on the first floor" of a Northwest Hills building, this Japanese establishment is "one of the best" spots for sushi in Austin, known for "fantastic", "fresh" Tokyo-style raw fin fare; the "talented chefs" will make you feel like you've "stepped into Japan" thanks to their "unique" offerings, including "incredible rolls" and "off-the-menu specials", although some surveyors are "rankled" by the "hostile staff", quipping they've "met friendlier kamikaze pilots."

☑ Salt Lick *BBQ* — 25 | 20 | 20 | $19

Driftwood | 18300 FM 1826 (FM 967) | 512-858-4959 |
www.saltlickbbq.com

☑ Salt Lick 360 *BBQ*

West Lake Hills | Davenport Vill. | 3801 N. Capital of Texas Hwy.
(Westlake Dr.) | 512-328-4957 | www.saltlickthreesixty.com

"Even a New Yorker will feel like a cowboy" at these "classic" meat meccas; "a tradition" since 1969, the Driftwood original features a "casual" Hill Country setting with "family-style" service on "picnic tables" ("it's BYO" too), while the West Lake Hills outpost is "as close to upscale BBQ as it gets", with "inventive" cuisine and a "nice wine list", but both are "a real experience for out-of-towners."

Starlite *American* — 25 | 25 | 23 | $38

Warehouse District | 407 Colorado St. (4th St.) | 512-374-9012 |
www.starliteaustin.net

"Starlite, star brite, eat and drink your fill tonight" say surveyors savoring another visit to this "sophisticated" eatery in the Warehouse District, where the New American cuisine is "divine" and the chef has an enviable "sensibility for food, flavor and matching ingredients"; you can also "trust your server and your bartender to delight you" with their "excellent" ministrations, including suggestions on choosing from the list of "unique drinks."

TRIO *Seafood/Steak* — - | - | - | E

Downtown | Four Seasons Hotel | 98 San Jacinto Blvd. (1st St.) |
512-685-8300 | www.fourseasons.com

After a complete makeover, the dining room at the Four Seasons has reopened as this vibrant, contemporary restaurant where longtime executive chef Elmar Prambs puts forth a new menu that's anchored by the classics: fresh seafood and prime steaks with an emphasis on local and seasonal ingredients; a floor-to-ceiling wine wall holds the offerings from a well-crafted list (including flights of two-ounce pours), and diners can also sit out on the terrace to take in the views of Lady Bird Lake.

☑ Uchi *Japanese* — 26 | 27 | 24 | $40

Zilker | 801 S. Lamar Blvd. (Barton Springs Rd.) | 512-916-4808 |
www.uchiaustin.com

"Superlatives don't do justice" to the "amazing fusion flavors" featured in the "inventive" Japanese cuisine at this Zilker "mecca for foodies", an "oasis of culinary fun and adventure" that's "outstanding in every way" thanks to the "creative genius" of "soon-to-be celebrity chef Tyson Cole", whose "always-fresh" dishes "truly are art"; the "sumptuous", "chic" interior is also a "nice mix of formal and casual", so though it's "expensive, it's really worth" it for such a "world-class sushi experience."

☑ Vespaio Ⓜ *Italian* — 28 | 23 | 25 | $36
SoCo | 1610 S. Congress Ave. (Monroe St.) | 512-441-6100 | www.austinvespaio.com

"Believe the buzz" about this "hip" "but unpretentious" SoCo Italian ranked No. 1 for Food in Austin thanks to a "creative" kitchen that "expertly prepares" "sublime", "complex" creations ("amazing daily specials", "tempting antipasti"), which are served in a "small, romantic" space by "attentive staffers" who are "knowledgeable about the incredible food selection" and "extensive wine list"; its "popularity" can mean "long waits" and "noisy" acoustics, "but who cares" when there's so much to "be dazzled" by?

☑ Wink Ⓑ *American* — 28 | 21 | 26 | $44
Old West Austin | 1014 N. Lamar Blvd. (11th St.) | 512-482-8868 | www.winkrestaurant.com

"Hidden in a strip mall" in Old West Austin is this "boutique" "gem" (with "adjoining wine bar") whose "amazing, interesting" menu changes daily "depending on" "the local fresh" ingredients, rendering "exquisitely well-prepared" and "impeccably served" French-inspired New American dishes of "jaw-dropping quality"; some "can't overcome" the "overpriced, under-filled plates", while others say that "noise is an issue" "when a big crowd" is crammed into the "too-close-together tables", but all agree that "the food is above reproach."

Zoot Ⓜ *American* — 26 | 22 | 26 | $43
Old West Austin | 509 Hearn St. (Lake Austin Blvd.) | 512-477-6535 | www.zootrestaurant.com

Set in a "charming" home in Old West Austin, this stylish New American is praised for its "exquisitely prepared" menu, "thoughtfully selected wine list" and an "intelligent, unpretentious" staff that offers "mature, traditional service"; also appreciated is its "quiet, elegant", "romantic" interior, which cements its status as the "place for a serious date"; P.S. "the chef's tasting menu with wine pairings is a treat for the fat-wallet crowd."

Baltimore/Annapolis

TOP FOOD RANKING

	Restaurant	Cuisine
28	Sushi Sono	Japanese
	Joss Cafe/Sushi	Japanese
27	Charleston	American
	Samos	Greek
	Peter's Inn	American
	Prime Rib	Steak
	Lemongrass	Thai
	Tersiguel's	French
	Mari Luna	Mexican
26	Chameleon Cafe	American
	O'Learys*	Seafood

OTHER NOTEWORTHY PLACES

Restaurant	Cuisine
Bicycle, The	Eclectic
Boccaccio	Italian
Clyde's	American
Corks	American
Helmand	Afghan
Linwoods	American
McCormick & Schmick's	Seafood
Mr. Bill's Terrace Inn	Crab House
Pazza Luna	Italian
Ruth's Chris	Steak

Bicycle, The *Eclectic*
– | 21 | 23 | $45

South Baltimore | 1444 Light St. (bet. Birckhead St. & Fort Ave.) | Baltimore | 410-234-1900 | www.bicyclebistro.com

Admirers who hoped that an ownership change would "not diminish the quality" of this "special place" in South Baltimore will be relieved to know that the current chef-owner has made only subtle alterations to the "inventive" Eclectic menu; it remains the type of "lighthearted" place that "buzzes" – due to its "small" setting *and* its "don't-miss 18 bottles for $18 wine list."

Boccaccio *Italian*
25 | 21 | 23 | $53

Little Italy | 925 Eastern Ave. (bet. Exeter & High Sts.) | Baltimore | 410-234-1322 | www.boccaccio-restaurant.com

Try to catch this "solid performer" on "a good night" and you'll find that the "flavorful" Northern Italian cuisine "will be the best you ever had", as will the usually "professional" service; with "tables far apart", it lends itself to dinner with friends, "romance or closing the big deal", so while the unimpressed protest about "mega bills", the majority agrees it's "a cut above the other Little Italy restaurants" and "worth it."

---

* Indicates a tie with restaurant above

	FOOD	DECOR	SERVICE	COST

Chameleon Cafe 🗵 Ⓜ American
26 | 18 | 24 | $37

Northeast Baltimore | 4341 Harford Rd. (3 blocks south of Cold Spring Ln.) | Baltimore | 410-254-2376 | www.thechameleoncafe.com

Husband-and-wife-team Jeffrey Smith and Brenda Wolf Smith's "dedication shines through" at this NE Baltimore "foodie's find" featuring "innovative, artistic, delicious" French-inflected New American entrees; while the "small" setting strikes some as "too casual for the menu", an open kitchen and "adept" servers "with a lot of heart" make you feel like you're "eating in the owners' home"; N.B. sidewalk seating adds appeal.

🗵 Charleston 🗵 American
27 | 26 | 27 | $74

Inner Harbor East | 1000 Lancaster St. (S. Exeter St.) | Baltimore | 410-332-7373 | www.charlestonrestaurant.com

"One of Baltimore's best" is "even better" thanks to a "strikingly elegant" makeover and a relatively new set-price format that lets diners "try more" of chef/co-owner Cindy Wolf's "cutting-edge", "Southern-style" New American small plates offered in three-, five- and six-course "create-your-own tasting menus"; though a few are perturbed about the now-"tiny portions", the "celestial" tabs at this Harbor East experience are justified by the "exceptional service" and an "exquisite wine list" from co-owner Tony Foreman.

🗵 Clyde's American
18 | 21 | 19 | $30

Columbia | 10221 Wincopin Circle (Little Patuxent Pkwy.) | 410-730-2829 | www.clydes.com

While this "original" American "dining saloon" has "created a vast legion of copycats", it remains a "staple" that's "always good, year after year" (it's the Most Popular restaurant in the Baltimore area); with "delicious" crab cakes, "the best" burgers and other "bar food, par excellence", all served amid "nostalgic decor", it's a "reliably good" choice.

Corks Ⓜ American
25 | 19 | 23 | $51

South Baltimore | 1026 S. Charles St. (bet. Cross & Hamburg Sts.) | Baltimore | 410-752-3810 | www.corksrestaurant.com

This "hidden gem" in a South Baltimore row house keeps the "passionate" oenophile "in mind", pairing its "sublime", seasonal New American menu with an "outstanding" "all-American wine list" featuring "little-known vineyards"; "attentive, knowledgeable servers" help compensate for the "intimate (read: small, but nice)" space and "costly" tabs.

Helmand Afghan
26 | 20 | 23 | $28

Mt. Vernon | 806 N. Charles St. (bet. Madison & Read Sts.) | Baltimore | 410-752-0311 | www.helmand.com

At this Mt. Vernon "institution", "your taste buds will dance" to the "delicious diplomacy" of "complex, eye-opening" Afghan dishes that "go far, far beyond the kebab" (don't miss the "bliss-on-a-plate pumpkin appetizer"); "vegetarians and meat eaters alike" "may fall in love with" its "exotic character" and "reasonable prices", and if "seating can be crowded", most feel "the food is worth the coziness."

🗵 Joss Cafe & Sushi Bar Japanese
28 | 16 | 23 | $34

Annapolis | 195 Main St. (Church Circle) | 410-263-4688 | www.josscafe-sushibar.com

"You'd have to catch it yourself to get fish any fresher" than at this "adventurous" "source of pride" in Annapolis, where sushi-philes savor

FOOD DECOR SERVICE COST

"heaven-in-a-wrapper" rolls plus "yummy options that don't involve raw" fin fare; claustrophobes complain it's "cramped" and "crowded" and "doesn't take reservations", but once you're in, expect "efficient" service and "kitschy" if "sparse" decor.

Lemongrass *Thai*

27 | 19 | 21 | $28

Annapolis | 167 West St. (Colonial Ave.) | 410-280-0086
Annapolis | Gateway Village Shopping Ctr. | 2625A Housely Rd. (bet. General Hwy. & Rte. 450) | 410-224-8424
www.lemongrassannapolis.com

"Annapolis rejoices!" – "finally, decent Thai" comes to wild West Street in the guise of this "hip" "oasis for absolutely top-notch" fare "beautifully served" by a "relaxed staff"; the "innovative" dishes are proffered in a setting that's "too damn small" but "lively, noisy and hot" – "both the spices and the clientele"; N.B. a second site (with a covered patio) opened post-Survey just west of 'Naptown.

Linwoods *American*

26 | 25 | 25 | $49

Owings Mills | 25 Crossroads Dr. (bet. McDonogh & Reisterstown Rds.) | 410-356-3030 | www.linwoods.com

After nearly 20 years, surveyors can still "count on" this "upscale" Owings Mills "gold standard" "blessed with many" "consistently delicious" "spins on New American fare"; "owner Linwood Dame knows his business well", and his "clubby" restaurant "is all class" "without pretense", with an open kitchen and "professional service" to boot; some note, however, that a meal here can "put a dent in your wallet."

Mari Luna Mexican Grill Ⓜ *Mexican*

27 | 13 | 20 | $18

Pikesville | 102 Reisterstown Rd. (Seven Mile Ln.) | 410-486-9910 | www.mariluna.com

"Located in a converted Carvel store", this Pikesville "gem" "may not have a ton of curb appeal", but it does have "authentic" "Mexican (not Tex-Mex)" fare that's "divine"; locals say it's "easy to get hooked on" this "friendly, family-owned" "find" that's both "small" and "popular as all get-out", so be "prepared to fight for a table"; P.S. a BYO policy makes it even more of a "value."

Ⓩ McCormick & Schmick's *Seafood*

21 | 20 | 20 | $41

Inner Harbor | Pier 5 Hotel | 711 Eastern Ave. (S. President St.) | Baltimore | 410-234-1300 | www.mccormickandschmicks.com

The "daily fresh-catch offering can't be beat" say habitués hooked on this "clubby" chain "classic" where the "plethora of choices" "cooked as simply or as complicated as one would like" and "knowledgeable servers" make it "a safe bet for a business lunch" or "excellent for a family celebration"; though the "disappointed" suggest that the "over-priced", "uninspired" fare is a "let-down", barflies insist that "great specials" during happy hour deliver "real value."

Mr. Bill's Terrace Inn Ⓜ *Crab House*

▽ 24 | 11 | 18 | $30

Essex | 200 Eastern Blvd. (Helena Ave.) | 410-687-5996

"It's all about the crabs" at this Essex joint where there's "no terrace" and "beer and linoleum are de rigueur"; the "noisy, crowded" house of hardshells is considered the "best place" to "crack claws" according to "cops and carpenters" who claim that "any bad point" – like the "un-bearable waits" – "is forgotten once you taste" the crustaceans.

O'Learys Seafood *Seafood*   26 | 21 | 23 | $50

Eastport | 310 Third St. (Severn Ave.) | 410-263-0884 |
www.olearysseafood.com

Skip the Annapolis "circus" and head to Eastport for this "lovely", "white-linen" "fish palace" "proudly featuring the Chesapeake's bounty" on a "creative", "mouthwatering" menu served by a "knowledgeable, on-its-toes" staff; it's "very popular", but fans feel it's "worth the noise and crowding" – as well as the "pricey" bill; P.S. it's dinner-only and "reservations are a must."

Pazza Luna *Italian*   – | – | – | E

Locust Point | 1401 E. Clement St. (Decatur St.) | Baltimore | 410-962-1212 | www.pazzaluna.us

Recently reopened under new ownership, this veteran Italian ensconced in a Locust Point row house is luring locals with its authentic, non-Americanized cuisine; gone is the Sinatra- and celestial-themed decor, replaced by a sleek, sophisticated aesthetic that includes an open kitchen, a bar area and a harlequin-esque upstairs dining room.

Z Peter's Inn 🅂🅼 *American*   27 | 15 | 20 | $28

Fells Point | 504 S. Ann St. (Eastern Ave.) | Baltimore | 410-675-7313 | www.petersinn.com

"Defining Baltimore quirkiness" with its "strange collision" of "leather-clad biker" and "gourmet", this "teeny-tiny" Fells Point "hangout" may "look like a dive" but it's "as culinary as places twice as fancy and four times as dull" with a "limited" but "surprisingly ambitious" New American menu that "rotates weekly"; "get there early" since "it can get crowded" and "noisy", though regulars reveal "it's much more pleasant" "now that it's nonsmoking."

Z Prime Rib ⬤ *Steak*   27 | 24 | 26 | $62

Downtown North | 1101 N. Calvert St. (Chase St.) | Baltimore | 410-539-1804 | www.theprimerib.com

"Classy, swanky and all dressed up", this black-lacquered "old-fashioned supper club" in Downtown North is the quintessential spot to celebrate anniversaries or the "close of a big deal" over "massive cuts of buttery, beefy, masculine prime rib", the "most succulent" crab and "perfect" martinis brought to table by "impeccable" tuxedoed waiters; although a few find it "ripe for a makeover", it has that "old-school", "sophisticated ambiance" that enables "everyone to pretend they're a power broker, bon vivant or participant in a clandestine tryst – and maybe they are."

Z Ruth's Chris Steak House *Steak*   24 | 21 | 23 | $57

Inner Harbor | 600 Water St. (bet. Gay St. & Market Pl.) | Baltimore | 410-783-0033
Inner Harbor | Pier 5 Hotel | 711 Eastern Ave. (S. President St.) | Baltimore | 410-230-0033
Pikesville | 1777 Reisterstown Rd. (Hooks Ln.) | 410-837-0033
Eastport | 301 Severn Ave. (3rd St.) | 410-990-0033
www.ruthschris.com

"Everything is big" at these "high-end" "budget-busting" houses of beef – the steaks "sizzling in butter, the sides, the drinks, the bill!" but "so what?" since you'll "check your diet at the door and rip into" a slab that "melts in your mouth", augmented by a "great bottle of wine"; the

FOOD DECOR SERVICE COST

"well-timed" service further "pampers" and the dark-wood interiors are just right for business, but some insist these choices are "not as good" as the area's other chophouse options.

Ⓩ Samos Ⓑ⚏ *Greek* | 27 | 12 | 20 | $18 |

Greektown | 600 S. Oldham St. (Fleet St.) | Baltimore | 410-675-5292 | www.samosrestaurant.com

Meet the "Greektown family you never knew you had": chef-owner Nick Georgalas, "there every day" with "capable son Michael at his side", along with "hometown waitresses" who "call you 'hon' and mean it" as they bring around "huge portions" of "divinely zesty" "delights"; it's "no-frills" and "doesn't take reservations", but diners have determined it's "far and away" "Baltimore's top Greek", with a "BYO that makes it easy on the wallet" too; N.B. cash-only.

Ⓩ Sushi Sono Ⓑ *Japanese* | 28 | 19 | 24 | $34 |

Columbia | 10215 Wincopin Circle (Little Patuxent Pkwy.) | 410-997-6131 | www.sushisonomd.com

"Lovely views" "overlooking serene Lake Kittamaqundi" "add to the Zen ambiance" at "Columbia's pristine Japanese haven", rated No. 1 for Food in the Baltimore area; "unmatched sushi and sashimi" and a "mouthwatering" "selection of specialty rolls" are "served with grace and charm" by a "kimono-clad" staff that has "a way of making you feel welcome"; "it's like being in another world" (especially after a few cups of sake), but it can be "quite pricey" and "packed."

Tersiguel's *French* | 27 | 23 | 26 | $51 |

Ellicott City | 8293 Main St. (Old Columbia Pike) | 410-465-4004 | www.tersiguels.com

"Allow chef/co-owner Michel Tersiguel to take you on a tour" of "fine French country cuisine" at this "first-rate", family-run Gallic "in the heart of Ellicott City"; it "has a following" for its "rich", "fabulous food" (they even "grow their own vegetables"), and the "extensive wine" list and "wonderful service" help to ensure it's "perfect for a special occasion"; a "whopping bill" doesn't deter fans who note they've "paid three times as much for offerings that don't compare."

Boston

	Restaurant	Cuisine
28	L'Espalier	French
	Oishii	Japanese
	Clio/Uni	French
27	No. 9 Park	French/Italian
	Aujourd'hui	French
	Lumière	French
	La Campania	Italian
	Blue Ginger	Asian Fusion
	Saporito's	Italian
	Oleana	Mediterranean
	Mistral	French/Mediterranean
	Coriander Bistro	French
	Zabaglione*	Italian
	Sweet Basil	Italian
	Craigie Street Bistrot	French
	Helmand	Afghan
26	Hamersley's Bistro	French
	Il Capriccio	Italian
	Sage	American/Italian
	Meritage	American

OTHER NOTEWORTHY PLACES

Baraka Cafe	African
Butcher Shop	French/Italian
East Coast Grill	BBQ/Seafood
Eastern Standard	American/European
Franklin Café	American
Legal Sea Foods	Seafood
Locke-Ober	American/Continental
Neptune Oyster	Seafood
Oak Room	Steak
o ya	Japanese
Petit Robert Bistro	French
Pigalle	French
Rendezvous	Mediterranean
Rialto	Italian
Salts	American/French
Sorellina	Italian
Taberna de Haro	Spanish
Taranta	Italian/Peruvian
Ten Tables	American/European
Toro	Spanish

---

* Indicates a tie with restaurant above

subscribe to zagat.com

	FOOD	DECOR	SERVICE	COST

Z Aujourd'hui *French* | 27 | 27 | 28 | $74 |

Back Bay | Four Seasons Hotel | 200 Boylston St. (bet. Arlington & Charles Sts.) | 617-351-2037 | www.fourseasons.com

All of "life should be lived" as it is at the Four Seasons' "lavish" dining "retreat" overlooking the Common in the Back Bay: you'll be surrounded by "smooth-as-silk" staffers who appear "devoted to your table" throughout an "exquisite" New French "experience" that's "worth the extra credit cards"; factor in a "fabulous Sunday brunch", and you'll be chiming in when the Francophiles chant *"oui, oui, j'adore Aujourd'hui!"*

Baraka Cafe M⊄ *African* | 24 | 19 | 20 | $23 |

Central Square | 80½ Pearl St. (bet. Auburn & William Sts.) | Cambridge | 617-868-3951 | www.barakacafe.com

Some seek out this "hidden jewel" near Central Square "just to meet" its "hoot" of a hostess, owner Alia Meddeb, whose "passion and wisdom" suffuse the "homey" venue – but don't leave without sampling her "dazzling" array of North African dishes; the service is deliberately "unhurried", but "be patient" and you'll enjoy a "charming" experience, "hampered only by the lack of alcohol" (simply indulge in the "blissfully habit-forming spiced lemonade").

Z Blue Ginger Z *Asian Fusion* | 27 | 22 | 25 | $52 |

Wellesley | 583 Washington St. (Church St.) | 781-283-5790 | www.ming.com

Celebrity chef Ming Tsai all but "defined East-meets-West" cuisine, and his Asian fusion "classic" – still "the shining star" of "swanky Wellesley" – "continues to wow" with its "fantabulous" "explosion of flavors"; indeed, the "luxuriousness" of the food leaves some "surprised" by the comparatively "sparse" surroundings and service that, though "unfailingly" "well-versed", isn't always "warm" – but "Master" "Sigh" compensates ("when present") by giving "personal attention" to "each dish" and "every table", justifying the "exorbitant prices."

Butcher Shop, The *French/Italian* | 24 | 22 | 22 | $40 |

South End | 552 Tremont St. (Waltham St.) | 617-423-4800 | www.thebutchershopboston.com

At Barbara Lynch's "stylish" French-Italian "combination butcher shop and wine bar", an "interesting mix" of South Enders spends hours perched on barstools or "standing around the giant butcher block" while indulging in some "high-class noshing" on "awesome charcuterie" and other "meaty offerings"; it's all paired with an "ever-changing", "wide-ranging selection of hard-to-find wines" that "helpful" stewards let diners "taste before committing" – good thing too, because the "high prices" can cause "credit-card whiplash."

Z Clio/Uni *French* | 28 | 25 | 26 | $73 |

Back Bay | Eliot Hotel | 370A Commonwealth Ave. (Mass. Ave.) | 617-536-7200 | www.cliorestaurant.com

Whether or not it "holds the local record for the highest price per calorie served", this "swanky" New French "supernova" in the Back Bay's Eliot Hotel "transports" "serious gourmets" who taste "brilliance" "beyond belief" in "every morsel" of chef Ken Oringer's "arresting", "complex" and "dramatic" presentations; even the miffed minority to whom the "extremely professional" staffers' "show of knowledge" comes across as "condescending" admits that Uni, the "incredible" sashimi bar right next door, reestablishes "cozy" "intimacy."

Coriander Bistro 🖼️🅼 *French* | 27 | 22 | 26 | $49 |

Sharon | 5 Post Office Sq. (bet. Billings & S. Main Sts.) | 781-784-5450 | www.corianderbistro.com

As "reasons to leave the city" go, this Sharon bistro is "difficult to top": a chef who "loves doing what he does best" and his "affable" wife know how to deliver "fantastic" "gourmet" French goods "artfully", using ingredients from "the farm down the street"; abetted by a "solicitous staff", they "make recommendations" from a wine list of "carefully chosen treasures", "adding a homey touch" to a "simple" space that's as "welcoming" as it is "welcome."

Craigie Street Bistrot 🅼 *French* | 27 | 19 | 25 | $53 |

Harvard Square | 5 Craigie Circle (bet. Brattle St. & Concord Ave.) | Cambridge | 617-497-5511 | www.craigiestreetbistrot.com

In this "wee, cozy" "basement from heaven" (transported to Harvard Square), "daring" "gourmets" "stop all conversation" except "oohs and aahs" as chef-owner Tony Maws makes their culinary "dreams come true" via "constantly new", "unfailingly memorable" French "challenges" that incorporate "whatever's freshest that day", while "sincere" servers offer "terrific" tips on "phenomenal" wines; if a few "meat-and-potato" types, "claustrophobes" and thwarted walk-ins feel "alienated", most swear its "stars are aligned"; P.S. the twice-weekly Chef's Whim prix fixe "blows away" "thrifty adventurers."

East Coast Grill & Raw Bar *BBQ/Seafood* | 26 | 18 | 21 | $36 |

Inman Square | 1271 Cambridge St. (Prospect St.) | Cambridge | 617-491-6568 | www.eastcoastgrill.net

"After all these years", Inman Square's "sultan of spice", Chris Schlesinger, "still finds ways" to "rock your world" with his "idiosyncratic" surf 'n' turf – "impeccable seafood" and "masterful" barbecue that merge "whimsy" with "edge" in "raucous", "tight but not confining" tiki-tinged digs; but "amateurs" beware: though the staff "doesn't take itself too seriously", "the wait is no joke" – and neither are the "infamous Hell Nights" ("if they say it's spicy, believe them").

Eastern Standard 🌓 *American/European* | 21 | 23 | 20 | $38 |

Kenmore Square | Hotel Commonwealth | 528 Commonwealth Ave. (Brookline Ave.) | 617-532-9100 | www.easternstandardboston.com

"Good karma" permeates this "classy, brassy" scene in Kenmore Square, a "striking" "facsimile" of an "old Paris" "train station", where the "soigné" set throngs a "kick-ass bar" and "rocking" heated patio for cocktails you "mustn't underestimate" before digging into "soul"-"satisfying" (if "a wee bit" "salty") American-European fare "in the brasserie tradition"; though some servers seem more like "players" than "professionals", at least the "wonderful host" compensates.

Franklin Café *American* | 24 | 18 | 20 | $34 |

South End | 278 Shawmut Ave. (Hanson St.) | 617-350-0010 🌓
Gloucester | 118 Main St. (bet. Hancock & Porter Sts.) | 978-283-7888
www.franklincafe.com

"Everyone loves" this ever-"festive" South End "scene" where your "reward" for "the most ridiculous wait" – which you'll spend "mingling"

	FOOD	DECOR	SERVICE	COST

with "cool" "bohemians" lubricated by "wonderful bartenders" – is an unfailingly "interesting", "expertly prepared" New American meal from a "small, frequently changing menu" that's "cheap considering what you're getting"; if it's just "too hard to get into" (it remains "busy, even late at night"), try the Gloucester branch, "an oasis in a fairly barren landscape."

☑ Hamersley's Bistro *French*

26 | 23 | 25 | $58

South End | 553 Tremont St. (Clarendon St.) | 617-423-2700 | www.hamersleysbistro.com

The South End's "pacesetter" for 20 years and counting, "master chef" Gordon Hamersley still runs the kitchen of his "handsome", "sunny-yellow" country French bistro, and "it shows on the plate": though "uncontrived", the cooking "pops" with "complex flavors" (the famed chicken has "changed lives"); his "dedicated longtime staff" also continues to serve with "silver-spoon" "verve", so it's no wonder upstarts who opine it "needs a shot of 'now'" are drowned out by worshipers who pray it never "succumbs to trendiness."

Helmand *Afghan*

27 | 23 | 20 | $32

East Cambridge | 143 First St. (Bent St.) | Cambridge | 617-492-4646 | www.helmandrestaurantcambridge.com

"In the desert" of East Cambridge, an exquisite "oasis" filled with "beautiful blues and maizes" and an "aroma they could charge for" awaits; as it is, you get "exceptional value" from the "distinctive", "hearty" and "intriguingly spiced" assortment of Afghan specialties that "never change, but neither do their quality" – from "smashing" baby pumpkin to "savory" lamb to "piping-hot flatbread" that warms your cockles – even when servers as "distant" as Kabul don't.

Il Capriccio ☑ *Italian*

26 | 21 | 24 | $56

Waltham | 888 Main St. (Prospect St.) | 781-894-2234

"Leave the kids at home" for "an evening to remember" at this "dark, private" Waltham "hideaway" where "rich" yet "crystal-pure" *piatti* complement a "world-class wine list" that has remained "devout in its homage to all things Italian" "for some 26 years"; while its "very seriousness" leaves a few fun-lovers chirping "lighten up!", most just wish they "could afford to eat here more" often.

La Campania ☑ *Italian*

27 | 25 | 25 | $55

Waltham | 504 Main St. (bet. Cross & Heard Sts.) | 781-894-4280 | www.lacampania.com

"Are we in Waltham" or a "rustic" "village" "inn"? wonder suburban Italophiles "swept away" by this "small" "blessing" with an "artist" for a chef and "a wine god" for a manager (oenophiles dream of running "loose in his cellar"); while some balk at the "steep" bill, they'll have to "get over" it, as most agree it's "sublime from start to finish."

☑ Legal Sea Foods *Seafood*

22 | 18 | 20 | $37

Back Bay | Copley Pl. | 100 Huntington Ave. (bet. Dartmouth & Exeter Sts.) | 617-266-7775
Back Bay | Prudential Ctr. | 800 Boylston St. (Ring Rd.) | 617-266-6800
Park Square | 26 Park Plaza (Columbus Ave.) | 617-426-4444 ◑
Waterfront | Long Wharf | 255 State St. (Atlantic Ave.) | 617-227-3115
(continued)

(continued)
Legal Sea Foods

Harvard Square | 20 University Rd. (Eliot St.) | Cambridge | 617-491-9400
Kendall Square | 5 Cambridge Ctr. (bet. Ames & Main Sts.) | Cambridge | 617-864-3400
Chestnut Hill | Chestnut Hill Shopping Ctr. | 43 Boylston St. (Hammond Pond Pkwy.) | 617-277-7300
Braintree | South Shore Plaza | 250 Granite St. (I-95, exit 6) | 781-356-3070
Peabody | Northshore Mall | 210 Andover St./Rte. 114 (Rte. 128) | 978-532-4500
Framingham | 50-60 Worcester Rd./Rte. 9 (Ring Rd.) | 508-766-0600
www.legalseafoods.com

"Come one, come all" to the "Ellis Island of fish", the "Oktoberfest of lobster", the "seafood-starved tourist" "zoo": "after all these years and all that expansion", Boston's Most Popular "institution" still draws the "teeming hordes" by providing more "impeccable consistency" "than any chain has a right to", all while getting the balance between culinary "simplicity" and "innovation" "down to a science" and honing its formula for "cheerful" decor and service; in short, it may be a "cliché", but it's a largely "beloved" one.

☑ L'Espalier *French*   28 | 28 | 28 | $89

Back Bay | 30 Gloucester St. (bet. Commonwealth Ave. & Newbury St.) | 617-262-3023 | www.lespalier.com

The city's "best all-around dining experience" is how many view this "luxe-to-the-max" gourmet "adventure", rated No. 1 in Boston for Food, where chef-owner Frank McClelland "takes you beyond the stretch of your imagination" with "*fantastique*" prix fixe menus that incorporate "impeccable" New England ingredients into "transcendent" New French meals; it's all set in an "opulent" Back Bay brownstone you'll "wish you could live in" and overseen by "beyond impeccable" servers who "think about everything for you"; of course, you'll pay a "staggeringly" "cost-prohibitive" price for such "culinary genius."

Locke-Ober ⑤ *American/Continental*   24 | 25 | 24 | $61

Downtown Crossing | 3 Winter Pl. (bet. Tremont & Washington Sts.) | 617-542-1340 | www.lockeober.com

You couldn't find this "historical monument" to Brahmin gastronomy "anywhere else in the world": "restored to glory" by Lydia Shire, the "fabulously overdone" Downtown Crossing "classic" – all mahogany, crystal and "dark corners" – still "pampers" the "upper crust" with "JFK's favorite" Continental dishes alongside "interesting" New American creations; still, it's just a "snooty", "overpriced" "Old Boston theme park" to cynics who "don't see the attraction."

Lumière *French*   27 | 22 | 25 | $56

Newton | 1293 Washington St. (Waltham St.) | 617-244-9199 | www.lumiererestaurant.com

A "surefire" "*bon soir*" awaits both "special-occasion" observers and "lucky" regulars at this "splendid" West Newton bistro where a "clean and cool", "quiet and refined" design sets the tone for "really classy service" and "cleverly" "streamlined" New French output from a "precision" kitchen that aims to "let the ingredients show through"; P.S. cost-conscious types who value "'oomph' for the price" might try the "superb" "weekday prix fixe."

	FOOD	DECOR	SERVICE	COST

Meritage ▯ *American* | 26 | 26 | 26 | $63 |

Waterfront | Boston Harbor Hotel | 70 Rowes Wharf (Atlantic Ave.) | 617-439-3995 | www.meritagetherestaurant.com

Gourmet "synergy" suffuses "exceptional chef" Daniel Bruce's Waterfront monument to pairing, where guests essentially "make their own tasting menus" from an "opulent, indulgent" array of seasonal New American dishes, available in small or large sizes, and selections from an "enormous wine list" – though "distinguished" servers can "provide direction" too; of course, "those little plates add up to big $$$", but "no one whines" – perhaps because the "dynamite" harbor view takes their breath away.

Mistral *French/Mediterranean* | 27 | 26 | 25 | $64 |

South End | 223 Columbus Ave. (bet. Berkeley & Clarendon Sts.) | 617-867-9300 | www.mistralbistro.com

Still "the Rolls-Royce" of restaurants in the South End, Jamie Mammano's French-Mediterranean "stronghold" "has it all": "out-of-this-world" "indulgences" paired with a "wide spectrum" of wines presented by a veritable "battalion" of "polished" floor staffers in a "regal", "high-ceilinged" space; granted, given the "buzz" the bar crowd of "young power brokers" and "models" generates, the noise level can rise to "absurd" levels – just like the "eye-popping" checks.

Neptune Oyster *Seafood* | 26 | 21 | 21 | $40 |

North End | 63 Salem St. (Cross St.) | 617-742-3474 | www.neptuneoyster.com

Devotees declare their "dying wish" "would be the hot lobster roll" at this "tiny" but "always jumping" North End "pearl" – "preceded by a dozen oysters", of course, chosen from a daily changing "panoply" that "overwhelms and delights"; meanwhile, the "bold flavors" of the "well-constructed fish dishes" on the frequently "morphing" menu give "squished" conversationalists something to talk about with "relaxed" owners who make the place "neighborly."

❷ No. 9 Park ▤ *French/Italian* | 27 | 24 | 26 | $67 |

Beacon Hill | 9 Park St. (bet. Beacon & Tremont Sts.) | 617-742-9991 | www.no9park.com

"You have arrived" when you enter Barbara Lynch's "suave" flagship on Beacon Hill – and you'll "stay for the duration" as "superior mixologists", a "wonderful sommelier" and "passionate" "servers who speak like chefs" administer an "extraordinary" "crossover French-Italian" meal you're actually "excited to eat", coming from a kitchen that's "on a different level altogether"; so while the usual holdouts harrumph over "minuscule portions" that leave them "hungry but appreciably poorer", the "'in' crowd" insists this fledgling "legend" is "worth your arm and your leg."

Oak Room *Steak* | 24 | 26 | 25 | $63 |

Back Bay | Fairmont Copley Plaza | 138 St. James Ave. (bet. Dartmouth & Trinity Sts.) | 617-267-5300 | www.theoakroom.com

"Dress up" and live out your "old world–romance" fantasies against the "so very baroque", "baronial" backdrop of this locally "legendary" Back Bay steakhouse where "individualized attention" "makes you feel special" as you feast on "gigantic", "decadent" chops and "classic" sides, followed by nightcaps (poured from "little carafes on ice") in the piano bar; sure, from another angle "it's a self-satisfied, old-money enclave" with "unimaginable" "billing practices" – but where else can you live "like the other half"?

Ζ Oishii M *Japanese*   28 | 14 | 21 | $43

Chestnut Hill | 612 Hammond St. (Boylston St.) | 617-277-7888
Sudbury | Mill Vill. | 365 Boston Post Rd./Rte. 20 (Concord Rd.) | 978-440-8300

Ζ Oishii Boston ●M *Japanese*

South End | 1166 Washington St. (E. Berkeley St.) | 617-482-8868
www.oishiiboston.com

The Chestnut Hill senior's "smaller than a Tokyo karaoke bar", the Sudbury junior's a "neighborhood joint" and the "ultracontemporary" South End freshman defines "chichi" – but all three serve as "shrines to the art of sushi" and "what it's supposed to taste like"; you may "panic at the cost" (not to mention the "hour-plus waits"), but once you've had one "mmm-worthy" bite of some "dreamy" "departure" from the spicy tuna norm, you'll be "ready to spend exorbitant" sums on "the omakase – a guaranteed thrill ride."

Oleana *Mediterranean*   27 | 22 | 23 | $47

Inman Square | 134 Hampshire St. (bet. Elm & Norfolk Sts.) | Cambridge | 617-661-0505 | www.oleanarestaurant.com

Inman Square's intelligentsia consider it "an unbelievable privilege" to "educate their taste buds" at this "remarkable" Mediterranean "destination": "each bite" of chef-owner Ana Sortun's "refreshingly" "gutsy" and "complex" creations shows she "knows her spices", and her "well-versed" "staff can describe every ingredient" (if in an occasionally "condescending" manner); quick studies have also learned to "sharpen their elbows" when seated at the "closely placed tables" – or arrive early for a spot on the "magical" patio.

o ya 🔳M *Japanese*   – | – | – | VE

Leather District | 9 East St. (South St.) | 617-654-9900

Tucked into a narrow old firehouse in the Leather District, this Japanese tavern sets a striking stage by blending elements of its former self (brickwork, concrete floors, high ceilings) with traditional Asian materials like blond wood and rice paper; complemented by high-end sakes, chef Tim Cushman's budget-breaking menu offers serious nigiri, sashimi and cooked delicacies featuring luxe global ingredients.

Petit Robert Bistro *French*   23 | 19 | 20 | $37

Kenmore Square | 468 Commonwealth Ave. (Charlesgate W.) | 617-375-0699
South End | 480 Columbus Ave. (Rutland Sq.) | 617-867-0600
www.petitrobertbistro.com

"Kudos" to Jacky Robert for "finally" filling a crucial "niche" – or rather two: in a "tight" but "charming" Kenmore Square townhouse and its South End spin-off, he "replicates" the "Left Bank" "experience to a T" via "luscious" yet "straightforward" *plats* and an "impressive" *carte des vins*; it's all presented "at true bistro prices" by waiters "with French accents" but skills from "all over the map", leading a few critics to conclude it's "satisfactory but overhyped."

	FOOD	DECOR	SERVICE	COST

Pigalle ☑ French
| | 25 | 21 | 24 | $56 |

Theater District | 75 Charles St. S. (bet. Stuart St. & Warrenton Pl.) | 617-423-4944 | www.pigalleboston.com

"Way ahead" of the Theater District pack, this "dimly lit" "jewel box" of a bistro "defines understated elegance" for foodies "brought to their knees" by chef Marc Orfaly's "expertise" in "updating" traditional French fare ("the cassoulet is one of Boston's best"); the "professional" floor staff brings a similar "flourish" to service, making the entire experience, in short, "worth every cent."

Rendezvous Mediterranean
| | 26 | 19 | 24 | $43 |

Central Square | 502 Mass. Ave. (Brookline St.) | Cambridge | 617-576-1900 | www.rendezvouscentralsquare.com

"Blue Room veteran" and "born restaurateur" Steve Johnson is back – and what an "out-and-out phenomenal" reentry he's made, bringing "enticing", "bright" Mediterranean cuisine that balances "comfort" with "creativity" to a "former Burger King" in still-"unfashionable Central Square" ("who'd a thunk?"); though you can "vaguely" picture its earlier incarnation "if you know where to look", "very educated" servers will erase the recollection while "answering questions you didn't think to ask."

Rialto Italian
| | 26 | – | 25 | E |

Harvard Square | Charles Hotel | 1 Bennett St. (Eliot St.) | Cambridge | 617-661-5050 | www.rialto-restaurant.com

After generating years of "euphoria" among Harvard Square's "glitterati" with her "special-occasion" "splurge" at the Charles Hotel, Jody Adams is staking her reputation as "one of the greats" with its complete reinvention (which may outdate the above scores): not only has she streamlined her kitchen to focus solely on regional Italian cuisine, but she's brightened up the entire space, from the harvest-toned dining room to the onyx-accented bar, proving she "knows how to please" pundits who proclaimed it was time for "an update."

Sage American/Italian
| | 26 | – | 22 | $50 |

South End | 1395 Washington St. (bet. Pelham & Union Park Sts.) | 617-248-8814 | www.sageboston.com

For edible "art", head to Anthony Susi's "serious" New American–Italian "standout" where the seasonal menu is "short" but "refined", "thoughtful" and "spot-on", from "unsurpassed gnocchi" to "melt-in-your-mouth meats"; plus, after more than a decade, it's moved to more spacious South End digs, with more seating and a full bar to round out the "well-selected" wine list.

Salts ☒☑ American/French
| | 26 | 22 | 26 | $56 |

Central Square | 798 Main St. (bet. Cherry & Windsor Sts.) | Cambridge | 617-876-8444 | www.saltsrestaurant.com

Balance is this "quiet" "little" Central Square destination's "brilliant" gift: a "manicured yet homey" dining room sets the tone for New American–French cuisine that's simultaneously "earthy" and "ethereal", "approachable" and "elegant"; plus, the "earnest" owners head up a staff of "class acts" that embody both "amiability" and "total professionalism"; P.S. if your heart's set on the signature duck for two, "order it in advance" – sometimes "they run out."

	FOOD	DECOR	SERVICE	COST

Saporito's 🄼 Italian
27 | 20 | 24 | $43

Hull | 11 Rockland Circle (George Washington Blvd.) | 781-925-3023 |
www.saporitoscafe.com

A "summer cottage" to the diplomatic, a "beach shack" to the blunt,
Hull's "gold standard" for Northern Italian cuisine is a "little treasure"
by most accounts, including those of urbanites who "schlep" south-
ward to be "accommodated" by "stellar" servers bearing "frequently
changing" creations; indeed, even the downsides – "uncomfortable"
"wooden booths" and "NYC prices" – are upsides, insofar as they
"turn off" "the tourists, who leave it alone."

Sorellina Italian
25 | 27 | 24 | $63

Back Bay | 1 Huntington Ave. (Dartmouth St.) | 617-412-4600 |
www.sorellinaboston.com

Boasting an all black-and-white interior that's a "conversation piece"
in itself, Mistral's "gorgeous", "slick" Italian "boutique" of a "little sister" teems with "intelligent" "metropolitans" "prancing about" – and
they just work here; the Back Bay's "chosen" also stream in to sample
"modern" creations whose surprisingly "genuine" "warmth" elicits
questions like "who knew meatballs could be so exquisite?" and "how
come everything costs so much?"

Sweet Basil 🄼🚭 Italian
27 | 11 | 20 | $30

Needham | 942 Great Plain Ave. (Highland Ave.) | 781-444-9600
Long generating "conspiratorial excitement" among BYO-toting
Needhamites with the "garlicky" "intensity" of its "abundant" "belly-
warmers", this Italian "walk-in closet" has finally upped the ante with
a recent size-doubling expansion (which may outdate the Decor
score); provided the "adorable" chef-owner and his much-"appreciated"
staff "continue their legacy" of "down-to-earth" "personality and flavor" at "prices that allow frequent visits", the space "to breathe"
should be "sweet indeed."

Taberna de Haro 🅂 Spanish
25 | 18 | 20 | $33

Brookline | 999 Beacon St. (St. Mary's St.) | 617-277-8272
"A hundred Spanish wines" don't lie: this eternally "red-hot Brookline
date spot" is your ticket to "Madrid without the smokers"; the open
kitchen sends a "nonstop flow" of "diverse" tapas, alternately "traditional" and "exotic", to the "rustic" corner space's "tightly" packed tables; it may be "expensive", but the small plates are "actually good-
sized", so "a little goes a long way" – if only the sometimes "flaky"
servers got the job done as efficiently (luckily, "ever-present" owners
compensate with "charm").

Taranta Italian/Peruvian
25 | 21 | 23 | $44

North End | 210 Hanover St. (Cross St.) | 617-720-0052 |
www.tarantarist.com

Attend the "intriguing marriage" of Southern Italian and Peruvian cuisines held nightly at this "intimate, brick-lined" "three-story charmer"
in the North End; it's a match that "exceeds expectations" as much for
its "hearty" "richness" as its "novelty" ("unusual" pastas like *gnocchi
di yuca* are "divine"), and it further benefits from an "excellent wine
list" – but the "extra-special ingredient" is the "outgoing personality"
of chef-owner José Duarte and his "totally delightful" staff.

	FOOD	DECOR	SERVICE	COST

Ten Tables *American/European*
26 | 20 | 24 | $38

Jamaica Plain | 597 Centre St. (bet. Pond & Spencer Sts.) | 617-524-8810 | www.tentables.net

Take the name "literally" and book "in advance", because this "cute" "closet" is a "pearl in the Jamaica Plain shell", where an open kitchen "hand-crafts" "every detail" of "refined" yet "luscious" New American-European cuisine that's "served with aplomb" alongside "fantastic" wines by a "warm and amusing staff"; though selections tend to be as "minimal" as the space itself, so are the relative costs – amounting to some of the most "remarkable" "values in [greater] Boston."

Toro *Spanish*
25 | 21 | 19 | $42

South End | 1704 Washington St. (W. Springfield St.) | 617-536-4300

Hit the "hot spot" for tapas where the tapas "hit the spot": Ken Oringer's "energetic" South End addition that "lives up to the hype" with a "terrific range" of "taste sensations" complemented by "wonderful wines"; though some suggest the servers are "too hip to be servers" and note the "prices add up fast", most agree "this place is worth it"; P.S. it's no-reservations, so "be prepared to wait."

Zabaglione *Italian*
27 | 18 | 24 | $42

Ipswich | 10 Central St. (Market St.) | 978-356-5466

Zabaglione Cafe *Italian*
Ipswich | 1 Market St. (Central St.) | 978-356-6484

"It's hard to choose just one entree" at this "intimate" Ipswich "secret" where "out-of-this-world" Italian creations – abounding in "clever", "artfully showcased" ingredients – are supplemented by "evening specials" "brought out to view" by a "staff that dotes on you"; whatever you select will be "worth every penny", so "don't pass up dessert"; P.S. the "cute cafe" "right down the street" keeps things "informal" and more "affordable."

Charlotte

TOP FOOD RANKING

	Restaurant	Cuisine
29	Barrington's	American
28	Volare	Italian
27	McIntosh's	Seafood/Steak
	Sullivan's	Steak
26	Nikko	Japanese
	Upstream	Seafood
	Toscana	Italian
	Noble's	Eclectic
	Luce	Italian
	Carpe Diem	American

OTHER NOTEWORTHY PLACES

Bonterra	American
Customshop	American
Fiamma	Italian
ilios noche	Greek/Italian
Lulu	French/Mediterranean
Mickey & Mooch	Steak
Palm	Steak
Restaurant i	Asian Fusion
Sonoma	American
Zebra	French

Z Barrington's Ⓢ *American* ⟨29⟩ ⟨21⟩ ⟨25⟩ ⟨$46⟩

SouthPark | FoxCroft Shopping Ctr. | 7822 Fairview Rd. (bet. Carmel & Colony Rds.) | 704-364-5755 | www.barringtonsrestaurant.com

No wonder it can be "impossible to get in to": No. 1 for Food and Popularity in Charlotte, this SouthPark New American "delights" and "surprises" with "memorable", "understated" creations from chef-owner Bruce Moffett, who has the "most sophisticated palate" in the area; it's "tiny", but that means service will be "as good as it gets."

Z Bonterra Dining & Wine Room ⓈAmerican ⟨25⟩ ⟨25⟩ ⟨25⟩ ⟨$48⟩

Dilworth | 1829 Cleveland Ave. (E. Worthington Ave.) | 704-333-9463 | www.bonterradining.com

It's "only fitting to be served such heavenly food in a former church" proclaim patrons who sing the praises of this Dilworth New American that's akin to a "religious experience" given the "imaginative" menu ("amazing" fried lobster tail) and a wine selection with enough "breadth" to "astonish" oenophiles (there's a "superb" by-the-glass lineup); plus, the staff is so "considerate", they'll "make you want to say 'amen.'"

Carpe Diem ⓈAmerican ⟨26⟩ ⟨25⟩ ⟨24⟩ ⟨$39⟩

Elizabeth | 1535 Elizabeth Ave. (Travis Ave.) | 704-377-7976 | www.carpediemrestaurant.com

"Everybody wins" at this "staple" in Elizabeth that impresses admirers with its winning combination of "artful", "stellar" New American cuisine (including "sophisticated" vegetarian options) and "gorgeous" art nouveau-style interior; further abetting the "wow" factor is an "attentive" staff that adds to the "eclectic" "charm."

Customshop ⊠ American
–	–	–	M

Elizabeth | 1601 Elizabeth Ave. (Travis Ave.) | 704-333-3396 | www.customshopfood.com

Consulting chef Dave Pasternack (NYC's Esca) lends his expertise to this New American in Elizabeth, where the Italian-accented dishes – think squid ink pasta with crabmeat – are crafted using locally sourced ingredients and paired with an atypical wine list; the intimate corner space is as contemporary as the cuisine, with candle-lined walls and a well-turned-out staff providing warm undertones.

Fiamma *Italian*
–	–	–	M

Dilworth | Park Square Shopping Ctr. | 2418 Park Rd. (Ordermore Ave.) | 704-333-3062

The owners may be Ecuadorian, but you can expect the menu at this Dilworth ristorante to be filled with enough homemade pastas, thin-crust pizzas and regional Italian specialties to make any paesano proud; there is also a Tuscan-heavy wine list, and the unfussy room features an open kitchen with a wood-burning oven (the moniker means 'flame' in Italian) and a cozy, family-friendly atmosphere.

ilios noche ⊠ *Greek/Italian*
24	19	21	$26

Ballantyne | 11508 Providence Rd. (I-485) | 704-814-9882 | www.iliosnoche.com

This "unique" Greek-Italian "knows what it's doing", serving up "excellent" food that lures an "attractive clientele" to its "suburban" location east of Ballantyne; if the "edgy" quarters don't provide enough entertainment, the "loud, loud, loud" ambiance may do the trick.

Luce ⊠ *Italian*
26	25	25	$45

Uptown | Hearst Tower | 214 N. Tryon St. (bet. 5th & 6th Sts.) | 704-344-9222 | www.luceristorante.net

A "Tuscan oasis in a sea of barbecue", this "first-class" Uptown Italian shines with "luscious" food, a "wonderful" Boot-centric wine list and "excellent" service; further enhancing the "rich" experience is "exquisite" decor that features Moreno glass and works by local artist Ben Long; in short, restaurateur Augusto Conte has "done it again!"

Lulu *French/Mediterranean*
–	–	–	M

Plaza-Midwood | 1911 Central Ave. (Nandina St.) | 704-376-2242

Its seasonal menu may feature playful dish names like 'Duck Duck Jus', but this Plaza-Midwood bistro produces comfortable French-Med cuisine that focuses on simple, vivid flavors with a Southern twist; true to its unpretentious style, it's located in a renovated '30s-era house and is staffed with servers who stick to a relaxed, amiable approach.

⊠ McIntosh's Steaks & Seafood ⊠ *Seafood/Steak*
27	22	25	$53

South End | 1812 South Blvd. (East Blvd.) | 704-342-1088 | www.mcintoshs1.com

There's "no better steak in town" crow content constituents who "don't leave a speck of food" on their plates at this "superb", locally owned South End surf 'n' turfer where "impeccable" service, a dark-wood interior with piano bar (Wednesday–Saturday) and a patio with fireplace make it "feel like a private club" – though "not a stuffy" one; it's "just what a steakhouse should be" and "worth every penny."

☑ Mickey & Mooch *Steak*   23 | 21 | 20 | $33

Arboretum | The Arboretum | 8128 Providence Rd. (Hwy. 51) | 704-752-8080
Huntersville | 9723 Sam Furr Rd. (I-77) | 704-895-6654
www.mickeyandmooch.com

"So low-key" yet "so well done", this chophouse pair off Highway 51 and in Huntersville wins kudos for "mammoth" portions of consistently "excellent" prime steaks and chops at "reasonable prices"; the "always hopping" settings are reminiscent of "a '50s New York supper club" (with "Frank playing on the sound system"), so don't be taken aback by the "long waits" or a "noise level [that's] off the charts."

☑ Nikko *Japanese*   26 | 18 | 22 | $30

Ballantyne | Ballantyne Commons E. | 15105 John J. Delaney Dr. (Ballantyne Commons Pkwy.) | 704-341-5550
South End | 1300 South Blvd. (Arlington Ave.) | 704-370-0100
www.nikkosushibar.net

Charlotte can "thank God" that "superb" sushi's "finally come to town": chef/co-owner Joanna Nix "proves" that "fabulous" raw fare "doesn't require you to be near the water" at her Japanese duo; they're "the standard" for "fresh" fish, so don't be surprised if they get a little "disco"-like on weekends (i.e. "loud, like a party's going on").

Noble's ☒ *Eclectic*   26 | 26 | 25 | $45

SouthPark | 3 Morrocroft Ctr. at SouthPark | 6801 Morrison Blvd. (Cameron Valley Pkwy.) | 704-367-9463 | www.noblesrestaurant.com

A "temple of gastronomic pleasure", this SouthPark "treasure" showcases chef-owner Jim Noble's "spectacular" French-, Italian- and Med-influenced Eclectic creations; the "elegant", "Tuscan-retreat" setting and "superb" staff enhance what some consider a "magical" experience – albeit one that may require you to "save your pennies" in advance.

☑ Palm *Steak*   24 | 21 | 24 | $52

SouthPark | 6705B Phillips Place Ct. (bet. Fairview & Sharon Rds.) | 704-552-7256 | www.thepalm.com

"Consistency" gets you far in the steakhouse game, and this national chain's "tried-and-true" formula draws devotees to SouthPark to sample "serious", "well-prepared" cuts; you'll also find caricatures of "local personalities" on the walls and a "buzzy" "banker bar scene" ("why pay the power bill when the noise alone could cook the food?"), so be prepared to pay "dearly" for the experience.

Restaurant i ☒ *Asian Fusion*   – | – | – | E

Dilworth | 1524 East Blvd. (Scott Ave.) | 704-333-8118 | www.restaurant-i.com

Its name is a play on the Japanese word for love (*ai*), and the culinary i-fuls at this fusion restaurant in Dilworth come courtesy of chef Masa Kokubu, who relies on the freshest of ingredients and over a decade of experience in French technique; his architectural entrees have equally artistic names (e.g. 'Rhapsody in Blue Ocean'), while the more standard sushi and sashimi selections complement the simple decor.

	FOOD	DECOR	SERVICE	COST

Sonoma Modern American 🗲 *American* — 24 | 22 | 23 | $40

Uptown | Bank of America Corporate Ctr. | 100 N. Tryon St. (Trade St.) | 704-332-1132 | www.sonomarestaurants.net

You'll "feel transported" to NYC at this "trendy" Uptowner attracting acolytes with its "terrific", "innovative" New American cuisine and "excellent wine list"; owner Pierre Bader helps deliver a "great experience" to diners, who find the "modern", "minimalist" space either "chic" or "cold"; P.S. be sure to check out the "must-see bathrooms."

🗲 **Sullivan's Steakhouse** *Steak* — 27 | 24 | 25 | $48

South End | 1928 South Blvd. (Tremont Ave.) | 704-335-8228 | www.sullivansteakhouse.com

Bring "fellow carnivores" to this "classy" South End steakhouse serving "huge portions" ("wear elastic waistbands") of "consistently excellent" beef and "scrumptious" seafood amid a "swanky", "boxing-themed" setting; a "great bar scene" and nightly live jazz enhance the "happenin'" vibe, and though it may be "pricey", it also "can't be beat."

Toscana 🗲 *Italian* — 26 | 23 | 25 | $42

SouthPark | Specialty Shops on the Park | 6401 Morrison Blvd. (Roxborough Rd.) | 704-367-1808

You just "won't be able to go wrong" at serial restaurateur Augusto Conte's SouthPark standby that "deserves" – and gets – high marks for "insanely good" Northern Italian specialties ("bravo!" to the "wonderful" white bean and olive oil overture) as well as "cordial", "attentive" service; P.S. opt for the "lovely patio" if weather permits.

🗲 **Upstream** *Seafood* — 26 | 25 | 24 | $46

SouthPark | Phillips Pl. | 6902 Phillips Place Ct. (bet. Colony & Sharon Rds.) | 704-556-7730 | www.upstreamit.com

Surveyors sup on "outrageously good" seafood at this "chic" SouthPark eatery where chef Tom Condron's "exotic", "outside-the-box" cooking "amazes", and the "attentive", "enthusiastic" staff "pampers" both the "ladies who lunch and the chaps who cut deals"; it manages to be "upscale" and "not uptight", and if some balk at the prices, more maintain it's "worth every dime"; N.B. there's also a covered, heated patio.

🗲 **Volare** 🗲 *Italian* — 28 | – | 26 | $43

Elizabeth | 1523 Elizabeth Ave. (bet. N. Torrence St. & Travis Ave.) | 704-370-0208 | www.volareristoranteitaliano.com

Dinner "can qualify as foreplay" at this "very romantic" "gem" in Elizabeth that scores with "serious", "heavenly" Italian food that's "magic" to the eyes and "perfection" to the palate; "passionate" service and a "charming" owner produce "pampering done right", so "reserve early" and get ready for a "splurge" that's a "must."

Zebra Restaurant & Wine Bar 🗲 *French* — 25 | 24 | 22 | $50

SouthPark | 4521 Sharon Rd. (bet. Fairview Rd. & Morrison Blvd.) | 704-442-9525 | www.zebrarestaurant.net

"Attention to detail" abounds at this SouthPark New French, from the "fantastic" fare featuring "superb flavors" that are exceeded only by the dishes' "visual appeal" to "unobtrusive" service to an "impressive" 800-label wine list; they keep the "noise level well under control", which pleases those interested in business or romance; P.S. "lunch is a steal", but you may want to "pack your platinum card" for dinner.

Chicago

Restaurant	Cuisine
29 Carlos'	French
28 Les Nomades	French
Tru	French
Alinea	American
Tallgrass	French
Arun's	Thai
27 Topolobampo	Mexican
Charlie Trotter's	American
Everest	French
Vie	American
Spring	American/Seafood
Barrington Country	French
Oceanique	French/Seafood
Blackbird	American
26 Courtright's	American
Frontera Grill	Mexican
Spiaggia	Italian
Mirai Sushi	Japanese
Avenues	French/Seafood
mk*	American

OTHER NOTEWORTHY PLACES

Aigre Doux	American
Avec	Mediterranean
BOKA	American
Chicago Chop House	Steak
DeLaCosta	Nuevo Latino
Gage, The	American
Gibsons	Steak
Green Zebra	Vegetarian
Joe's Sea/Steak	Seafood/Steak
Lou Malnati's	Pizza
Morton's	Steak
Nacional 27	Nuevo Latino
Naha	American
Niche	American
NoMI	French
North Pond	American
one sixtyblue	French
Osteria di Tramonto	Italian
Sepia	American
Wildfire	Steak

* Indicates a tie with restaurant above

subscribe to zagat.com

Aigre Doux *American*

— | — | — | E

River North | 230 W. Kinzie St. (bet. N. Franklin & Wells Sts.) | 312-329-9400 | www.aigredouxchicago.com

With a culinary pedigree that most recently includes LA's Chateau Marmont, husband-and-wife cooking duo Mohammad Islam and Malika Ameen – he's savory, she's sweet – helms this pricey, sophisticated New American in River North, where the linear, spartan-chic dining room is intimately illuminated with rows of dangling bulbs; a smart wine list and an adjacent bakery complete the experience.

⚡ Alinea Ⓜ *American*

28 | 27 | 28 | $168

Lincoln Park | 1723 N. Halsted St. (bet. North Ave. & Willow St.) | 312-867-0110 | www.alinearestaurant.com

Astronomic scores support the "sheer genius" of chef-owner Grant Achatz and the "astonishing flavors" of his "fabulous" New American cuisine at this Lincoln Park "thrill ride" that "engages all of your senses" and "expands your concept of fine dining"; the space is "lovely, understated and serene", the nearly 700-bottle wine list is "superb" and the "polished service" is near "perfect" too; be prepared, however, as this "surreal" "journey" will be "loooong" and "ungodly expensive" – though "worth it"; N.B. closed Mondays and Tuesdays.

Arun's Ⓜ *Thai*

28 | 24 | 26 | $88

Northwest Side | 4156 N. Kedzie Ave. (bet. Belle Plaine & Berteau Aves.) | 773-539-1909 | www.arunsthai.com

Arun Sampanthavivat's "completely inventive", "customized" 12-course tasting-only menu of "transcendental" Thai is tantamount to "edible art", "served with care and courtesy" in a "simply" "elegant gallery" setting with a "great wine cellar"; sure, it's tucked away on the Northwest Side, but it's "as good as the best in Thailand" and "a whole lot easier to get to", even if it "can seem wildly expensive"; in other words, "make sure this is on your 'things to do before I die' list."

Avec ● *Mediterranean*

25 | 19 | 22 | $42

West Loop | 615 W. Randolph St. (Jefferson St.) | 312-377-2002 | www.avecrestaurant.com

"The fabulous people" "squeeze into" this "must-dine" Med small-plates specialist for the "incredible flavors" of Koren Grieveson's "fantasy" "peasant cuisine", paired with an "eclectic, affordable wine list" and served by a "knowledgeable staff"; its "metrosexual Paul Bunyan" setting with table sharing and bench seating is "not for the anti-social", who lambaste it as "loud" and "uncomfortable", but extroverts enthuse over the "hip" West Loop "scene"; P.S. "if only they took reservations."

Avenues Ⓜ *French/Seafood*

26 | 26 | 26 | $88

River North | Peninsula Hotel | 108 E. Superior St. (bet. Michigan Ave. & Rush St.) | 312-573-6754

A trio of 26s conveys surveyors' praise for this "posh", "gracious" River North New French–seafood sophisticate where boulevardiers are buoyed by Graham Elliot Bowles' "amazing tasting menus" and "innovative, avant-garde presentations" – plus the "champagne cart pre-dinner is a nice touch"; the "well-spaced" tables of its "luxurious" Peninsula Hotel setting provide "beautiful views", and service strikes most as "impeccable" (though a smidge "stuffy" to some); P.S. you might want to "come with an expense account or rich aunt" and, if you're a gent, a jacket is recommended as well.

Barrington Country Bistro 🗷 *French* | 27 | 21 | 24 | $42 |

Barrington | Foundry Shopping Ctr. | 700 W. Northwest Hwy. (Hart Rd.) | 847-842-1300 | www.barringtoncountrybistro.com

Toques off to the "top-quality traditional bistro fare" at this "hidden gem" situated in an "inauspicious" Northwest Suburban mall; it's a "continual favorite" for its "pleasant country-French setting" (including comfortable outdoor seating), "excellent service" and the presence of a particularly "gracious owner"; P.S. "lunch is a special treat."

Blackbird 🗷 *American* | 27 | 20 | 23 | $57 |

West Loop | 619 W. Randolph St. (bet. Desplaines & Jefferson Sts.) | 312-715-0708 | www.blackbirdrestaurant.com

Make sure this "polished" West Loop "classic" is on your list for "pure tastes in a pure space", featuring "local and organic ingredients" in "exquisite" New American cuisine that "makes you proud to be from Chicago"; the setting may be "stark" ("the whole white on white thing") and the "tables cramped", but there's "plenty of eye candy", plus "consummately professional" service and "one of the highest-quality wine selections in the city, at all price ranges"; N.B. the Food rating may not reflect the addition of Mike Sheerin (ex NYC's wd-50) as chef de cuisine, taking over the kitchen reins from owner Paul Kahan.

BOKA *American* | 23 | 22 | 22 | $46 |

Lincoln Park | 1729 N. Halsted St. (North Ave.) | 312-337-6070 | www.bokachicago.com

"Finally, a good pre-theater spot that you'd actually visit even when you don't have Steppenwolf tickets" fawn flatterers of this Lincoln Park eatery's "creative" small and large plates (from a seasonal New American "menu that changes all the time"), "attractive staff" and "sophisticated", "high-energy" "date" environment; hecklers, however, hiss about "hype for not a lot of substance", noting it "can be noisy" and "prices are a little steep", but all agree it has "one of the best outdoor seating areas"; N.B. the arrival of chef Giuseppe Tentori (ex Charlie Trotter's) is not reflected in the Food score.

🗷 Carlos' *French* | 29 | 25 | 28 | $89 |

Highland Park | 429 Temple Ave. (Waukegan Ave.) | 847-432-0770 | www.carlos-restaurant.com

For a "memorable evening", head to this 26-year-old North Shore "treasure", a "fine-dining" "temple on Temple Avenue" that's ranked No. 1 for Food among Chicagoland restaurants on the strength of its "superb", "very creative" New French fare, which is accompanied by a "fantastic wine list" and served by a "staff that knows when to be friendly and when to be reserved"; the feel is "formal yet extremely comfortable, with cozy booths and soft lighting", making it a "great celebration place" – "if you can afford it"; N.B. jackets required.

🗷 Charlie Trotter's 🗷 *American* | 27 | 25 | 27 | VE |

Lincoln Park | 816 W. Armitage Ave. (Halsted St.) | 773-248-6228 | www.charlietrotters.com

"A religious experience" "worth a mortgage payment" awaits at Chicagoland's Most Popular restaurant, this "epitome of [New]

	FOOD	DECOR	SERVICE	COST

American gastronomy" in Lincoln Park, where customers are "daz-zled" by "brilliant" chef Charlie Trotter's daily changing menu (with "fantastic pairings" from an "exceptional wine cellar") and "cosseted" by a "masterfully courteous and knowledgeable" staff; a few find the "formal" feel "churchlike" and the whole experience a bit "precious", but most maintain it's "absolutely sublime", especially if you "get a reservation at the kitchen table"; N.B. jackets required, and be aware that it's only open on occasional Mondays.

Chicago Chop House *Steak* 25 | 20 | 22 | $54

River North | 60 W. Ontario St. (bet. Clark & Dearborn Sts.) | 312-787-7100 | www.chicagochophouse.com

A "heavy hitter" "in a city that knows meat", this "quintessential Chicago steak joint" and "ol' boys club" in River North "is rich in tradition – and you can taste it in the food" (including "wonderful prime rib"), not to mention see it in the "historical" setting with tin ceilings plus a "great bar area with old-time drinks made the way they should be made"; P.S. "men with white collars" like to "expense this one."

Courtright's Ⓜ *American* 26 | 25 | 26 | $58

Willow Springs | 8989 S. Archer Ave. (Willow Springs Rd.) | 708-839-8000 | www.courtrights.com

Excursionists to the Southwest Surburbs eagerly enthuse about this "excellent out-of-the-way" "destination restaurant" where "marvel-ous", "creative seasonal" New American "meals are carefully planned, expertly prepared and exquisitely presented" in a "classic atmo-sphere" with "beautiful gardens" ("grazing deer appear magically as if on cue"); P.S. "the wine alone is worth the trip."

DeLaCosta *Nuevo Latino* - | - | - | E

River North | 465 E. Illinois St. (bet. Lake Shore Dr. & McClurg Ct.) | 312-464-1700 | www.delacostachicago.com

Chef Douglas Rodriguez (of Miami's OLA empire) makes his Midwestern debut with this River North supper club serving pricey Nuevo Latino cuisine paired with six styles of sangria and sexy 'pop-tails' (cocktail popsicles); the 12,000-sq.-ft. setting includes multiple high-style environments, including a ceviche bar, a private wine room and a 'solarium' overlooking Ogden Slip.

Everest ⓈⓂ *French* 27 | 26 | 27 | $91

Loop | One Financial Pl. | 440 S. LaSalle St., 40th fl. (Congress Pkwy.) | 312-663-8920 | www.everestrestaurant.com

This "romantic", "formal" "expense-account haven" is "still at its peak" thanks to Jean Joho's "delectable" New French–Alsatian cuisine, an "exemplary wine list", "totally professional service" and "a breath-taking view" from "the top of the [Loop] Financial District"; a recent face-lift may appease fans who felt that the "nouveau riche" decor was "stuck in the '80s", though it may do little for those concerned that the "attitude" "is loftier than the location."

Ⓩ Frontera Grill ⓈⓂ *Mexican* 26 | 21 | 22 | $39

River North | 445 N. Clark St. (bet. Hubbard & Illinois Sts.) | 312-661-1434 | www.fronterakitchens.com

"Top-of-the-line Mexican [food] with a focus on fresh ingredients" comes courtesy of "culinary hero Rick Bayless" at this River North "treasure"; "bold, bright" and "somewhat raucous", it's "less expensive and more casual" than its "refined big brother", Topolobampo, with the same "superb wine selections" and "great margarita-tequila menu", but some say "service can be spotty when it's busy – which is always."

Gage, The *American*   – | – | – | M

South Loop | 24 S. Michigan Ave. (Madison St.) | 312-372-4243 | www.thegagechicago.com

A welcome addition to the South Loop near Millennium Park and the Art Institute, this classy New American restaurant/tavern in a grand old Louis Sullivan building exudes an upscale, vintage feeling with its tin ceiling, green subway tile and massive bar; in the kitchen, chef Dirk Flanigan puts a foodie spin on the midpriced pub fare; N.B. for parking, try the nearby Grant Park garage.

Gibsons Bar & Steakhouse ● *Steak*   25 | 19 | 23 | $56

Gold Coast | 1028 N. Rush St. (Bellevue Pl.) | 312-266-8999
Rosemont | Doubletree Hotel | 5464 N. River Rd. (bet. Balmoral & Bryn Mawr Aves.) | 847-928-9900
www.gibsonssteakhouse.com

"Aggressive carnivores" take an "authentic Chicago power trip" at this Gold Coast "high-roller" haven "where everything is big", including the "excellent cuts of [prime] meat cooked to perfection", the personalities of the "outgoing staff" – and the "big check"; there's a "fantastic" "cigar-friendly" bar scene for those "long, crowded waits", so "make a reservation, arrive early and hope for your table before the seasons change"; P.S. "the Rosemont location is as good – and easier" to navigate.

Green Zebra *Vegetarian*   25 | 23 | 23 | $51

West Town | 1460 W. Chicago Ave. (Greenview Ave.) | 312-243-7100 | www.greenzebrachicago.com

"You don't have to be a tree-hugger to love" this West Town "winner" where Shawn McClain (Spring) "makes you want to eat your vegetables" with his "complex" "seasonal" "small plates" ("converts" crow "you'll never miss the meat" – though a few chicken and fish dishes are also offered); factor in "knowledgeable service" and "smart" "Zen" surroundings and you have a "haute" "heaven" – though critics contend "nothing impresses as much as the prices."

Joe's Seafood, Prime Steak & Stone Crab *Seafood/Steak*   26 | 21 | 25 | $57

River North | 60 E. Grand Ave. (Rush St.) | 312-379-5637 | www.joesstonecrabchicago.com

River North residents swear this "great Midwestern version of Joe's Stone Crab" is even "better than the Miami original" thanks to "wonderful seafood feasting", "terrific" prime steaks and "to-die-for sides and Key lime pie", all "professionally served" in a "clubby", sometimes "raucous" setting; still, there are "long waits" and "for this kind of money" you could almost "head south to SoBe for the real thing."

☑ Les Nomades 🅢 Ⓜ *French*   28 | 26 | 28 | $90

Streeterville | 222 E. Ontario St. (bet. Fairbanks Ct. & St. Clair St.) | 312-649-9010 | www.lesnomades.net

This "refined" former private club in Streeterville "still satisfies" thanks to chef Chris Nugent, who uses "generous quantities of luxury ingredients" in his "excellent" New French cuisine, which is backed by a "fine" wine list and "superb service"; the "formal" (some say "stuffy") setting has an "understated", "hushed" tone that befits "a romantic rendezvous" or "an important business dinner" for a "cut-above" clientele that can afford "top-of-the-line prices."

Lou Malnati's Pizzeria *Pizza*   24 | 13 | 17 | $18

River North | 439 N. Wells St. (Hubbard St.) | 312-828-9800
Lincoln Park | 958 W. Wrightwood Ave. (Lincoln Ave.) | 773-832-4030
Southwest Side | 3859 W. Ogden Ave. (Cermak Rd.) | 773-762-0800
Evanston | 1850 Sherman Ave. (University Pl.) | 847-328-5400
Lincolnwood | 6649 N. Lincoln Ave. (bet. Devon & Pratt Aves.) | 847-673-0800
Buffalo Grove | 85 S. Buffalo Grove Rd. (Lake Cook Rd.) | 847-215-7100
Elk Grove Village | 1050 E. Higgins Rd. (bet. Arlington Heights & Busse Rds.) | 847-439-2000
Schaumburg | 1 S. Roselle Rd. (Schaumburg Rd.) | 847-985-1525
Naperville | 131 W. Jefferson Ave. (Washington St.) | 630-717-0700
www.loumalnatis.com

This "local chain" boasts a "cult following" of "addicts" who relish its "ridiculously good", "real Chicago pizza" – both the "decadent deep-dish" and the "even-better thin-crust" version – and "love the butter crust", "pure, simple sauce" with "chunks of tomato" and "thick cheese"; still, its reign at the top of the pie charts "of the known world" (and the local competition) is "not undisputed", with some citing "inconsistent service" and "cookie-cutter decor" as drawbacks.

Mirai Sushi Ⓢ *Japanese*   26 | 20 | 20 | $46

Wicker Park | 2020 W. Division St. (Damen Ave.) | 773-862-8500
"In the face of a Chicago sushi explosion", this "hip" Wicker Park Japanese "remains the best" per raters who order its "pricey" but "pristine fish" à la carte – the "unusual" "maki don't disappoint but the quality of the straight-up sashimi sets this place apart" – or "put themselves in the chef's hands for a sublime omakase dinner"; add the "divine sake" (over 30 varieties) and the "scene", especially on the "darker and more swank" upstairs level, and it's no surprise satisfied surveyors make this their "go-to" for raw fin fare.

mk *American*   26 | 24 | 25 | $62

River North | 868 N. Franklin St. (bet. Chestnut & Locust Sts.) | 312-482-9179 | www.mkchicago.com

Chef Eric Simmons (ex Bradley Ogden in Las Vegas) has come aboard Michael Kornick's "suave", still-"humming" River North "hot spot" that's managed to "endure and reinvent itself" time and again, offering New American cooking that's "outstanding without being fussy or pretentious"; the "bi-level" "loft" interior is "sleek" and the "attentive, accommodating" staffers know the "masterful wine list" and cheeses "like it's their business", so even if some raters report "rushed service" and "dreadfully noisy" digs, more maintain it's a "favorite."

Ⓩ Morton's, The Steakhouse *Steak*   26 | 21 | 24 | $59

Loop | 65 E. Wacker Pl. (bet. Michigan & Wabash Aves.) | 312-201-0410
Gold Coast | Newberry Plaza | 1050 N. State St. (Maple St.) | 312-266-4820

(continued)

(continued)

Morton's, The Steakhouse

Rosemont | 9525 W. Bryn Mawr Ave. (River Rd.) | 847-678-5155
Schaumburg | 1470 McConnor Pkwy. (Meacham Rd.) | 847-413-8771
Westchester | 1 Westbrook Corporate Ctr. (22nd St.) | 708-562-7000
www.mortons.com

"Still the standard" for "scrumptious slabs of the best [prime] beef known to man", this "granddaddy" is a "candy store for carnivores" complete with the "show-and-tell" presentation cart, "huge sides" and "soufflés meant to be shared", plus a "great wine list" and a "professional staff"; decor at various locations may stray from the "quintessential", "manly" Gold Coast "mother ship", and some raters reckon it's "resting on its laurels", but a well-fed majority insists this "class act" is "worth" its "break-the-bank prices."

Nacional 27 🅂 *Nuevo Latino*   22 | 24 | 20 | $42

River North | 325 W. Huron St. (Orleans St.) | 312-664-2727 |
www.nacional27.net

It's "a carnival for the palate" at this River North "hot spot" with "breathtaking decor" that serves a Nuevo Latino "smorgasbord" of chef Randy Zweiban's "inventive", "well-prepared" fare, including "creative tapas", "from every country south of the Rio Grande"; it's usually "quiet" and "cool", but "turns into a dance floor" "later in the evening" Thursday–Saturday, with "salsa that doesn't come in a bowl."

Naha 🅂 *American*   26 | 23 | 24 | $59

River North | 500 N. Clark St. (Illinois St.) | 312-321-6242 |
www.naha-chicago.com

Expect "unfussy", "innovative fine dining" at this River North "favorite" that's considered "consistently among the best"; Carrie Nahabedian's "exciting menu" of "fresh" New American fare with Med flair is paired with a "thoughtful wine list", "seductively served" by a "cool staff" and "shown off" in a "clean-lined", "minimalist" space that "feels like a spa" – in fact, the "excellent" experience is "only marred by the high decibel level" "when it's crowded"; P.S. don't miss "one of the city's best burgers (lunch only)."

Niche 🅂🅜 *American*   - | - | - | E

Geneva | 14 S. Third St. (State St.) | 630-262-1000 |
www.nichegeneva.com

Veteran chef Jeremy Lycan and more than a dozen staffers from the late 302 West have regrouped to once again offer quality (and pricey) New American cooking in West Suburban Geneva; the intimate, white-and-wood space has a clean feel, with a granite bar and a walk-in wine room housing an all-American selection sourced from boutique vineyards.

NoMI *French*   26 | 27 | 26 | $71

Gold Coast | Park Hyatt Chicago | 800 N. Michigan Ave. (Chicago Ave.) |
312-239-4030 | www.nomirestaurant.com

At this Gold Coast "lap of luxury", the "ethereal" "Zen" environs (including an "unbeatable view" of the Water Tower) set the stage for the "intriguing flavor combinations" of chef Christophe David's "exquisite" New French cuisine; it's a "special-occasion" "splurge" where "quality sushi" and an "excellent wine list" are just the beginning: additional assets include "discreet service", a "killer Sunday brunch", a "lovely outdoor terrace" and a "very swishy bar"; still, a minority finds it "stuffy" and doesn't relish "paying for the view."

North Pond Ⓜ *American* | 25 | 27 | 23 | $59 |

Lincoln Park | 2610 N. Cannon Dr. (bet. Diversey & Fullerton Pkwys.) | 773-477-5845 | www.northpondrestaurant.com

The "uncommon combination" of Bruce Sherman's "wonderfully crafted" "seasonal" cuisine, an "excellent wine list" and a "tranquil", "idyllic setting" of "lovely Arts and Crafts rooms" with "great skyline views" makes this New American "on the pond in [Lincoln] Park" "one of Chicago's finest and most unique" places for a "romantic meal or special occasion"; most surveyors "feel transported a million miles away", but others are earthbound by "inconsistent food and service" and "prices that have crept up"; P.S. they serve summer lunch and "delightful Sunday brunch" year-round.

Oceanique Ⓩ *French/Seafood* | 27 | 21 | 24 | $52 |

Evanston | 505 Main St. (bet. Chicago & Hinman Aves.) | 847-864-3435 | www.oceanique.com

"Unpretentious" "fine dining" is the house special at this North Suburban New French "treasure" where chef-owner Mark Grosz creates "a flawless assortment" of dishes featuring the "best seafood in the Chicago area", plus "plenty of alternate choices for meat people"; expect an "excellent wine list" and a "well-educated staff" in a "pleasant" setting where you can "enjoy the food and your companions without being dressed to the nines" (though some luxe-lovers would "upgrade" the atmosphere); P.S. try "the $39 three-course dinner Monday–Friday."

one sixtyblue Ⓩ *French* | 25 | 24 | 23 | $56 |

Market District | 1400 W. Randolph St. (Ogden Ave.) | 312-850-0303 | www.onesixtyblue.com

"Exciting and adventurous meals" await at this "stylish" New French establishment co-owned by basketball icon Michael Jordan that's "worth the detour" to the fringe of the Market District for "terrific" cuisine "balancing creativity and simplicity" from Martial Noguier, "a chef who cares", plus "a good selection of reasonably priced wines" and a "beautifully designed" room by Adam Tihany; it's a package that leads satisfied respondents to describe it as a "perfect place" "for a romantic dinner" or "before a concert at the United Center."

Osteria di Tramonto *Italian* | - | - | - | M |

Wheeling | Westin Chicago North Shore | 601 N. Milwaukee Ave. (Apple Dr.) | 847-777-6570 | www.cenitare.com

Rick Tramonto (ex Tru) cooks up classic and contemporary multiregional Italian cuisine in Wheeling's new Westin Chicago North Shore hotel; the seasonal menu is at once rustic and modern, a philosophy that's carried through in the decor with its exposed brick, 10,000-bottle glass wine wall and an open kitchen with dining counter; N.B. breakfast includes goodies from partner Gale Gand's on-site coffee bar.

Sepia *American* | - | - | - | M |

Market District | 123 N. Jefferson St. (bet. Randolph & Washington Sts.) | 312-441-1920 | www.sepiachicago.com

At this sophisticated Market District newcomer, toque Kendal Duque's impressive string of celeb-chef mentors (Julian Serrano, Alice Waters, etc.) comes through in his seasonal, simply presented New American cuisine (with a wine list to match); set in a remodeled printing house, it blends modern and vintage elements, including extravagant light fixtures, an 800-bottle floor-to-ceiling wine wall and – in a nod to the name – a late-19th-century antique camera.

Spiaggia *Italian*   26 | 27 | 25 | $80

Gold Coast | One Magnificent Mile Bldg. | 980 N. Michigan Ave., 2nd fl. (Oak St.) | 312-280-2750 | www.spiaggiarestaurant.com

Expect a "peak dining experience" at this "honed-to-perfection", "luxury" Gold Coaster boasting "sublime", "incomparable Italian" cuisine from chef Tony Mantuano, an "extensive wine list", a "sumptuous" setting with "spectacular views" of the Michigans (both Lake and Avenue) and "superlative service"; most maintain it's "one of the few places where the high price tag is worth it", though some submit that the staff's "snooty" and the "small portions" are "overpriced" (served only in the cafe, "lunch is a lot less expensive"); N.B. jackets required, jeans not allowed.

Spring Ⓜ *American/Seafood*   27 | 25 | 25 | $59

Wicker Park | 2039 W. North Ave. (Damen Ave.) | 773-395-7100 | www.springrestaurant.net

"As fresh and exciting as the season it's named after", this "hip" New American seafooder in Wicker Park inspires acolytes to ask "is it impolite to lick the plate?" after devouring one of the "incredible", "perfectly prepared" "creations" ("with a slight Asian slant") from chef Shawn McClain (Green Zebra); the "quietly elegant setting" "in a converted bathhouse" is "beautiful and peaceful", the service is "polished but not overwhelming" and there's an "outstanding wine list" too, so if you don't have a legitimate "special occasion, just come up with one."

Ⓩ Tallgrass Ⓜ *French*   28 | 24 | 25 | $69

Lockport | 1006 S. State St. (10th St.) | 815-838-5566 | www.tallgrassrestaurant.com

"Spectacular", "innovative" New French fare and a "deep wine list" (600 labels strong) fuel this "venerable" "foodie's paradise" "in the middle of nowhere" – aka historic Southwest Suburban Lockport – that's "well worth the drive from anywhere"; gourmets gush they "would go broke if they [lived] nearby", returning for chef-partner Robert Burcenski's "fine haute cuisine" with "wonderful presentation" in a "very private", "romantic" space; N.B. jackets are suggested.

Topolobampo Ⓢ Ⓜ *Mexican*   27 | 23 | 25 | $57

River North | 445 N. Clark St. (bet. Hubbard & Illinois Sts.) | 312-661-1434 | www.rickbayless.com

"This is what the food in heaven must taste like" posit praisers of this "pinnacle" of Mexican *alta cucina* in River North, where "every bite" of "creative genius" Rick Bayless' cuisine is "utterly swoon-worthy", the tequila list is "to die for" and the "passionate staff" "pampers" patrons; most feel it's "more elegant than its attached sister restaurant, Frontera Grill", with fare that "really is better", even if a handful of heretics wonder "is it worth the price difference?"; P.S. "book well ahead", as getting "weekend reservations can take forever."

	FOOD	DECOR	SERVICE	COST

⚡ Tru ⚡ *French* — 28 | 27 | 28 | $117

Streeterville | 676 N. St. Clair St. (bet. Erie & Huron Sts.) | 312-202-0001 | www.trurestaurant.com

"Art and food meet and really, really like each other" at this jackets-required Streeterville "temple of excess" that "amazes" with "progressive, daring" New French plates plus sommelier Scott Tyree's "divinely inspired" 1,400-bottle wine selection, all borne by a virtually "flawless" staff within a "stark, simple" setting sporting an "original Andy Warhol" and "a lovely little tuffet for Madame's handbag"; "sticker shock" aside, it's a "magical experience" that "will become a lasting memory"; N.B. the Food score was tallied when founding chefs Rick Tramonto and Gale Gand were still at the helm.

Vie ⚡ *American* — 27 | 23 | 23 | $55

Western Springs | 4471 Lawn Ave. (Burlington Ave.) | 708-246-2082 | www.vierestaurant.com

West Suburbanites feel "lucky to have" this New American in the "quaint", "sleepy" town of Western Springs, where chef-owner "Paul Virant brings many of his Blackbird sensibilities" to his "haute" "seasonal" "dishes with excellent flavor combinations", paired with a "very interesting wine list"; just "steps from the train station", it's even "worth the reverse commute for adventurous Chicagoans", though some call the "modern, minimalist" decor "cold" and others wish "the service could catch up with the brilliance of the food."

⚡ Wildfire *Steak* — 23 | 21 | 21 | $40

River North | 159 W. Erie St. (bet. LaSalle & Wells Sts.) | 312-787-9000
Lincolnshire | 235 Parkway Dr. (Milwaukee Ave.) | 847-279-7900
Glenview | 1300 Patriot Blvd. (Lake Ave.) | 847-657-6363
Schaumburg | 1250 E. Higgins Rd. (National Pkwy.) | 847-995-0100
Oak Brook | Oakbrook Center Mall | 232 Oakbrook Ctr. (Rte. 83) | 630-586-9000
www.wildfirerestaurant.com

Spreading like their namesake, this "insanely popular" passel of Traditional American steakhouses from the Lettuce Entertain You group keeps carnivores "coming back" with "hearty Midwest-sized portions" from a "crowd-pleasing menu" of "awesome wood-fired" fare ("juicy" steaks and fresh seafood), "delicious chopped salad" and "great martini flights" in a "classy", "clubby" "'40s-style" setting; salivating surveyors swear it's "worth the wait" ("even with reservations"), but wet blankets rank these "noisy" "madhouses" "really rather ordinary, just on a grand scale."

Cincinnati

TOP FOOD RANKING

	Restaurant	Cuisine
29	Jean-Robert at Pigall's	American/French
28	Daveed's at 934	Eclectic
27	Boca	Italian
	Nicola's	Italian
	BonBonerie	Bakery/Tearoom
	Precinct, The	Steak
26	Carlo & Johnny	Seafood/Steak
25	Jeff Ruby's Steak	Steak
	Morton's*	Steak
	Pho Paris	French/Vietnamese

OTHER NOTEWORTHY PLACES

cumin	Indian
Dewey's Pizza	Pizza
JeanRo	French
Jo An Japanese	Japanese
Montgomery Inn	BBQ
Nectar	Eclectic
Primavista	Italian
Slims	Puerto Rican
Teak Thai	Thai
Tinks Cafe	Eclectic

🇿 **Boca** 🅂🅼 *Italian*   27 | 23 | 25 | $66

Oakley | 3200 Madison Rd. (bet. Braizee St. & Ridge Rd.) | 513-542-2022 | www.boca-restaurant.com

At this "bustling" Oakley Italian, "adventurous" chef/co-owner David Falk has "created the perfect storm": "innovative" "seasonal dishes" "with a contemporary spin", "fantastic wine pairings", a "cozy dining room" and "intuitive service" all help to make it one of "the most sought-after reservations in town"; though wallet-watchers warn "it'll cost ya" (particularly the "special" chef's tasting menu), most agree this "hipster's paradise" is "worth" it.

🇿 **BonBonerie** 🅱 *Bakery/Tearoom*   27 | 18 | 19 | $15

O'Bryonville | 2030 Madison Rd. (Grandin Rd.) | 513-321-3399 | www.thebonbon.com

The "to-die-for opera cream cake" and other "superb desserts" have sweet tooths singing arias of praise about this "cute" bakery and tearoom in O'Bryonville; set in a "charming", fanciful space that feels just "like being inside of a cupcake", it's the "perfect place for the girls to lunch" on sandwiches, salads and soups, or to "meet your mother" for a reservations-required afternoon high tea – "she'll love you forever"; N.B. no dinner.

---

* Indicates a tie with restaurant above

	FOOD	DECOR	SERVICE	COST

Carlo & Johnny ⧈ *Seafood/Steak* | 26 | 25 | 25 | $60 |
Montgomery | 9769 Montgomery Rd. (Bunker Hill Ln.) | 513-936-8600 |
www.jeffruby.com
"Another Jeff Ruby extravaganza", this "over-the-top" Montgomery
meat mecca serves up "sublime steaks" and "fresh seafood" (including a "terrific raw bar") in a "charming" supper-club setting "done to
the max" with "themed rooms that make you feel like the Godfather is
going to walk in"; a "lovely" staff provides "attentive service", and
though the "big prices" are "not for the faint of wallet", the "oversized
portions make it easy to share."

cumin ⧈ *Indian* | 22 | 22 | 21 | $39 |
Hyde Park | 3520 Erie Ave. (Pinehurst St.) | 513-871-8714 |
www.cuminrestaurant.com
After a recent move "just a few doors down", this "innovative" Indian in
Hyde Park is now housed in a "spare, modern setting" that's larger and
"more cosmopolitan than ever before" – you'll feel as though you've
"left Cincinnati for a much hipper city"; although most "keep cumin
back" for chef-owner Yajan Upadhyaya's "fresh takes" on traditional
fare, a minority finds the new "fusion-style" menu "not as tempting"
and misses the "more low-key" original.

⧉ Daveed's at 934 ⧈Ⓜ *Eclectic* | 28 | 21 | 25 | $60 |
Mt. Adams | 934 Hatch St. (Louden St.) | 513-721-2665
Scale "trendy" Mt. Adams for "a real dining adventure" in the form of
this "quirky, ambitious" "gem" where chef/co-owner David Cook's
"cutting-edge" Eclectic fare is "an absolute delight" and served by an
"impeccable" staff with a "remarkable ability to pair wines with each
course"; it's all set in a "charming" "old house" with a patio and several
dining rooms that are "colorful" but "much too crowded", thus proving
this "favorite" has "a loyal following."

Dewey's Pizza *Pizza* | 24 | 16 | 19 | $18 |
Clifton | 265 Hosea Ave. (Clifton Ave.) | 513-221-0400
Oakley | Oakley Sq. | 3014 Madison Rd. (bet. Markbreit Ave. &
Romana Pl.) | 513-731-7755
Newport | Newport on the Levee | 1 Levee Way (Monmouth St.) |
859-431-9700
Kenwood | 7767 Kenwood Rd. (Montgomery Rd.) | 513-791-1616
Symmes | Shops at Harper's Point | 11338 Montgomery Rd.
(bet. E. Kemper Rd. & Harper's Point Dr.) | 513-247-9955
www.deweyspizza.com
"Prepare to be wowed" by the "wonderful" pies at this "bustling" local
mini-chain where a "large variety of toppings" ("from traditional pep-
peroni" to "exotic" goat cheese) makes for "imaginative, tasty combinations"; given "tantalizing salads", "friendly, efficient service" and "a
beer and wine menu to boot", these parlors seem "perfect in every
way" –except, perhaps, for the "long waits"; P.S. "kids will be enthralled watching them make the pizza."

⧉ JeanRo *French* | 24 | 22 | 23 | $39 |
Downtown | 413 Vine St. (bet. 4th & 5th Sts.) | 513-621-1465 |
www.bistrojeanro.com
For "five-star food at two-star prices" from "the best chef in town",
Jean-Robert de Cavel, head to this "little bit of Paris" "in the heart" of

Cincinnati, where a "personable" staff serves up "authentic bistro food" that's "more reasonably priced" than at sibling Pigall's; the "simple", "warm", "unpretentious" atmosphere is "always a treat", and business types find it "as good as a Downtown lunch can get."

☑ Jean-Robert
at Pigall's ⬛Ⓜ *American/French*

| 29 | 27 | 27 | $81 |

Downtown | 127 W. Fourth St. (bet. Elm & Race Sts.) | 513-721-1345 | www.jean-robertatpigalls.com

"Jean-Robert de Cavel is the Zeus of Cincinnati restaurateurs and this is his Mt. Olympus" attest admirers of this "elegant" Downtown destination that's "the absolute best the city has to offer", ranking as No. 1 for Food and Popularity; while set-price menus spotlight the "truly astonishing" New American–New French food, "lovely", "modern decor" sets the stage for the staff's "almost telepathic" ministrations; in sum, "everything is first-class – including the check!"

☑ Jeff Ruby's Steakhouse ⬛ *Steak*

| 25 | 23 | 25 | $62 |

Downtown | 700 Walnut St. (7th St.) | 513-784-1200 | www.jeffruby.com

"Sinatra would have loved this "old-school Downtown steak joint" where "everything is big", including "huge" "slabs of red meat", "generous portions" of "spectacular" sides and "a tome of a wine list", all served in a "glitzy", "see-and-be-seen" setting with a "lively bar" and "big-city flair"; you'll be "treated like a king" by the "exemplary" staff, but expect the "prices to match" the service – "expensive" tabs have some grousing "it's beef, not gold."

Jo An Japanese Cuisine ⬛ *Japanese*

| 25 | 14 | 19 | $36 |

Erlanger | 3940 Olympic Blvd. (Mineola Pike), KY | 859-746-2634

"Hidden in an office park near the airport" in Kentucky, this "real-deal" Japanese draws "die-hard devotees" and employees from Toyota's nearby headquarters for an "insanely good" menu that "goes well beyond sushi" to include "authentic, unusual" dishes ("if you don't know what to order, try the bento box"); the "utilitarian" decor is "nothing to speak of", which has some fans hopeful this spot will "stay a secret."

☑ Montgomery Inn *BBQ*

| 21 | 18 | 20 | $32 |

Downtown | 925 Riverside Dr. (Pete Rose Way) | 513-721-7427
Ft. Mitchell | 400 Buttermilk Pike (I-75) | 859-344-5333
Montgomery | 9440 Montgomery Rd. (bet. Cooper & Remington Rds.) | 513-791-3482
www.montgomeryinn.com

"The best places to take a ribbing", these "Cincinnati legends" are the "kings of BBQ in the Queen City", offering "falling-off-the-bone" babybacks and "killer sauce"; "everyone has to visit once" to savor the "fun atmosphere" that includes "beautiful views of the Ohio River" at Downtown's Boathouse branch and "lots of sports memorabilia" at the Montgomery location; still, their "staggering popularity" means you'll "wait with the masses" and then feel compelled to "eat fast."

Morton's, The Steakhouse *Steak*

| 25 | - | 24 | $60 |

Downtown | Carew Tower Arcade | 411 Vine St. (5th St.) | 513-621-3111 | www.mortons.com

"For steak you can count on", "there is no comparison to the taste of the beef" at this Downtown link in a "reliable" national chain that's a "classic" "place to entertain clients" given its "spot-on" staff and "gargantuan portions" of "mouthwatering" meat ("well worth the high prices"); it recently moved up in the world – from the basement of the Tower Place Mall to the second floor of the Carew Tower Arcade – and now sports a view onto Fountain Square.

Nectar ⓜ *Eclectic*   24 | 18 | 22 | $41
Mt. Lookout | 1000 Delta Ave. (Linwood Ave.) | 513-929-0525 | www.thenectarrestaurant.com

"Fresh local ingredients meet inspired preparation" at chef-owner Julie Francis' "seasonal restaurant in Mt. Lookout Square"; despite its "limited menu", it's "a steal" for "astonishingly delicious" Eclectic food that is "consistently creative" ("but not weird") and served by a "subtle, knowledgeable" staff; still, some surveyors feel stung by the minimalist dining room's "hard benches and loud surroundings."

ⓩ Nicola's Ⓢ *Italian*   27 | 24 | 24 | $55
Downtown | 1420 Sycamore St. (Liberty St.) | 513-721-6200 | www.nicolasrestaurant.com

At this "truly fine ristorante" just north of Downtown, chef Cristian Pietoso draws praise from paesani for his "imaginative takes" on "marvelous Northern Italian cuisine", including "exquisite homemade pastas" that are topped with "sauces as good as in Italy" and accompanied by "personalized service"; although it's located "in an iffy neighborhood", you'll "feel at home" in the "beautiful", "soaring interior" or out on the "lovely patio."

Pho Paris *French/Vietnamese*   25 | 23 | 24 | $43
Covington | 318 Greenup St. (bet. 3rd & 4th Sts.), KY | 859-643-1234 | www.phoparis.com

Chef-owner Jean-Robert de Cavel "does it again", this time delivering "a remarkable fusion of French and Vietnamese cuisine" that's "consistently superb" and complemented by an "interesting wine list" and "friendly, knowledgeable" service; after its recent move to a "charming building" in Covington, KY, "all has come together" in a "colorful", "modern" space that's a "bit more casual" in keeping with prices that are also "slightly lower."

Precinct, The *Steak*   27 | 20 | 25 | $57
Columbia Tusculum | 311 Delta Ave. (Columbia Pkwy.) | 513-321-5454 | www.jeffruby.com

Set in a "charming old police precinct", this arresting Columbia Tusculum chophouse is a "classic" "Jeff Ruby restaurant", which means big portions, delicious steaks and killer service" that some find "even better" than the aged beef; the "lobster and veal are nothing to sneeze at" either, but "expect to spend a lot" and "to make new friends" with your "classy" neighbors – "tight seating" means you'll be "dining in [their] laps"; N.B. jacket and tie preferred.

Primavista *Italian*   24 | 23 | 23 | $47
Price Hill | Queen's Tower | 810 Matson Pl. (bet. 8th St. & Price Ave.) | 513-251-6467 | www.pvista.com

At this "underappreciated" option in "out-of-the-way" Price Hill, "you come for the view" – "go on a clear night" for a "primo" peek at the Downtown skyline and the Ohio River – "and leave loving" the "hearty portions" of "classic", "dependable" Northern Italian fare; though "a bit pricey", it gets "busy on weekends" with couples who consider it an "incredibly romantic" "place for a date."

Slims M *Puerto Rican*   24 | 15 | 17 | $36
Northside | 4046 Hamilton Ave. (Blue Rock St.) | 513-681-6500 | www.slimsrestaurant.com
"Cincinnati's answer to Chez Panisse" is this Northside Puerto Rican where "the ingredients are always fresh" and very "local" (chef-owner Patrick McCafferty "grows his own lettuce"), and the "interesting space" – think "shared tables" – fills up with an "eclectic clientele" that favors the "amazing" no-corkage-fee BYO policy; still, while it's a "master of the Slow Food movement", some say "everything is slow" here: "don't come if you're in a rush"; N.B. it's closed Monday-Wednesday and now accepts credit cards.

Teak Thai Cuisine *Thai*   21 | 14 | 17 | $28
Mt. Adams | 1051 St. Gregory St. (Jerome St.) | 513-665-9800
Mt. Adams means Thai for those who crave this "casual" venue's "varied" selection of "traditional" fare, including options "for the adventurous" as well as "above-average sushi"; "service is hit-or-miss", and since there's also "no emphasis on décor", some regulars recommend "waiting for beautiful weather and then eating outside" on the "festive" two-story patio; P.S. it "offers parking", but finding a space can still be "a real nuisance."

Tinks Cafe *Eclectic*   20 | 17 | 19 | $38
Clifton | 3410 Telford St. (Ludlow Ave.) | 513-961-6500 | www.tinkscafe.com
A "sophisticated" standout amid Clifton's "jungle of casual college eateries", this "oasis" offers up "imaginative, well-presented" Eclectic entrees with a dollop of "friendly" service and a side of "nice live jazz"; set in a "charming" former post office building, it draws "an older crowd" that has stamped it a "favorite for before or after a movie" at the "indie theater around the corner"; P.S. "reasonable" prices make it even more of a "wonderful surprise."

Cleveland

TOP FOOD RANKING

	Restaurant	Cuisine
29	Chez François	French
28	Downtown 140	American
27	Three Birds	American
	Johnny's Bar	Italian
	Lola	American
	Parallax	Eclectic/Seafood
	Red The Steakhouse	Steak
26	Blue Point	Seafood
	Giovanni's	Italian
	Johnny's Downtown	Italian

OTHER NOTEWORTHY PLACES

Restaurant	Cuisine
Baricelli Inn	American/Continental
Fahrenheit	American
fire food & drink	American
Flying Fig	American/Eclectic
Lolita	American/Mediterranean
Michaelangelo's	Italian
Momocho	Mexican
Moxie	American
One Walnut	American
Sérgio's Saravá	Brazilian

Baricelli Inn 🗷 *American/Continental* | 26 | 25 | 26 | $62 |

Little Italy | Baricelli Inn | 2203 Cornell Rd. (Murray Hill Rd.) | 216-791-6500 | www.baricelli.com

Although the aged, artisanal "cheeses alone are worth a trip" to this "Little Italy institution", the "outstanding selection" of *fromage* is but a prelude to an "imaginative" New American–Continental menu (a "symphony of flavors") from chef-owner Paul Minnillo plus a "substantial wine list" and "attentive service"; it's all set in a "lovely" historic mansion featuring several "elegant" rooms, an "intimate" garden patio and overnight accommodations; P.S. it's "expensive", but a recent menu revamp has added some lower-priced options.

⊠ Blue Point Grille *Seafood* | 26 | 25 | 25 | $50 |

Warehouse District | 700 W. Saint Clair Ave. (6th St.) | 216-875-7827 | www.hrcleveland.com

"The ultimate for oysters in Cleveland", this "upscale" Warehouse District destination offers "superb" seafood (which surveyors say is "surprisingly well-executed for an inland restaurant"), an "excellent" wine list and an "attentive, knowledgeable" staff that's "not just going through the motions"; though "a bit noisy" at times, the "airy", "nautically themed" interior is a "vibrant" setting that comes complete with a "lively bar" and floor-to-ceiling windows for "watching the crowds go by."

	FOOD	DECOR	SERVICE	COST

☒ Chez François Ⓜ French
29 | 27 | 28 | $58

Vermilion | 555 Main St. (Liberty Ave.) | 440-967-0630 |
www.chezfrancois.com

"If you're a serious foodie" or "if romance is calling, sail on up" – literally – to this "French gem" on the Vermilion River, where the "sumptuous" menu earns it the top rating for Food in the Cleveland area; "well worth the drive" west of Downtown, this "ethereal experience" ("the perfect place to propose!") also includes a "phenomenal wine list" and "professional" staff plus a "charming dining room" and "relaxing" waterside patio – "the only letdown is it's closed for winter"; N.B. jacket required.

☒ Downtown 140 ⓈAmerican
28 | 27 | 26 | $53

Hudson | 140 N. Main St. (Rte. 303) | 330-656-1294 |
www.downtown140.com

Though "hidden in a basement" in "suburban Hudson", this subterranean "gem" is a "lovely, intimate restaurant" offering "outstanding ambiance" to go with its "imaginative" Asian- and French-accented New American menu, "wonderful wine list" and "top-notch service"; its "specialty is small plates with big taste" that "encourage culinary exploration", and though the "tantalizing tidbits" add up to "pricey" tabs, diners declare this "unique experience" is "not to be missed."

Fahrenheit Ⓢ American
25 | 23 | 22 | $46

Tremont | 2417 Professor Ave. (Jefferson Ave.) | 216-781-8858 |
www.fahrenheittremont.com

Just like its "trendy Tremont" locale, this "funky", "hip", "high-energy" bistro is a "hot place to see and be seen" while sampling "inventive" New American fare from chef-owner Rocco Whalen's "ever-evolving" menu ("to-die-for" Kobe beef short ribs, "tasty" pizzas); though it's a "fabulous value", it "can get a little loud at peak hours", so "arrive early" to sip a "frosty cocktail" at the bar or take advantage of the weekend's "great late-night dining" possibilities.

☒ fire food & drink Ⓜ American
26 | 22 | 23 | $46

Shaker Square | 13220 Shaker Sq. (N. Moreland Blvd.) | 216-921-3473 |
www.firefoodanddrink.com

"Always a hot place to be", this New American "gem" lights up Shaker Square with a "superb" "seasonal menu" from chef-owner Doug Katz, who "never runs out of creativity" as he makes use of organic and "locally grown ingredients"; while gourmets gush about the tandoor-roasted dinner entrees and the "unbelievable" Sunday brunch, a few confess the "crowded" space is too "noisy" "for comfortable conversation"; P.S. check out the "patio in summer for people-watching."

Flying Fig Ⓜ American/Eclectic
26 | 22 | 24 | $41

Ohio City | 2523 Market Ave. (W. 25th St.) | 216-241-4243 |
www.theflyingfig.com

"Fabulous" chef-owner Karen Small flies "ahead of the curve" at this "cool" Ohio City hangout where her New American–Eclectic menu is like "a feast for the senses", starring "creative yet still recognizable" small plates made with "local, seasonal ingredients"; a "casually sophisticated" setting, "attentive" service and "affordable" prices all make it "great for a cozy date", while "the best happy-hour specials" keep the the bar "hopping" with a "fun crowd."

	FOOD	DECOR	SERVICE	COST

Giovanni's Ristorante 🗷 *Italian* — 26 | 24 | 27 | $62
Beachwood | 25550 Chagrin Blvd. (Richmond Rd.) | 216-831-8625 |
www.giovanniscleveland.com

"Elegant", "old-fashioned" and "more formal than most", this "wonderful" Beachwood "fixture" is "everything a high-end restaurant should be and more", wowing its admirers for over 30 years with "superb" Northern Italian cuisine, a 700-bottle wine list, "impeccable" service and a "lovely" interior that belies its office-building locale; hipsters claim it "can be stuffy" and "expensive", but those who "walk away feeling pampered" consider it "well worth" the price.

☑ Johnny's Bar 🗷 *Italian* — 27 | 21 | 25 | $55
West Boulevard | 3164 Fulton Rd. (Trent Ave.) | 216-281-0055

"Don't mind the name", the nondescript exterior or the "out-of-the-way" setting west of Downtown, because you'll find "nirvana" inside the doors of this "fine" Northern Italian that's been an "institution" for over 80 years, with a "classic art deco interior" to prove it; it's "a real experience" that "gives you the feeling of a great New York restaurant", from the "awesome food" and "well-heeled clientele" to "waiters with personality" and a bill that necessitates "taking out a second mortgage"; N.B. lunch on Thursdays and Fridays only.

Johnny's Downtown *Italian* — 26 | 23 | 25 | $55
Warehouse District | 1406 W. Sixth St. (bet. St. Clair & Superior Aves.) |
216-623-0055

"An oasis of good things" in the Warehouse District, this "upscale", "masculine" little brother to Johnny's Bar combines "amazing" Northern Italian cuisine with "friendly, old-style" service and a "classy" setting that comes complete with a "great bar" and a "delightful patio"; while "the place smells like suits" to more casual customers, the city's "power brokers" find it ideal "for business entertaining", especially when "on an expense account" – it's "pricey but worth it."

☑ Lola *American* — 27 | 27 | 25 | $52
Downtown | 2058 E. Fourth St. (Prospect Ave.) | 216-621-5652 |
www.lolabistro.com

Chef/co-owner Michael Symon has reopened his flagship in Downtown's nascent entertainment district, and this "long-awaited" incarnation is "a welcome breath of urban sophistication" thanks to its "cutting-edge" New American cuisine and "fabulous" setting – don't miss the "stunning bar"; it can get "noisy", but it's emerged as the "hottest table in town" (it's ranked No. 1 for Popularity in the Cleveland area), with "professional service" and a "trendy atmosphere" adding to its widespread appeal.

Lolita 🅼 *American/Mediterranean* — 26 | 23 | 25 | $42
Tremont | 900 Literary Rd. (Professor Ave.) | 216-771-5652 |
www.lolabistro.com

It may be Lola's "more informal baby sister", but this "sexy, romantic" Tremont bistro boasts an equally "craveworthy" menu from celebrity chef Michael Symon: the "creative" New American–Med offerings include "spectacular" house-cured meats, artisanal cheeses and "gourmet comfort food" like mac 'n' cheese with roasted chicken; "attentive" service, a "reasonably priced" wine list and "amazing" happy-hour specials help attract an "eclectic clientele" that considers it "great for impressing [someone] without blowing a budget."

Michaelangelo's Italian
25 | 23 | 23 | $47

Little Italy | 2198 Murray Hill Rd. (Cornell Rd.) | 216-721-0300
"Tucked away" in Little Italy, this "romantic" retreat offers "authentic" Northern Italian cuisine from chef/co-owner Michael Annandono along with an "extensive" selection of wines from California and The Boot; service can be "spotty" at times, but it's set in a renovated 1880s building that's "warm" and "inviting", with a "stylish bar" area, a "large fireplace for winter" and a patio for warmer weather, making it an ideal choice for that "special night out."

Momocho Ⓜ Mexican
24 | 20 | 22 | $34

Ohio City | 1835 Fulton Rd. (Bridge Ave.) | 216-694-2122 | www.momocho.com
"Not your typical taco and burrito joint", this "hip cafe" in Ohio City is "a must-stop" for "delicious, inspired Mexican food" that can be supplemented with "*muy bueno* guacamole samplers" and "killer" margarita flights ("the blood-orange version is divine!"); what's more, the "fun, high-energy" ambiance helps make it "perfect for a date" – especially for those lucky enough to snag a seat on the "charming patio"; P.S. "try the [monthly] tequila tasting dinners."

Moxie Ⓢ American
24 | 22 | 23 | $47

Beachwood | 3355 Richmond Rd. (Chagrin Blvd.) | 216-831-5599 | www.moxietherestaurant.com
"Jumping with excitement", this "busy" New American is "well worth the drive" to suburban Beachwood for a seasonal menu of "creative cooking" (try the "out-of-this-world baked hot chocolate") that's served by a "warm staff" in a "tasteful but acoustically challenged" "New York–style" setting; "it's the place where movers and shakers make their deals" during lunch, but it also remains a "favorite" for a "lively" dinner or simply "to see and be seen."

One Walnut Ⓢ American
24 | 22 | 24 | $54

Downtown | Ohio Savings Bldg. | 1 Walnut Ave. (bet. 9th & 12th Sts.) | 216-575-1111 | www.onewalnut.com
At this "elegant" New American set "in one of those beautiful old buildings" Downtown, veteran chef-owner Marlin Kaplan will "excite your senses" via three-, four- or five-course prix fixe dinner menus that can be "seriously enhanced" with wine pairings from an "all-American list"; "attentive service" adds to its appeal as the city's "power-lunch capital", but you can expect to pay "top dollar for top-quality", so "go on the company's dime."

Ⓩ Parallax Restaurant & Lounge Ⓢ Eclectic/Seafood
27 | 24 | 25 | $48

Tremont | 2179 W. 11th St. (Fairfield Ave.) | 216-583-9999 | www.parallaxtremont.com
"The attention to detail is unparalleled" at this "trendy" Tremont Eclectic where "amazing chef"-owner Zack Bruell turns out "inventive preparations" of "incredibly fresh seafood" – including "fabulous sushi" – that incorporates "superb ingredients"; it's all served up by a "friendly staff" in an "intimate" space that's ideal "for unwinding after

a busy day" but can also get "crowded", leading admirers to advise "stand in line if you must, but don't miss this slice of heaven."

Red The Steakhouse *Steak*   27 | 25 | 25 | $61

Beachwood | 3355 Richmond Rd. (Chagrin Blvd.) | 216-831-2252 | www.redthesteakhouse.com

Though it "hardly looks like a traditional steakhouse" with its "rich, modern", monochromatic decor, this Beachwood "hot spot" is considered an "A-1" choice – even in this "city of red meat eaters" – for its "phenomenal" cuts of prime and certified Angus beef; while "high prices" alarm some cost-conscious carnivores, a "superb wine list", "top-of-the-line" service and a covered patio help to make the experience "worth every penny."

Sérgio's Saravá *Brazilian*   24 | 24 | 22 | $42

Shaker Square | 13225 Shaker Sq. (bet. N. Moreland & Shaker Blvds.) | 216-295-1200 | www.sergioscleveland.com

"A taste of Ipanema, right here in Shaker Heights!" exclaim fans of this "lively" "escape from quotidian Cleveland life", where a "reasonably priced" Brazilian menu includes both "traditional dishes" and "inventive small plates" (wash either down with a "fun" caipirinha); plus, the "layout lets you choose your experience": the "fireplace is a nice touch" in the "warm, inviting" interior, while "sultry" live music and "people-watching" perk up the outdoor patio.

⊠ Three Birds ⊠ *American*   27 | 26 | 25 | $46

Lakewood | 18515 Detroit Ave. (Riverside Dr.) | 216-221-3500 | www.3birdsrestaurant.com

No fly-by-night, this Lakewood "favorite" has kept foodies "atwitter" for over four years with an "ever-changing menu" of "original", "eclectic" New American cuisine that's "full of flavor" and "always first-rate"; "friendly service" and a "comfortable" interior also help it "soar", but it's the "unrivaled" garden patio – a shady, "secluded" former tennis court – that leads admirers to assert "the question is not whether you come here, but how often."

Connecticut

Restaurant	Cuisine
29 Thomas Henkelmann	French
28 Cavey's	French/Italian
Le Petit Cafe	French
Ibiza	Spanish
27 Jean-Louis	French
Max Downtown	American/Steak
Restaurant du Village	French
Luca Ristorante	Italian
Frank Pepe's/Spot	Pizza
26 Union League Cafe	French
Sally's Apizza	Pizza
Bernard's	French
Ondine	French
Frank Pepe	Pizza
Carole Peck's	American
Coromandel	Indian
Da Pietro's	French/Italian
Rebeccas	American
Bonda	American
Métro Bis	American

OTHER NOTEWORTHY PLACES

Barcelona	Spanish
Bentara	Malaysian
Bespoke	American/Eclectic
Bricco	American
Cafe Routier	French
Ching's	Pan-Asian
Dressing Room	American
Grant's	American
L'Escale	French
Match	American
Max's Oyster	Seafood
Mayflower Inn	American
Meigas	Spanish
Morton's	Steak
Napa & Co.	American
Still River Café	American
Telluride	Southwestern
Thali	Indian
Valbella	Italian
Zinc	American

	FOOD	DECOR	SERVICE	COST

☑ Barcelona Restaurant & Wine Bar *Spanish*

| 22 | 20 | 20 | $40 |

Fairfield | 4180 Black Rock Tpke. (Rte. 15, exit 44) | 203-255-0800
Greenwich | 18 W. Putnam Ave. (Greenwich Ave.) | 203-983-6400
New Haven | 155 Temple St. (bet. Chapel & Elm Sts.) | 203-848-3000
South Norwalk | 63 N. Main St. (bet. Ann & Marshall Sts.) | 203-899-0088
West Hartford | 971 Farmington Ave. (Main St.) | 860-218-2100
www.barcelonawinebar.com

These "tapas temples" deliver "big flavors on small plates" that are "pure heaven for those who like to taste a little of everything" while sipping something from an "amazing" Spanish wine list; "eternally hip", with "flirty waitresses" and "scantily clad ladies and slick-haired men crowding the bar", they make for "one of the best going out experiences around", but cynics shout the decibel level will have you "screaming at your date" while you're dining on "el blando" dishes.

Bentara *Malaysian*

| 25 | 22 | 20 | $35 |

New Haven | 76 Orange St. (Center St.) | 203-562-2511 | www.bentara.com

"Bring a towel to wipe the sweat off your brow" after you've eaten the "fantastic (and spicy) Malaysian food" at this "outstanding" Southeast Asian in Downtown New Haven; the "creative cuisine" "never disappoints" and the "very Zen-like setting and wonderful service" leave reviewers raving about what a "truly hip and happening place" it is.

Bernard's Ⓜ *French*

| 26 | 25 | 26 | $65 |

Ridgefield | 20 West Ln./Rte. 35 (Rte. 33) | 203-438-8282 | www.bernardsridgefield.com

Fans feel like "royalty in Ridgefield" at this "friendly yet formal family-run" French, a favorite for "special occasions" that's "awesome in every way"; Bernard Bouissou's "food is perfection, the decor is romance at its finest", the service is "cosseting" and the "wine list is impressive"; just "be ready to leave your wallet with the waiter", and beware: "tables by the piano are a bit loud"; N.B. jacket suggested.

Bespoke Ⓜ *American/Eclectic*

| - | - | - | E |

New Haven | 266 College St. (Chapel St.) | 203-562-4644 | www.bespokenewhaven.com

Located in Downtown New Haven across from the Shubert Theater, this yearling from chef/co-owner Arturo Franco-Camacho turns out New American–Eclectic cuisine in a space that's capable of satisfying any mood: it includes a bar with a communal table, a lively mezzanine with a fireplace and a quiet, candlelit wine room; those who prefer to dine à la carte can also head to the rooftop.

Bonda Ⓢ Ⓜ *American*

| 26 | 17 | 25 | $49 |

Westport | 30 Charles St. (Franklin St.) | 203-454-0840 | www.bondarestaurant.com

"The owners exude a love of great food" and it shows in "beautifully crafted dishes" that utilize "pristine" "seasonal ingredients" at this "unsung gem" of a New American in Westport; a gourmet deli by day, in the evenings it morphs into a "very good place to impress a first date" with a "wonderful wine list" and "service that could not be friendlier"; the only downside to the small space is "noise."

Bricco *American* | 24 | 21 | 21 | $40
West Hartford | 78 LaSalle Rd. (Farmington Ave.) | 860-233-0220 | www.restaurantbricco.com
"An experience not to be missed", chef-owner Billy Grant's "benchmark" New American in West Hartford offers "enticing" food that helps to make it a "winner"; still, it "doesn't take reservations" and it's "always packed" with a "very trendy" clientele, so expect the "chic" open-kitchen setting to occasionally be "crowded and loud."

Cafe Routier *French* | 26 | 22 | 23 | $46
Westbrook | 1353 Boston Post Rd. (I-95, exit 65) | 860-399-8700 | www.caferoutier.com
Chef "Jeff Renkel is the force behind the stove" at this "fabulous" Westbrook French bistro, which reviewers regard as the "best spot for sophisticated dining" "on the shoreline", singling out "the camp-style trout alone as being worth the drive from an hour away"; the "dining room and staff are welcoming", and the addition of a 30-seat lounge adds a lively note to the already-appealing mix.

Carole Peck's Good News Cafe *American* | 26 | 20 | 22 | $48
Woodbury | 694 Main St. S./Rte. 6 (Rte. 64) | 203-266-4663 | www.good-news-cafe.com
"Napa Valley comes to CT" at this Woodbury New American where the namesake chef "utilizes as much local organic produce as possible" and the result is "ever-innovative, fabulously fresh food" (like mile-high coconut layer cake) that "never fails to delight"; the art-gallery atmosphere is "funky", which to some means "cute as the proverbial button", but to others is "like looking at a yard sale on acid."

Ⓩ Cavey's Restaurants Ⓢ Ⓜ *French/Italian* | 28 | 24 | 25 | $59
Manchester | 45 E. Center St. (Main St.) | 860-643-2751
Whether you choose the more casual upstairs Italian or more formal downstairs French at this "two-level establishment" in Manchester, the result will be "a divine dining experience" with "sublime food, exquisite service" and a stellar 20,000-bottle wine cellar; the Tuscan fare, as in "heavenly osso buco", is "fairly priced" and "perfect for any occasion", while reviewers recommend reserving the "unparalleled" foie gras experience "for a special evening."

Ching's Table *Pan-Asian* | 25 | 17 | 18 | $38
New Canaan | 64 Main St. (Locust Ave.) | 203-972-8550 | www.chingsrestaurant.com
Ching's Kitchen *Pan-Asian*
Darien | 971 Post Rd. (Center St.) | 203-656-2225
Since there's "not a clunker on the menu", "it's hard to pass up old favorites in order to try new dishes" that spring from the chef-owner's "great imagination" at this New Canaan Pan-Asian that's "still the gold standard" for fusion cuisine in the area; it can be "noisy and crowded" and expect to hear a big "ka-ching" when it comes to the check, but the main reason it's "not a place to linger" is "a staff that rushes you out" – leaving snarky surveyors to suggest: "park out front and leave the car running"; N.B. the Darien outpost opened post-Survey.

	FOOD	DECOR	SERVICE	COST

⊿ Coromandel *Indian* — 26 | 17 | 21 | $33

Darien | Goodwives Shopping Ctr. | 25-11 Old Kings Hwy. N. (Sedgewick Ave.) | 203-662-1213
Orange | 185 Boston Post Rd. (Lindy St.) | 203-795-9055
www.coromandelcuisine.com

"Bring on the heat!" boast boosters of these "top-rated" subcontinentals in Darien and Orange offering "wonderful regional selections" that appeal to "both Indian émigrés and the hair-band set"; the "outstanding cuisine and impeccable service are marred only by decor that seems not to have changed since the Moghuls ruled Delhi"; N.B. proponents particularly praise the all-you-can-eat lunch buffets.

Da Pietro's ⊠ *French/Italian* — 26 | 18 | 24 | $63

Westport | 36 Riverside Ave. (Boston Post Rd.) | 203-454-1213

"Pietro Scotti is the prince of perfection" proclaim those who adore his "exquisite, little" French–Northern Italian in Westport, where you "definitely need a reservation" to sample "his sublime creations" and "surprising wine list"; some "love the intimacy" of the space and "feel like a guest in the chef-owner's home", but a minority is put off by "pricey-to-be-sure" tabs and a setting "so tiny and cramped" "you could eat off your neighbor's plate without stretching."

Dressing Room – A Homegrown Restaurant Ⓜ *American* — 24 | 24 | 21 | $50

Westport | 27 Powers Ct. (Compo Rd.) | 203-226-1114 | www.dressingroomhomegrown.com

"Don't ask for his autograph or snap his picture" if you happen to see Paul Newman chowing down at his "nifty" New American that sits adjacent to his wife Joanne Woodward's beloved Westport Country Playhouse; admirers applaud the "auspicious opening" of this "organic cuisine" collaboration with celebrity chef Michel Nischan, who uses local farmer's market ingredients to create "sophisticated comfort food" that's served against a warm, wood-beamed backdrop; the only boos come for paying what some call "movie star prices."

⊿ Frank Pepe Pizzeria *Pizza* — 26 | 11 | 15 | $18

Fairfield | 236 Commerce Dr. (bet. Berwick Ct. & Brentwood Ave.) | 203-333-7373
New Haven | 157 Wooster St. (Brown St.) | 203-865-5762
www.pepespizzeria.com

The "waits are interminable", the "ambiance is austere" and depending on your outlook, the service is either "rude" or "wonderfully irreverent", but one thing at this New Haven "institution" makes it all "worth it": "mind-boggling" "white clam pie" that "is among the best pizza in the Northeast and maybe the universe"; even though the Fairfield outpost's brick oven is still "being broken in", it hasn't prevented the "nonstop crowds from flowing in"; N.B. a Manchester branch is scheduled to open in fall 2007.

Frank Pepe's The Spot Ⓜ *Pizza* — 27 | 11 | 16 | $19

New Haven | 163 Wooster St. (Brown St.) | 203-865-7602

Surveyors say sotto voce "don't let out the locals' secret" ("because, really, who wants to wait in line"): "those who crave Wooster Street pizza" "walk across the parking lot to this perfectly fine sibling" "when the mother ship is full"; after all, this spot too "has a doctorate in dough-making" and the white clam pie is just as much of a "religious experience" as the "next-door" New Haven original's – and considering the slightly higher Food score here, perhaps more of one.

Grant's *American* 24 | 23 | 22 | $44

West Hartford | 977 Farmington Ave. (Main St.) | 860-236-1930 | www.billygrant.com

"Excellent", "cutting-edge food" like "delightful truffle frites" and "standout desserts" make Billy Grant's New American "a consistent winner" and "among the best in West Hartford"; "dark wood and even darker lighting" add up to "a casual yet beautiful atmosphere" that appeals to the "young and hip", but "courteous service" also means it's "a great place to take the parents."

☑ Ibiza ⑤ *Spanish* 28 | 23 | 26 | $51

New Haven | 39 High St. (bet. Chapel & Crown Sts.) | 203-865-1933 | www.ibizanewhaven.com

"Simply a genius" rave respondents describing "adventurous gourmet chef" Luis Bollo (of Norwalk's Meigas), whose "stunning" "modern Spanish" dishes are "works of art" and a "marvel of Iberian tastes"; throw in "a superb wine list", "impeccable service" and a "sleek", "sexy" setting and no wonder many consider this the "best place to eat in New Haven" and "as good as anything in Manhattan."

☑ Jean-Louis ⑤ *French* 27 | 22 | 26 | $75

Greenwich | 61 Lewis St. (bet. Greenwich Ave. & Mason St.) | 203-622-8450 | www.restaurantjeanlouis.com

At this "grown-up" Greenwich "foodie nirvana" "for people who appreciate the best cooking with the best ingredients", chef-owner Jean-Louis Gerin "continues to strive for and attain new heights" while staying "true to his French roots"; "gorgeous decor and superb service" lead surveyors to surmise it's a "special-occasion place" that's "worth taking someone whom you want to impress", although they admit "it's a good thing the tab is not in euros."

☑ Le Petit Cafe Ⓜ *French* 28 | 20 | 26 | $52

Branford | 225 Montowese St. (Main St.) | 203-483-9791 | www.lepetitcafe.net

Respondents remark that "ever-gracious" chef-owner Roy Ip routinely "follows up his five-star French meals" by "greeting guests during dessert", but you also know he "really cares about his customers" from the "outstanding preparation and presentation" of the "value" four-course prix fixe menu for $42.50; no wonder they say it's "well-worth inching along I-95 to enjoy this pot-of-gold" Branford bistro.

L'Escale *French* 21 | 24 | 20 | $63

Greenwich | Delamar Hotel | 500 Steamboat Rd. (I-95, exit 3) | 203-661-4600 | www.lescalerestaurant.com

Sit under the chandeliers or out on the terrace and enjoy the "beautiful view" of the Long Island Sound at this Greenwich "power-dining scene" and "fabulous summer spot" ensconced in "a wonderful boutique hotel"; "hedge-fund honchos and their diamond-clad trophy wives" favor the "excellent" French Provençal cuisine, but others find it "overpriced" and "overhyped" and observe that the bar is often "filled with throngs of fortysomething cougars looking to secure their futures by picking up a banker."

Luca Ristorante Italiano ☒ *Italian*   27 | 22 | 26 | $53
Wilton | 142 Old Ridgefield Rd. (Godfrey Pl.) | 203-563-9550 |
www.lucaristoranteitaliano.com
Enthusiasts exclaim *"molto bene!"* over this small, "outstanding Italian" "in the heart of Wilton", with "dynamite food" like osso buco and "homemade pastas"; the chef-owner and staff are "delightfully friendly", the "wine list is wonderful" and the earth-toned, low-lit room is "romantic", so though it may be "packed and pricey", it's "worth it."

Match   *American*   25 | 21 | 19 | $44
South Norwalk | 98 Washington St. (bet. Main & Water Sts.) | 203-852-1088 |
www.matchsono.com
Co-owner and chef Matt Storch "rocks on" at this matchless New American in South Norwalk, where "food is really the focal point", even though it's also a "noisy", "high-energy hangout" for "nubile young people"; however, your attention will return to your plate once you've tasted the "incredible seared tuna appetizer" and "warm chocolate-chip cookies"; in short, it's "trendy" but still "top-notch."

Max Downtown   *American/Steak*   27 | 25 | 25 | $51
Hartford | City Place | 185 Asylum St. (bet. Ann & Trumbull Sts.) |
860-522-2530 | www.maxrestaurantgroup.com
"As good as it gets in Hartford", Rich Rosenthal's New American steakhouse "caters to upscale, established" "business types" and is the "power place" to go for lunch Downtown; the "creative martinis", "great beef" and "daring specials" are all "still good to the max", as is the "knowledgeable staff"; sure, "a totally fine experience from start to finish" "is going to cost you, but it's worth it."

Max's Oyster Bar   *Seafood*   25 | 23 | 23 | $46
West Hartford | 964 Farmington Ave. (S. Main St.) | 860-236-6299 |
www.maxrestaurantgroup.com
"Tall towers of fresh-shucked shellfish", "outstanding oysters" and "first-rate seafood" "prepared in seemingly infinite ways" – "it's like low tide gone wild" at this West Hartford "staple" of the Max empire; the "always buzzing" "happening bar" is "very popular with local singles", which makes things "so noisy you can't hear yourself chew", and wry reviewers say it "reminds them of Yogi Berra's line – no one goes there anymore because it's too crowded."

Mayflower Inn & Spa, The   *American*   24 | 27 | 25 | $67
Washington | The Mayflower Inn & Spa | 118 Woodbury Rd./Rte. 47
(Rte. 199) | 860-868-9466 | www.mayflowerinn.com
"Not fortunate enough to have been born into royalty?" – "no matter, save your pennies and splurge" at this "romantic" Relais & Châteaux inn set among "the serene sights and sounds" of a "lovely" Washington locale; "delectable" New American cuisine is "impeccably served" in three "handsome" "formal dining rooms" that "shout special occasion"; a few critics complain the food "doesn't live up to the setting" and the prices are "ridiculous", but concede that following "an afternoon at the spa, you may be too blissed out" to care.

	FOOD	DECOR	SERVICE	COST

Meigas Ⓜ *Spanish* — 26 | 22 | 24 | $53

Norwalk | 10 Wall St. (bet. High & Knight Sts.) | 203-866-8800 |
www.meigasrestaurant.com

Located "in a neat little part of old Norwalk that's being revived", chef
Luis Bollo's (also of New Haven's Ibiza) "world-class", "high-end"
Spanish cuisine "abounds with original combinations" like "touches of
fruit or vegetable foams, goat cheese ice cream" and dishes like the
signature bacalao that "amaze the palate" and are complemented by
"wonderful wines"; the "romantic setting" is enhanced by "gracious
service" and the added "blessing" that it's possible to "carry on a conversation" and eat "dinner without a din."

Métro Bis Ⓔ *American* — 26 | 20 | 25 | $48

Simsbury | Simsburytown Shops | 928 Hopmeadow St./Rte. 10
(bet. Massaco St. & Plank Hill Rd.) | 860-651-1908 |
www.metrobis.com

"Full of class, from the owner-chef" to his hostess-wife, this "bustling"
Simsbury bistro serves "top-notch" New American cuisine "based on
available fresh ingredients", which, along with the "seasoned service",
makes for an "unexpected delight in a nondescript" strip-mall location; too bad it can "get so noisy" it precludes the place from being romantic unless "eye contact is the extent of your communication."

Morton's, The Steakhouse *Steak* — 24 | 21 | 23 | $64

Hartford | 852 Main St. (Asylum St.) | 860-724-0044
Stamford | UBS Investment Bank | 377 N. State St. (bet. Canal & Elm Sts.) |
203-324-3939
www.mortons.com

"Carnivores, start your engines" and rev up for prodigious pórter-
house steaks "properly prepared" and "baked potatoes the size of
small footballs" at this "very high-end" steakhouse chain; while most
maintain the meats are "the best" and the "service is great", some surveyors balk at "overpriced, ogre-sized servings" and say they're
"turned off by the Saran-wrapped" ingredient display – "do they really
think we need to be shown a tomato and told what it is?"

Napa & Co. *American* — - | - | - | E

Stamford | Courtyard Marriott Hotel | 75 Broad St. (Summer St.) |
203-353-3319 | www.napaandcompany.com

This New American restaurant brings together the former owners of
Telluride and talented chef Bill Taibe, who indulges his passion for
combining unlikely ingredients (many of them organic) in dishes like
duck breast braised in honey and thyme; located in Downtown
Stamford's Courtyard Marriott Hotel, the dining room features 18-ft.
ceilings, a chandelier and a wall of wine.

Ondine Ⓜ *French* — 26 | 24 | 25 | $62

Danbury | 69 Pembroke Rd./Rte. 37 (Wheeler Dr.) | 203-746-4900 |
www.ondinerestaurant.com

"A treasure" "tucked away in Northern Danbury", this "romantic",
chef-owned "country French" stalwart serves dishes like "memorable
venison" and "not-to-be-missed soufflés"; *amis* applaud the "expert
service" and deem the five-course "$55 fixed-price menu a bargain";
N.B. no children allowed and jackets are suggested.

	FOOD	DECOR	SERVICE	COST

Rebeccas ⧄Ⓜ *American* — 26 | 20 | 22 | $68

Greenwich | 265 Glenville Rd. (Riversville Rd.) | 203-532-9270 |
www.rkateliers.com

This "classy" New American "is a gift to Greenwich" and a "foodie's
delight" say supporters sold on chef/co-owner Reza Khorshidi's "perfectly executed", "imaginative" cuisine and his wife Rebecca's "warm
and genuine welcome"; some critics cite "atrocious acoustics", "too
many tables" and a "too-big-for-its-britches" attitude and conclude
it's "overpriced and underwhelming", but they're outvoted.

Restaurant du Village Ⓜ *French* — 27 | 24 | 25 | $59

Chester | 59 Main St. (Maple St.) | 860-526-5301 |
www.restaurantduvillage.com

"The food shines" at this "excellent" "country French" that's a de
rigueur "stop before the Goodspeed Theater at Chester"; "everything on
the menu is wonderful", thanks to the husband-and-wife chef-owners,
whose efforts in the kitchen remain "superb"; plus, "service is perfect"
and the "small, elegant room is "charming"; N.B. jacket suggested.

Sally's Apizza Ⓜ⇗ *Pizza* — 26 | 10 | 13 | $18

New Haven | 237 Wooster St. (bet. Olive & Warren Sts.) | 203-624-5271
For "the Holy Grail of pizza", head to this "crusty" New Haven place
where "pictures of celebrities adorn the wall, the vinyl seats are a bit old
and worn and the service can be a tad curt"; while fans insist "the brutal
waits of up to two hours are worth it", foes fume "they play favorites and
let some people in the back door", "while the rest have to wait on line."

Still River Café Ⓜ *American* — – | – | – | E

Eastford | 134 Union Rd./Rte. 171 (Centre Pike) | 860-974-9988 |
www.stillrivercafe.com

Set on a 27-acre farm in Eastford, this New American may be off the
beaten track, but it's found itself on the GPS of foodies who declare it
a "dining destination par excellence"; it's co-owned by former corpo-
rate lawyers Robert and Kara Brooks – he grows 95 percent of their organic produce, while she heads up the kitchen, resulting in "the
highest quality cuisine with prices to match"; N.B. it's only open for
dinner on Friday–Saturday and for brunch on Sundays.

Telluride *Southwestern* — 24 | 22 | 21 | $45

Stamford | 245 Bedford St. (bet. Broad & Spring Sts.) | 203-357-7679 |
www.telluriderestaurant.com

"This cool bit of Colorado" in Downtown Stamford is the place to go for
"eclectic Southwestern fare" (made mostly from organic ingredients)
complemented by "an excellent wine list"; "romantic lighting", "big
wooden tables and a mellow bar" give it such "good buzz", "it's harder
to get into than an audience with the pope" despite its "pricey" tabs.

Thali *Indian* — 24 | 21 | 22 | $37

New Canaan | 87 Main St. (bet. East & Locust Aves.) | 203-972-8332
New Haven | 4 Orange St. (George St.) | 203-777-1177
Ridgefield | Ridgefield Motor Inn | 296 Ethan Allen Hwy./Rte. 7
(Florida Hill Rd.) | 203-894-1080
www.thali.com

"Awesome" is what admirers say about the Konkan crab appetizer and
rack of cardamom lamb chops, both signature dishes at this "expen-

sive", "upscale" trio of chef-owned Indians; the decor varies widely with the location (New Canaan boasts a "way-cool overhead waterfall", New Haven is enormous and Ridgefield is in a "no-tell motel"), but the food is "consistently outstanding"; P.S. the $16.95 Sunday brunch buffet is a "fantastic deal."

☑ Thomas Henkelmann ☒ *French* | 29 | 28 | 28 | $80 |

Greenwich | Homestead Inn | 420 Field Point Rd. (bet. Bush Ave. & Merica Ln.) | 203-869-7500 | www.thomashenkelmann.com

Once again, chef Thomas Henkelmann and his wife, Theresa, achieve "the peak of perfection" with their "truly exceptional" New French – housed in "an absolutely gorgeous" Greenwich inn – which respondents voted Most Popular and No. 1 for Food in CT; considered the culinary "Matterhorn north of Manhattan", it "pampers" its clientele with a "beautiful" setting, "impeccable service", "sublime entrees, ethereal desserts" and a "superb wine list", albeit at prices that "would make J.P. Morgan wince"; N.B. jacket required.

Union League Cafe ☒ *French* | 26 | 27 | 26 | $54 |

New Haven | 1032 Chapel St. (bet. College & High Sts.) | 203-562-4299 | www.unionleaguecafe.com

With "impeccable service" and a stained-glass interior that "sets the standard" for "sophisticated elegance in the center of Yale's campus", this French is "so good it even makes Harvard men jealous"; chef-owner "Jean Pierre Vuillermet makes no mistakes" in his "delicious variations on classic dishes", and fans find it "fun people-watching everyone from parents feeding their offspring to professors with 'daughters'"; so, despite "a little stuffiness", this is "still the restaurant by which everything else in New Haven is judged."

Valbella ☒ *Italian* | 25 | 23 | 25 | $67 |

Riverside | 1309 E. Putnam Ave./Rte. 1 (Sound Beach Ave.) | 203-637-1155 | www.valbellact.com

There are "celebrity sightings nightly" at this *"magnifico"* Riverside Northern Italian where "Tony the maitre d' is always ready with tricky trivia questions for customers" and the "fantastic" dishes include seasonal seafood and a "special Napoleon for two that's worth the money"; service is "solicitous" and the ambiance throughout is "memorable", but "for a real treat, eat in the wine cellar" amid the vinous treasure trove of "great" bottles; there's only one caveat: "make sure your credit limit can handle the bill."

Zinc *American* | 24 | 22 | 23 | $46 |

New Haven | 964 Chapel St. (bet. College & Temple Sts.) | 203-624-0507 | www.zincfood.com

"Located on the green" in Downtown New Haven, this "sleek" New American has become "a top spot in a city overflowing with excellent dining", thanks to chef/co-owner Denise Appel, who "leads the way in new tastes" with her "adventurous" "Asian-influenced food" – "sometimes a little contrived, but that's just the risk of innovation" – while partner "Donna Curran and staff take pains" to keep the service on track; kudos, too, to the "fashionable modern setting" that "makes you feel hip to eat here."

Dallas/Ft. Worth

TOP FOOD RANKING

	Restaurant	Cuisine
29	French Room	American/French
28	York Street	American
	Abacus	Eclectic
	Aurora	American
	Lola	American
	Saint-Emilion	French
27	Tei Tei Robata	Japanese
	Lonesome Dove	Southwestern
	Pappas Bros.	Steak
	Café Pacific	Seafood
	Teppo Yakitori	Japanese
	Del Frisco's	Steak
	Nana	American
	Bonnell's	Southwestern
	Local	American
26	Al Biernat's	Steak
	Mercury Grill	American
	Goodhues	American
	Hôtel St. Germain	Continental/French
	Mansion on Turtle Creek	American

OTHER NOTEWORTHY PLACES

Restaurant	Cuisine
Angelo's Barbecue	BBQ
Babe's Chicken	American
Bice	Italian
Bijoux	French
Cafe Aspen	American
Capital Grille	Steak
Chow Thai	Thai
Craft Dallas	American
Fearing's	Southwestern
Grape, The	American
Joe T. Garcia's	Tex-Mex
La Duni Latin	Pan-Latin
Lavendou	French
Mi Cocina	Tex-Mex
Nobu Dallas	Japanese
Oceanaire	Seafood
Reata	Southwestern
62 Main	American
Steel	Pan-Asian
Stephan Pyles	Southwestern

	FOOD	DECOR	SERVICE	COST

☑ Abacus ⑤ *Eclectic* | 28 | 27 | 27 | $60

Knox-Henderson | 4511 McKinney Ave. (Armstrong Ave.) | Dallas | 214-559-3111 | www.abacus-restaurant.com

A "crown jewel of high-end, new-style dining", this "chic" Knox-Henderson "favorite" from "genius" chef Kent Rathbun is a "proven winner" that's ranked Most Popular among Dallas/Ft. Worth restaurants thanks to "inventive", "fabulous" Eclectic fare, "divine service" and a "modern" and "elegant" (if somewhat "loud") interior; a few outsiders opine that the "excellent staff" is "a tad snooty" "if you're not a regular", but most maintain that it's "always a treat."

Al Biernat's *Steak* | 26 | 24 | 25 | $55

Oak Lawn | 4217 Oak Lawn Ave. (Herschel Ave.) | Dallas | 214-219-2201 | www.albiernats.com

"Who doesn't love Al" Biernat, the "gracious host" and owner who "never forgets a name" at this Oak Lawn "steak haven", "a local favorite" of "power brokers and beautiful people alike", where "succulent" cuts and "imaginative salads" are served in "huge portions" that are "easily shared"; the "personable service", "dark, clubby atmosphere" and "exceptional wine list" are other pluses, but "high prices" mean it's "best to do this one on someone else's nickel – or $100 bill."

Angelo's Barbecue ⑤⇄ *BBQ* | 24 | 15 | 16 | $14

Near West | 2533 White Settlement Rd. (University Dr.) | Ft. Worth | 817-332-0357 | www.angelosbbq.com

This "classic" Near West Ft. Worth spot is "a longtime institution" and an "almighty shrine to smoked meat", dishing up "Texas beef at its very finest" along with "schooners of cold draft beer"; with its "authentic Texana surroundings", including a weathered wood interior and an infamous "big bear in the foyer", it "may look like a hole-in-the-wall, but isn't that usually where one finds the best BBQ?"

☑ Aurora ⑤ *American* | 28 | 27 | 28 | $87

Oak Lawn | 4216 Oak Lawn Ave. (Wycliff Ave.) | Dallas | 214-528-9400 | www.auroradallas.com

Chef/co-owner Avner Samuel, the "superbly talented enfant terrible of Dallas' culinary scene", "has outdone himself" at this "little jewel" in Oak Lawn, an "exotic and luxurious" "masterpiece" that's "over the top in every aspect" – from its "brilliant, creative" New American fare and "excellent service" to its "striking prices"; plus, "the focal point" of the "notable" interior is the "glass-enclosed kitchen", allowing you to "see the cooking theater", so "if your Gulfstream is in the shop and you can't go to Paris", "this is the place."

Babe's Chicken Dinner House *American* | 26 | 16 | 23 | $15

Carrollton | 1006 W. Main St. (S. Denton Dr.) | 972-245-7773
Garland | 1456 Belt Line Rd. (N. Garland Ave.) | 972-496-1041
Sanger | 204 N. Fourth St. (Cherry St.) | 940-458-0000 Ⓜ
Roanoke | 104 N. Oak St. (Main St.) | 817-491-2900
Burleson | 120 S. Main St. (Ellison St.) | 817-447-3400
www.babeschicken.com

Get ready to wait "with the rest of the crowd" at this small, suburban family-run chain noted for "awesome down-home" American cooking; "there are only six main courses to choose from, but that's all you need", and "if you run out of the very good side dishes, they'll bring more"; perhaps the interiors are a little too down-home, but "who cares about decor when you can get" "heavenly fried chicken" that's "probably the best you'll ever eat"?

Bice *Italian* | - | - | - | E |

Uptown | Crescent Court Complex | 100 Crescent Ct. (bet. Maple & McKinney Aves.) | Dallas | 214-922-9055 | www.bicedallas.com

A link in a haute Italian chain that was founded in Milan in 1926, this Uptown eatery inspires *amore* at first sight – and bite – with its trendy, opulent ambiance (two-toned hardwood flooring, flowing drapes) and its equally rich Italian cuisine, including standout seafood and classic pastas; white-jacketed servers preside over a happening scene that, given the high prices, is appropriately heavy on blue bloods.

Bijoux S M *French* | - | - | - | VE |

West Lovers Lane | 5450 W. Lovers Ln. (bet. Inwood Rd. & Preston Park Dr.) | Dallas | 214-350-6100 | www.bijouxrestaurant.com

Hidden on West Lovers Lane, this aptly named jewel is dazzling discerning gourmands with multicourse New French prix fixe menus (wine pairings are available) that are deftly crafted by local wunderkind Scott Gottlich; it's all served up in an intimate, elegant space by a professional cadre capable of explaining the preparations and ingredients, ensuring the pricey experience is worth its karat weight.

Bonnell's S M *Southwestern* | 27 | 23 | 26 | $42 |

Southwest | 4259 Bryant Irvin Rd. (Southwest Blvd.) | Ft. Worth | 817-738-5489 | www.bonnellsrestaurant.com

Chef-owner Jon Bonnell "must be the nicest chef in the city": he "makes sure his patrons have a wonderful time and a wonderful meal" at his discriminating Southwestern bistro in Southwest Ft. Worth; the combination of "inventive", "outstandingly presented" "Texas ranch cuisine" (featuring "interesting game" dishes), the room's "intimate ambiance" and his "friendly" staff's "great wine recommendations" help to ameliorate the "off-the-beaten-path" location.

Cafe Aspen S *American* | 22 | 20 | 20 | $33 |

West | 6103 Camp Bowie Blvd. (Bryant Irvin Rd.) | Ft. Worth | 817-738-0838 | www.cafeaspen.com

How nice for West Ft. Worth to have this "popular spot" offering "consistently" "excellent" New American fare, a "knowledgeable staff" and a "wonderful community feeling, where people know one another and the owner knows everyone" – be it the "blue-haired ladies at lunch" or those seeking "a great place for a business or pleasure" meal; some say the "setting leaves a bit to be desired", but more find the "nice, soothing decor" (including a covered patio) "charming."

Z **Café Pacific** S *Seafood* | 27 | 25 | 26 | $49 |

Highland Park Village | 24 Highland Park Vill. (bet. Mockingbird Ln. & Preston Rd.) | Dallas | 214-526-1170

The "accommodating kitchen" at this "classy, longtime favorite" in Highland Park Village "consistently turns out excellent dishes", especially "first-class seafood", that are "superbly served" within an "upscale environment"; it's known as a meeting place for a "slightly older crowd" of "old-money" "Dallas blue bloods", nouveau "billionaires (seriously)", celebrities and assorted sundry "beautiful people", making for "great people-watching."

Capital Grille *Steak*

25 | 25 | 24 | $55

Uptown | Crescent Shops & Galleries | 500 Crescent Ct. (Cedar Springs Rd.) | Dallas | 214-303-0500 | www.thecapitalgrille.com

Carnivores call this national chain the embodiment of the "classic Texas steakhouse", with "fabulous" meat, "huge" sides, an "excellent" wine selection and "devoted", "timely but unobtrusive" service; the "plush", "clubby" ambiance and "expensive" fare befit business meals – "don't forget your platinum card" – though a cadre of critics calls these meateries "overrated" and "pretentious."

Chow Thai *Thai*

23 | 19 | 20 | $23

Addison | 5290 Belt Line Rd. (Montfort Dr.) | 972-960-2999
Plano | 3309 Dallas Pkwy. (Parker Rd.) | 972-608-1883
www.chowthai.com

"Go once and you'll be hooked" by these "upscale" spots owned by West Coast transplants Vinnie and Sam Virasin, a husband-and-wife duo that delivers with "wonderful" food that's a "fresh, California-style Thai (i.e. don't expect authentic)"; "despite the strip-mall locations", both branches are "quiet places for lunch or dinner", with "lightning-fast service" and "fun decor."

Craft Dallas *American*

- | - | - | VE

Uptown | W Dallas – Victory | 2440 Victory Park Ln. (N. Houston St.) | Dallas | 214-397-4111 | www.craftdallas.com

Bi-coastal chef-owner Tom Colicchio (of the NYC and LA eateries of the same name) transports his flavor-packed New American cuisine to this ultrachic space in the W hotel at Uptown's Victory Park, where plush interiors set the tone for indulgent dishes that can be coupled with a selection from the two-story glass wine tower; the sum effect takes the city's price point to new heights, and does the same with the lengthy valet lines; N.B. reservations required on weekends.

☑ Del Frisco's Double Eagle Steak House *Steak*

27 | 24 | 25 | $59

North Dallas | 5251 Spring Valley Rd. (Dallas N. Tollway) | Dallas | 972-490-9000
Downtown Ft. Worth | 812 Main St. (8th St.) | Ft. Worth | 817-877-3999
www.delfriscos.com

"A top contender" for "best steakhouse" ("which means a lot" in these parts), these North Dallas and Downtown Ft. Worth "gut- and wallet-busting à la carte" outposts not only have "excellent steaks" but also "spectacularly executed appetizers, sides and desserts", all served with "individual attention"; "don't be in a hurry", though, as you might have "a long wait" "even with reservations", and "be prepared for the bill", as the "wine list is off-the-chart expensive."

Fearing's *Southwestern*

- | - | - | VE

Uptown | Ritz-Carlton | 2121 McKinney Ave. (Olive St.) | Dallas | 214-922-4848 | www.ritzcarlton.com

Megawatt chef Dean Fearing (ex Mansion on Turtle Creek) is cooking up his unique brand of Southwestern cuisine – ranging from comfort food signatures to Asian-accented entrees – at this multivenue extravaganza in the Ritz-Carlton; the palatial digs include several indoor and outdoor spaces, and whether you sit at the counter near the busy open kitchen, in the posh gallery or at one of the bars, you can expect to see the showman himself as he circulates, ensuring every budget-breaking bite is worth it.

☑ French Room ⓈⓂ *American/French* | 29 | 29 | 29 | $80 |

Downtown Dallas | Hotel Adolphus | 1321 Commerce St. (Field St.) | Dallas | 214-742-8200 | www.hoteladolphus.com

"There aren't enough superlatives to describe" this "gorgeous" "grande dame" in Downtown's Hotel Adolphus that's ranked No. 1 for Food among Dallas/Ft. Worth restaurants courtesy of "spectacular", "expensive" French-American cuisine served by an "impeccable but unpretentious" staff; it's a "wonderful experience" "to be savored", with "beautiful surroundings" that include "hand-painted ceilings" (swooning surveyors insist it's like "eating in a cathedral"), so "if you're looking for a romantic, old-world" venue in which "to celebrate an event, this is the place"; N.B. jacket required.

Goodhues Wood Fired Grill ☑ *American* | 26 | 22 | 22 | $31 |

McKinney | 204 W. Virginia St. (Wood St.) | 972-562-7570 | www.goodhuesgrill.com

It's "always a lovely evening" at this "true spot of light" in "historic Downtown McKinney", where the "great menu" "changes subtly from visit to visit" but always offers "imaginative", "high-end" New American "home cooking", including "fancy pastas"; "most importantly, it's quiet", guaranteeing it's "a special-occasion place."

Grape, The *American* | 25 | 21 | 23 | $36 |

Greenville Avenue | 2808 Greenville Ave. (Vickery Blvd.) | Dallas | 214-828-1981 | www.thegraperestaurant.com

"One of the darkest and oldest wine bars in Dallas", this "intimate" Greenville Avenue "neighborhood bistro" is a "foodie favorite", boasting "terrific" New American fare that's "consistently good, even with different chefs over the years"; "comparatively low markups" on its vino and an "educated, attentive staff" are other selling points, and the "romantic atmosphere" with its "cozy, close quarters" makes it the "perfect place to get engaged."

Hôtel St. Germain ⓈⓂ *Continental/French* | 26 | 29 | 27 | $83 |

Uptown | Hôtel St. Germain | 2516 Maple Ave. (bet. Cedar Springs Rd. & McKinney Ave.) | Dallas | 214-871-2516 | www.hotelstgermain.com

Set within a "beautiful hotel" "in an old Victorian house" Uptown, this "romantic getaway" is a "perfect" place to celebrate any "special occasion" thanks to a "fantastic" prix fixe Continental-French menu served "off silver trays" by a host of "waiters in white gloves"; reserve "weeks in advance" and your reward will be an "elegant", "formal dining experience" (jacket and tie required).

Joe T. Garcia's ⌿ *Tex-Mex* | 20 | 22 | 21 | $19 |

North Side | 2201 N. Commerce St. (22nd St.) | Ft. Worth | 817-626-4356 | www.joets.com

Sprawling across "several homes joined by a courtyard", this cash-only North Side "Ft. Worth landmark" is definitely "for the indecisive, because there's not much to select from" on its "simple menu" of "quintessential Tex-Mex" that fans describe as *"muy bueno"*; still, those who lament the "long waits" (no reservations for parties of less than 20) and "touristy" vibe insist it's "not about the food – it's about" "their famous margaritas"; P.S. the "fantastic grounds" provide "great outdoor dining", "especially near the pool."

La Duni Latin *Pan-Latin* 25 | 22 | 20 | $29

Knox-Henderson | 4620 McKinney Ave. (Knox St.) | Dallas | 214-520-7300 **M**
Oak Lawn | 4264 Oak Lawn Ave. (Herschel Ave.) | Dallas | 214-520-6888
www.laduni.com

A "great take on Latin, Caribbean and South American food" can be found at this "happening" Pan-Latin pair from "warm and friendly" chef-owner-partners Espartaco and Dunia Borga, who whip up "top-notch" fare, especially their "sinful", "luscious desserts" and "scrumptious, puffy popover sandwiches" ("a fantastic bargain" considering they're "still charging half of what they could/should ask"); in fact, "the only downside" is "slow service."

Lavendou 🅂 *French* 24 | 22 | 23 | $40

North Dallas | 19009 Preston Rd. (bet. Frankford Rd. & President George Bush Tpke.) | Dallas | 972-248-1911 | www.lavendou.com

For "a touch of France", visit this far North Dallas bistro, a "lovely, serene place" offering "the feel and taste of Provence", with a "nice country interior" and "plants on the patio that screen the traffic noise and view of the parking lot so that you can forget you are in a strip shopping center"; some say the staff "occasionally exhibits a little bit of attitude", but the service is generally "caring"; N.B. reservations required for the weekday high tea.

Local 🅂🅜 *American* 27 | 24 | 25 | $46

Deep Ellum | 2936 Elm St. (S. Malcolm X Blvd.) | Dallas | 214-752-7500 | www.localdallas.com

An "exquisitely minimalist-chic" space "is the perfect setting for" a "savory" New American menu "combining upscale and down-home" cuisine at this "trendy", "intimate" spot in Deep Ellum's historic Boyd Hotel building ("book several weeks in advance"); the clientele is "gorgeous", and the "excellent food" "is fresh, organic and wonderful", though some fret over the "fairly small portions", saying these examples of "minuscule nouvelle cuisine of days past" are "expensive for what's received."

🆉 Lola 🅂🅜 *American* 28 | 24 | 26 | $59

Uptown | 2917 Fairmount St. (Cedar Springs Rd.) | Dallas | 214-855-0700 | www.lola4dinner.com

Foodies are "hard-pressed to think of a better meal" than the prix fixe menus (two, three or four "courses of heaven", each a "sensational treat") offered at this Uptown New American, "one of this city's top" spots for "romantic dinners" backed by an "extensive", "impeccable wine list" and "knowledgeable", "friendly" service; the "old-house setting with great charm" includes the Tasting Room, where diners can indulge in a 10-course degustation menu.

Lonesome Dove
Western Bistro ⚫Ⓜ *Southwestern*

27	24	24	$50

Stockyards | 2406 N. Main St. (24th St.) | Ft. Worth | 817-740-8810 |
www.lonesomedovebistro.com

"Highly recommended", the "satisfying" "gourmet Texan fare" at this "artfully winning" outpost "in a rustic, restored building" in Ft. Worth's Stockyards district comes from "celebrity chef" Tim Love, whose Southwestern cuisine (heavy on "wild game") is "cowboy fusion cooking that actually tastes as good as the menu descriptions"; the "helpful" servers are "ready and willing to explain anything", while the "cozy" yet "chic" decor includes a prominent bar "set for fine dining."

ⓩ Mansion on Turtle Creek *American*

26	27	27	$73

Uptown | Mansion on Turtle Creek | 2821 Turtle Creek Blvd. (Gillespie St.) | Dallas | 214-559-2100 | www.mansiononturtlecreek.com

"Still just about the best around for a truly memorable outing", this "classic" in the Uptown hotel of the same name is a "Dallas institution" that now serves a New American menu from chef John Tesar but has nevertheless retained a few of its "marvelous" Southwestern classics; savvy surveyors insist it's the "perfect place for a fancy night out" – jackets are required – thanks to "gracious staffers" providing "impeccable service" in a setting that should be even more "beautiful" after renovations are completed in late October 2007.

Mercury Grill *American*

26	22	24	$46

Preston Forest | Preston Forrest Vill. | 11909 Preston Rd. (Forest Ln.) | Dallas | 972-960-7774 | www.mcrowd.com

For a "little NYC in Dallas", saunter into this "sophisticated" Preston Forest eatery where there's "always something innovative" on "nationally known chef" Chris Ward's menu of "high-priced", "stylishly presented" New American fare; adding to its "deserved reputation" is the "superb service", which also "far exceeds expectations of a restaurant located in a strip mall at a busy North Dallas intersection."

ⓩ Mi Cocina *Tex-Mex*

21	20	20	$22

Lake Highlands | 7201 Skillman St. (Kingsley Rd.) | Dallas | 214-503-6426
Highland Park Village | 77 Highland Park Vill. (bet. Mockingbird Ln. & Preston Rd.) | Dallas | 214-521-6426
Preston Forest | Preston Forrest Vill. | 11661 Preston Rd. (Forest Ln.) | Dallas | 214-265-7704
West Village | West Vill. | 3699 McKinney Ave. (Lemmon Ave.) | Dallas | 469-533-5663
Richardson | 1370 W. Campbell Rd. (Coit Rd.) | 972-671-6426
Las Colinas | 7750 N. MacArthur Blvd. (Lyndon B. Johnson Frwy.) | Irving | 469-621-0452
Plano | Lakeside Mkt. | 4001 Preston Rd. (Lorimar Dr.) | 469-467-8655
Plano | Shops at Legacy | 5760 Legacy Dr. (Parkwood Blvd.) | 972-473-8777
Downtown Ft. Worth | Sundance Sq. | 509 Main St. (bet. 4th & 5th Sts.) | Ft. Worth | 817-877-3600
Southlake | Southlake Town Sq. | 1276 S. Main St. (Carroll Ave.) | 817-410-6426
www.mcrowd.com
Additional locations throughout the Dallas/Ft. Worth area

Extremely "popular", this "locally owned chain" dominates the Tex-Mex field courtesy of "consistent", "very-good-all-around" fare and decor with an "upscale" edge that's "welcoming to both singles and families"; sure, it's a "little noisy", but that's because many "go here as much for the scene and the drinks", which, with the "multiple-hour wait", can mean you'll get "more than just dinner – this place can be your entire night's entertainment."

Nana *American*   27 | 28 | 26 | $65

Market Center | Hilton Anatole Hotel | 2201 Stemmons Frwy., 27th fl. (Market Center Blvd.) | Dallas | 214-761-7470 | www.nanarestaurant.com
A "spectacular setting" featuring a "panoramic view of the Dallas skyline" instantly "elevates" this New American foodie temple on the 27th floor of the Market Center's Hilton Anatole Hotel to the realm of "very special special-occasion place", but fans insist it'd be "worthy even on the ground floor" thanks to a "top-drawer" staff and "amazingly creative chef" Anthony Bombaci's "exceptional food"; a few feel he's "a bit stingy" with the "expensive" portions, but a "dazzled" majority declares that "everything is outstanding."

Nobu Dallas *Japanese*   25 | 24 | 21 | $72

Uptown | Hotel Crescent Ct. | 400 Crescent Ct. (bet. Cedar Springs Rd. & Maple Ave.) | Dallas | 214-252-7000 | www.noburestaurants.com
Dallas foodies feel "lucky to have this" "world-class" restaurant in Uptown's Crescent Court complex, an outpost of Nobu Matsuhisa's "famous" Peruvian-influenced Japanese chain and a "true dining experience" thanks to "fabulous food" (including "awesome" "melt-in-your-mouth sushi") and "way-cool decor"; be warned, though, that the "noise" from the "trendy" clientele can make it "hard to converse", while the "outrageous" "expense-account pricing" has some insisting that "better value can be found elsewhere."

Oceanaire Seafood Room *Seafood*   26 | 24 | 24 | $49

North Dallas | Westin Galleria Hotel | 13340 N. Dallas Pkwy. (bet. Dallas N. Tollway & Lyndon B. Johnson Frwy.) | Dallas | 972-759-2277 | www.theoceanaire.com
"Am I on a coast?" wonder wags wowed by the "beautifully presented" and "wonderfully fresh" seafood that "never fails to satisfy" at this "amazing" national chain with a retro "nautical theme"; it's "a little pricey", but the "service is impeccable", as is the "classy, old-time luxury" decor that makes it easy to imagine you're on a "1930s liner."

Pappas Bros. Steakhouse ⓩ *Steak*   27 | 24 | 25 | $57

Love Field | 10477 Lombardy Ln. (bet. I-35 & Northwest Hwy.) | Dallas | 214-366-2000 | www.pappasbros.com
"There's a lot of competition" but cognoscenti confide that this handsome steakhouse stands out from the herd thanks to "perfectly cooked" "slabs o' cow", "tasty sides", a "comprehensive wine cellar", "sommeliers who truly know what they're talking about" and "attentive, respectful" servers who "treat everyone like a VIP"; a vocal few, however, consider it an "overpriced", "inconsistent" bum steer.

Reata *Southwestern*   23 | 25 | 23 | $40

Downtown Ft. Worth | Sundance Sq. | 310 Houston St. (3rd St.) | Ft. Worth | 817-336-1009 | www.reata.net
This "fun cowboy-style" "Ft. Worth favorite" – "a true taste of Cowtown" and "a must for any visitor" – "looks as though it's straight

off the *Giant* movie set" and always draws "a crowd"; its Southwestern menu has "inventive entrees and salads, as well as wonderful margaritas", and the staff is "accommodating", but the talk inevitably returns to the "amusing", "retro" Western decor and "rooftop dining" space "that's one of the prettiest places Downtown."

Saint-Emilion ⓈⓂ *French* | 28 | 25 | 27 | $48 |

Cultural District | 3617 W. Seventh St. (Montgomery St.) | Ft. Worth | 817-737-2781

"For a special evening" of "romance (especially if your significant other is a foodie)", this "wonderful French" "classic" set in a "charming little house" in Ft. Worth's Cultural District is a "fabulous" option for "elegantly executed preparations" of "incredible food" and a "unique wine list" "with the namesake Bordeaux well represented"; P.S. "stick to the blackboard specials" for the best meal.

62 Main Restaurant ⓈⓂ *American* | 23 | 21 | 23 | $49 |

Colleyville | 62 Main St. (bet. Hwy. 26 & Main St.) | 817-605-0858 | www.62mainrestaurant.com

"Master" chef David McMillan (ex Nana) "amazes everyone" at this "small, chic" "gourmet dining" spot that's "surprisingly located in suburban Colleyville"; its "creative, daily changing menu" of "blue-ribbon" New American fare features "fresh, quality ingredients" and is ferried by an "enthusiastic staff", sealing its status as an "excellent addition to the area" and "a lovely place for a grown-up evening out."

Steel *Pan-Asian* | 24 | 25 | 20 | $48 |

Oak Lawn | Centrum Bldg. | 3102 Oak Lawn Ave. (Cedar Springs Rd.) | Dallas | 214-219-9908 | www.steeldallas.com

Yes, this "trendy" Oak Lawn "place to be seen" is filled with "sports figures" and "young", "beautiful people", but supporters insist its "fantastic wine list" and "amazing" combination of Chinese, Japanese and Vietnamese cuisines (including "creatively presented sushi") "back up the flash"; a few find it "pretentious" and "noisy", but most say it's "a favorite place to take out-of-towners, who are surprised to find something other than steak in Dallas."

Stephan Pyles Ⓢ *Southwestern* | - | - | - | E |

Downtown Dallas | 1807 Ross Ave. (N. St. Paul St.) | Dallas | 214-580-7000 | www.stephanpyles.com

Local celebrity chef Stephan Pyles has returned from sabbatical to open this eponymous eatery in Downtown Dallas' Arts District, where he turns out globally inflected Southwestern dishes plus a few signature items from his days at the now-closed Star Canyon (bone-in rib-eye, anyone?); it's all set in a swanky space done up with etched glass, copper curtains, a cascading waterfall and an urban patio, plus a bar that serves an array of tapas and ceviche.

Tei Tei Robata Bar Ⓜ *Japanese* | 27 | 24 | 23 | $44 |

Knox-Henderson | 2906 N. Henderson Ave. (Willis Ave.) | Dallas | 214-828-2400 | www.teiteirobata.com

A Knox-Henderson "hot spot", this "authentic robata grill" ("Teppo's more expensive brother") is "popular" for its "excellent Japanese cuisine" – including "rare options" of "outstanding" "high-end sushi", plus "hot rock–cooked Kobe beef" you "sear yourself"; the room is "chic" and the service "excellent", but those not content to "hobnob" at the "trendy bar" "rarely visit due to the no-reservations policy" during peak hours and the "unbearable waits."

Teppo Yakitori & Sushi Bar Ⓜ *Japanese*

27 | 22 | 22 | $38

Greenville Avenue | 2014 Greenville Ave. (Prospect Ave.) | Dallas | 214-826-8989 | www.teppo.com

Bringing "consistently great" "West Coast–style sushi to Dallas", this Greenville Avenue sibling of Tei Tei (with a slightly younger but no less devout following) features a "big selection" of "excellent, super-fresh" raw-fish fare, and "the added bonus" of "amazing yakitori", enjoyed amid a pleasingly "cavelike atmosphere"; N.B. it now accepts reservations for parties of three or more.

Ⓩ York Street Ⓢ Ⓜ *American*

28 | 22 | 27 | $56

Lakewood | 6047 Lewis St. (Skillman St.) | Dallas | 214-826-0968

A "showcase of fine dining", this "sublime" New American is "the place for foodies who want to experiment", as "only the finest and freshest ingredients make it onto" chef-owner Sharon Hage's "exquisite revolving menu"; "tucked on a side street in a converted house", it sits in a "strange location" next to a Lakewood gas station and seats fewer than four dozen – making reservations "essential."

Denver Area & Mountain Resorts

	Restaurant	Cuisine
28	Mizuna	American
	Frasca	Italian
	Fruition	American
	Sushi Den	Japanese
27	Sushi Sasa	Japanese
	Six89 Kitchen/Wine	American
	Matsuhisa	Japanese
	Keystone Ranch	American
	Del Frisco's	Steak
	Kevin Taylor	French
	Splendido at the Chateau	American
26	Sweet Basil	American
	Piñons	American
	Flagstaff House	American
	Luca d'Italia	Italian
	rioja	Mediterranean
	La Tour	French
	Barolo Grill	Italian
	Z Cuisine Bistrot	French
	Juniper	American

OTHER NOTEWORTHY PLACES

Bistro Vendôme	French
Cafe Brazil	Brazilian/Colombian
Capital Grille	Steak
Deluxe	Californian
Duo	American
Highland's Garden	American
India's	Indian
Kitchen, The	Eclectic
L'Atelier	Eclectic
Montagna	American
Morton's	Steak
Palace Arms	American
Panzano	Italian
Potager	American
Samplings	American
Solera Restaurant/Wine	American
Summit	American
Super Star Asian	Chinese
240 Union	American
Vesta Dipping Grill	American

⚡ Barolo Grill 🔒Ⓜ️ *Italian* | 26 | 23 | 25 | $54 |

Cherry Creek | 3030 E. Sixth Ave. (bet. Milwaukee & St. Paul Sts.) | Denver | 303-393-1040 | www.barologrilldenver.com

"You'd have to travel to Tuscany to find better fare" than at this "elegant" Cherry Creek "favorite" where "beautiful people" sit by the "romantic fireplace" and savor "heavenly" (if "pricey") Northern Italian cuisine that's "a study in flavor", especially when paired with selections from the "amazing wine list"; in fact, the staff itself "visits Italy every year", resulting in service that surveyors describe as "somewhat pretentious" but "knowledgeable and eager to help."

Bistro Vendôme Ⓜ️ *French* | 24 | 23 | 22 | $40 |

Larimer Square | 1424H Larimer St. (15th St.) | Denver | 303-825-3232 | www.bistrovendome.com

"A fabulous spot for Francophiles who can't afford the airfare to Paris", this "vivacious" "French jewel" "tucked behind Larimer Square" boasts an "authentic bistro menu" (including what some call "addictive pommes frites") that's best enjoyed on the "fetching outdoor patio fragrant with blooming foliage"; if you prefer to sit inside, the dining room is also a "*très charmant*" choice for relaxing over a "romantic" dinner or a "lovely" weekend brunch.

Cafe Brazil 🔒Ⓜ️ *Brazilian/Colombian* | 24 | 17 | 21 | $37 |

North Denver | 4408 Lowell Blvd. (44th Ave.) | Denver | 303-480-1877 | www.cafebrazildenver.com

"For something different, but not too different", try this "vibrant" North Denver "favorite" where the "authentic" Brazilian-Colombian cuisine is "fabulous", especially the "super-fresh seafood dishes featuring spicy, tropical fruit accents"; the cuisine pairs well with "unique cocktails" and a "bold, colorful" interior that may be "a little kitschy" but has a "wonderful atmosphere overall."

Capital Grille *Steak* | 25 | 23 | 25 | $57 |

Larimer Square | 1450 Larimer St. (15th St.) | Denver | 303-539-2500 | www.thecapitalgrille.com

"If you wish to splurge, look no further" than this Larimer Square link in an "always consistent" national chain, where a "flawless" staff "meets your every desire" as it delivers "luscious hunks of red meat" plus "fresh seafood" and selections from an "extensive wine list"; the "clubby dark-wood" setting fills up with "Downtown VIPs" who don't mind paying the "big prices" you'd expect from a "sure-to-impress" "steakhouse institution."

Del Frisco's Double Eagle Steak House *Steak* | 27 | 24 | 26 | $64 |

Greenwood Village | Denver Tech Ctr. | 8100 E. Orchard Rd. (I-25, Ext. 198) | 303-796-0100 | www.delfriscos.com

This "clubby" Greenwood Village "cow palace" corrals all types – from "power brokers" and "local sports celebrities" to "high rollers and those looking to hit on them" – for "consistently excellent" steaks "prepared to perfection" plus "huge sides" and an "extensive wine list" that "reads like *War and Peace*"; "exceptional service" and a "separate cigar lounge" add appeal, but be prepared – you'll need "some large bills" to pay the tab at this "carnivore's delight."

Deluxe 🄢🄼 *Californian*
| 24 | 19 | 20 | $37 |

Downtown Denver | 30 S. Broadway (W. Ellsworth Ave.) | Denver | 303-722-1550 | www.deluxedenver.com

At this "hidden gem" set in a "little storefront on Broadway", "the best place to sit is at the chef's counter, where you can watch the culinary magic unfold right before your eyes" as chef-owner Dylan Moore and his "highly competent" crew turn out "creative" Californian cuisine that's "full of memorable flavor combinations"; the space is "tiny" but "dressed to impress, just like the va-va-voom clientele."

Duo *American*
| 24 | 21 | 22 | $37 |

Highlands | 2413 W. 32nd Ave. (Zuni St.) | Denver | 303-477-4141 | www.duodenver.com

The "inventive food" is the highlight of this "bustling" "neighborhood favorite" in Highlands, where chef John Broening incorporates "fresh, seasonal ingredients" in his "tasty", "well-prepared" New American cuisine; it's all served by a "friendly" staff in an "earthy" space featuring a "warm and inviting open kitchen" and a "unique communal table", leading some to say it's "a keeper" that's as "lovely for brunch" as it is "for a romantic date night."

Flagstaff House *American*
| 26 | 27 | 27 | $76 |

Boulder | 1138 Flagstaff Rd. (on Flagstaff Mtn.) | 303-442-4640 | www.flagstaffhouse.com

"Make the drive up" Flagstaff Mountain to this "treasure in the sky" where "resplendent views" "overlooking Boulder and beyond" ("so beautiful at sunset!") are just the beginning: chef Mark Monette's "simply superb" New American cuisine, an "amazing wine list with incredible sommeliers to match" and "impeccable" service "timed to the second" also add to the "absolutely first-class" package; it's "not for the weak of wallet", but you "need to go at least once in a lifetime."

☑ Frasca Food and Wine 🄢 *Italian*
| 28 | 24 | 27 | $62 |

Boulder | 1738 Pearl St. (18th St.) | 303-442-6966 | www.frascafoodandwine.com

"Words cannot adequately express how divine" Colorado's Most Popular restaurant really is, so you'll just have to "call two months ahead and pray" that you get a reservation at this "beacon in Boulder", where chef Lachlan Mackinnon-Patterson and master sommelier Bobby Stuckey (both French Laundry alums) "specialize in the food and wine of [Italy's] Friuli" region; there's also a "friendly, knowledgeable staff" to help make this a "truly world-class" option that's "deserving of all the hype" – and "worth every cent."

☑ Fruition 🄼 *American*
| 28 | 21 | 26 | $52 |

Country Club | 1313 E. Sixth Ave. (bet. Lafayette & Marion Sts.) | Denver | 303-831-1992 | www.fruitionrestaurant.com

"Absolutely incredible" "plates that look like a Cézanne still life" are the hallmark of this "top-tier destination" situated between Capitol Hill and Country Club that has come to "fruition indeed" courtesy of "talented" chef/co-owner Alex Seidel, who "goes above and beyond" with his "fantastic", "expertly crafted" New American cuisine; "deft and friendly service" adds to the "sterling experience", which means "the only chink in the armor" is the "cozy" but "very tiny space."

Highland's Garden Cafe *American*

`25` `25` `24` `$49`

Highlands | 3927 W. 32nd Ave. (bet. Osceola & Perry Sts.) | Denver | 303-458-5920 | www.highlandsgardencafe.com

"Take your sweetheart" to this "charming" Highlands restaurant that's a "memorable experience" thanks to chef-owner Patricia Perry's "inventive" menu of "just plain lovely" New American cuisine, a "superb" spread that "lives up to the atmosphere": a converted 1890s Victorian with a "cozy", "inviting" interior and "delightful" garden dining on several "lush", "carefully tended" patios; what's more, there's a "wonderful", "pampering" staff to ensure "nothing is amiss."

India's *Indian*

`25` `19` `18` `$28`

South Denver | Tamarac Sq. | 3333 S. Tamarac Dr. (Hampden Ave.) | Denver | 303-755-4284 | www.indiasrestaurant.com

It's "not your average curry joint", so "don't let the strip-mall location turn you away" from this South Denver Indian where the "powerfully addictive", "perfectly spiced" cuisine will have you "salivating just approaching the restaurant" and the "regally appointed" dining room "boasts billowy fabrics and white tablecloths"; while a few feel the "inconsistent service" "needs some improvement", most agree you "come here for the food, which tastes awesome."

Juniper *American*

`26` `20` `22` `$51`

Edwards | 97 Main St. (Hwy. 6) | 970-926-7001 | www.juniperrestaurant.com

"A charming surprise" situated a few miles from Vail in "unassuming" Edwards, this New American "gem" is "well worth the drive" for "excellent" "seasonal" cuisine served by an "enthusiastic" staff, plus its "happening local scene" and "sublime" deck with tables "overlooking the Eagle River"; nevertheless, a few fret about "cramped quarters" and a "snooty attitude", recommending patrons "sit at the bar for optimal location and attention."

Kevin Taylor ☒ *French*

`27` `25` `26` `$67`

Downtown Denver | Hotel Teatro | 1106 14th St. (Arapahoe St.) | Denver | 303-820-2600 | www.ktrg.net

Step into "a magical world where all your desires come true" at this "benchmark of excellence" in the Downtown theater district offering "exquisite" New French cuisine from "accomplished" and "uncompromising" chef-owner Kevin Taylor; situated in a "classic white-tablecloth" setting in the Hotel Teatro, it's an "elegant" (if "pricey") experience that's elevated by a "superior wine list" and "attentive but unobtrusive service."

Keystone Ranch ☒ *American*

`27` `27` `26` `$82`

Keystone | Keystone Ranch Golf Course | 1437 Summit County Rd. 150 (Rd. D) | 970-496-4386 | www.keystone.snow.com

"As good as it gets", this "rustic" "reminder of a time gone by" offers "consistently wonderful" regional New American cuisine and "superb" service amid the "spectacular" ambiance of an "elegant" "turn-of-the-century" Keystone ranch house; such a "memorable" evening could only end with dessert in a "cozy" sitting room that comes "complete with roaring fire and overstuffed leather sofas"; in short, it may be "costly, but who cares?"

Kitchen, The *Eclectic*

| 25 | 21 | 23 | $43 |

Boulder | 1039 Pearl St. (bet. 10th & 11th Sts.) | 303-544-5973 | www.thekitchencafe.com

"Even if you don't wear Birkenstocks, drive a Prius or oppose globalization, you'll love" this "quintessential Boulder eatery" where the "creative", "well-executed" Eclectic cuisine is crafted from "fresh", "local and sustainable ingredients", and wind power, food composting and recycling are the norm; the "lively setting" includes a "hip" but "noisy" dining room with a 12-ft.-long communal table and a "cool upstairs wine lounge" that offers monthly vino classes.

L'Atelier *Eclectic*

| 25 | 22 | 24 | $54 |

Boulder | 1739 Pearl St. (18th St.) | 303-442-7233 | www.latelierboulder.com

"If you like food as art", head to this Boulder "treasure" where chef-owner Radek Cerny "does a magnificent job" with his "extravagant" "French-influenced world cuisine" (the "fabulous tasting menu is worth the price tag") and "outstanding wine list"; while some insist the 50-seat space is "cramped", "attentive service" and an "elegant" "formal atmosphere" help to make it an ideal choice "for a special occasion."

La Tour *French*

| 26 | 20 | 24 | $62 |

Vail | 122 E. Meadow Dr. (I-70) | 970-476-4403 | www.latour-vail.com

Have your "French food and wine fantasy fulfilled" at this "hidden" "must-do in the Vail Valley", where chef/co-owner Paul Ferzacca offers "heaven on a plate" in the form of "creative", contemporary Gallic cuisine ("the Dover sole is truly inspired"); it's all served by a "friendly", "attentive staff that knows the menu" and can suggest the "perfect wine pairing", helping to make this both a "place to impress a date" and "a tough ticket in-season."

Luca d'Italia 🈹 Ⓜ *Italian*

| 26 | 19 | 26 | $48 |

Capitol Hill | 711 Grant St. (bet. 7th & 8th Aves.) | Denver | 303-832-6600 | www.lucadenver.com

Overseen by chef-owner Frank Bonanno ("the mind behind Mizuna"), this "splendid Italian noshery" on Capitol Hill is "a truly superior experience" offering "interesting culinary combinations" full of "unexpectedly wonderful flavors" plus homemade "pastas from the heavens"; although a few frown upon the "simple", "sterile" surroundings, they're outvoted by those who appreciate the "excellent tasting menu", "knowledgeable staff" and "great people-watching."

Matsuhisa *Japanese*

| 27 | 23 | 24 | $71 |

Aspen | 303 E. Main St. (Monarch St.) | 970-544-6628 | www.matsuhisaaspen.com

"A mile-high Nobu" that "lives up to its reputation", this Aspen eatery from the eponymous restaurateur is a "fabulous" "treat" delivering "jaw-dropping Japanese fusion" fare and "amazingly fresh" sushi; the "food outshines everything else", but the basement-level dining room has a "hip vibe" and the upstairs lounge is also a "happening" place to sip "chilled sake served in bamboo carafes"; still, "astronomical prices" have some insisting "it's not the the lack of oxygen in the air that leaves you breathless – it's the bill."

Z Mizuna S M *American* 28 | 23 | 27 | $57

Capitol Hill | 225 E. Seventh Ave. (bet. Grant & Sherman Sts.) | Denver | 303-832-4778 | www.mizunadenver.com

Rated No. 1 for Food in Colorado, this "consistently excellent" Capitol Hill "favorite" "still leads the pack" when it comes to "culinary genius" Frank Bonanno's "undeniably brilliant" New American menu (including "to-die-for lobster mac 'n' cheese"); it has "all the components of a wonderful evening" – a "well-rounded wine list", "impeccable service" and an "intimate, romantic" ambiance – so although prices are steep, it's "worth every penny" in order to "sweep a first date or long-time girlfriend off her feet."

Montagna *American* 26 | 26 | 25 | $73

Aspen | The Little Nell Hotel | 675 E. Durant Ave. (Spring St.) | 970-920-6330 | www.thelittlenell.com

"Nestled in The Little Nell Hotel" in Aspen, this "place to see and be seen" draws a "fabulous crowd" with its "equally fabulous food": chef Ryan Hardy's "sophisticated menu" of "inventive, well-executed" New American cuisine is coupled with an "opulent", "encylopedic wine list" overseen by "maestro Richard Betts"; "unsurpassed service" adds to a "beautiful experience" that's costly and to some "a bit stuffy", but for most is "just magnificent" – "what more could you want?"

Morton's, The Steakhouse *Steak* 24 | 22 | 24 | $65

LoDo | 1710 Wynkoop St. (17th St.) | Denver | 303-825-3353
Greenwood Village | Denver Crescent Town Ctr. | 8480 E. Belleview Ave. (DTC Blvd.) | 303-409-1177
www.mortons.com

Carnivores claim "you cannot beat the steaks" at these "reliable, up-scale" chain links where the "quality" cuts are "perfectly done" and brought "sizzling" to the table by a "friendly, efficient" staff; as you might expect from an "old-school" "beef eater's paradise", the "dark, serious" "men's club feel" is coupled with "astronomical prices", so "bring plenty of dough" or "hope someone else is paying."

Palace Arms *American* 25 | 26 | 26 | $64

Downtown Denver | Brown Palace Hotel | 321 17th St. (Tremont Pl.) | Denver | 303-297-3111 | www.brownpalace.com

"Beaming with sophistication and poise", this "classy, old-fashioned" "grande dame" in the "historic" Brown Palace Hotel is "everything a first-class restaurant should be", offering "outstanding" New American cuisine, an "extensive wine list" and "snappy service" amid "opulent decor"; "not everyone enjoys this level of formality", but those who do "come in an armored car stacked with money" and "splurge on a special occasion"; N.B. jackets are recommended.

Panzano *Italian* 24 | 21 | 23 | $43

Downtown Denver | Hotel Monaco | 909 17th St. (Champa St.) | Denver | 303-296-3525 | www.panzano-denver.com

"Not your typical hotel restaurant", this "lovely venue" "in the heart of Downtown" "continues to excel" courtesy of "amazing chef" Elise Wiggins, who turns out "superb" Northern Italian cuisine in a "romantic", recently remodeled setting; an "extensive wine selection" and "attentive, cordial service" also help to make this "the place you take your friends and business associates if you really want to treat them right"; P.S. it "has a gluten-free menu."

Piñons *American* | 26 | 24 | 26 | $71 |

Aspen | 105 S. Mill St. (E. Main St.) | 970-920-2021

Still "an outstanding dining experience" "after all these years", this "timeless" Aspen "favorite" draws "locals and VIPs" (hence there's "excellent people-watching") with "superb" "Rocky Mountain haute cuisine", including meats that "practically 'moo' from your plate"; but whether you relax in the "elegant" interior or "outside on a perfect summer evening", be sure to take note of the "great mountain views" and take advantage of the "bargain", "early prix fixe dinner."

Potager ⑤Ⓜ *American* | 25 | 21 | 23 | $43 |

Capitol Hill | 1109 Ogden St. (bet. 11th & 12th Aves.) | Denver | 303-832-5788

"A seasoned toque in every sense", chef/co-owner Teri Rippeto is "truly dedicated" to using "seasonal, locally raised and mostly organic" ingredients at her "lovely" Capitol Hill New American, a "unique" option with "something for everyone" on a menu that's "ever-changing" yet "never bends to hip food trends"; "a boutique wine list just adds to the culinary magic", as does an "attentive but not obtrusive" staff and an "intimate backyard garden"; P.S. get here "early since they don't take reservations."

Z rioja *Mediterranean* | 26 | 23 | 23 | $46 |

Larimer Square | 1431 Larimer St. (bet. 14th & 15th Sts.) | Denver | 303-820-2282 | www.riojadenver.com

Chef/co-owner Jennifer Jasinski "is nothing short of amazing", and her "cosmopolitan" restaurant in "hip Larimer Square" rewards its "loyal following" with "mouthwatering" Med cuisine that "makes use of seasonal and local ingredients" and is paired with "some fine Spanish wines"; a "knowledeable" staff that "goes above and beyond" adds to the "inviting" and "always energetic" (if occasionally "noisy") ambiance; P.S. try to "get a seat at the chef's counter."

Samplings Ⓜ *American* | 25 | 22 | 21 | $46 |

Frisco | 320 Main St. (bet. Streamside Ln. & W. Creekside Dr.) | 970-668-8466 | www.samplingswine.com

"Like nothing else in the mountains", this "gem" in "the heart of beautiful Frisco" is the place "to go with some friends" to feast on "artfully crafted" New American small plates and "incredible dessert samplers" in a "cozy" but "sophisticated" setting; there's also an "amicable and highly trained" staff on hand to suggest "creative wine pairings" and "to guide you" through your "tantalizingly long dinner"; P.S. be sure to "ask for a seat by the fireplace."

Six89 Kitchen/Wine Bar Ⓜ *American* | 27 | 22 | 25 | $54 |

Carbondale | 689 Main St. (7th St.) | 970-963-6890 | www.six89.com

"Skip the scene in Aspen" and take a "trip down-valley" to this "swanky" "favorite" that's "worth the drive" to Carbondale for "unusual", "truly creative" New American cuisine from chef-owner Mark Fischer, a proprietor who "knows no wrong"; the "food and wine combinations" are "coveted by locals", who also appreciate the "exceptional staff" and a "fantastic atmosphere" that includes a welcoming patio and a dining room "where you can carry on a conversation."

Solera Restaurant & Wine Bar 🅜 *American* | 24 | 19 | 22 | $45 |

East Denver | 5410 E. Colfax Ave. (Grape St.) | Denver | 303-388-8429 | www.solerarestaurant.com

"Leave bustling Colfax Avenue behind" at this "superb" East Denver "hideaway" from chef-owner Goose Sorensen, a "top talent" who "takes diners on a culinary journey" via his "creative" New American menu; though the "elegantly lit" dining room is "nicely appointed", "the best seat" is out on the "wonderful" garden patio, a "quiet little oasis" tended to by the same "friendly, engaging" staff; P.S. there are "excellent wine tastings on Wednesday evenings."

Splendido at the Chateau *American* | 27 | 27 | 26 | $74 |

Beaver Creek | Beaver Creek Resort | 17 Chateau Ln. (Scott Hill Rd.) | 970-845-8808 | www.splendidobeavercreek.com

"An outstanding experience" "from start to finish", this New American in the Beaver Creek Resort offers a "splendid blending of food, service and atmosphere": chef David Walford "runs a first-class kitchen" that turns out "imaginative" preparations of local game, while a "fantastic" staff treats guests "like royalty" as they dine in the "beautiful", "elegant room" or sip cocktails in the "delightful piano bar"; yes, it's "expensive", but it's "worth the cost" "for a special occasion."

Summit 🅜 *American* | 25 | 27 | 26 | $56 |

Colorado Springs | The Broadmoor | 19 Lake Circle (off Mesa Ave.) | 719-577-5896 | www.summitatbroadmoor.com

"The Broadmoor reinvents itself once again" with the addition of this "absolutely stunning" New American "success", "a step into modernity" featuring an "exciting", "deliciously prepared" brasserie menu and an "exquisite" Adam Tihany–designed dining room (complete with an "amazing wine tower"); "genuinely interested and knowledgeable" servers tend to the "buzzy" crowd amid a "fun, vibrant atmosphere" that's bolstered by a "lovely bar."

Super Star Asian *Chinese* | 24 | 8 | 15 | $21 |

West Denver | 2200 W. Alameda Ave. (Yuma St.) | Denver | 303-727-9889

"Welcome to Hong Kong" announce locals who "love" this West Denver Chinese enough to endure "wretched waits" in order to sample "marvelous dim sum" "paraded around on carts" by "smiling, attentive servers"; the "chaotic, loud, impossibly busy" dining room is "not much to look at but is fun to be in" as you devour "authentic" entrees and "out-of-this-world wonderful" dumplings.

🅩 Sushi Den *Japanese* | 28 | 23 | 21 | $44 |

South Denver | 1487 S. Pearl St. (E. Florida Ave.) | Denver | 303-777-0826 | www.sushiden.net

For "absolutely flawless" "fish so fresh you can't believe you're eating it in Colorado", set sail for this South Denver Japanese where "shockingly" "inspired sushi" and "unique rolls" are served in a "stylish" space that gets "crowded" with "local stars, sports celebrities" and other "beautiful people"; there are often "outrageous waits" and servers can be "a bit snooty", but most agree it's "worth the suffering" to "watch the magic unfold"; P.S. "they don't take reservations."

☑ Sushi Sasa *Japanese*

27 | 22 | 23 | $45

Highlands | 2401 15th St. (Platte St.) | Denver | 303-433-7272 | www.sushisasadenver.com

At this "upscale" Japanese in the "increasingly popular Highlands neighborhood", chef-owner Wayne Conwell "is a magician" who will "tantalize your taste buds" with his "delicious seafood dishes" and "brilliantly crafted", "impeccably fresh sushi"; a "simple", "modern space" with "white everything" serves as a counterpoint to the "dynamic cuisine", while a "friendly" staff adds to the "pleasant experience."

☑ Sweet Basil *American*

26 | 23 | 24 | $59

Vail | 193 E. Gore Creek Dr. (Bridge St.) | 970-476-0125 | www.sweetbasil-vail.com

"Still as sweet as ever", this "high-altitude gem" is "the gold standard of the Vail Valley" courtesy of "cutting-edge", "practically flawless" New American cuisine from chef Paul Anders plus a "killer wine list" and an "engaging staff"; a "glitzy crowd" gathers here "after a hard day playing in the powder", so although the "delightful setting" was "just refurbished and enlarged", it remains "tough to score a reservation" ("go for lunch"); P.S. "ask for a creekside window table."

240 Union *American*

25 | 19 | 24 | $42

Lakewood | 240 Union Blvd. (bet. 6th Ave. Frwy. & W. Alameda Pkwy.) | 303-989-3562 | www.240union.com

"Legions of fans enjoy" the "exquisite" "seasonal" New American fare at this Lakewood "favorite" serving up "superb meat and seafood entrees" along with "fabulous desserts" and an "affordable wine list" in an "upscale" room with a view of the open kitchen; the "gracious staff" "always delivers a nice dining experience", so even if a few feel it's "way too loud", most maintain it's "worth the ride" to the Western suburbs.

Vesta Dipping Grill *American*

24 | 24 | 22 | $42

LoDo | 1822 Blake St. (bet. 18th & 19th Sts.) | Denver | 303-296-1970 | www.vestagrill.com

A "clever concept that still has legs after 10 years", this "way hip" LoDo New American from "risk-taking young gun" Matt Selby combines "perfectly grilled meats and vegetables" with a "never-ending list" of "amazing" dipping sauces for a "unique", "interactive dinner" with friends; it all unfolds in a "sexy" "see-and-be-seen" setting with a "buzzing" (if "noisy") ambiance, so it's "worth the wait for a table if you aren't savvy enough to snag a reservation."

Z Cuisine Bistrot & Parisian Bar ⑤ Ⓜ *French*

26 | 20 | 22 | $36

Highlands | 2239 W. 30th Ave. (Wyandot St.) | Denver | 303-477-1111 | www.zcuisineonline.com

Be "transported to Paris" "without the jet lag" at this "labor of love" located "off the beaten path" in Highlands, where "talented" chef/co-owner Patrick DuPays pleases patrons with a "terrific" blackboard menu of "truly incredible, authentic bistro" classics that "pair perfectly with the lovely wine list"; the "intimate", "postage stamp–sized" space is being expanded, which is certain to appease frustrated Francophiles who say "the no-reservations policy is a crock of cassoulet"; N.B. closed Sunday–Tuesday.

Detroit

TOP FOOD RANKING

	Restaurant	Cuisine
28	Lark, The	Continental
27	Bacco	Italian
	Zingerman's	Deli
	Tribute	French
	Beverly Hills Grill	American
	Ristorante Café Cortina	Italian
26	No. VI Chop House	Seafood/Steak
	West End Grill	American
	Common Grill	Seafood
	Five Lakes Grill	American

OTHER NOTEWORTHY PLACES

Assaggi	Mediterranean
Atlas Global Bistro	Eclectic
Capital Grille	Steak
Coach Insignia	Seafood/Steak
Fiddleheads	American
Grill/Ritz-Carlton	American
Rattlesnake, The	Seafood/Steak
Rugby Grille	American/Continental
Sweet Georgia Brown	Southern
Whitney, The	American

Assaggi Bistro Ⓜ *Mediterranean*　　26 | 19 | 23 | $40
(fka Assaggi Mediterranean Bistro)
Ferndale | 330 W. Nine Mile Rd. (Woodward Ave.) | 248-584-3499 |
www.assaggibistro.com
Diners happily invest time and money at this "hot" Ferndale Med
showcasing "consistently excellent" food (much of it created in the
open kitchen's wood-fired oven), "personable" service from both staff
and owners George Gize and Josephine Knapp, and a "lovely" courtyard;
the "sophisticated" ambiance is even ideal for a "romantic" rendezvous.

Atlas Global Bistro *Eclectic*　　23 | 21 | 20 | $38
Downtown | 3111 Woodward Ave. (Charlotte St.) | 313-831-2241 |
www.atlasglobalbistro.com
The "original", "globally influenced" menu pleases "the most discerning
diners" at this Eclectic "oasis" near Downtown; the floor-to-ceiling windows are draws, as is the "trendy", "big-city" vibe and "one of the
best" Sunday brunches around.

Ⓩ Bacco Ristorante Ⓢ *Italian*　　27 | 25 | 26 | $56
Southfield | 29410 Northwestern Hwy. (bet. Inkster & 12 Mile Rds.) |
248-356-6600 | www.baccoristorante.com
"Movers and shakers" and other "highbrow clientele" with "money to
burn" "fill the seats" of this "fine-dining" spot in Southfield whose "out-

standing", "rich" Italian preparations are abetted by an all-Boot wine list
that's *"magnifico"* and staff that defines "attentive"; the "elegant" trap-
pings frame the food and help give the restaurant "top-notch" status.

☑ Beverly Hills Grill *American* `27` `18` `24` `$37`
Beverly Hills | 31471 Southfield Rd. (bet. 13 & 14 Mile Rds.) | 248-642-2355
"Always jammed, with good reason" sums up the sentiment about this
20-year-old Beverly Hills New American that continues to please customers with its "consistently high-quality" menu including "fresh" fish
specials, "phenomenal" breakfasts and "top-notch" Sunday brunches;
"no reservations" and a "small bar/waiting area" make for long waits,
but given the "excellent" offerings, it's "worth the effort."

☑ Capital Grille *Steak* `25` `25` `25` `$56`
Troy | Somerset Collection-North | 2800 W. Big Beaver Rd. (bet. Coolidge &
Crooks Rds.) | 248-649-5300 | www.thecapitalgrille.com
"Big shots" and "local celebs" partake of the "delicious" chops that arrive with "heaping" sides at this Troy steakhouse chain outlet that's part
of the Somerset Collection – just expect tabs that require a "second
mortgage"; fans applaud a setting that's equally conducive to "high-
level" deals and pickups at the "smoky" "meat market" of a bar.

Coach Insignia ☒ *Steak* `23` `27` `23` `$58`
Downtown | Renaissance Ctr. | 100 Renaissance Ctr., 72nd fl. (Jefferson Ave.) |
313-567-2622 | www.mattprenticerg.com
Panoramic "knock-your-socks-off" views of Detroit and Canada leave
visitors amazed at Matt Prentice's "pricey" 72nd-story Renaissance
Center chophouse whose kitchen puts "twists on old" steakhouse
standards; "one of the best wine lists" (overseen by master sommelier
Madeline Triffon) helps place this site "a cut above" the competition.

☑ Common Grill, The Ⓜ *Seafood* `26` `21` `24` `$38`
Chelsea | 112 S. Main St. (bet. Middle & South Sts.) | 734-475-0470 |
www.commongrill.com
There's "nothing common" about chef-owner Craig Common's "true
gem" of a seafooder "stashed away" an hour's drive from Detroit in
"quaint little" Chelsea; all agree the drawback of "long waits" caused
by the reservations policy (only for six or more) is effectively overcome by the "bustling" atmosphere, "good-humored service" and, of
course, the "meticulously" crafted cooking.

Fiddleheads Ⓜ *American* `23` `19` `21` `$37`
Royal Oak | 4313 W. 13 Mile Rd. (Greenfield Rd.) | 248-288-3744 |
www.fiddleheadsroyaloak.com
"Tucked away where you wouldn't expect" it in "residential" Royal
Oak, this New American offers "inspired" seasonal dishes from chef
Tim Voss (formerly of Forté), a "friendly" wine list, "sexy cocktails"
and a "low-key" style; aside from varying perspectives on service
("helpful" vs. "inattentive"), most concede it's "worth the hunt."

Five Lakes Grill ☒ *American* `26` `20` `24` `$47`
Milford | 424 N. Main St. (Commerce St.) | 248-684-7455 |
www.fivelakesgrill.com
"Culinary leader" Brian Polcyn is the driving force behind this New
American producing "memorable" meals (devised from "local" produce)

in Milford; P.S. the monthly prix fixe dinners are not to be missed, and neither is the "excellent" charcuterie, for which the chef is famed.

Grill at the Ritz-Carlton, The *American* | 26 | 25 | 26 | $59 |

Dearborn | Ritz-Carlton Dearborn, Fairlane Plaza | 300 Town Center Dr. (bet. Hubbard Dr. & Southfield Frwy.) | 313-441-2100 | www.ritzcarlton.com
"The Ritz is the Ritz anywhere in the world . . . and that's a good thing" for those who seek out this "classy" New American in Dearborn for "top-notch" dining enhanced by "pro" service; the "excellent kitchen dishes up old faves and inventive cuisine with equal facility", making the "expense-account" prices relatively easy to digest.

Z Lark, The Ⓢ Ⓜ *Continental* | 28 | 27 | 28 | $85 |

West Bloomfield | 6430 Farmington Rd. (W. Maple Rd.) | 248-661-4466 | www.thelark.com
"Every superlative you can think of" applies to this West Bloomfield Continental, the "best of the best" for surveyors who've voted it tops for Food, Decor and Service in the Detroit area, thanks to "heavenly", "gorgeous" food, a "lovely" "flower-filled" setting reminiscent of a "country inn" and "tuxedo-clad" servers who provide "all the pampering you could want" or need; overall, this "pinnacle of fine dining" is "worth every penny of the splurge"; N.B. jackets required.

No. VI Chop House & | 26 | 24 | 24 | $55 |
Lobster Bar *Seafood/Steak*

Novi | Hotel Baronette | 27790 Novi Rd. (12 Mile Rd.) | 248-305-5210 | www.mattprenticerg.com
This "hidden wonder" inside the Hotel Baronette delivers a "high-end experience for its high-end" diners via "fabulous" steaks and other signatures, notably a "divine" morel bisque, served in "dark" quarters accented by "deep leather chairs"; they also deliver "premium" pricing, but in light of the quality, fans find this chophouse "easy to recommend."

Rattlesnake, The Ⓢ Ⓜ *Seafood/Steak* | 26 | 25 | 25 | $57 |

River Place | Stroh's River Pl. | 300 River Place Dr. (Joseph Campau St.) | 313-567-4400
"Fabulous" views of Canada across the river enhance the all-around appeal of this "upscale" River Place endeavor (going into its 20th year) that presents its "delectable" steaks and seafood with "class and elegance"; factor in an "extensive drinks" selection, and it's clear you've got a "diamond" in an "unassuming part of town."

Ristorante Café Cortina Ⓢ *Italian* | 27 | 25 | 25 | $52 |

Farmington Hills | 30715 W. 10 Mile Rd. (Orchard Lake Rd.) | 248-474-3033 | www.cafecortina.com
"Feeling like royalty" comes naturally at this Farmington Hills staple prized for its Italian slate, especially the "incredible" pastas served in the "most romantic" setting featuring a fireplace that roars in winter or a vine-covered patio perfect in warmer weather; true, the price "figure may be a little high", but "superlative" service helps sweeten the deal.

Rugby Grille ● *American/Continental* | 25 | 23 | 25 | $66 |

Birmingham | Townsend Hotel | 100 Townsend St. (Pierce St.) | 248-642-5999 | www.townsendhotel.com
Located in Birmingham's "classy" Townsend Hotel, this Continental-American boasts a "refined" "European" atmosphere" to accompany the

	FOOD	DECOR	SERVICE	COST

"equally refined, classic" fare, most notably the "fantastic" Dover sole done tableside; given the "hefty prices", it's no surprise that "famous people" tend to make their way here, most of whom are likely to get a table in the coveted "grill room rather than in the outside hallway."

Sweet Georgia Brown 🅜 *Southern* | 23 | 23 | 21 | $50 |

Downtown | 1045 Brush St. (Monroe St.) | 313-965-1245 | www.sweetgb.com

"High-end" Southern cooking brings "high rollers" to this "urban" Downtown draw selling "huge" portions of "first-rate" fare that'll "blow your low carb diet out the window" as well as jazz on weekends and an atmosphere that "hums"; N.B. there's a new patio, and the restaurant offers a buffet to go along with Sunday's jazz brunch.

🆉 Tribute 🅢 *French* | 27 | 27 | 26 | $84 |

Farmington Hills | 31425 W. 12 Mile Rd. (Orchard Lake Rd.) | 248-848-9393 | www.tributerestaurant.com

Don Yamauchi's Asian-influenced French cuisine is "delectable art" and "out of this world", and the staff makes you "feel like you are celebrating" as it "helps you pair your meal" with selections from the "exceptional" wine list at this Farmington Hills venue showcasing a "dramatic", vaulted dining room; the kitchen-side chef's table provides "a great floor show", and the "platinum-card" pricing doesn't deter diners from visiting this "Paris- and New York–worthy competitor."

West End Grill 🅢🅜 *American* | 26 | 20 | 25 | $50 |

Ann Arbor | 120 W. Liberty St. (Main St.) | 734-747-6260 | www.westendgrilla2.com

Pre-entree beignets "in lieu of bread" help set apart this Ann Arbor New American whose candlelit, "elegantly simple" setting frames the "delicious" offerings; clients who "can't stop praising" the quality of this "truly professional" operation are also amazed by the staff's "savantlike" memory when reciting all those menu descriptions.

Whitney, The 🅜 *American* | 22 | 27 | 24 | $56 |

Wayne State | 4421 Woodward Ave. (Canfield St.) | 313-832-5700 | www.thewhitney.com

"Go to be treated like a royal", or at least "a lumber baron of yore", at this "pricey" Wayne State New American "grande dame" housed in an "opulent" Victorian showplace that's "elegant in every regard", featuring Tiffany chandeliers, stained-glass windows, marble fireplaces and rich woods throughout; the desserts are "to die for", but the savories are "quite good" too, and lunch is "an especially good deal."

🆉 Zingerman's Delicatessen *Deli* | 27 | 16 | 22 | $19 |

Ann Arbor | 422 Detroit St. (Kingsley St.) | 734-663-3354 | www.zingermans.com

"The lines can be daunting" at this nationally acclaimed "juggernaut of sandwich making", an Ann Arbor "institution" (Detroit's Most Popular eatery) that some consider "better than NYC's Zabar's", with a sandwich board "longer than the yellow brick road" that lists all the "high-quality" housemade breads and cheeses; it "ain't cheap", but the "amazing" goods effectively quash any gripes about pricing; P.S. you can purchase online their "incredible" artisanal offerings, such as olive oils, vinegars and charcuterie.

TOP FOOD RANKING

Restaurant	Cuisine
27 Cafe Maxx	American/Eclectic
La Brochette	Eclectic
Eduardo de San Angel	Eclectic/Mexican
Casa D'Angelo	Italian
26 Cohiba	Eclectic
Canyon	Southwestern
Capital Grille	Steak
25 Mark's Las Olas	American
3030 Ocean	American/Seafood
Galanga	Japanese/Thai

OTHER NOTEWORTHY PLACES

Anthony's Pizza	Pizza
Blue Moon Fish	Seafood
Bonefish Grill	Seafood
Four Rivers	Thai
Greek Islands Taverna	Greek
Grille 66	Seafood/Steak
Hi-Life Café	American
Johnny V's	Floribbean
Seasons 52	American
Sunfish Grill	American/Seafood

Anthony's Coal-Fired Pizza *Pizza* | 23 | 15 | 19 | $21 |

Ft. Lauderdale | 2203 S. Federal Hwy. (SE 22nd St.) | 954-462-5555
Pompano Beach | 1203 S. Federal Hwy. (SE 12th St.) |
954-942-5550
Weston | Weston Commons | 4527 Weston Rd. (Griffin Rd.) |
954-358-2625
Plantation | 512 N. Pine Island Rd. (SW 6th St.) | 954-474-3311
www.anthonyscoalfiredpizza.com
"Holy smokes" shout surveyors smitten with the "crisp, charred" coal-fired-oven pizzas at this "lively", "always packed" quartet; there's a "limited menu" – "it's pretty much [the pies], salad and chicken wings" – but "what they do, they do very well" (ok, occasionally "the crust gets a little burnt").

Z Blue Moon Fish Co. *Seafood* | 25 | 23 | 22 | $49 |

Ft. Lauderdale | 4405 W. Tradewinds Ave. (E. Commercial Blvd.) |
954-267-9888
Coral Springs | 10317 Royal Palm Blvd. (Coral Springs Dr.) | 954-755-0002 **M**
www.bluemoonfishco.com
Once in a blue moon you find a "place that has it all": "superb" seafood, an "incredibly accommodating staff" and "killer views" of the Intracoastal ("sit outside and watch the yachts go by") – so it's small wonder "fish aficionados" have voted this the Ft. Lauderdale area's Most Popular, even if it's "a little expensive"; while not on the water,

its younger cousin is one of "Coral Springs' finest", and both offer "the most amazing brunch on Sundays."

Bonefish Grill *Seafood*   22 | 19 | 21 | $35

Ft. Lauderdale | 6282 N. Federal Hwy. (NE 62nd St.) | 954-492-3266
Coral Springs | 1455 N. University Dr. (Shadow Wood Blvd.) | 954-509-0405
Davie | Weston Commons | 4545 Weston Rd. (Griffin Rd.) | 954-389-9273
www.bonefishgrill.com

Make "no bones about it" – there's "nothing on the menu you'll throw back" at these "casual, comfortable" seafooders; converts "can't believe it's a chain", given the "intimate" atmosphere and "pleasant" servers who "know their fish"; perhaps it's a bit "predictable", but the principal problem with these "popular" *poissoneries* is, you gotta "go early or late or expect a wait."

☑ Cafe Maxx *American/Eclectic*   27 | 20 | 24 | $60

Pompano Beach | 2601 E. Atlantic Blvd. (NE 26th Ave.) | 954-782-0606 | www.cafemaxx.com

"Never mind the cost, it doesn't get any better" than this "longtime champ", "Pompano Beach's must-go restaurant" for 23 years (and Ft. Lauderdale's No. 1 for Food this year); the kitchen dishes up "terrific New American"–Eclectic cuisine, supplemented by a "can't-be-beat wine list" – and "now a full bar" – and served by a staff that's "knowledgeable but not pretentious"; some sigh "if only the decor were up to the food" (the strip-mall "location is a challenge"), but overall this storefront "is never disappointing."

Canyon *Southwestern*   26 | 21 | 22 | $48

Ft. Lauderdale | 1818 E. Sunrise Blvd. (N. Federal Hwy.) | 954-765-1950 | www.canyonfl.com

It's "so busy" diners are advised to "come early or prepare for a long wait" – really, that "no-reservations policy needs rethinking" – but for an "addictive" "prickly pear margarita pick-me-up", plus "grand" Southwestern fare, this "intimate" Ft. Lauderdale bistro is "worth every dollar"; if possible, opt for "the draped booth-area tables, which make a cozy" oasis within the "crowded" confines.

Capital Grille *Steak*   26 | 25 | 25 | $63

Ft. Lauderdale | 2430 E. Sunrise Blvd. (Bayview Dr.) | 954-446-2000 | www.thecapitalgrille.com

"Dealmakers" and Florida's "who's who" bring their appetites and expense accounts to this "mighty mecca of meat" where the "melt-in-your-mouth" steaks (including a "to-die-for" Kona-crusted sirloin), "clubby atmosphere" and service that is "beyond reproach" make it "ideal for business lunches or making good impressions"; "you may have to sell your first-born" to afford it, but converts claim "local steakhouses simply can't compete" with this chain link.

☑ Casa D'Angelo *Italian*   27 | 20 | 25 | $55

Ft. Lauderdale | Sunrise Square Plaza | 1201 N. Federal Hwy. (bet. E. Sunrise Blvd. & NE 13th St.) | 954-564-1234 | www.casa-d-angelo.com

"The best Italian in Lauderdale" . . . "in Broward County" . . . "in South Florida" fawn fans of the casa created by celebrity chef Angelo Elia, a "master" of "authentic", "deeply satisfying" Northern Italian fare, paired with "extraordinary wines" and proffered by "gracious, intelligent servers"; true, the "tables are getting closer and closer, the noise level higher and higher", and there are "long waits" even with reservations, but "taste the food – it's worth it"; P.S. "mama's pasta is not to be missed when she's in town."

☑ Cohiba Brasserie ☒ *Eclectic*   26 | 17 | 24 | $43

Pembroke Pines | 17864 NW Second St. (NW 178th Ave.) | 954-442-8777 | www.cohibabrasserie.com

"Well-hidden" in a Pembroke Pines medical complex, this Eclectic eatery is "hard to find", but the hunt "is worth it" given chef Robert Ferrer's "outstanding" menu of Latin dishes that are "cooked with care" in "Continental-like" preparations and served by a "staff that aims to please" and is overseen by wife/co-owner Celia Ferrer; P.S. the once-"cozy" digs are undergoing a post-Survey expansion.

☑ Eduardo de San Angel ☒ *Eclectic/Mexican*   27 | 22 | 26 | $53

Ft. Lauderdale | 2822 E. Commercial Blvd. (bet. Bayview Dr. & NE 28th Ave.) | 954-772-4731 | www.eduardodesanangel.com

"This is not your typical tacos and enchiladas place" – rather, it's a "haute" dining destination where "inspired" chef-owner Eduardo Pria creates "swoonworthy", "unexpected" Eclectic-Mexican fare that poetic patrons describe as "heaven on a plate"; not only that, but the "cozy" Ft. Lauderdale confines boast "the kindest and most customer-oriented staff around."

Four Rivers *Thai*   ▽ 26 | 28 | 18 | $47

Ft. Lauderdale | Sunrise Square Plaza | 1201 N. Federal Hwy. (NE 13th St.) | 954-616-1152

"Not your usual Thai", this Ft. Lauderdale newcomer charms with both "contemporary decor and menu"; the former is dark, dramatic and generally "incredible", while the latter, focusing on organic ingredients, is "delicious"; it's "expensive" ("bring two credit cards"), but "definitely worth a trip" for a culinary adventure.

Galanga *Japanese/Thai*   25 | 24 | 23 | $40

Wilton Manors | 2389 Wilton Dr. (NE 8th Terr.) | 954-202-0000 | www.galangarestaurant.com

"Alive on the Drive", this "hip" Wilton Manors haven "has it all": an "unusual" but "fantastic" "mix of Japanese and Thai" fare, "gorgeously presented" by "helpful servers", and a "relaxed" ambiance whether you're on the "nice, breezy" terrace – "great for people-watching" – or occupying the "posh", "stylishly modern" interior that's decked out with candlelight, an illuminated sushi bar and a "mesmerizing" 700-gallon fish tank; clearly, it's "a place to impress that special someone."

☑ Greek Islands Taverna *Greek*   24 | 14 | 21 | $32

Ft. Lauderdale | 3300 N. Ocean Blvd. (Oakland Park Blvd.) | 954-565-5505 | www.greekislandstaverna.com

"A cut above any other Greek place in the area" aver aficionados of this Hellenic haven on the Galt, where the "reasonably priced", "traditional delicacies" include "the best lamb chops off Mt. Olympus"; "lines abound, but they move quickly", and it gets "a little cramped but that adds to the lively taverna feel"; in short, "people never seem to go away unhappy" from here.

	FOOD	DECOR	SERVICE	COST

Grille 66 *Seafood/Steak*

| | 25 | 26 | 23 | $59 |

Ft. Lauderdale | Hyatt Regency-Pier 66 | 2301 SE 17th St. (SE 23rd Ave.) | 954-728-3500 | www.grille66andbar.com

"Grab a window seat to watch the yachts rolling by" at this "expensive" but "beautiful" Hyatt Regency eatery that features a "fabulous view" overlooking the Intracoastal; from the "elegant" surf 'n' turf menu to the "awesome" 400-label wine list to the "lovely service", "everything works incredibly well."

Hi-Life Café ◪ *American*

| | 23 | 19 | 24 | $43 |

Ft. Lauderdale | Plaza 3000 | 3000 N. Federal Hwy. (south of Oakland Park Blvd.) | 954-563-1395 | www.hilifecafe.com

Chef/co-owner Carlos Fernandez may not have triumphed on *Top Chef*, but he's "still a winner" to Ft. Lauderdale loyalists who keep coming back for a "special dining experience" that features "Southern-accented" New American fare and "servers who are a delight" (thanks to "gracious" co-owner/manager Chuck Smith); the "friendly atmosphere" "attracts a mix of gay and straight diners, so no matter who you are, there's someone interesting to look at."

Johnny V's *Floribbean*

| | 24 | 20 | 21 | $56 |

Ft. Lauderdale | 625 E. Las Olas Blvd. (Federal Hwy.) | 954-761-7920 | www.johnnyvlasolas.com

For "sophisticated" dining "in the heart of Las Olas", this "pricey" site is the go-to place for chef-owner Johnny Vinczencz's "original", "sexy" Floribbean cuisine, plus "a dream of a cheese menu" and tapas at the bar; cynics grouse it's "lost a bit of its edge" of late, but groupies gush it remains "one of Ft. Lauderdale's finest."

☑ La Brochette Bistro ◪ *Eclectic*

| | 27 | 20 | 25 | $44 |

Cooper City | Embassy Lakes Plaza | 2635 N. Hiatus Rd. (Sheridan St.) | 954-435-9090 | www.labrochettebistro.com

"What a find" – this "romantic" "little" Eclectic from chef-owner Aboud Kobaitri and wife Lori is "a font of fine dining tucked away in a shopping center" in Cooper City; it specializes in "creative" fish, and although rack of lamb is a "favorite", regulars recommend you "wait for the daily [specials] instead of ordering off the menu"; whatever you choose, you can expect "professional", "friendly" service.

☑ Mark's Las Olas *American*

| | 25 | 22 | 23 | $59 |

Ft. Lauderdale | 1032 E. Las Olas Blvd. (SE 11th Ave.) | 954-463-1000 | www.chefmark.com

When ready "for a night out", Ft. Lauderdale's movers and shakers migrate to Mark Militello's mainstay, which "still has that buzz" after nearly 20 years; the namesake chef-owner "continues to delight and surprise" patrons with "ambitious" New American cuisine served by an "attentive, efficient" staff, and though critics complain it's too "crowded, noisy" and "in need of an overhaul" (both decor- and menu-wise), the majority maintains "it never lets you down."

Seasons 52 *American*

| | 23 | 24 | 23 | $40 |

Ft. Lauderdale | Galleria Mall | 2428 E. Sunrise Blvd. (Bayview Dr.) | 954-537-1052 | www.seasons52.com

"Everything's under 475 calories and it tastes fantastic" proclaim "pleasantly surprised" surveyors captivated by the "clever concept" of this "always busy" New American chain; staffers who can describe the ingredients and calorie counts of any dish serve "small portions" of grilled "seasonal veggies, lean meats and whole grains" "without trans fats", a "terrific wine-by-the-glass" selection and "delicious desserts" "in shot glasses" ("just a tiny sin").

Sunfish Grill ☒ *American/Seafood* | 24 | 20 | 22 | $55 |

Ft. Lauderdale | 2761 E. Oakland Park Blvd. (bet. Bayview Dr. & NE 27th Ave.) | 954-564-6464 | www.sunfishgrill.com

Fans of this "innovative" New American seafooder "loved the place when it was a little hole-in-the-wall", but now that it's moved to still "homey" but "more spacious accommodations" in Ft. Lauderdale, some fear "they've bitten off more than they can chew"; still, most remain sunny when it comes to the "fabulous fish" and "to-die-for" desserts, presented by a "helpful" (if sometimes "stressful") staff.

3030 Ocean *American/Seafood* | 25 | 22 | 24 | $56 |

Ft. Lauderdale | Marriott's Harbor Beach Resort & Spa | 3030 Holiday Dr. (Seabreeze Blvd.) | 954-765-3030 | www.3030ocean.com

"Way better than you'd expect for a Marriott", this Ft. Lauderdale New American is actually "a serious foodie establishment", with "seafood so good it's hard to believe you're in a hotel" – though the fact "you're in the lobby" quickly reminds you; still, the "service is attentive", and many find the steps-from-the-sand setting "lovely."

Honolulu

TOP FOOD RANKING

	Restaurant	Cuisine
28	Alan Wong's	Hawaii Reg.
27	La Mer	French
26	Hoku's	Pacific Rim
	Roy's	Hawaiian
	Chef Mavro	French/Hawaii Reg.
	Roy's Ko Olina	Hawaiian
	Orchids	American
	3660 on the Rise	Pacific Rim
	Hy's Steak	Steak
25	Ruth's Chris	Steak

OTHER NOTEWORTHY PLACES

Cassis	French
Diamond Head Grill	Eclectic
Duke's Canoe Club	Seafood
Indigo	Asian Fusion
Kaka'ako Kitchen	Hawaii Reg.
Nico's at Pier 38	French
Nobu Waikiki	Japanese
Ola	Hawaii Reg.
Pineapple Room	Hawaii Reg.
town	Italian

☑ Alan Wong's   *Hawaii Reg.*   28 | 20 | 26 | $58

Ala Moana | McCully Ct. | 1857 S. King St., 3rd fl. (bet. Hauoli & Pumehana Sts.) | 808-949-2526 | www.alanwongs.com

Ranked Most Popular and No. 1 for Food in Honolulu, this restaurant located "away from the tourist fray" in Ala Moana "never ceases to amaze" fans of notable chef Alan Wong's "creative brilliance"; with Hawaii Regional dishes like the "heavenly ginger-crusted onaga", "amazing" tasting menus and "stealthlike", "unobtrusive service", it's "Pacific meets perfection", despite its "nondescript" second-floor space and "limited street parking"; P.S. be sure to make reservations "well in advance."

Cassis by Chef Mavro   *French*   - | - | - | E

Downtown | 66 Queen St. (Nimitz Hwy.) | 808-545-8100 | www.cassishonolulu.com

Top chef George Mavrothalassitis (of the highly regarded Chef Mavro in Ala Moana) draws on his Provençal heritage at this trendy Downtown addition where an attractive staff serves up island-inflected French bistro fare – think grilled ahi niçoise – and a hip wine bar offers daily flights; the cavernous former Palomino space retains a slightly institutional feel despite an extensive renovation, so aesthetes are advised to grab a window seat to take in the Honolulu Harbor views; N.B. it gets packed at lunch.

	FOOD	DECOR	SERVICE	COST

Z Chef Mavro M *French/Hawaii Reg.*

	26	23	26	$72

Ala Moana | 1969 S. King St. (McCully St.) | 808-944-4714 | www.chefmavro.com

"From the moment you enter until the end of your meal", dining here is an "experience for all the senses" say fans of the "inspired" New French–meets–Hawaii Regional cuisine of chef George Mavrothalassitis, who "often greets guests himself"; service is very "knowledgeable", the "wine pairings are outstanding" and the interior is "beautiful", so even if its Ala Moana location "leaves a bit to be desired" and "portions are tiny", most take one bite of the "homemade malasadas" dessert and declare it "fabulomavrous!"

Diamond Head Grill *Eclectic*

	–	23	21	$51

Waikiki | W Honolulu Hotel | 2885 Kalakaua Ave. (Diamond Head) | 808-922-3734 | www.w-dhg.com

At this "trendy" venue in the "oh-so-hip" W Honolulu Hotel, "innovative" Eclectic fare with a Hawaiian touch is brought to table by a "superb" staff; though there's "no view" to be had, the "cool" quotient steps up a notch after 10 PM, when the restaurant "turns into a dance club"/"hangout" for twentysomethings sipping "great martinis."

Z Duke's Canoe Club *Seafood*

	17	22	17	$31

Waikiki | Outrigger Waikiki on the Beach | 2335 Kalakaua Ave. (bet. Dukes Ln. & Kaiulani Ave.) | 808-922-2268 | www.dukeswaikiki.com

"Wild, wacky" and "tons of fun", this "always packed", open-air, ocean-front seafooder in the Outrigger Waikiki on the Beach is a "tourist mecca" with a "great" breakfast buffet, "classic mahi sandwiches", "kitschy Hawaiian cocktails" and a "famous hula pie", all delivered with "a smile"; there's lots of "memorabilia" honoring the "great surfing legend" Duke Kahanamoku, and when the "hotties" show up for live music after sunset, it becomes *the* happening place."

Z Hoku's *Pacific Rim*

	26	26	26	$60

Kahala | Kahala Hotel & Resort | 5000 Kahala Ave. (Kealaolu Ave.) | 808-739-8780 | www.kahalaresort.com

For "sublime dining" with a "beautiful view of the ocean", this Kahala Hotel & Resort restaurant is a "stunning" choice; feast on a recently revamped menu of "creative", "phenomenal" Pacific Rim fare among the "movers and shakers", revel in the "gracious" service and soak up the "romantic" ambiance "at sunset" with the one you love; sure, it may "break the bank", but it leaves you "happy to pay"; N.B. no casual attire allowed in the evenings.

Hy's Steak House *Steak*

	26	23	25	$56

Waikiki | Waikiki Park Heights Hotel | 2440 Kuhio Ave. (Uluniu Ave.) | 808-922-5555 | www.hyshawaii.com

"Excellent" slabs of beef grilled "exactly how you ordered" right "before your eyes" on a kiawe-wood fire make this "wonderful anachronism" in the Waikiki Park Heights Hotel a "superb" steakhouse "throwback to the '60s or '70s"; a dimly lit, "old-world" setting complete with "curved booths for cuddling" and "impeccable" service add to its appeal, and meat mavens maintain they'd "eat there nightly" if they could; N.B. there's live guitar Wednesday–Saturday.

	FOOD	DECOR	SERVICE	COST

Indigo 🗷 M *Asian Fusion* — 23 | 23 | 21 | $38

Chinatown | 1121 Nuuanu Ave. (Hotel St.) | 808-521-2900 |
www.indigo-hawaii.com

"Wow your taste buds" with "irresistible" Asian fusion eats from chef Glenn Chu, who "blends unique flavors for a multicultural feast" at this "exotic" "*Sex-and-the-City*-meets-*South-Pacific*" "hipster" in Chinatown; it's a "favorite for the Downtown lunch crowd", and "trendy twenty- and thirtysomethings" seeking a "killer happy hour" can head to the attached Green Room lounge; it can get "noisy", but it's one of the most "provocative" settings around; P.S. "valet parking is recommended."

Kaka'ako Kitchen *Hawaii Reg.* — 20 | 10 | 15 | $14

Ala Moana | Ward Ctr. | 1200 Ala Moana Blvd. (Kamakee St.) |
808-594-3663

"Gourmet food" at "automat prices" earns accolades at chef Russell Siu's (3660 on the Rise) Hawaii Regional in Ala Moana's Ward Center; here, a "friendly, efficient" staff serves "hearty portions" of a "healthy alternative to the plate lunch" – factor in "outdoor seating", and you have what some call "a poor man's taste of fine dining."

🗷 La Mer *French* — 27 | 28 | 27 | $78

Waikiki | Halekulani Hotel | 2199 Kalia Rd. (Lewers St.) | 808-923-2311 |
www.halekulani.com

Although "each bite" of chef Yves Garnier's "delectable" New French cuisine "with an island touch" "is a taste of heaven", don't forget this Halekulani Hotel landmark's other "unforgettable" attributes: a "breathtaking" location overlooking "seductive" ocean waves and "flawless" service; so even if you need to wear a jacket and the "cost rivals that of NY's" top eateries, it's the "ultimate special date" choice.

Nico's at Pier 38 🗷 *French* — - | - | - | I

Iwilei | Pier 38 | 1133 N. Nimitz Hwy. (Alakawa St.) | 808-540-1377 |
www.nicospier38.com

This tiny eatery located on the docks at Iwilei lures commercial fisher- men, business executives and tourists alike for gourmet, island-style French bistro fare from chef-owner Nicolas 'Nico' Chaize; you can ex- pect low prices along with a no-frills, open-air setting offering casual seating and a view of the harbor; N.B. no dinner.

Nobu Waikiki *Japanese* — - | - | - | VE

Waikiki | Waikiki Parc Hotel | 2233 Helumoa Rd. (Lewers St.) | 808-237-6999 |
www.noburestaurants.com

Celebrity chef Nobu Matsuhisa has brought his innovative interna- tional chain to a town known for its Asian restaurants, and Honolulu foodies are already flocking to the Waikiki Parc Hotel to sample Peruvian-accented Japanese fare that's as pricey as it is unique; it's set in a 7,500-sq.-ft. lobby space – complete with lounge, sushi bar and private dining room – that's been transformed by the Rockwell Group to include sophisticated Hawaiian and Asian touches.

Ola *Hawaii Reg.* — - | - | - | M

Kahuku | Turtle Bay Resort | 57-091 Kamehameha Hwy. (Kuilima Dr.) |
808-293-0801 | www.olaislife.com

Located literally on the beach next to Kahuku's Turtle Bay Resort, this restaurant offers a romantic open-air setting to go with the globally in-

FOOD DECOR SERVICE COST

fluenced island cuisine of chef-owner Fred DeAngelo, who uses fresh seafood and locally grown produce ('ola' means healthy in Hawaiian) in his dishes; fine views of the North Shore waves are but another reason to make the hour-long drive from Waikiki.

Orchids *American* | 26 | 27 | 26 | $57 |

Waikiki | Halekulani Hotel | 2199 Kalia Rd. (Lewers St.) | 808-923-2311 | www.halekulani.com

With "amazing breakfasts", a "fantastic Sunday brunch" and a "view over the water at sunset", this open-air, beachside American in the Halekulani Hotel (just downstairs from La Mer) is a "relaxing" choice; so "sip the most fabulous mai tai", feast on "superb" fare served by an "impeccable" staff, listen to the "lapping waves" and be "transported."

Pineapple Room *Hawaii Reg.* | 24 | 18 | 21 | $35 |

Ala Moana | Macy's, Ala Moana Shopping Ctr. | 1450 Ala Moana Blvd. (Atkinson Dr.) | 808-945-6573 | www.alanwongs.com

At this "little-known outpost" from "mega-talented" chef Alan Wong ("oddly located" in the Ala Moana Shopping Center Macy's and "a gift to the ladies who lunch"), the "master's touch" is discernible in the "excellent" Hawaii Regional fare, especially the "to-die-for Kahlua pig BLT", but the prices "will leave some padding in your wallet" compared to his eponymous King Street spot; still, sour sorts snap over "inconsistent service" and an underwhelming "view of the rooftop mall parking" lot; P.S. "reservations are a must."

⚡ Roy's *Hawaiian* | 26 | 21 | 24 | $50 |

Hawaii Kai | 6600 Kalanianaole Hwy. (Keahole St.) | 808-396-7697 | www.roysrestaurant.com

This "original" Hawaii Kai "flagship" (of a 30-plus-location chain) "put Hawaiian fusion cuisine on the culinary map" and continues to thrill patrons with its "unpretentious, eye-appealing and always delicious" offerings and seemingly "choreographed" service; while some suggest dining in the "quieter" downstairs section, others say "come early", head upstairs and "watch the beautiful sunset."

Roy's Ko Olina *Hawaiian* | 26 | 23 | 25 | $47 |

Kapolei | Ko Olina Resort & Marina | 92-1220 Aliinui Dr. (Kamoana Pl.) | 808-676-7697 | www.roysrestaurant.com

"There's a reason Roy has become so ubiquitous" in the islands, the Mainland and abroad: "fabulous" Hawaiian fusion fare with "twists" and "creativity" that differ from location to location; for some, this Kapolei outpost is even "better than the [Honolulu-area] original" due to its "beautiful setting overlooking the Ko Olina Golf Course", its aloha "hospitality" and its "fabulous" fare (especially the signature macadamia-encrusted mahi mahi); so even if it's far away, most find it "well worth the drive"; N.B. also open for lunch.

Ruth's Chris Steak House *Steak* | 25 | 21 | 23 | $55 |

Restaurant Row | Restaurant Row | 500 Ala Moana Blvd. (bet. Punchbowl & South Sts.) | 808-599-3860
Waikiki | Waikiki Beach Walk | 226 Lewers St. (Helumoa Rd.) | 808-440-7910 www.ruthschris.com

"If you want a good steak" served "exactly how you like it", this chainster is "the place to go"; with dishes "generous enough for the local army", a "comfortable", "clubby" atmosphere on Restaurant Row and a "courteous" staff, it attracts locals as well as expense-accounters for a "very urban" yet "genteel" experience; N.B. a second location has opened in the Waikiki Beach Walk development.

3660 on the Rise Ⓜ Pacific Rim   26 | 20 | 24 | $50

Kaimuki | 3660 Waialae Ave. (Wilhelmina Rise) | 808-737-1177 | www.3660.com

The "innovative" Pacific Rim cuisine of chef Russell Siu (a "master of food and wine") "amazes" diners at this Kaimuki "favorite" where the menu includes an "ahi katsu appetizer that will melt in your mouth", a "to-die-for bread pudding" and a "delicious" lychee martini brought to table by an "engaging", "informal" staff; there's "no view" and the interior "looks like a coffee shop" to some, but others counter "who cares?" – this one "rises" higher than most.

town Ⓢ Italian   - | - | - | M

Waialae | 3435 Waialae Ave. (9th St.) | 808-735-5900 | www.townkaimuki.com

A hi-tech ambiance (concrete floors, highly polished steel tables) draws a hip crowd to this Waialae eatery where chef-owner Ed Kenney creates modern Italian fare with fresh, organic ingredients; along with lunch and dinner, it also serves breakfast Monday–Saturday, so drop by at any time of the day for a seat in the orange-and-white dining room or out on the lanai.

Houston

TOP FOOD RANKING

	Restaurant	Cuisine
28	Mark's American	American
27	Da Marco	Italian
	Brennan's	Creole
	Bistro Moderne	French
	Pappas Bros.	Steak
	Chez Nous	French
26	Cafe Annie	Southwestern
	Frenchie's	Italian
	Indika	Indian
	Vic & Anthony's	Steak
	Remington	American
	Oceanaire	Seafood
	Tony's	Continental
	Churrascos	S American
	Fogo de Chão	Brazilian/Steak
25	Kiran's	Indian
	Strip House	Steak
	Capital Grille	Steak
	Shade	American/Eclectic
	Artista	American

OTHER NOTEWORTHY PLACES

Restaurant	Cuisine
Américas	S American
Amici	Italian
Arcodoro	Italian
Backstreet Café	American
Carrabba's Italian	Italian
Catalan Food/Wine	American
Dolce Vita	Italian/Pizza
Glass Wall	American
Goode Co. Seafood	Seafood
Gravitas	American
Hugo's	Mexican
Ibiza	Mediterranean/Spanish
Mockingbird Bistro	American
Pesce	Seafood
Quattro	Italian
Red Onion	Pan-Latin/Seafood
Reef	Seafood
17	American
t'afia	American
Tony Mandola's	Seafood

	FOOD	DECOR	SERVICE	COST

Américas ⓈS American
25 | 26 | 22 | $41

Galleria | The Pavilion | 1800 Post Oak Blvd. (bet. San Felipe St. & Westheimer Rd.) | 713-961-1492 | www.cordua.com

With "over-the-top" decor so "whimsical" it sends fans on flights of fancy ("Dr. Seuss goes Mayan", "Disney on Quaaludes"), the Cordúa family's "high-end" Galleria-area standby is an undisputed showplace; fortunately, the "unforgettable" South American specialties ("melt-in-your-mouth" churrasco steaks, "amazing tres leches cake") are equally "dazzling" and well presented by an "attentive" staff; just be ready for the "ambient din."

Amici *Italian*
- | - | - | M

Sugar Land | Sugar Land Town Sq. | 16089 City Walk (Plaza Dr.) | 281-242-2800 | www.amicitownsquare.com

The latest from the Vallone family (Tony's), this boisterous but polished suburbanite lures Inner Loopers to Sugar Land to sample chef Bruce McMillian's Neapolitan-rooted Italian fare; the menu ranges from robust meat and seafood entrees to zesty salads and thin-crust pizzas, all complemented by an ample wine list and and served either in a sprawling, modern interior or out on a cozy patio.

Arcodoro *Italian*
23 | 21 | 21 | $40

Galleria | 5000 Westheimer Rd. (S. Post Oak Rd.) | 713-621-6888 | www.arcodoro.com

"Actual Italians would approve" of the "friendly service" and "reliable" dishes (including "exotic Sardinian specialties") at this "upmarket" ristorante near the Galleria; during the day it's a "convenient" haven for "business-lunchers" and "shopping tourists", while the "hopping" bar is popular "after work" and as a "late-night watering hole for Gen-Xers."

Artista Ⓢ *American*
25 | 25 | 23 | $41

Downtown | Hobby Center for the Performing Arts | 800 Bagby St. (Walker St.) | 713-278-4782 | www.cordua.com

"The theater has a tough act to follow" applaud admirers of the Cordúa family's "minimalist" New American in Downtown's Hobby Center, featuring an ensemble of "stunning urban views" and "superb", "creative" fare that spotlights the "tastes of South America"; though the mix-and-match menu "confuses" some and parking can be "tough", it's "ideal" for a curtain-conscious clientele.

Backstreet Café *American*
24 | 22 | 21 | $32

River Oaks | 1103 S. Shepherd Dr. (W. Clay St.) | 713-521-2239 | www.backstreetcafe.net

"Good ol' Southern food with a creative flair" – paired with "exquisite" wines and served up by a "knowledgeable" staff – attracts aficionados to this River Oaks New American "gem"; its "laid-back" yet "sophisticated" setting with a "fabulous" courtyard provides the "perfect atmosphere" for "a quiet business lunch or a romantic dinner"; P.S. the "Sunday jazz brunch is wonderful."

☑ Bistro Moderne Ⓢ *French*
27 | 26 | 24 | $52

Galleria | Hotel Derek | 2525 West Loop S. (Westheimer Rd.) | 713-297-4383 | www.bistromoderne.com

In its latest incarnation ("third time's the charm"), this "refreshing" Galleria-area bistro at the Hotel Derek is a "piece of Paris right here in the Lone Star State" – its "innovative" French cuisine is proffered by "first-rate" servers in a "chic" room populated with "beautiful people"; *amis* assert that this "winner" is even "worth the aggravation" of trying to navigate the "impossible intersection" outside.

Z Brennan's Creole — 27 | 26 | 26 | $48

Midtown | 3300 Smith St. (Stuart St.) | 713-522-9711 | www.brennanshouston.com

For a "true taste of N'Awlins", this Midtown "tradition" is a "must" for its "extravagant", "refined" Texas-inflected Creole cuisine, its "unmatched" 500-label wine cellar and an "elegant", "aristocratic" atmosphere that, of course, includes "exquisite service"; though weekenders relish the "decadent jazz brunch", regulars who "go there to be pampered" report dinner at the private kitchen table is "a marvelous experience"; N.B. jackets preferred.

Z Cafe Annie ⊠ Southwestern — 26 | 24 | 25 | $59

Galleria | 1728 Post Oak Blvd. (San Felipe St.) | 713-840-1111 | www.cafe-annie.com

"Still grand" swoon supporters of Robert Del Grande's Galleria-area "classic" – now over 25 years old – where the chef-owner's "inventive", "beautifully presented" and "incredibly delicious" Southwestern cuisine is paired with a wine list "as wide and deep as the Gulf"; the "treasure map" of a menu is matched by "professional and discreet service" and "posh" digs that provide "first-rate people-watching"; yet after so many years of "superior quality", some sense a "downhill" drift and suggest this "pricey" place is "resting on its laurels."

Capital Grille Steak — 25 | 25 | 24 | $55

Galleria | 5365 Westheimer Rd. (Yorktown St.) | 713-623-4600 | www.thecapitalgrille.com

Carnivores call this national chain the embodiment of the "classic Texas steakhouse", with "fabulous" meat, "huge" sides, an "excellent" wine selection and "devoted", "timely but unobtrusive" service; the "plush", "clubby" ambiance and "expensive" fare befit business meals – "don't forget your platinum card" – though a cadre of critics calls these meateries "overrated" and "pretentious."

Z Carrabba's Italian Grill Italian — 23 | 20 | 21 | $25

Champions | Champions Vill. | 5440 FM 1960 W. (Champion Forest Dr.) | 281-397-8255
Galleria | 1399 S. Voss Rd. (bet. San Felipe & Woodway Drs.) | 713-468-0868
Northwest Houston | 7540 Hwy. 6 N. (Longenbaugh Dr.) | 281-859-9700
Upper Kirby District | 3115 Kirby Dr. (Branard St.) | 713-522-3131
West Houston | 11339 Katy Frwy. (N. Wilcrest Dr.) | 713-464-6595
Webster | 502 W. Bay Area Blvd. (I-45) | 281-338-0574
Kingwood | 750 Kingwood Dr. (Chestnut Ridge Rd.) | 281-358-5580
Sugar Land | 2335 Hwy. 6 S. (Southwest Frwy.) | 281-980-4433
The Woodlands | 25665 North Frwy. (Rayford Rd.) | 281-367-9423
www.carrabbas.com

Loyalists insist that the two "still-family-owned" locations (Galleria and Upper Kirby District) in this group – now an Outback subsidiary – are "far superior" to their brethren, with "outstanding" "classic" Italian dishes and "personal" service in a "warm, friendly" if often "noisy" atmosphere; the other branches, equally loud, are labeled "consistent", with "unusually competent" service and "value" tabs.

Catalan Food and Wine M *American*   – | – | – | M

Heights | 5555 Washington Ave. (TC Jester Blvd.) | 713-426-4260 | www.catalanfoodandwine.com

At this Heights-area eatery, the Spanish-inspired New American menu offers interesting small plates (along with a few entree-sized dishes) such as crabmeat-and-piquillo gratin, foie gras bonbons and calamari with a jalapeño-lime dipping sauce; there's also an extensive, extremely reasonable wine list (a hallmark of Catalan's older sibling, Ibiza), and its snazzy white-tableclothed space features metallic chandeliers, brick arches and abstract glass butterflies.

Chez Nous Z *French*   27 | 23 | 26 | $50

Humble | 217 S. Ave. G (Main St.) | 281-446-6717 | www.cheznousfrenchrestaurant.com

For "magnificent" French cuisine "prepared to perfection" ("every plate a work of art"), even far-flung foodies will "drive two hours on a fairly regular basis" to this chef-owned Humble "favorite"; the "intimate" atmosphere is enhanced by staffers who "make you feel like they want you there"; the only caveat is that this "jewel" – set in a residential neighborhood – can be "difficult to find."

Churrascos *S American*   26 | 21 | 22 | $37

Upper Kirby District | 2055 Westheimer Rd. (S. Shepherd Dr.) | 713-527-8300
West Houston | 9705 Westheimer Rd. (Gessner Rd.) | 713-952-1988
www.cordua.com

It's a trip to "Buenos Aires minus the airfare" proclaim gourmet gauchos who gallop over to Michael Cordúa's "still fabulous" South American duo in Upper Kirby and West Houston; the namesake "mouthwatering" steaks "you can cut with a fork" are a "carnivore's delight", sides and appetizers are "delicious" ("nothing beats those plantain chips") and the regional wines are "excellent"; factor in "professional service" in "upscale" surroundings and you've got "a Houston tradition"; P.S. the $15 three-course lunch is a "bargain."

Z Da Marco Z M *Italian*   27 | 21 | 24 | $50

Montrose | 1520 Westheimer Rd. (bet. Montrose Blvd. & Shepherd Dr.) | 713-807-8857 | www.damarcohouston.com

Thanks to "amazing, sophisticated" *cucina* ("wonderful fried artichokes", "first-class" pastas), voters declare Marco Wiles' "intimate" Montrose "villa" "easily the best Italian in town"; they credit "flawless" execution, a "short" but "great" wine list, an "unpretentious atmosphere" and "knowledgeable" servers, but note that "excellence" has its price: "traffic jams" in the "tiny" bar, "cramped" seating and a "migraine-inducing" din – so head to the enclosed patio instead.

Dolce Vita Pizzeria Enoteca M *Italian/Pizza*   – | – | – | M

Montrose | 500 Westheimer Rd. (Whitney St.) | 713-520-8222 | www.dolcevitahouston.com

Scenesters are flocking to this Montrose pizzeria and wine bar that serves inventive thin-crust pizzas (e.g. taleggio with pears and arugula) and original antipasti such as a shaved Brussels-sprout salad,

	FOOD	DECOR	SERVICE	COST

proving it's not your regular pie parlor; tables are close – all the better to people-watch – and noise levels get high.

Fogo de Chão *Brazilian/Steak* | 26 | 21 | 25 | $51

West Houston | 8250 Westheimer Rd. (Dunvale Rd.) | 713-978-6500 | www.fogodechao.com

An "insane onslaught" of flesh fare is ferried on skewers by "super-attentive gauchos" and paired with an "amazing salad bar" that "will even get respect from carnivores" at this West Houston "temple of gluttony", a "Brazilian-import" chain that remains "true to its original concept"; its "all-the-meat-you-can-eat gimmick attracts lots of businessmen (not so many businesswomen) on expense accounts", but remember that it's "not for vegetarians – or the fainthearted."

Frenchie's 🗷 *Italian* | 26 | 13 | 23 | $24

Clear Lake | 1041 NASA Pkwy. (Egret Bay Blvd.) | 281-486-7144 | www.villacaprionclearlake.com

"Despite the name", Italian's the game at this "casual", family-owned and family-friendly Clear Lake "standard" where "NASA eats lunch" and astronaut pics adorn the walls; regulars "treasure" the "tasty" *cucina* that comes in "huge", "steaming-hot" portions, and though the "popular" place can be a "zoo", service is usually "fast."

Glass Wall 🗷Ⓜ *American* | - | - | - | E

Heights | 933A Studewood St. (bet. Merrill & Omar Sts.) | 713-868-7930 | www.glasswalltherestaurant.com

Make way for another culinary destination in the Heights: chef-owner Lance Fegen's latest endeavor is drawing attention, not only for its simple decor – river rock and aqua with a wave of resin tiles above the dining space – but also for its regularly changing menu of bistro-style seasonal New American dishes, featuring game, seafood, risottos and signature crab cakes, plus a 'happy ending' dessert du jour; N.B. though fun for people-watching, it can get loud.

Goode Co. Texas Seafood *Seafood* | 23 | 18 | 19 | $24

West U | 2621 Westpark Dr. (Kirby Dr.) | 713-523-7154
Memorial | 10211 Katy Frwy./I-10 W. (Gessner Dr.) | 713-464-7933
www.goodecompany.com

Goode friends gloat this piscatory pair "proves that Texas food can be excellent even if it's not barbecue or Mexican"; the "fresh" and "perfectly seasoned" fish comes in many forms ("don't leave without trying" the signature campechana), including Gulf Coast specialties, all ferried by "quick" servers; also transporting is the vehicle-themed decor – West U's "neat old" converted train car and an "antique racing boat" at the "more upscale" Memorial location.

Gravitas *American* | 22 | 18 | 16 | $34

Midtown | 807 Taft St. (bet. Allen Pkwy. & W. Dallas St.) | 713-522-0995 | www.gravitasrestaurant.com

Owner-slash-"food genius" Scott Tycer lends his air of gravitas to this "hot" Midtown bistro, a "hip", "stark" space spotlighting "inventive" New American fare and "interesting" wines; prices are "reasonable" and "prospects look bright" but "growing pains" include "uneven", "uninformed" service and "terrible acoustics."

Hugo's *Mexican*

23 | 22 | 20 | $34

Montrose | 1600 Westheimer Rd. (Mandell St.) | 713-524-7744 | www.hugosrestaurant.net

It's "not Tex-Mex", it's "haute Mexican" at Hugo Ortega's "sophisticated", "upscale" Montrose establishment, where the "brilliant, innovative spins" on regional cuisine are complemented by "killer" wine and tequila lists and "terrific" margaritas; thanks in part to "accommodating" servers, the "urban-chic" restored building is imbued with a "wonderful, festive air", especially at Sunday brunch when there's "great live music from local mariachi bands."

Ibiza *Mediterranean/Spanish*

24 | 22 | 22 | $36

Midtown | 2450 Louisiana St. (McGowen St.) | 713-524-0004 | www.ibizafoodandwinebar.com

Intrigued oenophiles do "double takes" when they see the "practically give-away prices" on this Midtowner's 500-label wine list, but the "buzzy", "happening" Iberian is also favored by the "young and beautiful" for its "creative" and "savory" Med-Spanish fare ("innovative small plates") served by "knowledgeable", "friendly" personnel; as a result, this "trendy" yet "comfortable" setting remains "popular for business lunches" and pre-theater dining.

Indika Ⓜ *Indian*

26 | 22 | 24 | $32

Montrose | 516 Westheimer Rd. (Whitney St.) | 713-984-1725 | www.indikausa.com

Ensconced in Montrose digs complete with a patio overlooking buzzing Lower Westheimer, chef-owner Anita Jaisinghani's Indian "jewel" continues to "challenge diners" with "sophisticated, stylized cuisine" – so "imaginative" that at times it's "more like fusion" – matched with a "surprisingly good" wine list; "prompt", "helpful" servers "explain everything" so even "neophytes can make delicious choices."

Kiran's *Indian*

25 | 23 | 23 | $30

Galleria | 4100 Westheimer Rd. (Midlane St.) | 713-960-8472 | www.kiranshouston.com

Kiran Verma, the chef-owner of this "attractive" colonial-style Galleria-area subcontinental, "loves her work and it shows"; her "first-class", "seasoned-to-perfection" "aromatic delights" "take Indian cuisine to new heights" with the help of an "affordable, varied" 400-label wine list; service is usually "efficient and friendly" to boot; P.S. the five-course tasting menu may well be the area's "best value", and now there's Sunday brunch too.

ⓩ Mark's American Cuisine *American*

28 | 26 | 27 | $55

Montrose | 1658 Westheimer Rd. (bet. Dunlavy & Ralph Sts.) | 713-523-3800 | www.marks1658.com

Worshipers at this converted Montrose church – a "cathedral to food" anointed Houston's No. 1 for Food and Popularity – sing hosannas over Mark Cox's "breathtaking", "divinely inspired" seasonal New American creations ("amazing presentations") and "outstanding" 275-label wine list; the "spectacular" setting and "impeccable" service are two more reasons it's been christened a downright "religious experience, as it should be"; yes, it's "expensive" ("you'll need to pray for a raise at work") and often "noisy" but most wouldn't alter a thing.

Mockingbird Bistro Wine Bar *American*

24	20	23	$39

River Oaks | 1985 Welch St. (bet. Hazard & McDuffie Sts.) |
713-533-0200

River Oaks' "excellent neighborhood hideaway" has surveyors warbling the praises of its "creative", "upscale" New American cuisine and "superb" 500-label wine list that can be explicated by "knowledgeable" servers; maybe the "eclectic" decor turns a few off, but the majority finds it "quaint" and "charming."

Oceanaire Seafood Room *Seafood*

26	24	24	$49

Galleria | Galleria | 5061 Westheimer Rd. (Sage St.) | 832-487-8862 |
www.theoceanaire.com

"Am I on a coast?" wonder wags wowed by the "beautifully presented" and "wonderfully fresh" seafood that "never fails to satisfy" at this "amazing" national chain with a retro "nautical theme"; it's "a little pricey", but the "service is impeccable", as is the "classy, old-time luxury" decor that makes it easy to imagine you're on a "1930s liner."

⊠ Pappas Bros. Steakhouse ⊠ *Steak*

27	24	25	$57

Galleria | 5839 Westheimer Rd. (Bering Dr.) | 713-780-7352 |
www.pappasbros.com

"There's a lot of competition" but cognoscenti confide that this handsome steakhouse stands out from the herd thanks to "perfectly cooked" "slabs o' cow", "tasty sides", a "comprehensive wine cellar", "sommeliers who truly know what they're talking about" and "attentive, respectful" servers who "treat everyone like a VIP"; a vocal few, however, consider it an "overpriced", "inconsistent" bum steer.

Pesce ⊠ *Seafood*

23	24	21	$47

Upper Kirby District | Upper Kirby Shopping Ctr. | 3029 Kirby Dr.
(W. Alabama St.) | 713-522-4858 | www.pescehouston.com

Pescavores are hooked on the "wonderful" fin fare and "pristine" oysters at this "reliable" Upper Kirby District seafooder, ensconced in "elegant" environs with a marble bar, "starched linens" and a "beautiful aquarium"; service ranges from "wonderful" to "pretentious", though, and both noise and cost can be high.

Quattro *Italian*

25	25	25	$51

Downtown | Four Seasons Hotel Houston | 1300 Lamar St. (Austin St.) |
713-276-4700 | www.fourseasons.com

A "must for gourmands", this Italian at Downtown's Four Seasons (hence the name) is as "excellent" as "you'd expect from" this posh hotel chain – to wit, "spectacular" cuisine, hundreds of wines, "first-class" service and an "exceptionally tasteful" atmosphere "perfect for business lunches" or an "exquisite" Sunday brunch; the bar's happy hour is "popular" with nearby office workers; N.B. it also boasts four private dining rooms.

Red Onion Seafood y Mas ⊠ *Pan-Latin/Seafood*

24	22	23	$28

Northwest Houston | 12041 Northwest Frwy. (43rd St.) | 713-957-2254 |
www.caferedonion.com

Planted in the Northwest Houston spot once occupied by the original Café Red Onion, this "upscale" Pan-Latin pescatorium reels in aficionados with "creative" seafood ("addictive" snapper, "unusual ceviche"), solid service and an "exotic" environment; even those who call it "costly" admit it's "worth every penny."

Reef Ⓢ Seafood
— | — | — | M

Midtown | 2600 Travis St. (McGowen St.) | 713-526-8282 | www.reefhouston.com

At this buzzy Midtown addition, Bryan Caswell and Bill Floyd (both formerly of Bank by Jean-Georges) have created a cool, modern seafood house that avoids the clichés as it delivers globally inspired fin fare from around the world, including long-neglected Gulf fish like tripletail and grouper; it fills up with a trendy crowd that's also likely to appreciate the wares at the separate cocktail bar: a food menu served until 2 AM and a view of the Houston skyline.

Remington, The American
26 | 25 | 27 | $51

Galleria | St. Regis Hotel | 1919 Briar Oaks Ln. (San Felipe St.) | 713-403-2631 | www.theremingtonrestaurant.com

Comparatively "unsung", this New American in the Galleria-area St. Regis Hotel triggers a 21-gun salute in honor of its "impeccable" staff's "unobtrusive" ministrations; the "meticulous" chef's "melt-in-your-mouth" cookery and the recently "updated" lipstick-red dining room are more reasons why this "oasis" is deemed "great" for a "romantic rendezvous" (or "people-watching" in the dark, wood-paneled bar), even if its elevated prices raise some eyebrows.

17 American
25 | 24 | 23 | $50

Downtown | Alden Houston Hotel | 1117 Prairie St. (San Jacinto St.) | 832-200-8888 | www.17food.com

This "hip" eatery at Downtown's Alden Houston Hotel highlights "innovative" New American fare and a list of "reasonable" wines amid sleek, "absolutely fabulous" surroundings; "great" service and a "see-and-be-seen" clientele make this "surprising oasis" a "wonderful place to impress a date" – unless you're with one of the jaded few who find it "expensive and overrated."

Shade American/Eclectic
25 | 21 | 21 | $32

Heights | 250 W. 19th St. (Rutland St.) | 713-863-7500 | www.shadeheights.com

Fans feel they have it made in the shade at this "hip", "minimalist" New American–Eclectic in the Heights – "a breath of fresh air" "without a trace of stuffiness" thanks to "adventurous" yet "unpretentious" cuisine, a "laid-back" bar and a "narrow urban patio", plus "friendly, knowledgeable" service that includes the input of a "top-notch" sommelier; though a few take a dim view of the "long waits", most think it's all cool.

Strip House Steak
25 | 25 | 23 | $52

Downtown | Shops at Houston Ctr. | 1200 McKinney St. (San Jacinto St.) | 713-659-6000 | www.theglaziergroup.com

Patrons lick their chops at this "pricey" Downtowner where "strip means more than steak": "flavorful" cuts of meat and "great" wines are served by a "sharp" crew in a "bordello" setting tricked out with "extremely sexy" "naked-lady" artifacts (e.g. photos of vintage burlesque queens, as at the NYC original); the theme – "risqué" and "edgy" to some, "hackneyed" "'50s-style porn" to others – has all agreeing it's "probably not a place to bring the family."

	FOOD	DECOR	SERVICE	COST

t'afia 🏠 Ⓜ American
24 | 17 | 22 | $40

Midtown | 3701 Travis St. (bet. W. Alabama & Winbern Sts.) | 713-524-6922 | www.tafia.com

At this Midtown "gem", "culinary alchemist" Monica Pope conjures up "cutting-edge", "foodies'-delight" New American cuisine out of "wonderfully fresh" local ingredients and pairs it with a "terrific" Texas-accented wine list; most appreciate the efforts of "welcoming" staffers in the "hip", "minimalist", "loftlike" room, though a minority shrugs the whole scene's too "austere" and "avant-garde"; N.B. there's a farmer's market here on Saturday mornings.

Tony Mandola's Gulf Coast Kitchen Seafood
24 | 18 | 22 | $33

River Oaks | River Oaks Ctr. | 1962 W. Gray St. (McDuffie St.) | 713-528-3474 | www.tonymandolas.com

"You can't go wrong" with this "dependable" River Oaks seafooder's "delectable variety" of Gulf Coast–style shellfish, "perfectly seasoned" slaw or gumbo that'll "make you weep"; "Tony runs a tight ship" in this "lively", "friendly" "hangout", so though a few find the fare "overpriced", "no one seems to care."

Tony's 🏠 Continental
26 | 26 | 26 | $64

Greenway Plaza Area | 3755 Richmond Ave. (Timmons Ln.) | 713-622-6778 | www.tonyshouston.com

Ensconced in a "sumptuous", "modern" space "with great art and a water wall", this tony Greenway Plaza–area "standard" is still the "best place to see and be seen" say the socially conscious; "exceptional" Continental cuisine is complemented by a "first-class wine list", and "the welcome is always gracious" even if the "excellent" service is occasionally "intrusive"; mere mortals find the vibe "snobby" and prices "very high" unless they're "celebrating special occasions."

Vic & Anthony's Steak
26 | 26 | 24 | $53

Downtown | 1510 Texas Ave. (La Branch St.) | 713-228-1111 | www.vicandanthonys.com

A "guys' kinda place", this Downtown steakhouse "near MLB and NBA venues" bases its appeal on "outstanding" steaks, a "variety of non-beef alternatives", "rich, decadent sides" and "excellent wines", all served up by an "obliging staff"; the "luxurious", "clubby" atmosphere also features a "terrific" bar that "makes you feel like Sinatra in 1962", so despite "close-together" tables, a "high" noise level and "astronomical" prices, a meal here is an "enjoyable" experience; N.B. lunch on Fridays only.

Kansas City

TOP FOOD RANKING

	Restaurant	Cuisine
27	Bluestem	American
26	Oklahoma Joe's	BBQ
	Le Fou Frog	French
	Tatsu's	French
	40 Sardines	American
	Plaza III	Steak
	Room 39	American
	MelBee's	American
	American Restaurant	American
25	Danny Edwards'	BBQ

OTHER NOTEWORTHY PLACES

Café Sebastienne	American
Fiorella's Jack Stack	BBQ
Grand St. Cafe	Eclectic
Lidia's	Italian
McCormick & Schmick's	Seafood
1924 Main	American
PotPie	French
Starker's Reserve	American
Swizzle	American
Trezo Mare	Italian/Seafood

American Restaurant ⑤ *American* | 26 | 24 | 27 | $60 |

Crown Center | Crown Ctr. | 200 E. 25th St. (Grand Ave.) | 816-545-8000 | www.theamericankc.com

"Outstanding" chef Celina Tio produces "stellar" New American food at this "formal" Crown Center stalwart where the menu is complemented by "fantastic" service and a deep wine list showcasing 1,500 selections; the "tired" decor "could use an upgrade", but the interior setting is trumped anyway by the "amazing" city views.

☑ Bluestem *American* | 27 | 22 | 24 | $60 |

Westport | 900 Westport Rd. (Roanoke Rd.) | 816-561-1101 | www.bluestemkc.com

The "brilliant", "cutting-edge" dishes and their "remarkably" beautiful presentations add up to "high art" at this Westport New American (No. 1 for Food), a "nirvana" for gourmets that's guided by chef-owners Colby and Megan Garrelts, the latter the hand behind the "fabulous" desserts; it's a "big-city" experience where the urbane, "hip" space includes a lounge, the site of "delightful" libations and nicely priced fare.

Café Sebastienne Ⓜ *American* | 24 | 25 | 22 | $36 |

Country Club Plaza | Kemper Museum of Contemp. Art | 4420 Warwick Blvd. (bet. 44th & 45th Sts.) | 816-561-7740 | www.kemperart.org

Chef Jennifer Maloney's "delicious" dishes show "balanced flavors" and are a perfect fit with the "super" setting at this New American housed

	FOOD	DECOR	SERVICE	COST

within the Kemper Museum of Contemporary Art; more may know it as a "lovely" lunch spot since its nighttime hours are limited (Fridays and Saturdays until 9:30 PM).

Danny Edwards' Famous Kansas City Barbecue ⊠ BBQ

25	–	19	$22

Downtown KCMO | 2900 Southwest Blvd. (W. 29th St.) | 816-283-0880
"Now, this is what I'm talking about" echoes the sentiment of 'cue pros who've tried this Downtown eatery "living up to its rep" thanks to the "best" burnt ends and other "tasty", "messy" chow; it's "what BBQ is meant to be", but just follow the smell – they're in new digs these days.

Z Fiorella's Jack Stack BBQ

25	21	22	$24

Crossroads | 101 W. 22nd St. (Wyandotte St.) | 816-472-7427
Country Club Plaza | 4747 Wyandotte St. (Ward Pkwy.) | 816-531-7427
Overland Park | 9520 Metcalf Ave. (95th St.) | 913-385-7427
Martin City | 13441 Holmes Rd. (135th St.) | 816-942-9141
www.jackstackbbq.com
"Don't even think of going to KC without eating here" say regulars of this relatively "fancy" (Most Popular) trio that proves barbecue "doesn't have to be eaten in a dive", especially when the vittles are all "downright fabulous", from the "best" babybacks to "to-die-for" burnt ends; the "amazing" quality makes the sometimes "long waits" no big deal.

Z 40 Sardines American

26	22	24	$44

Overland Park | 11942 Roe Ave. (W. 119th St.) | 913-451-1040 | www.40sardines.com
"Clever", "fabulous" and "soulful" justly describe chef Debbie Gold's food at her "high-style", blue-hued Overland Park New American, a "peerless" performer whose "standards remain high" including service that "excels"; the restaurant "deserves all the credit it gets", and there's "value" here to boot, with "nicely priced" wines and a 'martini and panini' night on Wednesdays.

Grand St. Cafe Eclectic

24	21	23	$35

Country Club Plaza | 4740 Grand Ave. (47th St.) | 816-561-8000 | www.eatpbj.com
From the "quite-good" Eclectic cooking (e.g. "delish" lobster gnocchi and "addictive" fried chicken salad) to servers who "care" about their customers, it's "tough to beat a meal" at this eatery near the Plaza; the "botanical-themed" digs may "need remodeling", but overall, fans like the "bustling" vibe here.

Z Le Fou Frog M French

26	19	22	$42

City Market | 400 E. Fifth St. (Oak St.) | 816-474-6060 | www.lefoufrog.com
Serving up "a little slice of Paris" in the "rugged" City Market area, this "funky" French "doesn't look like much on the outside", but "marvelous" food and a perpetually changing chalkboard menu put folks at ease; the "incredible" early-bird specials make the "tight" quarters palatable.

Z Lidia's Italian

23	26	23	$35

Crossroads | 101 W. 22nd St. (Baltimore Ave.) | 816-221-3722 | www.lidiasitaly.com
TV- and NYC-celeb Lidia Bastianich is a "star" in KC too, "brightening the Italian scene" with her durable Crossroads restaurant (housed in

a refurbed warehouse) that operates in "arguably the most beautiful" room in the city, thanks in part to the "gorgeous" chandeliers; the "gutsy", "high-quality" cooking is part of the toque's trademark, all made even better by "attentive" service.

☑ McCormick & Schmick's *Seafood*   23 | 24 | 23 | $41

Country Club Plaza | 448 W. 47th St. (Pennsylvania Ave.) | 816-531-6800 | www.mccormickandschmicks.com

"Great" seafood in a "land-locked town" means lots of customers show up at this Country Club Plaza standby also prized for its extensive variety of "fresh" fish; sit under the stained-glass ceiling that covers most of the restaurant, or opt for the outdoor patio – either way, the "good" servers "work pretty hard at making you forget the fact" that it's a chain.

MelBee's *American*   26 | 22 | 23 | $43

Mission | 6120 Johnson Dr. (bet. Beverly Ave. & Horton St.) | 913-262-6121 | www.melbees.com

Allies quip "the best thing to happen to Mission" is this New American small-plates expert serving a "tasty", and "tastefully prepared", roster of fare; the "modern" decor frames all those "beautiful women and men dressed so hip they'd make Sinatra look like a hobo", another reason this restaurant dispels the notion that "not all the good places are in Midtown."

1924 Main 🅂🅜 *American*   24 | 22 | 22 | $42

Crossroads | 1924 Main St. (19th St.) | 816-472-1924 | www.1924main.com

"Epicureans who desire something beyond the norm" look to this "attractive" Crossroads New American (housed in the restored, turn-of-the-century Rieger Building) that "takes advantage of the best ingredients available" for its "excellent" dishes that "change weekly"; the "bargain" prix fixes and "solid" service seal the deal; P.S. the wood-burning oven is pure "eye candy for foodies."

☑ Oklahoma Joe's
Barbecue & Catering 🅢 *BBQ*   26 | 12 | 18 | $14

Olathe | 11950 S. Strang Line Rd. (119th St.) | 913-782-6858
Downtown KCKS | Shamrock Gas Station | 3002 W. 47th Ave. (Mission Rd.) | 913-722-3366
www.oklahomajoesbbq.com

No-nonsense types insist the "gas-station location is perfect" for enjoying "some of the world's best" pulled pork, "tender" ribs and other "amazing" low-cost cooking at this "great" barbecue joint in Roeland Park; if the Olathe spot's ambiance seems "less authentic", at least there's more space for gnawing.

☑ Plaza III The Steakhouse *Steak*   26 | 22 | 25 | $51

Country Club Plaza | Country Club Plaza | 4749 Pennsylvania Ave. (Ward Pkwy.) | 816-753-0000 | www.plazaiiisteakhouse.com

Packing "enough testosterone to make Chuck Norris blush" is this "quintessential" steakhouse that gets props for "melt-in-your-mouth" meats, a "legendary" steak soup and even "sensational" desserts; "be prepared to pay", and for those who can swing with the tabs, "check out the jazz" on weekends.

PotPie ⑤Ⓜ *French*
25 | 18 | 21 | $28

Westport | 904 Westport Rd. (Roanoke Rd.) | 816-561-2702 |
www.kcpotpie.com

You're as likely to see "someone with a tongue ring and pierced nose as you are to see someone in a suit and tie" at this homey, "funky" Westport French known for "delicious" homestyle cookery and a chalkboard menu that's updated regularly; modest prices and the "most friendly" service further guarantees "repeat" business.

Room 39 ⑤ *American*
26 | 20 | 22 | $33

39th Street | 1719 W. 39th St. (bet. Bell & Genessee Sts.) | 816-753-3939 |
www.rm39.com

A "favorite" for breakfast and lunch but also offering "marvelous", "clever twists on American originals" at dinner, this "funky", affordable address has become a "staple" on 39th Street; it's "highly recommended", as one can see from "all the chefs in town eating there come Saturday morning."

Starker's Reserve ⑤ *American*
25 | 24 | 26 | $50

Country Club Plaza | 201 W. 47th St. (Wyandotte St.) | 816-753-3565 |
www.starkersrestaurant.com

Get treated like "royalty" at this "romantic, secluded" "special-occasion" mainstay purveying chef-owner John McClure's "splendid" New American preparations that are "meticulously" executed and served; it's no secret that the restaurant is "favored" by oenophiles, who delight in the "incredible" 1,500 wine list.

Swizzle Martini & Wine Bistro ⑤Ⓜ *American*
▽ 23 | 18 | 19 | $32

Waldo | 7100 Wornall Rd. | 816-361-3333 | www.swizzlekc.com

The "talents of the chef" explain the "good experiences" at this Waldo eatery serving a "limited" albeit number of "creative" New American options; if the "service needs work", most applaud the "reasonably priced" wines and overall quality here.

Ⓩ Tatsu's *French*
26 | 19 | 24 | $41

Prairie Village | 4603 W. 90th St. (Roe Ave.) | 913-383-9801 |
www.tatsus.com

"Sturdy", "reliably delicious" Classic French specialties (think Grand Marnier soufflés) set the tone for this "genteel" Prairie Village restaurant where meals are enhanced by "attentive" service; if you can abide the "staid", "granny's parlor" decor, you shouldn't have trouble enjoying this stalwart's "high standards."

Trezo Mare *Italian/Seafood*
▽ 24 | 28 | 24 | $44

Kansas City, North | 4105 N. Mulberry Rd. | 816-505-3200 |
www.trezomare.com

"Unique" Italian seafood compositions advocates call the "best in the area" bring notice to this upscale North KC entry whose dishes fans enjoy "from appetizers to desserts"; the "Cirque du Soleil meets Tuscany" decor is widely hailed as a "beautiful setting fit for a king."

Las Vegas

Restaurant	Cuisine
28 Rosemary's	American
Lotus of Siam	Thai
27 Nobu	Japanese
Picasso	French
Michael Mina	Seafood
André's	French
Prime Steak	Steak
26 Steak House	Steak
Delmonico Steak	Steak
Sterling Brunch	American
SW Steak	Steak
Fleur de Lys	French
Alex	French/Mediterranean
Medici Café	American
Le Cirque	French
Nobhill	Californian
Bradley Ogden	American
Okada	Japanese
Pamplemousse	French
Todd's Unique Dining	Eclectic

OTHER NOTEWORTHY PLACES

Aureole	American
Bartolotta	Italian/Seafood
Bellagio Buffet	Eclectic
Bouchon	French
Craftsteak	Seafood/Steak
David Burke	American
Eiffel Tower	French
Emeril's	Seafood
Guy Savoy	French
Joël Robuchon	French
Joe's Sea/Steak	Seafood/Steak
L'Atelier de Joël Robuchon	French
Le Provençal	French/Italian
Mesa Grill	Southwestern
Mix	American/French
Ping Pang Pong	Chinese
Pullman Grille	Steak
Rao's	Italian
Spago	American
Tableau	American

	FOOD	DECOR	SERVICE	COST

Alex ⑤Ⓜ *French/Mediterranean*　　26 | 27 | 26 | $114

Strip | Wynn Las Vegas | 3131 Las Vegas Blvd. S. (Spring Mountain Rd.) |
702-770-9966 | www.wynnlasvegas.com

One of Sin City's "very best" chefs, Alex Stratta, has earned the first-
name clout to head up this "Wynn top draw" where diners "descend a
grand staircase" to a "lavish" room to savor "extraordinarily conceived" French-Med cuisine in the form of either a $145 three-course
prix fixe meal or a $195 seven-course tasting menu; the staff "goes out
of its way to ensure a wonderful evening" that includes "perfect
touches" like a "seat-side purse ottoman" aimed at a clientele "who
actually remembers to dress" up; N.B. no children under five allowed.

André's *French*　　27 | 25 | 26 | $69

Downtown | 401 S. Sixth St. (bet. Bonneville St. & Bridger Ave.) |
702-385-5016 ⑤
Strip | Monte Carlo Resort | 3770 Las Vegas Blvd. S. (bet. Harmon &
Tropicana Aves.) | 702-730-7777
www.andrelv.com

"Go to the original for homey and the hotel for classy", but enjoy the
same "fantastic" French fare at André Rochat's eponymous eateries
located in a "rustic, charming" "cottage" Downtown and tucked behind "soundproof doors" in a "Louis XIV–style" room in the Monte
Carlo; "everything is rich, rich, rich", but diners "basking in the full
glory of butter, cream and foie gras" "done to perfection" and presented by a "gracious" staff find it all *magnifique!*

☑ Aureole *American*　　25 | 27 | 24 | $76

Strip | Mandalay Bay Resort | 3950 Las Vegas Blvd. S. (Mandalay Bay Rd.) |
702-632-7401 | www.charliepalmer.com

"Book your bachelor party" in the "vaulted" front room (or let the "attentive" staff usher you to the back for a "romantic" evening) at Charlie
Palmer's Mandalay Bay outpost of an NYC original, where the "super-
sexy" "dining fantasy" comes complete with "sublime" New American
offerings and "acrobatic" "angels" "on bungees" "who fetch the good
stuff" from the "extravagant wine tower"; but "bring your bank book",
as the bill "can rise as high as those lovely ladies."

Bartolotta Ristorante　　26 | 26 | 24 | $70
di Mare *Italian/Seafood*

Strip | Wynn Las Vegas | 3131 Las Vegas Blvd. S. (Spring Mountain Rd.) |
702-770-9966 | www.wynnlasvegas.com

Namesake chef Paul Bartolotta's Wynn palazzo offers "exceptional"
Italian seafood thanks to fish previously "unheard of west of
Appalachia" that are flown in daily from the Mediterranean and oven-
roasted or charcoal-grilled; the neo-rustic interior is "lovely", and the
property's exclusive lake makes for "beautiful" outdoor dining, but
wherever you sit, "if you watch what you order", your meal "can be
reasonably priced for the high-end."

☑ Bellagio Buffet *Eclectic*　　24 | 19 | 19 | $31

Strip | Bellagio Hotel | 3600 Las Vegas Blvd. S. (Flamingo Rd.) | 702-693-8255 |
www.bellagio.com

"Loosen your belt" because "all anyone could want" to eat is "deftly
prepared" and "well presented" at the Bellagio's "high-end" Eclectic

paean to "pigging out"; the "feast" (from "unlimited cracked crab" and Kobe beef to "Asian specialties like congee") is so "fresh and flavorful", it "elevates the genre", so despite "hungry" "hordes" and a "banquet-hall" atmosphere, gourmands ask "can I live here?"

Bouchon *French* — 24 | 24 | 23 | $57

Strip | Venetian Hotel | 3355 Las Vegas Blvd. S. (bet. Flamingo & Spring Mountain Rds.) | 702-414-6200 | www.bouchonbistro.com

"Genius" Thomas Keller "graces Vegas" with this French bistro (an outpost of the Yountville "classic") set "far away from the razzmatazz" in the Venetian Hotel's Venezia Tower; "casual" foodies flock here for "power breakfasts" featuring "light-as-a-feather sourdough waffles" or dinner's "luscious rotisserie chicken", nesting either in the "Parisian"-style interior or out on the "lovely" patio; some say the service is "so-so", but the kitchen earns its "buzz" by "proving you don't have to be expensive to be excellent."

Bradley Ogden *American* — 26 | 24 | 25 | $80

Strip | Caesars Palace | 3570 Las Vegas Blvd. S. (Flamingo Rd.) | 702-731-7731 | www.caesarspalace.com

"What a treat" it is to dine at this "wonderful" Caesars Palace destination where the "celebrity" namesake chef "is actually in", "working his wonders" with an "always changing" menu featuring "deliciously innovative" New American fare; the "portions are small" but the "flavors are big", and the "impeccable" staff is "without pretension" – they might even give you a "tour of the kitchen" to top off an "elegant" evening that's well "worth your hard-earned dollars."

Craftsteak *Seafood/Steak* — 25 | 24 | 24 | $70

Strip | MGM Grand Hotel | 3799 Las Vegas Blvd. S. (Tropicana Ave.) | 702-891-7318 | www.mgmgrand.com

"As expected", Tom Colicchio's chop-and-seafood house in the MGM Grand delivers "superior quality", "flawless execution" and culinary empowerment: you can "build your own meal with a bountiful selection" of sides to go with your "sublime" beef, lamb, pork, fowl or fish; the wine list is "tremendous", the staff is "helpful" and the "un-Vegas-like setting" ("not old boy, but metrosexual") is "delightfully unadorned", so if you can afford the "high prices", you're certain to "enjoy it."

David Burke Modern American Cuisine *American* — - | - | - | VE

Strip | Venetian Hotel | 3355 Las Vegas Blvd. S. (bet. Flamingo & Spring Mountain Rds.) | 702-414-7111 | www.venetian.com

Celebrity chef David Burke brings his inventive New American cuisine (pretzel-crusted crab cakes or cheesecake lollipop trees, anyone?) to Vegas with this eponymous eatery overlooking the lobby at the Venetian; surrounded by a lively color scheme of red, purple and white, guests can dine on budget-busting fare as they gaze at sculptured Himalayan salt bricks and a glass-walled, two-story wine room.

☑ Delmonico Steakhouse *Steak* — 26 | 23 | 25 | $67

Strip | Venetian Hotel | 3355 Las Vegas Blvd. S. (bet. Flamingo & Spring Mountain Rds.) | 702-414-3737 | www.emerils.com

"Everything Emeril touches turns to gold", including this "hunk-of-meat heaven" in the Venetian, where the beef is "impeccably aged" and "seasoned to perfection", the wine list is to "drool over" and the sides are so "orgasmic", "even the potato chips are divine"; what's more, the synchronized servers "know how to put on a great show", although the "dark, simple" room could be less "noisy" and "more interesting to match the quality of the fare"; P.S. book the pricey chef's table "for a feast to be remembered."

Eiffel Tower French
22 | 26 | 22 | $70

Strip | Paris Las Vegas | 3655 Las Vegas Blvd. S. (bet. Flamingo Rd. & Harmon Ave.) | 702-948-6937 | www.eiffeltowerrestaurant.com

Want to "fall in love again"? – then ride the glass elevator to this "romantic" "special-occasion" destination atop the namesake at the Paris and "get a window seat facing the Strip", because "watching the Bellagio water show is dreamy" from above, particularly when combined with a "classic" French meal; you may even make "a trip to The Little White Wedding Chapel" afterward, if your mood isn't dampened by "prices as high as the view", "disappointing" dishes and "lookie-loos who interfere with timely service."

Emeril's New Orleans Fish House Seafood
23 | 19 | 22 | $55

Strip | MGM Grand Hotel | 3799 Las Vegas Blvd. S. (Tropicana Ave.) | 702-891-7374 | www.emerils.com

"Kick your dinner plans up a notch" at this MGM Grand spot for "oh-my-God"-worthy, "spicy, down-home Louisiana" seafood, a "bam! bam!" "sign of the times that you can get fantastic food of all sorts in Vegas"; dishes "bursting" with "flavors, colors and textures" match a "trendy" remodel (which may outdate the Decor score), but while the staff manages to lend "a smaller feel to the huge" space, those who find the "TV chef's" empire "spread thin" say "the trouble with Emeril's is there's no Emeril here"; N.B. it also serves lunch.

Fleur de Lys French
26 | 26 | 25 | $90

Strip | Mandalay Bay Resort | 3950 Las Vegas Blvd. S. (Mandalay Bay Rd.) | 702-632-9400 | www.fleurdelyssf.com

Chef-owner Hubert Keller "nourishes all the senses" at the "Vegas branch of his SF legend", this "dreamy" "jewel box" in Mandalay Bay, where the "out-of-this-world" New French fare is "artistically impressive", the "spectacular service" helps to ensure a "peaceful" experience and the "sexy" decor features "3,000-plus roses on the wall"; choose one of the "exquisite" three-, four- or five-course prix fixe dinner menus and pair it with a flight from the "amazing wine list" to "impress anyone from a date to a client."

Guy Savoy ⓜ French
- | - | - | VE

Strip | Caesars Palace | 3570 Las Vegas Blvd. S., 2nd fl. (Flamingo Rd.) | 702-731-7731 | www.caesarspalace.com

The eponymous chef introduces his haute New French cuisine to the U.S. at this Caesars Palace offshoot of his Parisian original: set in a sleek yet intimate space, it includes three private dining rooms, a chef's table, a champagne and wine bar (boasting some 1,500 labels) and a glass-enclosed patio overlooking the Roman Plaza and the Strip; the bill of Savoy fare features à la carte options as well as a 10-course tasting 'menu prestige' at $290 and a four-course option for $190; N.B. closed Mondays and Tuesdays.

	FOOD	DECOR	SERVICE	COST

Joël Robuchon *French*

–	–	–	VE

Strip | MGM Grand Hotel | 3799 Las Vegas Blvd. S. (Tropicana Ave.) |
702-891-7925 | www.mgmgrand.com

Foodies aren't likely to be disappointed by acclaimed chef Joël
Robuchon's first stateside restaurant, a New French fete in the MGM
Grand featuring $225 six-course and $360 16-course tasting menus
full of inventive creations like truffled langoustine ravioli with stewed
cabbage; the cuisine is supported by a 750-bottle wine list and served
in an interior that's lavishly reminiscent of a 1930s Parisian mansion –
in other words, ooh-la-la.

Joe's Seafood, Prime Steak & Stone Crab *Seafood/Steak*

24	21	23	$59

Strip | Forum Shops at Caesars Palace | 3500 Las Vegas Blvd. S.
(Flamingo Rd.) | 702-792-9222 | www.leye.com

"Miami surf meets Chicago turf" at this Forum Shops collaboration by
the Sunshine State's namesake restaurant and the Windy City's Lettuce
Entertain You group; "if you like stone crabs – and who wouldn't? – this
is the only game in town" for claws "as good as in Florida", but the
bone-in filet is also "a wow!"; "smart, trendy" and full of "*Sex and the
City* types" (who "love the idea of half a piece" of Key lime pie), it's
also "huge and loud", but that's "what Joe's should be."

L'Atelier de Joël Robuchon *French*

–	–	–	E

Strip | MGM Grand Hotel | 3799 Las Vegas Blvd. S. (Tropicana Ave.) |
702-891-7358 | www.mgmgrand.com

The more casual of the namesake chef's two MGM Grand restaurants,
this New French eatery offers a small number of tables plus service
around a U-shaped counter for the ultimate open-kitchen experience;
the à la carte and tasting menus include specialties such as the
toque's legendary truffled mashed potatoes, roasted rack of lamb and
free-range quail stuffed with foie gras, as well as desserts like the
chartreuse soufflé with pistachio ice cream.

Le Cirque *French*

26	26	25	$88

Strip | Bellagio Hotel | 3600 Las Vegas Blvd. S. (Flamingo Rd.) |
702-693-8100 | www.bellagio.com

"Turn your frown upside down" when you step from the Bellagio casino into this "elegant" "temple of gastronomy", where ringmaster
Sirio Maccioni's "synchronized servers" deliver "superb" New French
cuisine and "delectable desserts", albeit at "steep prices"; "lusciously
colored" overstuffed seating makes the "intimate" room feel like "sitting inside a jewel box", and a window table ensures a "great view of
the fountains"; N.B. no children under 12 allowed.

Le Provençal *French/Italian*

21	20	19	$35

Strip | Paris Las Vegas | 3655 Las Vegas Blvd. S. (bet. Flamingo Rd. &
Harmon Ave.) | 702-946-4656 | www.parislasvegas.com

At this "well-kept secret" in the Paris, "singing servers" deliver French-
Italian bistro fare like "sublime crêpes" and bouillabaisse as well as
"some of the best pizza in Vegas"; some feel the "food is good enough
without the show", and others find the songs "fun" and "entertaining", but everyone agrees the "charming farmhouse"-style setting is
"excellent for lunch."

☑ Lotus of Siam *Thai*

28 | 12 | 21 | $23

E of Strip | Commercial Ctr. | 953 E. Sahara Ave.
(bet. Maryland Pkwy. & Paradise Rd.) | 702-735-3033 |
www.lotusofsiamlv.com

"Take a trip off the beaten path" to this "hidden treasure" east of the Strip and "don't let the location fool you": it may be in a shopping center, but whatever it's "lacking in decor", it makes up for with "transcendental" Northern Thai cuisine, like beef that will make you "weep with delight", "staggeringly good tom yum soup" and "ethereal sour sausage"; plus, each "authentic", "inexpensive" dish can be paired with one of the many "amazing Rieslings."

Medici Café *American*

26 | 26 | 26 | $51

Lake LV | Ritz-Carlton, Lake Las Vegas | 1610 Lake Las Vegas Pkwy.
(Grand Mediterra Blvd.) | Henderson | 702-567-4700 |
www.ritz-carlton.com

"Far in the boondocks" of Lake Las Vegas is this "out-of-the-way gem" where "sublime" New American cuisine is proffered amid "elegant", silk-and-brocade environs featuring a "wonderful view" of the Ritz-Carlton's Florentine gardens; "brunch is delicious", lunch is "fantastic" and dinner is "a special evening every time", thanks to a "romantic" setting (including patio seating) that "provides a serenity often hard to get in Las Vegas."

Mesa Grill *Southwestern*

24 | 22 | 22 | $54

Strip | Caesars Palace | 3570 Las Vegas Blvd. S. (Flamingo Rd.) |
702-731-7731 | www.caesarspalace.com

Sure, "it would be nice if he were present", but even if TV toque Bobby Flay is at his flagship in NYC, this "impressive" Caesars offshoot is "his place from the time you enter to leaving", offering "ultra-creative" Southwestern fare that "restores your faith in celebrity chefs" with "beautiful presentations" and "distinctive flavors"; it's all backed up by "personable service" in a "stylish" yet "relaxing" space, so "if you like a little spice in your meal", this "could become a regular haunt" – after all, it's "flay-bulous!"

☑ Michael Mina *Seafood*

27 | 24 | 26 | $82

Strip | Bellagio Hotel | 3600 Las Vegas Blvd. S. (Flamingo Rd.) | 702-693-8255 |
www.michaelmina.net

San Francisco "master chef" Michael Mina feeds fish to the whales (aka "high rollers") at this "inspired" destination for "exquisite" eating à "*la mer*" in the Bellagio conservatory – so "treat yourself to their caviar service", then "try the signature lobster" pot pie accompanied by a bottle from the "excellent wine list"; the dishes are so "outstanding", the service so "congenial" and the space (with open kitchen) so "chic and cosseting" (if "noisy") that the "sky-high prices" are "worth it."

Mix *American/French*

23 | 27 | 22 | $82

Strip | Mandalay Bay Resort | 3950 Las Vegas Blvd. S., 64th fl.
(Mandalay Bay Rd.) | 702-632-9500 | www.chinagrillmgt.com

"Dine in an egg-shaped pod" in a room "straight out of a Kubrick film" with "hundreds of glass spheres hanging from the ceiling", a "hip bar" and "the best view this side of a Vegas showgirl" from atop The Hotel at Mandalay Bay; the "outrageously decadent" experience extends to the New American–New French fare from über-chef/co-owner Alain Ducasse and chef de cuisine Bruno Davaillon, who "keep your *bouche* amused" throughout; all this and "mind-blowing service" make for a "top-of-the-world" "winner" – at "equally high prices."

Nobhill *Californian*
26 | 25 | 25 | $80

Strip | MGM Grand Hotel | 3799 Las Vegas Blvd. S. (Tropicana Ave.) | 702-891-7337 | www.michaelmina.net

"You'd think you're in the city" by the Bay at chef Michael Mina's "San Francisco treat" serving the "talented" toque's "creative" Californian cuisine in a "posh" MGM Grand setting; carb lovers say the "most delicious things ever tasted" are the complimentary mashed-potato sampler and the "steaming-hot bread fresh from the oven", but Atkins dieters focus on the "incredible wine list" and "attentive" staff.

☑ Nobu *Japanese*
27 | 22 | 23 | $71

E of Strip | Hard Rock Hotel | 4455 Paradise Rd. (bet. Flamingo Rd. & Harmon Ave.) | 702-693-5090 | www.noburestaurants.com

"Be adventuresome and trust your waiter – he won't steer you wrong" at this east-of-Strip outpost in Nobu Matsuhisa's "unique" empire famed for "cutting-edge sushi like you've never had", "don't-miss miso cod" and other "fabulous" Peruvian-accented Japanese fare; the "tranquil" garden setting is particularly "wonderful" for a "first date", provided you "come with your checkbook" and avoid it on "hotter-than-a-royal-flush" weekends, when "noisy crowds" turn it into a sort of "bass-pumping nightclub."

Okada *Japanese*
26 | 27 | 24 | $72

Strip | Wynn Las Vegas | 3131 Las Vegas Blvd. S. (Spring Mountain Rd.) | 702-770-9966 | www.wynnlasvegas.com

"Another Wynn winner", this Japanese restaurant specializes in "excellent teppanyaki" and "must-try robata" cooking, not to mention "fantastic sushi", all served in a "visually stunning" "Zen garden" featuring a "floating pagoda table" and "floor-to-ceiling windows" that showcase the hotel's "famous mountain", lake and "lit waterfall"; plus, there's "first-rate service" to match the "gorgeous food and decor."

Pamplemousse *French*
26 | 23 | 25 | $52

E of Strip | 400 E. Sahara Ave. (bet. Joe W. Brown Dr. & Paradise Rd.) | 702-733-2066 | www.pamplemousserestaurant.com

"Named by Bobby Darin", this traditional French "gem" once favored by the "Rat Pack" is an "oldie but still a goodie" thanks to a "classic", "quirky menu (they recite it to you)" from owner Georges LaForge and new chef-partner Jean-David Groff-Daudet; the "outstanding" meal comes complete with a "romantic shanty" setting east of the Strip and "fabulous" servers that ply you with "remarkable crudités."

☑ Picasso *French*
27 | 28 | 27 | $102

Strip | Bellagio Hotel | 3600 Las Vegas Blvd. S. (Flamingo Rd.) | 702-693-8255 | www.bellagio.com

Just like the "beautiful" namesake originals on the wall, chef Julian Serrano's "exquisite" Spanish-inflected New French dishes are "meticulously honed" "masterpieces" at this "MoMA-meets-Bacchus" "splurge" in the Bellagio (voted Most Popular in Las Vegas); other enticements include "perfect wines", a "gracious" staff and "a view of the dancing

FOOD · DECOR · SERVICE · COST

fountains"; of course it's "expensive", but "it still costs less than 15 minutes at blackjack"; N.B. closed on Tuesdays.

Ping Pang Pong ● *Chinese*

▽ 23 | 9 | 14 | $25

W Side | Gold Coast Hotel | 4000 W. Flamingo Rd. (bet. Valley View Blvd. & Wynn Rd.) | 702-367-7111 | www.goldcoastcasino.com

"The won-derful won ton soup, hall-of-fame walnut prawns" and all the rest of the "creative Chinese" dishes are "not to be expected in such simple" "cafeteria decor", but the food at this "real surprise" "belies its location" on the West Side; it serves dim sum at lunchtime and its 3 AM closing time makes it "good for a late-night snack", as long as you can deal with the staff – "either the servers won't leave you alone, or they won't come back."

☑ Prime Steakhouse *Steak*

27 | 27 | 26 | $83

Strip | Bellagio Hotel | 3600 Las Vegas Blvd. S. (Flamingo Rd.) | 702-693-8255 | www.bellagio.com

"Sink into the lavish seats" and "begin an evening of delight" at this steakhouse where Jean-Georges Vongerichten's "pampering" staff serves "heaven on a plate (and in a glass)"; "if the Rat Pack were still around, they'd congregate here" for "marvelous" meat, "martini-centric drinks", "theatrical decor" and "fantastic" views of the Bellagio fountains, "all of which scream 'ring-a-ding Vegas'"; just "know you'll be spending a ton" to dine among the "famous" folk.

Pullman Grille Ⓜ *Steak*

20 | 23 | 19 | $33

Downtown | Main Street Station Hotel | 200 N. Main St. (Ogden Ave.) | 702-387-1896 | www.mainstreetcasino.com

This "true find" Downtown in the Main Street Station is a "bit out of the way" but "worth getting on board" to enjoy "excellent" chophouse fare while "soaking up the atmosphere" of a "romantic Victorian" room that's "big on wood" and "antique furnishings"; polish off the evening with "after-dinner drinks" in the "actual rail car that belonged to Louisa May Alcott"; N.B. closed Mondays and Tuesdays.

Rao's *Italian*

- | - | - | E

Strip | Caesars Palace | 3570 Las Vegas Blvd. S. (Flamingo Rd.) | 702-731-7731 | www.caesarspalace.com

Thanks to a reservations line, you don't need to be connected to nab a table at this Caesars Palace re-creation of the East Harlem landmark, an old-world Southern Italian that's one of Gotham's toughest tickets; while twin 'Rao's Rooms' (with just 10 tables each) and the presence of chef Carla Pellegrino, daughter-in-law of owner Frank, evoke the original's all-in-the-family vibe, Vegas touches include an outdoor bocce court overlooking the Garden of the Gods pool as well as dining areas designed to look like NYC streets and parks.

☑ Rosemary's *American*

28 | 21 | 26 | $52

W Side | W. Sahara Promenade | 8125 W. Sahara Ave. (bet. Buffalo Dr. & Cimarron Rd.) | 702-869-2251 | www.rosemarysrestaurant.com

Tucked "way off the Strip" on the West Side, this "not-to-be-missed" New American from chef-owners Michael and Wendy Jordan may be Las Vegas' "ultimate epicurean event", a "hidden treasure" that's toppled Nobu to become No. 1 for Food in Las Vegas; "fabulous tastes and flavors" are served in a "pretty" space that "belies its strip-mall location", while "excellent prix fixe" options and "exceptional" service that "goes above and beyond expectations" make it "worth every penny of the cab ride" home.

Spago *American*

23	19	21	$48

Strip | Forum Shops at Caesars Palace | 3500 Las Vegas Blvd. S. (Flamingo Rd.) | 702-369-0360 | www.wolfgangpuck.com

Amid the "fancy chefs and restaurants [that have been] arriving in Vegas by the trainful", this 15-year-old "Wolfgang wonder" in the Forum Shops remains a "sure bet" for New American cuisine on a "high, yet highly accessible, plane"; "it's Puck, so what else do you expect?" ask acolytes who also appreciate the "knowledgeable staff", "people-watching" patio and an interior that was given a stylish update in 2006; plus, diversity-seekers can "delight" in a daily changing menu – "repeat visits mean trying new things."

Steak House *Steak*

26	21	24	$47

Strip | Circus Circus Hotel | 2880 Las Vegas Blvd. S. (Circus Circus Dr.) | 702-794-3767 | www.circuscircus.com

"Fred and Barney" could order a couple of "perfect" brontosaurus-sized steaks and "kick it old-school"-style at this "dark-wood-and-leather" chophouse in the "bizarre" Circus Circus Hotel, where the "excellent" cuts come at "amazingly" prehistoric prices with "soup or salad and sides included" (and are offset by a limited wine list); plus, there's one of "the best Sunday brunches" around to lure "real-deal" hunters "past the kiddies-and-clowns" crowd.

Sterling Brunch Ⓜ *American*

26	19	23	VE

Strip | Bally's Las Vegas Hotel | 3645 Las Vegas Blvd. S. (Flamingo Rd.) | 702-967-7999 | www.ballyslasvegas.com

Yes, it's only open on Sundays (9:30 AM–2:30 PM), but for a "delightful" brunch experience fueled by "free-flowing Perrier Jouët", this Bally's American is "absolutely grand"; "feel free to pile your plate five deep with grilled lobster and top them off with good-quality American sturgeon caviar", then finish your meal with a "decadent dessert"; just remember to reserve in advance, be prepared to deal with "crowds" and "bring a credit card with a large limit" – the set-price spread costs $65.

SW Steakhouse *Steak*

26	26	25	$74

Strip | Wynn Las Vegas | 3131 Las Vegas Blvd. S. (Spring Mountain Rd.) | 702-770-9966 | www.wynnlasvegas.com

Savor "steak you can cut with a fork" at this "fabulous" chophouse in the Wynn, where the "breathtaking" setting features a patio overlooking the "lake and forest with a water show at night"; "sensational service" and a "reasonable wine list" are just two more reasons this is an "excellent" part of the high-rolling scene.

Tableau *American*

▽ 26	26	26	$71

Strip | Wynn Las Vegas | 3131 Las Vegas Blvd. S. (Desert Inn Rd.) | 702-770-9966 | www.wynnlasvegas.com

At this "phenomenal" French-influenced New American "hidden" in the "beautiful atrium" of the Wynn's south tower, the "wonderfully attentive staff" may just suggest you "choose the chef's tasting menu" "with the wine pairing"; those who worry that this "great sleeper" might be "getting lost in the crowd" should note standout touches like the "cute copper saucepans that hold the bread" and – a rarity among "exclusive" Vegas spots – a vegetarian tasting menu.

Todd's Unique Dining ⑤ *Eclectic*   26 | 18 | 26 | $39
Henderson | 4350 E. Sunset Rd. (Green Valley Pkwy.) | 702-259-8633 | www.toddsunique.com

"Finally, fabulous food that doesn't cost an arm and a leg or involve a smoke-filled room" sigh surveyors who hail this "winner" in a "quiet" Henderson mall, where chef-owner Todd Clore brings his Eclectic sensibilities (honed at Sterling Brunch) to a daily changing dinner menu that features "innovations" like goat-cheese won tons with raspberry-basil sauce; also among its "charms" are "reasonably priced wines", "personal service" and a newly renovated interior.

Long Island

	Restaurant	Cuisine
28	Kotobuki	Japanese
	Maroni Cuisine	Eclectic/Italian
27	Kitchen à Bistro	French
	North Fork Table & Inn	American
	Jedediah's	American
	Mirabelle	French
	Le Soir	French
	Peter Luger	Steak
	Chachama Grill	American
	F.O.O.D.	American/French
	Piccolo	American/Italian
	La Plage	Eclectic
	Fifth Season	American
	Polo	American
	Panama Hatties	American
	Mill River Inn	American/Eclectic
	Dario's	Italian
	Plaza Cafe	American
26	La Piccola Liguria	Italian
	Mirko's	Eclectic

OTHER NOTEWORTHY PLACES

Restaurant	Cuisine
Barney's	American/French
Bravo Nader!	Italian
Bryant & Cooper	Steak
Cheesecake Factory	American
Dave's Grill	Continental/Seafood
Della Femina	American
Galleria Dominick	Italian
Giulio Cesare	Italian
Harvest on Fort Pond	Italian/Mediterranean
Il Mulino	Italian
Louis XVI	French
Nisen	Japanese
Orient	Chinese
Rialto	Italian
Siam Lotus	Thai
Starr Boggs	American/Seafood
Stone Creek	French/Mediterranean
Tellers	Steak
Vine Street Café	American
West End Cafe	American

	FOOD	DECOR	SERVICE	COST

Barney's ⓜ *American/French*   25 | 22 | 23 | $62

Locust Valley | 315 Buckram Rd. (Bayville Rd.) | 516-671-6300 |
www.barneyslv.com

"Amazing from start to finish" declare devotees of this "romantic",
"charming old house" on an "out-of-the-way" country road in Locust
Valley, where you can savor "imaginative", "impeccable" New
American–French cuisine ("the duck is especially fine"), matched by a
"tremendous wine list" and served by an "attentive staff"; sit by the
"roaring fire" with the "love of your life" for a "sublime experience."

Bravo Nader! *Italian*   25 | 13 | 24 | $52

Huntington | 9 Union Pl. (bet. New York Ave. & Wall St.) | 631-351-1200 |
www.bravonader.com

"Consummate host", chef and owner Nader Gebrin is renowned for his
"beaming" smile and "humongous" plates of "to-die-for" Southern
Italian cuisine at this 12-table "cult gem" in Huntington; though fans
fawn "you feel like you're going to a friend's house for a fabulous dinner", some say the "super-size portions in cramped quarters make for
an uncomfortable evening."

☒ Bryant & Cooper Steakhouse *Steak*   26 | 20 | 22 | $62

Roslyn | 2 Middle Neck Rd. (Northern Blvd.) | 516-627-7270 |
www.bryantandcooper.com

This "brilliant" Roslyn meatery offers "awesome", "old-fashioned"
steaks and "equally scrumptious fish"; the surroundings are "traditional"
and "clubby", and the service is "congenial" (especially "if you're a
regular"), so "crowds" and high "noise levels" on the weekend are no
surprise; P.S. their butcher shop/retail market next door "is a steal."

Chachama Grill *American*   27 | 16 | 23 | $50

East Patchogue | Swan Nursery Commons | 655 Montauk Hwy.
(S. Country Rd.) | 631-758-7640 | www.chachamagrill.com

It's a "miracle in a mall" proclaim acolytes of this "divine" New American
hidden in an East Patchogue shopping center, where chef-owner Elmer
Rubio turns out "consistently superior", "creative and flawless food";
the "staff is a pleasure", the "simple" surroundings are "serene"
enough to "encourage conversation" and you just "can't beat the prix
fixe menu" ($38) from 5–6 PM.

☒ Cheesecake Factory ● *American*   20 | 18 | 17 | $29

Westbury | Mall at the Source | 1504 Old Country Rd. (Evelyn Ave.) |
516-222-5500 | www.thecheesecakefactory.com

"Who doesn't love this place?" is the question posed by the fans of
this Westbury American, who say the "dinosaur portions" of "surprisingly exciting" food – "considering it's a chain" – from a "menu as long
as a recipe book" (with multiple flavors of that "amazing" eponymous
dessert) make it an "all-around favorite" as well as a "real value"; still,
folks are split on whether it's worth the "painfully long waits" and upbeat but "amateurish" service, with most saying yes.

Dario's ☒ *Italian*   27 | 18 | 25 | $55

Rockville Centre | 13 N. Village Ave. (bet. Merrick Rd. & Sunrise Hwy.) |
516-255-0535

"The South Shore has its Il Mulino" proclaim dazzled diners who "trot
out the superlatives" for the "spectacular food" – especially the "out-

of-this-world" veal and "fantastic" "fresh whole fish" – at this family-run Northern Italian in Rockville Centre; an "impeccable", "can-do" (but never "overbearing") staff also makes it a "treat" for "special occasions", and though the prices may be "steep" and the decor "hardly memorable", "who cares when the food and service are this good?"

Dave's Grill   *Continental/Seafood* | 26 | 16 | 21 | $53 |
Montauk | 468 W. Lake Dr. (bet. Flamingo Ave. & Soundview Dr.) | 631-668-9190 | www.davesgrill.com

Seafarers are smitten with the "sublime fish" "you see coming in fresh on the boats" at this tiny, seasonal "Montauk treat" where the "inventive" Continental menu includes turf selections too, all presented by "professional" servers "without the Hamptons attitude"; while there's frequent carping about the "outrageous" system for reservations (only taken the same day after 4:30 PM, or a bit earlier if you get on line at the door), "once you're finally seated" you'll be in "nirvana."

Della Femina   *American* | 25 | 22 | 21 | $60 |
East Hampton | 99 N. Main St. (Cedar St.) | 631-329-6666 | www.dellafemina.com

Boldface names and common citizens congregate at Jerry Della Femina's East Hampton "treasure" to feast on "fresh", "phenomenal" New American cuisine; the "professional" staff, "warm", "beautiful interior" and "terrific garden" all enhance a "totally unstuffy" social scene in which the "vibes are powerful and the mood exhilarating" (especially when you "catch a star"); in short, it remains "one restaurant in the Hamptons that's actually worth the money."

Fifth Season, The 🅼 *American* | 27 | 21 | 24 | $53 |
Greenport | 45 Front St. (bet. 1st & Main Sts.) | 631-477-8500 | www.thefifth-season.com

This Greenporter is graced by the talents of chef/co-owner Erik Orlowski, who brings "flair, imagination" and a "great knowledge of fresh local produce" to his "memorable" weekly roster of New American dishes, which are "thoughtfully" matched with LI wines and New York State beers; the dining room is "picturesque", with an "entertaining open kitchen", and the "servers are eager, well prepared" and "amazing", making this a bit of "NYC in wine country."

F.O.O.D.   *American/French* | 27 | 13 | 21 | $47 |
Hampton Bays | 122 E. Montauk Hwy. (Bittersweet Ave. S. exit) | 631-723-3663

"If you rate it, they will come" predict patrons of this "secret" seasonal "star" on the highway in Hampton Bays; many are "astonished at the quality" of its "unbelievable" New American–French cuisine – prepared by "caring" chef-owner Antonio Coelho and served by a "first-rate staff" – since the "cottage" is so "shabby-chic" (some call it a "rundown shack") and "tiny" that you might find yourself "squashed"; naturally, reservations are required in the summer.

Galleria Dominick   *Italian* | 25 | 21 | 25 | $52 |
Westbury | 238 Post Ave. (bet. Drexel & Winthrop Aves.) | 516-997-7373 | www.galleriadominick.com

"Top-notch" Northern Italian cuisine "flawlessly served" by an "outstanding" staff that "makes you feel special" earns many a *molto bene* for this upscale Westbury "classic" where touches like weekend piano music add to the "gracious dining" experience; though some report "regulars seem to get preferred treatment", the rejoinder is owner Dominick Zelko "recognizes repeat business – a smart man!"

Giulio Cesare Ristorante 🅩 *Italian*   26 | 15 | 23 | $53
Westbury | 18 Ellison Ave. (Old Country Rd.) | 516-334-2982
Caesar never had it so good, hail followers who praise this Westbury "favorite" for "outstanding" Northern Italian dishes (including "melt-in-your-mouth" veal meatballs) and "old-fashioned service" (that's a touch more "coddling" to regulars); while a few note that the decor is "something out of another era", others urge diners to "ignore the wood paneling and focus on the fabulous food."

Harvest on Fort Pond *Italian/Mediterranean*   26 | 21 | 21 | $48
Montauk | 11 S. Emery St. (Euclid Ave.) | 631-668-5574 |
www.harvest2000.com
"Amazing", "abundant" Northern Italian–Med food presented in a "family-style" cornucopia distinguishes this "festive", airy Montauk destination; sunset dinners are ideal for "magnificent views over Fort Pond", and the staff is all around "professional" and "courteous" – just remember it's "difficult to order for two", and be sure to make a reservation, as "everything about this place is divine."

Il Mulino New York *Italian*   26 | 22 | 24 | $81
Roslyn Estates | 1042 Northern Blvd. (bet. Old Northern Blvd. & Searingtown Rd.) | 516-621-1870 | www.ilmulinonewyork.com
A "jewel" for "phenomenal" Northern Italian food, this Roslyn Estates branch of the famed New Yorker delivers "tremendous portions" (tip: don't gorge on the "complimentary foreplay" of appetizers) in a "dark, sexy" dining room whose tables require "reservations well in advance"; the waiters "treat you like royalty", though some cite a little too much "hovering" – "maybe to catch you when you see the bill."

🄩 Jedediah's *American*   27 | 28 | 23 | $58
Jamesport | Jedediah Hawkins Inn | 400 S. Jamesport Ave. (bet. Main Rd. & Peconic Bay Blvd.) | 631-722-2900 |
www.jedediahhawkinsinn.com
"How many ways can you say superb?" – chef Tom Schaudel "brings it all together" at this "marvelous" Jamesport inn restaurant that's set in a "beautifully restored" and "stunningly" decorated 1863 building; the equally "wowing" New American dishes (which "should be photographed") "raise North Fork cuisine to a new level" laud reviewers, and though the service is "a little less polished than the setting", most simply concentrate on a "serious gastronomic experience" that exemplifies "event dining at its best."

🄩 Kitchen à Bistro 🅩🔁 *French*   27 | 9 | 21 | $39
St. James | 532 N. Country Rd. (Lake Ave.) | 631-862-0151 |
www.kitchenabistro.com
"Awed" admirers are "calling all foodies" to taste chef-owner Eric Lomando's "amazing", "inventive" French cooking – the seafood-focused blackboard menu "changes daily" – at this "teeny" St. James bistro that's recently been "spruced up"; though "hard to find" (and requiring weekend reservations that are "virtually impossible to get"),

it's "well worth the effort" given "helpful" service and a BYO policy
that makes the tabs here even more of a "bargain."

☑ Kotobuki Ⓜ *Japanese* 28 | 19 | 21 | $36
Roslyn | Harborview Shoppes | 1530 Old Northern Blvd. (Bryant Ave.) |
516-621-5312
Babylon | 86 Deer Park Ave. (Main St.) | 631-321-8387
Hauppauge | 377 Nesconset Hwy. (Rte. 347) | 631-360-3969
www.kotobukinewyork.com
"Nothing on the island compares" to the "supremely fresh", "pristine"
and "beautiful" sushi – including "butterlike" sashimi and fried oysters
"to die for" – that's "expertly prepared" at these Babylon and
Hauppauge "gems", again rated No. 1 for Food on Long Island; both locations are sparely decorated (though Babylon looks "better" post-
renovations), service is "lively" if "inconsistent" and the "wait can be
torture" (no reservations taken), but "once you finally sit down",
you're in for "a most pleasurable experience"; N.B. a Roslyn branch
opened post-Survey.

La Piccola Liguria Ⓜ *Italian* 26 | 19 | 26 | $56
Port Washington | 47 Shore Rd. (bet. Mill Pond & Old Shore Rds.) |
516-767-6490
"Waiters recite the impressive" roster of "seductive", "spectacular"
specials ("culinary theater at its best") that outnumber the equally
"superb" menu selections at this "elegant" Northern Italian destination favored by a "mature" Port Washington clientele; though fussy
folks fret the muralled, "muted" space "needs a face-lift", the service
is "marvelous" and the "exceptional" kitchen is still "on top of its
game", guaranteeing a "special evening out."

La Plage *Eclectic* 27 | 19 | 24 | $54
Wading River | 131 Creek Rd. (Sound Rd.) | 631-744-9200 |
www.laplagerestaurant.net
"It's still worth the trip into the wilds of Wading River" for chef-owner
Wayne Wadington's "glorious" Eclectic cuisine (the "quality and in-
ventiveness easily stand up to any Manhattan restaurant"); so what if
it resembles a "shrimp shack" and you "have to look over a parking lot"
to get a peekaboo view of Long Island Sound – the "service is attentive" and "professional" and "every mouthful of food is so delectable"
that few diners mind the "simple digs" or the "expense."

Le Soir Ⓜ *French* 27 | 20 | 24 | $48
Bayport | 825 Montauk Hwy. (west of Nicolls Rd.) | 631-472-9090
"*C'est formidable!*" say floored francophones about this "outstanding"
Bayport French where chef/co-owner Michael Kaziewicz prepares
"sublime" and "surprisingly plentiful" cuisine that's simply "a joy"; the
Tudor-style "relaxing, romantic" "hideaway" is staffed by "congenial"
servers, and its "bargain" weekday dinner special eases the way to a
"one-of-a-kind experience."

Louis XVI Ⓜ *French* 25 | 27 | 25 | $75
Patchogue | 600 S. Ocean Ave. (Masket Dock) | 631-654-8970 |
www.louisxvi.org
"Let them eat cake" along with the rest of the "unforgettable" New
French cuisine at this "absolutely beautiful" Patchogue palace, which

FOOD | DECOR | SERVICE | COST

is adorned with rich draperies and crystal chandeliers, but is most striking for its "magnificent view of the bay"; "white-glove" service makes guests "feel like the king and queen", and while Their Majesties will need "plenty of room" on the royal "credit limit", a special prix fixe menu cuts the cost; a few find the experience "too fussy", but most agree it's "simply superb"; N.B. jacket suggested.

ⓩ Maroni Cuisine 🛇Ⓜ⇄ *Eclectic/Italian* | 28 | 14 | 23 | $72

Northport | 18 Woodbine Ave. (bet. Main St. & Scudder Ave.) | 631-757-4500 | www.maronicuisine.com

Northport chef-owner Michael Maroni orchestrates "the most original dining experience on LI" according to the multitudes who find "magic in every bite" of his "unusual, outstanding" Eclectic-Italian tasting menu ("the way to go") that roams from exceptionally "tender duck" to sashimi to "oh those meatballs!"; despite the "thimble-sized" 20-seat space ("don't bring your elbows"), most "love the vibe" and the "ultrafriendly staff", and are happy to savor the "incredibly expensive" "miracles on a plate" at least once.

Mill River Inn *American/Eclectic* | 27 | 23 | 25 | $70

Oyster Bay | 160 Mill River Rd. (bet. Lexington Ave. & Oyster Bay-Glen Cove Rd.) | 516-922-7768

"Love is in the air" at this "perennial favorite" in Oyster Bay, a "cozy", "cottagelike hideaway" serving a "fantastic", "original" and "pricey" menu of New American–Eclectic cuisine that's worth "inventing a special occasion" for; the "service is sublime", the atmosphere "dignified and refined", and although less starry-eyed sorts scold "refurbish, please", it consistently enchants with "evenings to remember."

Mirabelle Ⓜ *French* | 27 | 21 | 26 | $67

St. James | 404 N. Country Rd./Rte. 25A (Edgewood Ave.) | 631-584-5999 | www.restaurantmirabelle.com

"Why drive to the city?" ask diners thrilled with the "sheer culinary artistry" of chef/co-owner Guy Reuge, who "impresses" "year after year" at this "French gem" in St. James; "top-flight" service and an "excellent" wine list add to the "delightful albeit expensive" experience, though costs can be lowered via the prix fixe lunch and dinner options; some say it can be "a little tight" on weekends and complain of "tiny servings", but overall it's the kind of place "you dream about."

Mirko's Ⓜ *Eclectic* | 26 | 23 | 24 | $65

Water Mill | Water Mill Sq. | 670 Montauk Hwy. (bet. Old Mill & Station Rds.) | 631-726-4444 | www.mirkos.com

"Elegant", "European-inflected" cuisine is "served with panache" and a bit of "formality" at this "hidden" Eclectic in Water Mill Square; it has a country look with a fireplace ("cozy on a winter evening") as well as a courtyard, and is staffed by an "efficient" crew, so although it's "hard to snag a table" and some snip that "only the regulars get top-notch service", "the food has always been the star here" anyway.

Nisen Ⓜ *Japanese* | 26 | 18 | 21 | $37

Commack | 5032 Jericho Tpke. (Larkfield Rd.) | 631-462-1000 | www.nisensushi.com

"Sublime sushi" and "beautiful rolls" (some named for customers) that "melt in your mouth" make afishionados flip over this "way hip"

	FOOD	DECOR	SERVICE	COST

Commack Japanese where "one-of-a-kind" chef-owner Tom Hayashi sets the "*Cheers*-like" tone; while the "small" dining room, bar and tatami rooms fill up early, most agree it's "worth the wait."

☑ North Fork Table & Inn *American*

27 | 23 | 23 | $69

Southold | North Fork Inn | 57225 Main Rd./Rte. 25 (bet. Boisseau & Laurel Aves.) | 631-765-0177 | www.northforktableandinn.com

Rapt reviewers applaud this "slice of the Upper East Side" in a restored Southold inn, where chef Gerry Hayden (ex Manhattan's Aureole) and pastry chef Claudia Fleming (ex NYC's Gramercy Tavern) turn locally farmed ingredients into a "spectacular", "well-rounded" New American menu of "original and intricate" dishes served by an "enthusiastic", "informative" staff; the soft blue walls and "spare" decor create an "elegant" setting, so even if some tut that it's "too noisy when full", most agree it's a "terrific" experience; N.B. closed Tuesdays.

Orient, The *Chinese*

26 | 10 | 18 | $23

Bethpage | 623 Hicksville Rd. (Central Ave.) | 516-822-1010

Mavens maintain that "maestro" Tommy Tan "orchestrates ingredients, spices and secrets" into some of "the most delicious food east of Chinatown" at this "affordable" Bethpage "treasure" where the staff can guide diners ("just go for it") toward the "large menu's" most "delicate, subtle" Cantonese, Hunan and Szechuan dishes, plus "nontraditional specials"; a weekend "wait for a table" is all but inevitable, but the "fabulous" dim sum is "not to be missed."

Panama Hatties *American*

27 | 23 | 25 | $67

Huntington Station | Post Plaza | 872 E. Jericho Tpke. (2 mi. east of Rte. 110) | 631-351-1727 | www.panamahatties.com

"Serendipitous", "stupendous" and "beautifully plated" New American fare shines through the "strip-mall setting" of this "hidden" "special-occasion place" in Huntington Station helmed by chef-owner Matthew Hisiger; pressed-tin ceilings adorn the "lovely" room, and return raters say the "professional" staff is "not as stuffy" these days, so "discriminating diners" are happy to shell out "the big bucks."

☑ Peter Luger ⇗ *Steak*

27 | 16 | 21 | $65

Great Neck | 255 Northern Blvd. (bet. Lakeville Rd. & Little Neck Pkwy.) | 516-487-8800 | www.peterluger.com

"A staple for eating cow" since 1960, this Great Neck branch of the Brooklyn original has been moo-ving patrons to vote it Long Island's Most Popular for 14 years by delivering "phenomenal" steak and sides ("porterhouse is the way to go"); it's served by a famously "gruff" staff and, yes, it looks like it's "time for a rehab", but "you don't come here for the decor", as this is the "quintessential steakhouse" – "the one others aspire to when they grow up"; P.S. "bring lots of cash, since they don't take plastic" (except for debit).

Piccolo *American/Italian*

27 | 21 | 25 | $52

Huntington | Southdown Shopping Ctr. | 215 Wall St. (bet. Mill Ln. & Southdown Rd.) | 631-424-5592 | www.piccolorestaurant.net

"Your taste buds will thank you" for the "exquisite", "succulent" New American-Italian dishes at this Huntington "foodie heaven" (known for its "amazing" homemade pasta), where the "fabulous" staff en-

FOOD | DECOR | SERVICE | COST

sures you'll "never lift a finger"; the dining room is "warm" and "lush", although a bit "tight", and a nightly pianist enhances the "romance", so it "lives up to the raves" – a "sheer gustatory delight."

Plaza Cafe *American*   27 | 23 | 25 | $61
Southampton | 61 Hill St. (bet. First Neck & Windmill Lns.) | 631-283-9323 | www.plazacafe.us
The New American fare is "transcendent" at this tucked-away Southampton "oasis" offering "innovative" dishes – headlined by "superb seafood" that's "so fresh it talks back" – and a "fabulous", "all-American wine list"; its lofty room is both "luxurious and comfortable" ("sit by the fireplace in winter"), and the "flawless" servers are highly "informative" about both food and vino, so the "expense" pays off in a genuine "epicurean experience."

Polo Restaurant Ⓜ *American*   27 | 27 | 27 | $67
Garden City | Garden City Hotel | 45 Seventh St. (bet. Cathedral & Hilton Aves.) | 516-877-9352 | www.gchotel.com
"Pampered" patrons call this "superb" New American in the Garden City Hotel the "crème de la crème" for its "inventive", "exquisite" food (including a "superior Sunday brunch"), "exceptional" staff and an "elegant" dining room with that "precious commodity – space between tables"; yes, the bill might elicit an "ouch!", but "it's worth the pain" for a meal that "excels in every way."

Rialto Ⓜ *Italian*   26 | 20 | 24 | $51
Carle Place | 588 Westbury Ave. (bet. Glen Cove Rd. & Post Ave.) | 516-997-5283
"Hidden inconspicuously" in a Carle Place "neighborhood setting", this "traditional", "cozy" Northern Italian is called "one of the best" by gratified guests who admire its "memorable" cuisine as well as its "old-school", "solicitous staff", including owners who are models of "graciousness and hospitality"; yes, it's "expensive", but "the price isn't painful" in light of the "wonderful, intimate" meal.

Siam Lotus Thai Ⓜ *Thai*   26 | 14 | 23 | $31
Bay Shore | 1664 Union Blvd. (bet. 4th & Park Aves.) | 631-968-8196
Just hearing the owner recite the day's "delectable" specials can "make your mouth water" at this stellar Siamese in Bay Shore, known for "amazing", "nicely plated" and "subtly spiced" cooking (though it can be "very, very" hot if you want), backed up by "charming", "devoted service"; the pink-and-green color scheme, inspired by the titular flower, "leaves a bit to be desired" – but on the other hand "who needs that" when the cost is modest and the "food is so damn good!"

Starr Boggs *American/Seafood*   26 | 24 | 23 | $58
Westhampton Beach | 6 Parlato Dr. (Library Ave.) | 631-288-3500
It's the "Union Square Cafe of the Hamptons" report rapt reviewers about this seasonal "Westhampton Beach winner" where the "mayor" of local dining, chef-owner Starr Boggs, is a "magician with fish" and other "beautiful" New American dishes conjured with "fresh ingredients and inventive preparations"; the breezy "Hamptons decor", adorned with original Warhol prints, is "gorgeous" and the "service is now top-notch", adding luster to one of the Island's "shining stars."

	FOOD	DECOR	SERVICE	COST

Stone Creek Inn *French/Mediterranean*

| 26 | 23 | 23 | $57 |

East Quogue | 405 Montauk Hwy. (bet. Carter Ln. & Wedgewood Harbor) | 631-653-6770 | www.stonecreekinn.com

"Unbelievably elegant and well-prepared" French-Med dishes with "lovely plate presentations" are the signature of this East Quogue "treasure"; "stylish service" enhances its "gorgeous" setting, a house that served as a speakeasy in the '20s, so no wonder lovers laud it as the "Le Bernardin of Long Island" – just "don't forget your wallet."

Tellers American Chophouse *Steak*

| 25 | 26 | 23 | $60 |

Islip | 605 Main St. (Rte. 111) | 631-277-7070 | www.tellerschophouse.com

The "fantastic experience" of eating at this Islip steakhouse comes in part from its "gorgeous" setting in a converted bank with 30-ft.-windows and "dramatic lighting", a "hot", "beautiful bar" and a second, "intimate" upstairs dining room, not to mention a walk-in wine cellar housed in a "must-see" former vault; meat mavens laud the "exceptional" steaks and "to-die-for" seafood, as well as the "outstanding" service, so even if some quip "they should have kept the ATMs", most agree "any money deposited here is well worth it."

Vine Street Café *American*

| 25 | 19 | 21 | $57 |

Shelter Island | 41 S. Ferry Rd. (1½ mi. north of S. Ferry on Rte. 114) | 631-749-3210 | www.vinestreetcafe.com

A "wonderful find" among a growing number of "upscale Shelter Island eateries", this little "hideaway" offers "phenomenal" French-influenced American dishes complemented by a "unique wine selection" (which some guests wish were "more affordable"); the service is largely "attentive", and the cottage "charming" and "country-esque"; P.S. "call ahead, as everyone seems to know about it."

☑ West End Cafe *American*

| 25 | 19 | 21 | $41 |

Carle Place | Clocktower Shopping Ctr. | 187 Glen Cove Rd. (Old Country Rd.) | 516-294-5608 | www.westendli.com

For "a bit of Manhattan in Carle Place", try this "wonderful" "date restaurant" "hidden in the back of a strip mall" that's a local "favorite" for its "artistic" New American dishes, which are "served graciously" by an "efficient" staff; since the atmosphere is so "warm" and "unpretentious", and the pricing is "fair" (particularly the "winning" twilight menu), it tends to "pack them in" – so "be sure to have reservations."

Los Angeles

Restaurant	Cuisine
28 Mélisse	American/French
Nobu Malibu	Japanese
Asanebo	Japanese
27 Matsuhisa	Japanese
Brandywine	Continental
La Cachette	French
Angelini Osteria	Italian
Providence	American/Seafood
Katsu-ya	Japanese
Piccolo	Italian
Derek's	Californian/French
Tuscany	Italian
Sona	French
Leila's	Californian
Water Grill	Seafood
Hatfield's	American
Spago	Californian
Josie	American
Sushi Nozawa	Japanese
Babita	Mexican

OTHER NOTEWORTHY PLACES

A.O.C.	Californian/French
bld	American
Brent's Deli	Deli
Brentwood, The	American
Café Bizou	Californian/French
Campanile	Californian/Mediterranean
Capo	Italian
Chaya Brasserie	Asian/Eclectic
Craft	American
Cut	Steak
Foundry on Melrose	American
Fraiche	Mediterranean
Grace	American
Grill on the Alley	American
Hamasaku	Japanese
JiRaffe	Californian
Mimosa	French
Mori Sushi	Japanese
Pizzeria Mozza	Pizza
Rustic Canyon	Californian/Mediterranean

Angelini Osteria 🅼 *Italian*
27 | 17 | 23 | $49

Beverly Boulevard | 7313 Beverly Blvd. (Poinsettia Pl.) | 323-297-0070 |
www.angeliniosteria.com

"Incomparable feasts" crafted by "masterful" chef Gino Angelini
"transport" guests at this "intimate" Beverly Boulevard Italian whose
"rustic" dishes like pork chop *alla Milanese* "put you in pig heaven"; "tight
seating" is part of the "bargain", but both "in-the-know locals and
celebs" sit "cheek-by-jowl" as they savor "personal" service and "exquisite" wines to accompany the "superb" fare; P.S. "reserve early."

ⓩ A.O.C. *Californian/French*
26 | 22 | 23 | $53

Third Street | 8022 W. Third St. (bet. Crescent Heights Blvd. &
Edinburgh Ave.) | 323-653-6359 | www.aocwinebar.com

Chef/co-owner Suzanne Goin's "small-plates heaven" presents "marvelous" Cal-French dishes complemented by "spectacular wines and
cheeses", which are all ideal for "sharing with a group" and "perfect for
dates" (whether romantic or "bacon-wrapped"); the "lovely, understated" interior hosts "enough of a scene to entertain but not intimi-
date", and the "informed", "attentive" staff can convince you to "nosh
all night", even if tabs do "add up quickly"; P.S. arrive early to "get a
seat at the bar" if you don't have a reservation.

ⓩ Asanebo 🅼 *Japanese*
28 | 15 | 24 | $61

Studio City | 11941 Ventura Blvd. (bet. Carpenter & Radford Aves.) |
818-760-3348

At this "superb find" on Studio City's "sushi row", Tetsuya Nakao
slices up "incredible" sashimi in a "traditional Japanese" style that's
"beautifully presented", though "sometimes not for the faint of heart"
and never "for the faint of budget"; both insiders and initiates appreciate the "excellent" servers who "explain each dish", adding there's
"no ambiance, but who cares?"

Babita Mexicuisine 🅼 *Mexican*
27 | 14 | 21 | $35

San Gabriel | 1823 S. San Gabriel Blvd. (Norwood Pl.) | 626-288-7265
"No burritos or taquitos here", this mecca for "haute Mexican cuisine"
by chef Roberto Berrelleza delivers a "superior", "sensual" dining experience that converts call "the best reason to go to San Gabriel"; true,
its 10-table space in a "humble building" is "far from ideal", but combined with the "warm family service", it provides an "extremely unpretentious" backdrop for the "awesome" food.

bld *American*
21 | 18 | 19 | $33

Beverly Boulevard | 7450 Beverly Blvd. (N. Vista St.) | 323-930-9744 |
www.bldrestaurant.com

Beverly Boulevard habitués "love the breakfast" (with "superb" pan-
cakes) at chef/co-owner Neal Fraser's "chicer, cheaper" New
American cousin to Grace; although some find the service "needs improvement" and call the "diner-inspired gourmet food" a little "less exciting at dinner", the "modern" dining room is "bright with lots of
windows", adding to its "refreshing" appeal.

ⓩ Brandywine Ⓢ *Continental*
27 | 20 | 25 | $58

Woodland Hills | 22757 Ventura Blvd. (Fallbrook Ave.) | 818-225-9114
For "amazing" albeit "rich" Continental cuisine encompassing foie
gras, sweetbreads and flourless chocolate cake, Valleyites flock to this

"teeny", "expensive" but "worth-every-penny" Woodland Hills "favorite" that's hard to find – "we drove by it three times" – but rewards diehards with "charming" live music and "top-notch" service; since the "special" lace-curtained booths are in high demand, reviewers recommend "reserving well in advance."

Brent's Deli *Deli* | 26 | 14 | 21 | $20
Northridge | 19565 Parthenia St. (bet. Corbin & Shirley Aves.) | 818-886-5679
Westlake Village | 2799 Townsgate Rd. (Westlake Blvd.) | 805-557-1882
www.brentsdeli.com

"Finally, a deli we can brag about in the Conejo Valley" effuse fans of the "fancier and more spacious" Westlake Village outpost of the "super-popular" 40-year-old Northridge original, both of which "richly reward" guests with "world-class pastrami", "righteous Reubens" and "shout-out"-worthy soups, as well as desserts that "require a derrick" to get from case to plate; "snappy" waitresses set down everything "with a smile", causing many to declare this "the daddy of all delis."

Brentwood, The *American* | 21 | 18 | 19 | $47
Brentwood | 148 S. Barrington Ave. (1 block south of Sunset Blvd.) | 310-476-3511

"Well-heeled Brentwood comes to dine" at this "deliberately dark", "clubby", "lively" scene where Bruce Marder creates "delicious" New American "homestyle favorites" (like Kansas City steak and fries) accompanied by a lengthy wine list; less comforted customers call the service "uneven" and the bill "one step too expensive", and while the dimness can be "seductive", some shout "who turned the lights out?"

☑ Café Bizou *Californian/French* | 23 | 19 | 21 | $32
Pasadena | 91 N. Raymond Ave. (Holly St.) | 626-792-9923
Sherman Oaks | 14016 Ventura Blvd. (bet. Costello & Murieta Aves.) | 818-788-3536
www.cafebizou.com

These "dependable", "all-occasion" Cal-French bistros in Pasadena and Sherman Oaks win praise for "well-prepared" fare that's a "wonderful value" (especially with an "unbelievably low" $2 corkage fee); though the "no-attitude" staff is "attentive", a few patrons frown on the "long waits", "even with reservations."

Campanile *Californian/Mediterranean* | 26 | 24 | 23 | $56
La Brea | 624 S. La Brea Ave. (bet. 6th St. & Wilshire Blvd.) | 323-938-1447 | www.campanilerestaurant.com

At this La Brea "must for LA dining", chef-owner Mark Peel delivers Cal-Med cuisine that's "sumptuous", "elegant" and "impervious to fashion"; enamored eaters call the weekend brunch the "discovery of the year", Thursday night's grilled cheese the "best you'll ever taste" and Monday's three-course family-style meal a "real steal", also noting the "properly attentive" service and the lofty space built by Charlie Chaplin – a "timeless" "part of Hollywood history."

Capo ☑ Ⓜ *Italian* | 26 | 24 | 24 | $77
Santa Monica | 1810 Ocean Ave. (Pico Blvd.) | 310-394-5550

"Bring the Gold Card" to this Santa Monica Italian where chef/co-owner Bruce Marder oversees a dining experience "fit for a king" ("yes, that's Tom Hanks in the corner"), encompassing "amazing" wood-grilled New York steaks, "excellent" homemade pastas and an "impressive wine list" inside a "charming" interior; even if some call it "too cool for school", "they never rush you" and you can reserve ahead to dine at the bar – "the best seat in town."

Chaya Brasserie *Asian/Eclectic* | 23 | 22 | 21 | $49 |

West Hollywood | 8741 Alden Dr. (bet. Beverly Blvd. & W. 3rd St., off Robertson Blvd.) | 310-859-8833 | www.thechaya.com

At this West Hollywood "favorite", the "innovative" Asian-Eclectic menu changes seasonally, but its "amazing" steaks, "out-of-this-world desserts" and "unique drinks" anchor the dining experience; with "un-stuffy" servers and a "gorgeous" room uplifted by a bamboo garden centerpiece, it hosts a "lively", "noisy" "scene" (especially at happy hour) that "never goes out of style."

Craft ⊠ *American* | – | – | – | E |

Century City | 10100 Constellation Blvd. (bet. Ave. of the Stars & Century Park E.) | 310-279-4180 | www.craftrestaurant.com

Top chef (and *Top Chef* judge) Tom Colicchio plants the first LA out-post of his popular NYC-bred New American right next to Century City's new Creative Artists HQ; featuring a glass-enclosed dining room, shiny glass-and-chrome bar and outdoor patio with cabanalike lounges, it's already being referred to as the 'CAA Commissary', so ex-pect much moving and shaking over the plates of seasonal fare.

Cut ⊠ *Steak* | 26 | 24 | 24 | $94 |

Beverly Hills | Beverly Wilshire | 9500 Wilshire Blvd. (Beverly Dr.) | 310-276-8500 | www.wolfgangpuck.com

"The new king" of Kobe, Wolfgang Puck has a "winner" with this "quintessential" steakhouse in the Beverly Wilshire hotel that "sets the bar" with "amazing" cuts of beef ("Wagyu as rich and tender as foie gras") and "inventive" sides served in a "professional", if "some-times over-the-top", manner befitting the "outlandish" prices (you may as well "just hand your wallet to the hostess when you walk in"); the "magnificent" Richard Meier–designed room is a "total scene" where "celeb-spotting is highly probable", but reservations are a "pain" "unless you've been nominated for an Academy Award"; N.B. a limited menu is available at the adjacent Sidebar.

Derek's ⊠Ⓜ *Californian/French* | 27 | 23 | 25 | $62 |

Pasadena | 181 E. Glenarm St. (bet. Arroyo Pkwy. & Marengo Ave.) | 626-799-5252 | www.dereks.com

It's "a real find!" exclaim enthusiasts of Derek Dickenson's "exceptional" bistro "hidden" away in a Pasadena strip mall, where the "inspired" menu of "adventurous and creative" Cal-French dishes "consistently delivers" as does the "fabulous wine list"; an "extremely knowledge-able" staff works the various dining rooms, which have a "high-end, but not stuffy" vibe; it may be "wildly expensive", but cognoscenti coo it's "worth every penny."

Foundry on Melrose, The Ⓜ *American* | – | – | – | M |

Melrose | 7465 Melrose Ave. (N. Gardner St.) | 323-651-0915 | www.thefoundryonmelrose.com

Chef-owner Eric Greenspan has transformed what used to be a neigh-borhood pizza parlor on Melrose into an impressive art deco–style cafe with a hand-carved bar; the midpriced New American menu features innovative dishes of the moment like short ribs with sunchoke purée and pork belly with corn velouté and wild mushroom agnolotti.

Fraiche *Mediterranean*

-	-	-	M

Culver City | 9411 Culver Blvd. (Main St.) | 310-839-6800 | www.fraicherestaurantla.com

Built to resemble a Tuscan villa, this moderately priced Mediterranean with a busy bar boasts one of the best-looking rooms in newly gentrified Culver City; its culinary team of Jason and Miho Travi, along with Providence veteran Thierry Perez in the front of the house, is bringing a touch of elegance to the neighborhood.

Grace 🅼 *American*

25	24	24	$62

Beverly Boulevard | 7360 Beverly Blvd. (Fuller Ave.) | 323-934-4400 | www.gracerestaurant.com

"East Coast sophistication" comes to Beverly Boulevard via chef-owner Neil Fraser's "ambitious" "neighborhood jewel" that marries "chic, modern" surroundings with "big-flavored" American fare, an "unbelievable wine list" and "delectable" desserts (Wednesday's Doughnut Night "rules"); "effortless" service exudes "class", and if the less-captivated are "underwhelmed" by what they deem "overpriced" fare, they're overruled by the majority that maintains this "grown-up" "culinary adventure" is "one of LA's top tables."

Grill on the Alley, The *American*

24	20	24	$56

Beverly Hills | 9560 Dayton Way (Wilshire Blvd.) | 310-276-0615 | www.thegrill.com

Beverly Hills' "dealmaking HQ", this "expensive" American plays host to "one of the best power-lunch scenes in the city" with "actors", "agents" and other "industry types" angling for a "coveted green-leather booth", all the better from which to enjoy "top-notch" filet mignon and Cobb salads ferried by a "polished" staff; non-celebs realize snagging a seat at this "old-line" "staple" "is a tough ticket" since "VIPs get priority."

Hamasaku 🅢 *Japanese*

27	17	21	$59

West LA | 11043 Santa Monica Blvd. (Sepulveda Blvd.) | 310-479-7636 | www.hamasakula.com

A sushi "scene" in West LA, this "expensive, but worth it" "celeb"-heavy hot zone is well-nigh "unparalleled" claim cognoscenti praising the "creative", "beautifully presented" rolls and "standout" signature dishes; the strip-mall digs are mostly "nondescript" though the "hip crowd" gives it "a touch of Hollywood" that appeases the "power" clientele; N.B. a branch on Melrose is in the works.

Hatfield's 🅢 *American*

27	19	24	$63

Beverly Boulevard | 7458 Beverly Blvd. (Gardner St.) | 323-935-2977 | www.hatfieldsrestaurant.com

"No feuds here" quip proponents of this "real McCoy" run by "gracious" married team Quinn and Karen Hatfield and set in a "sliver" of a space with "elegant", "modern" decor and a "beautiful" front patio; the "pitch-perfect" New American cuisine prepared from "impeccable" "farmer's market" ingredients "deserves all of its recent accolades" (and its high price), and if a few deem the "small portions" "a little precious", most "rave" this "darling" spot is shaping up to be "a real highlight" of the "burgeoning Beverly Boulevard" dining scene.

JiRaffe *Californian*   26 | 21 | 24 | $56
Santa Monica | 502 Santa Monica Blvd. (5th St.) | 310-917-6671 | www.jirafferestaurant.com
"Bravo to Raphael [Lunetta]" effuse fans of the chef-owner who "knows how to cook and create" "delicious surprises" at this "phenomenal" Santa Monica Californian; even though the chandelier-accented space has "tight seating" downstairs (with a "quieter" upper level), the "smashing martinis", "impeccable service" and Monday 'Bistro Night' "deal" elicit lots of "love" – indeed, as one admirer attests, "I went into labor and stayed to finish my meal."

Josie *American*   27 | 23 | 25 | $60
Santa Monica | 2424 Pico Blvd. (25th St.) | 310-581-9888 | www.josierestaurant.com
"Entirely pleasurable on all levels", this Santa Monica "favorite" "isn't trendy", but it's "pretty much perfect" say those praising chef Josie Le Balch's "sumptuous" New American fare that spotlights "fresh, local" ingredients and "excellent game"; "attentive service" and a "gorgeous" room with "romantic" fireside tables make it a "favorite haunt" for well-heeled locals, and if the "pricey" final tab intimidates some, insiders say "no-corkage Mondays" and Wednesday night's Farmers Market prix fixe are less expensive options.

Katsu-ya *Japanese*   27 | 15 | 19 | $40
Encino | 16542 Ventura Blvd. (Hayvenhurst Ave.) | 818-788-2396
Studio City | 11680 Ventura Blvd. (Colfax Ave.) | 818-985-6976
"Sublime sushi" and "phenomenal", "nontraditional" "handrolls that are a work of art" as well as the signature spicy tuna on crispy rice keep these Japanese twins in Encino and Studio City "mobbed" with a "hip crowd" of "locals" and "stars" in spite of somewhat "sterile", "claustrophobic" surroundings; "prices can add up fast" and service is "rushed", but supporters swear the "flat-out terrific" fare "makes you forget" any shortcomings.

La Cachette *French*   27 | 25 | 26 | $66
Century City | 10506 Little Santa Monica Blvd. (Thayer Ave.) | 310-470-4992 | www.lacachetterestaurant.com
A "dignified", "gorgeous" light-filled "retreat in the middle of Century City" is how admirers view this "real treasure" and its "very talented" chef-owner Jean François Meteigner, who "removes most of the butter and cream", but none of the "flavor", from his "exquisite" seasonal New French creations; "spot-on" service sometimes veers toward "stuffy", but that's no matter to the "posh" deep-pocket crowds who continue to celebrate it as "one of LA's finest" tickets – "it's outstanding in every way."

Leila's 🅂🄼 *Californian*   27 | 20 | 24 | $47
Oak Park | RE/MAX Plaza | 706 Lindero Canyon Rd. (Kanan Rd.) | 818-707-6939 | www.leilasrestaurant.com
Supporters call this Oak Park Californian the "Spago of the suburbs" for chef Richie De Mane's "exquisite", "cleverly crafted" cuisine that's finished with "fantastic wine pairings"; though its "shop-front setting"

FOOD | DECOR | SERVICE | COST

and "minimalist" decor are a "major drawback" for some, the "quality service" makes for a "mellow", "intimate" meal, leading locals to cry "Leila's is ours! – stay away."

◪ Matsuhisa *Japanese* 27 | 16 | 23 | $74

Beverly Hills | 129 N. La Cienega Blvd. (bet. Clifton Way & Wilshire Blvd.) | 310-659-9639 | www.nobumatsuhisa.com

"Place yourself in their hands and order omakase" advise those who've found sushi "nirvana" at Nobu Matsuhisa's "phenomenal" Beverly Hills original, which also excels with "exquisite" Peruvian-influenced Japanese cooking; space is so tight that "you might end up sitting in some famous person's lap", but the staff "makes everyone feel like a celebrity" according to grateful guests who find the "sublime" experience worth the "mighty" tab; N.B. his next restaurant in the former L'Orangerie is slated to open soon.

◪ Mélisse ⧠Ⓜ *American/French* 28 | 25 | 26 | $90

Santa Monica | 1104 Wilshire Blvd. (11th St.) | 310-395-0881 | www.melisse.com

"Incredible talent" Josiah Citrin earns this Santa Monica "temple" of French–New American dining the No. 1 Food score in the LA area for his "outstanding", "cutting-edge" dishes that strike a "balance between traditional and imaginative", matched with "always right-on" recommendations by sommelier Brian Kalliel; the "pristine" service and "sophisticated", "romantic" room ("love the purse stools") lend themselves to "three-hour" dinners that are "stratospherically" expensive but "stay in your memory as a beautiful experience."

Mimosa ⧠ *French* 22 | 18 | 20 | $47

Beverly Boulevard | 8009 Beverly Blvd. (bet. N. Edinburgh & N. Laurel Aves.) | 323-655-8895 | www.mimosarestaurant.com

After more than 10 years, this Beverly Boulevard bistro continues to serve, "as the French would say, 'correct'" Gallic "comfort food" prepared with "traditional" techniques by chef Jean Pierre Bosc; the recently renovated indoor/outdoor seating area and "warm service" bring "a touch of Lyon", even though the disenchanted "just don't get" the "nostalgic" approach.

Mori Sushi ⧠ *Japanese* 26 | 17 | 21 | $64

West LA | 11500 W. Pico Blvd. (Gateway Blvd.) | 310-479-3939 | www.morisushi.org

"Serious nigiri sushi" by Morihiro Onodera arrives in "elegant presentations" at this West LA haven whose "hipster" clientele advocates omakase as the best way to sample the "extraordinary", "sumptuous" cuisine; the food is served on unique plates (many of them handmade by the chef-owner) in a "simple" space, and though it's all suited to those with "deep pockets", it's "worth it" for special occasions.

◪ Nobu Malibu *Japanese* 28 | 21 | 24 | $71

Malibu | 3835 Cross Creek Rd. (PCH) | 310-317-9140 | www.nobumatsuhisa.com

"The food is off the charts" at Nobu Matsuhisa's "phenomenal" locale off PCH that presents "superb" "sushi as art" as well as other "unbelievable" Japanese cuisine; "celebrities" and "Malibu mogul sightings" add a spark to the "traditional room" – "who cares if it's in a strip-mall?" – while the staff "ensures every need is fulfilled", leaving just the "samurai"-strength bill to give one pause.

Piccolo *Italian*

27 | 17 | 24 | $51

Venice | 5 Dudley Ave. (Spdwy.) | 310-314-3222 | www.piccolovenice.com

"Just off the beach" in Venice, in what may be the "weirdest location for a fine-dining restaurant in LA", resides this "aptly named" "hole-in-the-wall" that "deserves its grand reputation" for fashioning "heavenly, inventive" Italian cuisine bursting with "big, authentic flavors" and coupled with an "impressive" (although "exceedingly expensive") wine list; "they don't take reservations", but "warm, helpful service" helps to allay the "hassle" of "waiting for a table."

Pizzeria Mozza ● *Pizza*

26 | 19 | 22 | $37

Hollywood | 641 N. Highland Ave. (Melrose Ave.) | 323-297-0101 | www.mozza-la.com

Mario Batali "has taken LA by storm" in partnership with Nancy Silverton, turning out "regional Italian" pies that "actually live up to the hype" with their "extravagantly bubbly" crust supporting an "amazing synthesis of ingredients" ("the fennel sausage is a definite favorite"); it's "so trendy it's almost silly", the "noise level is over the top" and seating's "tight", but the "buoyant" staff and "affordable wine list" keep Hollywood customers "rejoicing"; P.S. "book a month" in advance, or arrive early and "eat at the bar to avoid a hellacious wait."

Providence *American/Seafood*

27 | 24 | 26 | $84

Hollywood | 5955 Melrose Ave. (Cole Ave.) | 323-460-4170 | www.providencela.com

"Unstoppable" chef/co-owner Michael Cimarusti creates "absolutely sublime" New American seafood dishes ("of all stripes, colors and textures") at this "sensational" Hollywood "treasure chest" boasting a "memorable" tasting menu; the "seamless" staff "goes out of its way to serve you" amid a room that's "elegant", "subdued" and enlivened by aquatic touches, so while it demands a bit of "bling", gastronomes deem it "the Holy Grail" of LA dining experiences.

Rustic Canyon *Californian/Mediterranean*

21 | 19 | 21 | $46

Santa Monica | 1119 Wilshire Blvd. (bet. 11th & 12th Sts.) | 310-393-7050 | www.rusticcanyonwinebar.com

"Perfectly fresh ingredients" sourced from the Santa Monica farmer's market take the spotlight at this "unpretentious" newcomer where "imaginative" Cal-Med dishes (including several small-plates options) are paired with wines from a "smart" list; "enthusiastic" servers and a "happening" vibe mean it's off to a "great start", though a few find it "hampered" by "tight seating" and "deafening" noise levels.

Sona 🅢 Ⓜ *French*

27 | 24 | 26 | $87

West Hollywood | 401 N. La Cienega Blvd. (bet. Beverly Blvd. & Melrose Ave.) | 310-659-7708 | www.sonarestaurant.com

"Outstanding in every way" swoon smitten surveyors of David Myers' West Hollywood boîte that "pushes the culinary envelope" with "exquisite" New French fare "prepared with imagination and care" and best appreciated via the "brilliant" tasting menu (either with wine pairings or "let the sommelier guide you" through the "biblical" list); the "beautifully appointed" room is "elegant and warm" while service is "top-notch" (if sometimes "overbearing"); all in all, it's "a strong contender for one of LA's best restaurants" – just be prepared for some "major sticker shock."

Z Spago *Californian*   27 | 25 | 25 | $73

Beverly Hills | 176 N. Cañon Dr. (Wilshire Blvd.) | 310-385-0880 | www.wolfgangpuck.com

"Forget Gibraltar, this place is the rock of Los Angeles" sum up survey-ors who award the Most Popular title to this "flashy", "irresistible" "legend" that's "well worth" the "big-ticket prices" for its "flawless" Californian cuisine from Lee Hefter and "cutting-edge" desserts from pastry chef Sherry Yard; owner Wolfgang Puck "can often be seen ta-ble hopping" in the "flamboyant" room that opens onto a "tree-filled patio" dotted with celebrities, while his "hard-to-fault" servers have been "trained by Beverly Hills' most high-maintenance clientele."

Sushi Nozawa ☒ *Japanese*   27 | 6 | 15 | $58

Studio City | 11288 Ventura Blvd. (bet. Arch & Tropical Drs.) | 818-508-7017

"Master" chef-owner Kazunori Nozawa continues to "rule with an iron fist" at this "outstanding" Studio City "strip-mall" spot where the "fa-mously nonexistent decor" is "part of the shtick", as is the somewhat "intimidating" man behind the counter who doles out "melt-in-your-mouth perfect" slabs of "buttery" fish on "warm rice" (but "no California rolls"); "purists" know to simply "order the omakase", "shut up" and "revel in the experience" – it's "worth the punishment."

Tuscany II Ristorante *Italian*   27 | 22 | 24 | $48

Westlake Village | Westlake Plaza | 968 S. Westlake Blvd. (Townsgate Rd.) | 805-495-2768 | www.tuscany-restaurant.com

Widely considered the "crème de la crème" for Westlake Village, this "outstanding" Italian kitchen presents creations that "taste as good as they look", including "fine specials" and a "good wine selection"; add-ing to the feel of "formal dining in a casual atmosphere" ("even better since the redesign") are "servers who genuinely care about making you happy", themselves overseen by "delightful owners."

Z Water Grill *Seafood*   27 | 24 | 25 | $62

Downtown | 544 S. Grand Ave. (bet. 5th & 6th Sts.) | 213-891-0900 | www.watergrill.com

A "mind-boggling assortment" of fish prepared in a "brilliantly" "imagi-native manner" is what you'll find at this Downtown "favorite", which surveyors deem the "best damned seafood" spot in LA; a "terrific se-lection" of international wines adds to the "classy", "clubby" ambi-ance, as do the "sophisticated", "well-informed" servers, putting it "at the top" of the "short list" "for special occasions, business dinners" and other events that merit "ocean-deep pockets."

Miami

TOP FOOD RANKING

Restaurant	Cuisine
28 Michy's	American/French
27 Palme d'Or	French
Nobu Miami Beach	Japanese/Peruvian
Romeo's Cafe	Italian
Prime One Twelve	Seafood/Steak
Pascal's on Ponce	French
26 Francesco	S American
Azul	Mediterranean
Hiro's Yakko San	Japanese
Cacao	Nuevo Latino
Joe's Stone Crab	Seafood
Tropical Chinese	Chinese
Osteria del Teatro	Italian
Chef Allen's	New World
Oceanaire	Seafood
Caffe Vialetto	Italian
Quinn's	Seafood
Escopazzo	Italian
Capital Grille	Steak
Matsuri	Japanese

OTHER NOTEWORTHY PLACES

Barton G.	American
Bonefish Grill	Seafood
Blue Door	French
Café Pastis	French
Café Ragazzi	Italian
Casa Tua	Italian
Cheesecake Factory	American
Graziano's	Argentinean/Steak
Little Saigon	Vietnamese
Michael's Genuine Food	American
North One 10	American
Off the Grille	Caribbean
OLA	Nuevo Latino
Ortanique	Caribbean/New World
SushiSamba	Japanese/S American
Table 8	Californian
Talula	American
Tamarind	Thai
Timo	Italian/Mediterranean
Versailles	Cuban
Wish	American

Azul *Mediterranean*

26 | 27 | 25 | $74

Brickell Area | Mandarin Oriental Hotel | 500 Brickell Key Dr. (8th St.) | 305-913-8358 | www.mandarinoriental.com

"Creative, amazing food" – officially Med, but with "a touch of Asia, a touch of France and a touch of the U.S." – plus "excellent" wines and staffers who "know what you want before you do" make dining at the Mandarin Oriental an "orgasmic experience"; "you'll want to devour the view too", and the "as-chic-as-they-come" surrounds are "a great place to go spotting local celebs"; some sigh "prices rose after chef Michelle Bernstein left", but landing current toque Clay Conley "was quite a coup", and this remains "one of Miami's top innovative restaurants."

☑ Barton G...The Restaurant *American*

22 | 26 | 23 | $68

South Beach | 1427 West Ave. (14th Ct.) | Miami Beach | 305-672-8881 | www.bartong.com

"Good for celebrity spotting" and "for celebrations" too, it's always "showtime!" at SoBe's "DisneyWorld for foodies" where, amid a "beautiful garden" set, "ridiculously huge" size – and priced – New American dishes are "served in an unusual manner" (e.g. "popcorn shrimp in movie popcorn boxes"); if foes fear "this once-novel restaurant is becoming a novelty", with staff and cuisine "sacrificed to the humor, pomp and circumstance of the presentation", stalwarts swear "there may be places with better food, service or decor, but this puts all three together."

☑ Blue Door at Delano ● *French*

24 | 27 | 22 | $71

South Beach | Delano Hotel | 1685 Collins Ave. (17th St.) | Miami Beach | 305-674-6400 | www.chinagrillmgt.com

The "epitome of high-end SoBe decor", the Delano Hotel's "paradise in white" is a "fittingly swank location" for "checking out the rich and famous" as you consume "terrific" New French cuisine from *célébrité* chef Claude Troisgros, brought by "white-glove", if somewhat self-impressed, servers; skeptics sniff it's all "style over substance", but most deem the experience "worth it" – "even when they bring the check."

Bonefish Grill *Seafood*

22 | 19 | 21 | $35

Coral Gables | 2121 Ponce de Leon Blvd. (Alcazar Ave.) | 305-460-1888
Kendall | 12520 SW 120th St. (125th Pl.) | 786-293-5713
Westernmost Dade | 14220 SW Eighth St. (bet. SW 142nd & 143rd Aves.) | 305-487-6430
www.bonefishgrill.com

Make "no bones about it" – there's "nothing on the menu you'll throw back" at these "casual, comfortable" seafooders; converts "can't believe it's a chain", given the "intimate" atmosphere and "pleasant" servers who "know their fish"; perhaps it's a bit "predictable", but the principal problem with these "popular" *poissoneries* is, you gotta "go early or late or expect a wait."

Cacao ☒ *Nuevo Latino*

26 | 23 | 24 | $56

Coral Gables | 141 Giralda Ave. (bet. Galiano St. & Ponce de Leon Blvd.) | 305-445-1001 | www.cacaorestaurant.com

As its name suggests, "wonderful" chocolate desserts cap off Venezuelan chef-owner Edgar Leal's "gourmet riff on the best of Latin

American cuisine"; "superb" service, "cosmopolitan" white/orange decor and a "wine cellar second to none" all enhance his "sophisticated" menu, and while some hesitate at the "high prices", few deny this is "a wonderful alternative to the tried and tired Coral Gables offerings."

Café Pastis ⓩ French
23 | 13 | 18 | $35

South Miami | 7310 S. Red Rd. (bet. 73rd & 74th Sts.) | 305-665-3322 | www.cafepastis.com

"Oh, the amazing meals that come from the tiny kitchen" of this "small but precious jewel of Provençal delight" whose "real French bistro fare" "provides a little escape to Europe", though you're actually in a "nondescript South Miami strip mall"; "it's worth the wait", even if a few detractors say *non* to the "noisy, elbow-to-elbow" seating and "brusque", even "surly" service.

Café Ragazzi ● Italian
23 | 18 | 21 | $42

Surfside | 9500 Harding Ave. (95th St.) | 305-866-4495

If you want to be "treated like family" and eat "food that feels like it came straight from Italy", this "upscale neighborhood" spot in off the eatin' path Surfside is a "perennial local favorite"; expect "long waits" (eased somewhat by free wine) to get into a room that, even "with expansion", remains "overwhelmingly crowded" and "loud"; but to the faithful "that says 'life – enjoy it while it lasts.'"

Caffe Vialetto Italian
26 | 20 | 24 | $49

Coral Gables | 4019 Le Jeune Rd. (bet. El Prado Blvd. & Malaga Ave.) | 305-446-5659

"A small restaurant, but a big restaurant taste and experience" gush groupies of this "simple storefront" in Coral Gables, where the Latin- and Caribbean-tinged Italian cuisine is both "excellent and consistent" and the staff "treats you like family"; the "jammed", "noisy" dining room is strictly small-time, though, as is the no-weekend-reservations policy, even if you do get "complimentary glasses of wine while you wait."

Capital Grille Steak
26 | 25 | 25 | $63

Brickell Area | 444 Brickell Ave. (SE 5th St.) | 305-374-4500 | www.thecapitalgrille.com

"Dealmakers" and Florida's "who's who" bring their appetites and expense accounts to this "mighty mecca of meat" where the "melt-in-your-mouth" steaks (including a "to-die-for" Kona-crusted sirloin), "clubby atmosphere" and service that is "beyond reproach" make it "ideal for business lunches or making good impressions"; "you may have to sell your first-born" to afford it, but converts claim "local steakhouses simply can't compete" with this chain link.

Casa Tua Italian
24 | 26 | 22 | $81

South Beach | Casa Tua | 1700 James Ave. (17th St.) | Miami Beach | 305-673-1010 | www.casatualifestyle.com

"Cozy" and "discreet", this SoBe Northern Italian charms converts with "wonderful" fare, "service so attentive you may have to ask for some privacy" and most of all, "romantic" ambiance – like "eating at your sophisticated lover's summer home in Tuscany"; as "gorgeous as can be, it's a bit ridiculous when it comes to price and attitude" ("do you have to be a star to be in this show?"), but most are mellowed by a most "memorable" meal here.

	FOOD	DECOR	SERVICE	COST

☑ Cheesecake Factory ● *American*   20 | 19 | 19 | $28

Aventura | Aventura Mall | 19501 Biscayne Blvd. (NE 195th St.) |
305-792-9696
Coconut Grove | CocoWalk | 3015 Grand Ave. (Main Hwy.) |
305-447-9898
Kendall | Dadeland Mall | 7497 N. Kendall Dr. (88th St.) | 305-665-5400
www.thecheesecakefactory.com

"It's a chain but a great one" is the verdict of a veritable factory of fans
who delight in this American's "phonebook-like", region-ranging
menu offering "huge portions" of "something for everyone, from tacos
to tuna", plus "reliable" service and "incredibly good prices"; it's "always crowded" – but "always a crowd-pleaser" – so "be prepared for
roaring noise levels" and to "wait for hours for a table."

Chef Allen's *New World*   26 | 22 | 25 | $67

Aventura | 19088 NE 29th Ave. (bet. NE 191st St. & 28th Ave.) |
305-935-2900 | www.chefallens.com

Shining for over 20 years, "chef-owner Allen Susser is one of the
brightest stars on the Southern Florida culinary scene" say fans of this
"foodie paradise" that, despite its location in an Aventura strip mall,
delivers "consistently superb" if "expensive" New World cuisine
served by an "attentive, caring staff"; though a few feel the decor
"could do with modernization" and sense "a sameness in every
course", it definitely "remains a dependable high-end option."

Escopazzo ● *Italian*   26 | 19 | 23 | $60

South Beach | 1311 Washington Ave. (bet. 13th & 14th Sts.) | Miami Beach |
305-674-9450 | www.escopazzo.com

"Real culinary genius" hides behind this "simple storefront" on South
Beach, delivering "creative but classically inspired" Italian eats, an
"exemplary" roster of wines and "conscientious service"; the "romantic"
dining room contrasts with the decidedly "un-romantic street", but the
"high-test clientele" doesn't mind that, nor the "incredibly expensive"
tabs for a meal that "makes you feel like you're in the owners' home."

Francesco ☒ *S American*   26 | 16 | 23 | $50

Coral Gables | 325 Alcazar Ave. (bet. Salzedo St. & SW 42nd Ave.) |
305-446-1600 | www.francescorestaurant.com

"The best Peruvian north of Lima" say surveyors about this "quaint"
Coral Gables eatery specializing in seafood that is "absolutely fresh
and cooked perfectly" ("be sure to order the ceviche" too), brought by
"cordial" servers; and even if the decor's "nondescript" and the quarters "cramped", most deem it a "good value", given the "unique" fare
and "unusual South American wines."

Graziano's Restaurant *Argentinean/Steak*   24 | 19 | 21 | $48

Coral Gables | 394 Giralda Ave. (S. Le Jeune Rd.) | 305-774-3599
Westchester | 9227 SW 40th St./Bird Rd. (92nd Ave.) | 305-225-0008

You don't have to expire to ascend to "carnivore's heaven" – just go to
these "great Argentine *parrillas*" (grills) in Westchester and the Gables,
where "delectable steaks and chops" "of all kinds" meet a "fantastic",
"well-priced" roster of South American wines in a room "as romanti-
cally lit as any Buenos Aires hideaway"; "amiable" service plus "hefty"
portions equal "good value", though "vegetarians beware" – you can
see the meats roasting on the indoor pit.

	FOOD	DECOR	SERVICE	COST

Hiro's Yakko San ● *Japanese* — 26 | 12 | 20 | $28

North Miami Beach | 17040-46 W. Dixie Hwy. (bet. 170th & 171st Sts.) | 305-947-0064

"A treasure hidden" in North Miami Beach, this "authentic Japanese" dishes up "superlative", mostly cooked fare, including "innovative tapas" that pique the palates of "adventurous" diners who "like trying new and exotic foods"; it may be a "hole-in-the-wall" with "not-wonderful decor", but the "polite" staff, "great selection of sakes" and 3 AM closing time lead fish-o-philes to bubble "this is the real deal."

Ⓩ Joe's Stone Crab Ⓜ *Seafood* — 26 | 19 | 23 | $63

South Beach | 11 Washington Ave. (S. Pointe Dr.) | Miami Beach | 305-673-0365 | www.joesstonecrab.com

"Who doesn't love Joe's?" – no one, apparently, since this "South Beach classic", "a shrine to the stone crab", is voted Miami's Most Popular; the claws are simply "awesome", as are the "heavenly hash browns", and do "leave room for the best Key lime pie"; expect "excruciating" waits to get into the "cafeteria"-like dining room and, once inside, "astronomical" prices and "rushed" if "reponsive" service; even so, "you have to go once (then order takeout after that)."

Little Saigon ●♥ *Vietnamese* — ▽ 22 | 7 | 16 | $15

North Miami Beach | 16752 N. Miami Ave. (bet. NE 163rd & 164th Sts.) | 305-653-3377

"Good tasty eats" that "fill you up for little $$$", plus "fast", "friendly" service ("after two visits you'll be treated as a regular") make this "authentic", "hole-in-the-wall" North Miami Beach Vietnamese a "real find"; "don't forget to take cash" (no credit cards accepted).

Matsuri Ⓜ *Japanese* — 26 | 11 | 20 | $31

South Miami | 5759 Bird Rd. (Red Rd.) | 305-663-1615

"Visiting Japanese businessmen", "celebs in-the-know" and "some of the top sushi chefs in town" all flock to an "inauspicious" South Miami strip mall to scarf down "the best and freshest sushi and sashimi in South Florida"; "religiously faithful" fans also savor the "surprisingly low prices"; P.S. "desperately needed" decor renovations were underway post-Survey.

Michael's Genuine Food & Drink *American* — 25 | 21 | 23 | $47

Design District | Atlas Plaza | 130 NE 40th St. (bet. 1st & 2nd Aves.) | 305-573-5550 | www.michaelsgenuine.com

It's a "fantastic addition" to the "trendy Design District" say fans of longtime local chef Michael Schwartz's "simple New American bistro" with "freshly made, often organic food" ("dishes from the large [wood-burning] oven are especially good") and a "neighborly, comfortable vibe" amid the "dark espresso furnishings" and boxy red lights; throw in "super-friendly, unpretentious" service and you have a genuine "godsend."

Ⓩ Michy's Ⓜ *American/French* — 28 | 19 | 25 | $59

Upper East Side | 6927 Biscayne Blvd. (bet. NE 69th & 70th Sts.) | 305-759-2001

Chef "Michelle Bernstein stars" at this "cozy, intimate" Upper Eastsider where a "sophisticated menu for real foodies" – voted No. 1 in Miami – lists a variety of tapas-style, New American–French dishes that "blend Latin, Southern, comfort food and just plain delicious flavors"; "warm, friendly" service is another plus, and though the "dodgy" neighborhood and "quirky" orange/blue decor "leave something to be desired", this place "would proudly hold its own with the best in New York."

Nobu Miami Beach ◑ *Japanese/Peruvian*   27 | 23 | 22 | $79
South Beach | Shore Club | 1901 Collins Ave. (20th St.) | Miami Beach | 305-695-3232 | www.noburestaurants.com

"It's noisy, it's expensive, it's young, it's fabulous" – it's the "swanky" SoBe outpost of Nobu Matsuhisa's empire, with "the same incredible", "addictive" Japanese-Peruvian fare that features the "freshest, best-prepared sushi on the planet"; some say the staff, while "knowlegeable", is "more interested in being seen than in serving", and you better "be there exactly when it opens to avoid killer waits" (reservations for parties of six or more only), but most hail this "shining star" (indeed, "stay long enough and you may see a star").

North One 10 *American*   25 | 19 | 24 | $52
Biscayne Shores | 11052 Biscayne Blvd. (110th St.) | 305-893-4211 | www.northone10.com

"High-end food without the high-end attitude" means "it's a joy to be a diner" at this Biscayne Shores outpost of New American cookery where "hands-on" chef Dewey LoSasso dishes "delectable twists on traditional standbys", handled by "respectful service"; true, the "dated" decor is a minus, and it's "gotten pricier as time's gone on", but it's still a "great place for special occasions."

Oceanaire Seafood Room *Seafood*   26 | 25 | 24 | $66
Downtown | Mary Brickell Vill. | 900 S. Miami Ave. (10th St.) | 305-372-8862 | www.theoceanaire.com

This new, "elegant" fish house – "part of a chain but it doesn't feel chain-y" – blows a "welcome breath of fresh air into Downtown", dishing up an "amazing variety of seafood" "served steakhouse-style" (e.g. separately priced sides) in a dining room "that looks like a cruise ship"; to be sure, it's "pricey" and the "friendly staff is maybe too friendly", but the "super-sized portions" and super-"fresh" fare make those of the piscine persuasion want to "go back again and again."

Off the Grille Bistro *Caribbean*   ▽ 26 | 15 | 19 | $14
Kendall | 12578 SW 88th St. (bet. SW 125th & 127th Aves.) | 305-274-2300 | www.offthegrille.com

It may be "nothing to look at" from the outside, but inside, this industrial-"chic" Caribbean "hole-in-the-wall" in a Kendall shopping center is the source for "sizable portions" of "tasty", "healthy food" at "extremely reasonable prices"; the "only drawback is the wait, but it's definitely worth it", so stay loose, mon, and remember to "bring your own wine."

OLA *Nuevo Latino*   24 | 21 | 22 | $58
(fka OLA on Ocean)
South Beach | Sanctuary Hotel | 1745 James Ave. (bet. 17th & 18th Sts.) | Miami Beach | 305-695-9125 | www.olamiami.com

Chef "Doug Rodriguez is a genius" and his "exotic" Nuevo Latino "cuisine never fails to surprise and entice the taste buds", especially the "unmatched ceviche"; now situated in SoBe's "small, seductive"

Sanctuary Hotel, it's a "loud and bustling" place, but the "knowledge-able staff keeps pace"; tapas-style "small portions" encourage you to "try a little of everything."

Ortanique on the Mile _Caribbean/New World_   25 | 22 | 23 | $54

Coral Gables | 278 Miracle Mile (Salzedo St.) | 305-446-7710 | www.cindyhutsoncuisine.com

"Outstanding seafood" and "the best mojitos in Miami" are just two of the charms of this "chic" Coral Gables champion of Caribbean-New World cuisine, where the service remains "remarkable" from "decadent mains" through "fantastic desserts"; it may be "expensive as hell", with tables that are "too close for comfort" in a "loud" room, but that doesn't keep the place from always being "packed by 8:30, mostly with locals."

Osteria del Teatro ⑤ _Italian_   26 | 16 | 24 | $59

South Beach | 1443 Washington Ave. (Española Way) | Miami Beach | 305-538-7850

"There's no need to read the menu" at this "little bit of Italy in South Beach", but "you may want to take notes on the many specials" of "oh-so-simple, but oh-so-good" Northern Italian fare or risk "being over-whelmed with choices"; hungry throngs can overwhelm the "cramped" dining room, but servers who "anticipate your every need" help allevi-ate the pain of "paying dearly" for "food that reigns supreme."

☑ Palme d'Or ⑤Ⓜ _French_   27 | 26 | 26 | $73

Coral Gables | Biltmore Hotel | 1200 Anastasia Ave. (Granada Blvd.) | 305-445-1926 | www.biltmorehotel.com

Francophiles fawn life "doesn't get better" than at this "luxurious", "sophisticated" "Biltmore Hotel restaurant", a contemporary corner of the famed "shrine to turn-of-the-century Mediterranean architec-ture"; chef Philippe Ruiz's menu of New French small plates "brings new meaning to the word flavor", the wine list is "excellent" and the "formal, intelligent and well-trained personnel" are rated No. 1 in Miami; the experience "doesn't come cheaply", but you'll "leave with a sense of well-being."

Pascal's on Ponce ⑤ _French_   27 | 18 | 24 | $56

Coral Gables | 2611 Ponce de Leon Blvd. (bet. Almeria & Valencia Aves.) | 305-444-2024 | www.pascalmiami.com

Staffers "treat you like VIPs" while the kitchen turns out "artistic", "classically inspired New French fare" at this "high-end bistro" run by "incredibly creative" chef Pascal Oudin; "c'est magnifique!" crows a contented Coral Gables crowd, whose "only gripe is that tables are oh-so-Parisian close."

☑ Prime One Twelve ❶ _Seafood/Steak_   27 | 23 | 23 | $83

South Beach | 112 Ocean Dr. (1st St.) | Miami Beach | 305-532-8112 | www.prime112.com

"The hottest restaurant south of the Mason-Dixon line" caters to ce-lebrities from the "NBA to fashion to Hollywood, and everywhere in between" with "gargantuan" portions of "perfect seafood" and steaks that are "a religious experience"; "even with reservations, waits can be horrible" for a seat in the "crowded", "deafening" dining room, service swings from "surprisingly quick" to "standoffish" and critics crack it should be called "Crime One Twelve", given the "exceptionally expensive" tabs; nevertheless, this is "the ultimate SoBe" scene.

Quinn's Restaurant *Seafood* 26 | 23 | 24 | $56

South Beach | Park Central Hotel | 640 Ocean Dr. (bet. 6th & 7th Sts.) | Miami Beach | 305-673-6400 | www.quinnsmiami.com

To "enjoy the alfresco atmosphere without all the crowds" on Ocean Drive – and get in some "great people-watching" as well – "request a seat on the patio" of chef-owner Gerry Quinn's "pretty" seafooder, home of "the highly touted bam bam shrimp"; advocates aver "everything about this place says 'winner'", from the "upbeat service" to the nightly guitarist.

☑ Romeo's Cafe ⊠Ⓜ *Italian* 27 | 18 | 26 | $77

Coral Way | 2257 SW 22nd St. (bet. 22nd & 23rd Aves.) | 305-859-2228 | www.romeoscafe.com

For a "unique, romantic experience", get thee to this "jewel box" of a Northern Italian in Coral Way, where "there is no printed menu"; instead, namesake toque Romeo Majano "will visit your table to discern your likes and dislikes", then create an "incredible" multicourse meal; it's "like having your own personal chef", as well as your own "wonderful" staff for a "rich", elaborate and "expensive" evening – one that has "discerning diners" declaring "bravo Romeo!"

SushiSamba dromo ● *Japanese/S American* 22 | 21 | 18 | $49

South Beach | 600 Lincoln Rd. (Pennsylvania Ave.) | Miami Beach | 305-673-5337 | www.sushisamba.com

Swooning surveyors ask "did I just have an orgasm?" from the "awesome Japanese-Peruvian-Brazilian fare" – or was it the "spectacular scene" at this "vibrant" SoBe fusionista that swarms with models, hipsters "and those in search of the beautiful people" as they consume "crazy sushi and sashimi" and "strong drinks"; critics complain "quality doesn't meet the price" here, but everyone else is too busy having "fun, fun, fun" to notice.

Table 8 *Californian* 22 | 23 | 22 | $69

South Beach | South Beach Regent | 1458 Ocean Dr. (Ocean Ct.) | Miami Beach | 305-672-4554 | www.table8restaurants.com

"LA transplant" chef Govind Armstrong brings "a bit of California to our own backyard" with this novice that dishes "simple, delicious cuisine inspired by local ingredients" in a "mod", "loungey" space with a "hip bar" "looking up into the pool above" and "everyone-is-someone" crowd; some find the "menu limited", but savvy souls pre-order the salt-crusted porterhouse, urging "try it, you'll like it – though, as with many of the trendy SoBe offerings, your wallet might not."

Talula Ⓜ *American* 24 | 20 | 22 | $59

South Beach | 210 23rd St. (bet. Collins Ave. & Dade Blvd.) | Miami Beach | 305-672-0778 | www.talulaonline.com

Husband-and-wife chef-owners Frank Randazzo and Andrea Curto-Randazzo have created "home sweet home for true foodies" in an "intimate" space with a "romantic" "small courtyard" and "awesome" New American cuisine "in a distant corner of South Beach"; to naysayers, it's "nothing special" but fans insist "if it weren't so off the beaten path, it would be jammed nightly."

	FOOD	DECOR	SERVICE	COST

Tamarind ☒ *Thai*
| | 24 | 17 | 22 | $32 |

Miami Beach | 946 Normandy Dr. (71st St.) | 305-861-6222 | www.tamarindthai.us

"A great casual find" with "courteous service" and "none of the pretensions you find on SoBe", this "hidden Miami Beach gem" is "popular with neighbors", whose palates are pleased by its "reasonable", "delicious Thai favorites"; other senses are soothed by an art-filled dining room "quiet enough to actually have a conversation with your dining partner."

Timo *Italian/Mediterranean*
| | 25 | 21 | 23 | $46 |

Sunny Isles Beach | 17624 Collins Ave. (bet. 175th Terr. & 178th St.) | 305-936-1008 | www.timorestaurant.com

"Populated with locals who know a good thing when they see it", chef/co-owner Tim Andriola's Sunny Isles Beach venue is "one of the best-kept secrets in town", where the "inspired" Italian-Med cuisine "just gets better and better" and the "bistro ambiance" has "good energy" "despite the strip-mall surroundings"; bartenders who are "great fun" make the lounge a "perfect place to eat if you are alone."

Tropical Chinese *Chinese*
| | 26 | 16 | 20 | $32 |

Westchester | Tropical Park Plaza | 7991 SW 40th St./Bird Rd. (SW 79th Ave.) | 305-262-7576

The "nonstop gastronomic parade" of "incredible, inexpensive dim sum" is the "real attraction" of this "gourmet" Chinese where the "gruff" but "competent" waiters, "glassed-in kitchen" and "lazy Susans on large tables" make you "feel like you're in Hong Kong", even though you're really in an "out-of-the-way" Westchester strip mall; P.S. at night, "you must get the Peking duck – more than a dish, it's an art form."

Versailles ● *Cuban*
| | 21 | 13 | 17 | $24 |

Little Havana | 3555 SW Eighth St. (SW 35th Ave.) | 305-444-0240

"The ultimate Cuban restaurant, period" proclaim patrons of this "institution for the exile community", "a must" for anyone desiring an "authentic taste of Calle Ocho" (Eighth Street to you gringos) – which includes everyone from "Latin recording stars" to U.S. presidents; though the "cheesy mirrored interior" and "glorified diner" service get dings, the "late hours" and "large portions at reasonable prices" testify "if you want to know what Havana is like, go to Versailles."

Wish *American*
| | 24 | 25 | 22 | $67 |

South Beach | The Hotel | 801 Collins Ave. (8th St.) | Miami Beach | 305-674-9474 | www.wishrestaurant.com

"Fabulous outdoor dining under the stars" in a "lush", "romantic" garden brings a "hip crowd" to this "perfect combination of SoBe style and culinary invention"; chef Michael Bloise's "inspired", "exciting" Asian-influenced New American fare make foodies' "dreams come true", while "astute service" ensures that their "wishes are fulfilled"; P.S. "do not miss" a drink at the "cool" rooftop Spire Bar, with its panoramic view of the ocean and Miami skyline.

Milwaukee

TOP FOOD RANKING

	Restaurant	Cuisine
29	Sanford	American
26	Eddie Martini's	Steak
	Five O'Clock Steak	Steak
	Immigrant Room	American
	Bacchus	American
25	River Lane Inn	Seafood
	Coquette Cafe	French
	Riversite, The	American
	Osteria del Mondo	Italian
	Sake Tumi	Asian

OTHER NOTEWORTHY PLACES

Dream Dance	American
Elliot's Bistro	French
Jake's Fine Dining	Steak
Lake Park Bistro	French
Maggiano's	Italian
P.F. Chang's	Chinese
Potbelly Sandwich	Sandwiches
Ristorante Bartolotta	Italian
Roots	Californian
Singha Thai	Thai

ⓩ Bacchus *American*   26 | 26 | 26 | $56

Downtown | Cudahy Towers | 925 E. Wells St. (Prospect Ave.) |
414-765-1166 | www.bacchusmke.com

"Milwaukee arrives" courtesy of this "snazzy" Downtown "in-a-class-
by-itself" "jewel" that's "definitely a place to indulge" your taste for
New American cuisine (it "doesn't get much better" than this) served
within a "posh" setting; even admirers, though, assert that the "over-
attentive staff just needs to relax a bit"; P.S. lunch is served in the sun-
drenched, glass-enclosed conservatory.

Coquette Cafe Ⓢ *French*   25 | 21 | 23 | $36

Third Ward | 316 N. Milwaukee St. (St. Paul Ave.) | 414-291-2655 |
www.coquettecafe.com

"Is this France?" local Europhiles ask about this "lively" "little bit of
Paris" in the "newly hippified" Third Ward, "friendly and creative chef"
Sanford 'Sandy' D'Amato's source for "hearty", "innovative" French
cuisine "at affordable prices"; the "cozy", "casually elegant" atmosphere is "great for a pre-show meal" at one of the nearby theaters.

Dream Dance ⓈⓂ *American*   25 | 23 | 25 | $59

Downtown | Potawatomi Bingo Casino | 1721 W. Canal St. (16th St.) |
414-847-7883 | www.paysbig.com

They "treat you like royalty" at this "calming, romantic" Downtown
"refuge" attached to the Potawatomi Bingo Casino; factor in the "amaz-

ing combinations" on chef Jason Gorman's New American menu and "retail-priced wines", and you get a "foodie's heavenly experience, not merely a dream."

☑ Eddie Martini's *Steak* | 26 | 24 | 26 | $54

West Side | 8612 Watertown Plank Rd. (86th St.) | 414-771-6680 | www.eddiemartinis.com

"It's back to the '50s at this "real gem" of a West Side steakhouse "institution", a classic for "incredible" steaks ("my mouth is watering just thinking about them") and "unbelievable" martinis that's "popular with doctors" from the nearby medical complex and other "Milwaukee bigwigs"; its "sophisticated" "old supper club-like" interior has some convinced that "Frank and Dean are still with us", but remember that the "big drinks" are matched by "big tabs", so "bring extra cash."

Elliot's Bistro ● Ⓜ *French* | 20 | 18 | 20 | $37

East Side | 2321 N. Murray Ave. (North Ave.) | 414-273-1488 | www.elliotsbistro.com

"For the French bistro experience in Milwaukee", this "delightful" East Side "favorite" is "a definite must-do" "complete with an authentic [Gallic] chef", Pierre Briere, whose "traditional" cooking – from cassoulet to boeuf bourguignon – "rivals that of many Paris bistros"; P.S. "great for a dinner date or meeting old friends."

☑ Five O'Clock Steakhouse Ⓢ Ⓜ *Steak* | 26 | 12 | 22 | $46
(fka Coerper's 5 O'Clock Club)

Central City | 2416 W. State St. (24th St.) | 414-342-3553 | www.fiveoclocksteakhouse.com

Clock-watchers "can't stop eating once [they] start" tucking into the "enormous portions" of "to-die-for" steaks at this Central City standby; its "kitsch", "time-warp-into-the-'50s" decor "will bring back memories of the classic steakhouse experience of days gone by", and "the servers will make you feel like you're visiting an older relative's house" – though some "don't like" the "required stop at the bar", where you "order a drink and dinner before getting to your table."

☑ Immigrant Room & Winery, The Ⓢ Ⓜ *American* | 26 | 26 | 26 | $64

Kohler | American Club | 419 Highland Dr. (School St.) | 920-457-8888 | www.destinationkohler.com

For "a fine-dining experience of the highest caliber", "gourmets" go to this "wonderful" "Wisconsin treasure" in Kohler's American Club resort, one of the "finest hotels in the Midwest", where the "elegant" New American fare comes with a "nice wine list" and "doting service" ("at these prices, it should be") "now *this* is a place for romance and privacy" say fans of its six different dining rooms, which "take you back to the old days"; P.S. if the tab's too high, remember that "the prices on bottles and cheese in The Winery [next door] are extremely fair."

Jake's Fine Dining Ⓢ *Steak* | ▽ 25 | 20 | 22 | $39

Brookfield | 21445 W. Gumina Rd. (Capital Dr.) | 262-781-7995 | www.jakes-restaurant.com

"You only have to go once" to this "nostalgic" Brookfield steakhouse – an "established presence on the West Side" since 1967 – "to feel like a regular" thanks to its "wonderful presentation" of "awesome" "comfort food" (filet mignon and signature onion rings) and "comfortable service"; "ask for a seat by" the "huge fireplace" ("a great place on a winter day") or belly up to the bar and "enjoy some fine brandy."

☑ Lake Park Bistro *French* | 25 | 27 | 25 | $50 |

East Side | Lake Park Pavilion | 3133 E. Newberry Blvd. (N. Lake Dr.) | 414-962-6300 | www.lakeparkbistro.com

"It's wonderful to sit by the windows" and revel in the "exquisite" Lake Michigan view (especially "heavenly" at sunset) at this "treat" located in Frederick Law Olmsted–designed Lake Park, where "lots of new twists on old classics" make the "ooh-la-la fabulous French cuisine" "worth every decadent calorie"; factor in a "romantic atmosphere" and staffers who "pay attention to all the details" and it adds up to a "great place for a special occasion" or "the perfect date."

☑ Maggiano's Little Italy *Italian* | 20 | 19 | 20 | $31 |

Wauwatosa | Mayfair Mall | 2500 N. Mayfair Rd. (North Ave.) | 414-978-1000 | www.maggianos.com

Regulars "rely" on this "red-sauce" chain (Milwaukee's Most Popular) for its "affordable", "hearty" "standards" served "family-style" in a "boisterous" "retro" atmosphere where "everyone always seems to be having a great time"; but some dissenters who knock what they call a "faux" vibe and "obscenely large portions" of "blah", "cookie-cutter" cuisine say it's better to "bring the kids [than] the Italian food lovers."

Osteria del Mondo ⑤ *Italian* | 25 | 22 | 22 | $48 |

Downtown | 1028 E. Juneau Ave. (Astor St.) | 414-291-3770 | www.osteria.com

"Remaining solidly [near] the top of the ladder in Milwaukee", this Downtown Northern Italian delivers "outstanding meals" courtesy of chef/co-owner Marc Bianchini, who "never ceases to amaze" with "elegant fare" that's "inventive" "without being strange"; combined with "wonderful service" and a "comfortable setting" (including "a great patio"), it amounts to a "fine-dining" experience that's "not to be missed"; N.B. a separate cigar lounge and valet parking are available.

☑ P.F. Chang's China Bistro *Chinese* | 20 | 20 | 19 | $28 |

Wauwatosa | Mayfair Mall | 2500 N. Mayfair Rd. (North Ave.) | 414-607-1029 | www.pfchangs.com

Flatterers of this "friendly" Wauwatosa eatery favor its "nontraditional", "varied" Mandarin-style munchables made from "fresh", "identifiable ingredients", plus its "excellent cocktails" and Great Wall of Chocolate dessert ("as big as" the real thing) offered in "upscale-casual" confines with "tasteful decor"; but while adherents assert they "look for" outposts of the "consistent chain" "in every city", foes find the feel "formulaic" and the fare "faux Chinese", saying it's "not for purists."

☑ Potbelly Sandwich Works *Sandwiches* | 20 | 15 | 18 | $9 |

Downtown | 135 W. Wisconsin Ave. (Plankinton Ave.) | 414-226-0014
Brookfield | 17800 W. Bluemound Rd. (bet. Brookfield & Calhoun Rds.) | 262-796-9845
www.potbelly.com

"There's a reason the lines are out the door" at this beloved duo of "fast-food" "favorites" "at the top of their game" with "tasty, toasty sandwiches" that "satisfy" "addicts" from "vegetarians to the biggest carnivore"; though some "first-time"-ers complain of a "confusing ordering system", most insist the "unbelievably speedy" counter staff has it "down to a science", ensuring "you'll never waste a lot of time getting your food."

Ristorante Bartolotta *Italian* | 25 | 22 | 23 | $46 |
Wauwatosa | 7616 W. State St. (Harwood Ave.) | 414-771-7910 | www.bartolottaristorante.com

"You'll think you're in a big city" when visiting the "wonderful" 'Tosa Italian – "a total star of a restaurant", featuring executive chef Juan Urbieta's "varied menu" of "incredible" cuisine ("the risotto is positively orgasmic!"), "excellent service" and "lovely", "cozy atmosphere"; P.S. "reservations are a must", though some suggest the small venue always seems "to be overbooked."

River Lane Inn ⊠ *Seafood* | 25 | 18 | 24 | $37 |
North Shore | 4313 W. River Ln. (Brown Deer Rd.) | 414-354-1995

"From [Wednesday] lobster night to the always-changing fish specials on the chalkboard", this "longtime favorite" (sibling to Mequon's Riversite) set in a turn-of-the-century building in an "off-the-beaten-path" North Shore location "still delivers" "consistently great" seafood ferried by "friendly servers" in a "low-key" setting – no wonder it continues to "attract a crowd" ("regulars love it").

Riversite, The ⊠ *American* | 25 | 23 | 26 | $46 |
Mequon | 11120 N. Cedarburg Rd. (Mequon Rd.) | 262-242-6050

"The always reliable, elegant sister to the River Lane Inn" on the North Shore, this "very popular" place in Mequon keeps dinner "creative" thanks to "artist"-chef Tom Peschong, whose Traditional American specialties are "superb"; "fabulous warm service" from a "stellar staff" that's "knowledgeable about" the "unbeatable wine list" and a "glorious setting" affording a "great view of the Milwaukee River" also make it "worth the drive."

Roots Restaurant & Cellar *Californian* | 25 | 23 | 21 | $37 |
Brewers Hill | 1818 N. Hubbard St. (Vine St.) | 414-374-8480 | www.rootsmilwaukee.com

A "class act all the way", this "wonderful place" on Brewers Hill "puts together delicious creations" of Californian "comfort food" (using some "organically grown local produce" from co-owner Joe Schmidt's 67-acre Cedarburg farm) in "surprisingly inventive combinations that really work"; "perched above the city", its bi-level location also offers "drop-dead views" of Downtown Milwaukee, so "whether upstairs or down" expect an "always-enjoyable" experience; N.B. the Cellar offers a less-formal menu.

Sake Tumi ⊠ *Asian* | 25 | 24 | 23 | $34 |
Downtown | 714 N. Milwaukee St. (bet. Mason St. & Wisconsin Ave.) | 414-224-7253 | www.sake-milwaukee.com

"Don't let the corny", *Laugh-In*-style name "fool you into thinking this isn't a high-quality experience" advise addicts "hooked" on this "amazing" Asian, an "absolute must" Downtown whose "ambitious and well-executed menu has something for everyone" – from "trendy" fusion dishes to traditional Japanese and Korean BBQ fare; also, the "lively dining room" and "fun", "swanky" upstairs Buddha Lounge are "where the beautiful people go to eat sushi" and revel in a "cool vibe."

☑ Sanford ☒ American   29 | 26 | 28 | $66

East Side | 1547 N. Jackson St. (Pleasant St.) | 414-276-9608 | www.sanfordrestaurant.com

"Words can't describe" the "world-class" experience at this "hits-on-all-cylinders" East Side New American "gem" that's definitely "in a league by itself" (as evidenced by the fact that it's ranked No. 1 for both Food and Service in Wisconsin); eponymous toque-owner Sandy D'Amato gets "all the details right" – from the "sophisticated" "gourmet" fare, to the "unbeatable" service provided by "friendly caring staffers" who can "feel your table's mood", to the "intimate", "ultra-modern" dining room; P.S. "try the chef's 'Surprise'", an "especially fabulous seven-course" tasting menu.

Singha Thai _Thai_   24 | 13 | 18 | $19

West Side | 2237 S. 108th St. (Lincoln Ave.) | 414-541-1234
Singha Thai II _Thai_
Downtown | 780 N. Jefferson St. | 414-226-0288
www.singhathairestaurant.com

"Delicious food" at a "good value" makes for a "great Thai" experience at this West Side "favorite" "hidden in a strip mall"; to be sure, the "uninspired", "no-ambiance" decor keeps some diners away, but folks who flip for the "authentic" fare ("their pad Thai is a favorite") insist the "picturesque" cuisine more than compensates; N.B. the Downtown branch opened post-Survey.

Minneapolis/St. Paul

TOP FOOD RANKING

	Restaurant	Cuisine
28	La Belle Vie	French/Mediterranean
	112 Eatery	Eclectic
	Alma	American
	Bayport Cookery	American
27	Lucia's	American
	Vincent	French
	D'Amico Cucina	Italian
26	Fugaise	French
	Manny's	Steak
	Heartland	American

OTHER NOTEWORTHY PLACES

B.A.N.K.	American
Chambers Kitchen	Asian Fusion
Cosmos	Eclectic
Cue	American
Dakota Jazz	American
Oceanaire	Seafood
Solera	Spanish
St. Paul Grill	American
Town Talk	American
20.21	American

Z Alma *American* ⸻ 28 | 21 | 25 | $48

Dinkytown | 528 University Ave. SE (bet. 5th & 6th Aves.) | Minneapolis |
612-379-4909 | www.restaurantalma.com
"Food to move your soul (*alma*)" is the forte of this Dinkytown "neighborhood" New American whose dishes show "skill and balance" and
are fashioned from local, organic items, all served within an "intimate"
room whose "design reflects the restaurant's heartland roots"; true,
the menu is a bit "limited" (i.e. short), but the place is long on the
"price/quality ratio."

B.A.N.K. *American* ⸻ 21 | 28 | 21 | $46

Downtown | Historic Westin Hotel | 88 S. Sixth St. | Minneapolis |
612-656-3255 | www.bankmpls.com
All eyes are on the "drop-dead-gorgeous" looks of this "art deco"
Westin Hotel "masterpiece" crafted out of the infrastructure of a
former bank in the city's Downtown area; aside from disagreement on
the New American cuisine ("well done" vs. "ok"), folks agree the
"cocktail-friendly" bar and lounge are nice dividends.

Z Bayport Cookery M *American* ⸻ 28 | 23 | 25 | $60

Bayport | 328 Fifth Ave. N. (Rte. 95) | 651-430-1066 |
www.bayportcookery.com
Road-trippers recommend this "dreamy" Bayport "perennial" for its
"excellence" on all fronts, whether it's the pricey but "wonderful" New

American cooking, "top-notch" service or "date"-ready setting; it's "worth the gasoline" money, and insiders insist you order the "fantastic" morel dishes when the 'shrooms are in season.

Chambers Kitchen *Asian Fusion*   25 | 25 | 23 | $51

Downtown | Chambers Hotel | 901 Hennepin Ave. (9th St.) | Minneapolis | 612-767-6900 | www.chambersminneapolis.com

Star chef Jean-Georges Vongerichten's "exceptional" menu "works magic" on Minneapolitans at this "pricey" basement-level Asian in Downtown's Chambers Hotel where the food is as much a magnet for the "glitzy" crowds as the "trendy" bar, "ultramodern" David Rockwell design and Damien Hirst artworks ("the best art gallery in town"); if some say service can be "so-so", the overall quality begs the question: "what's not to like?"

Cosmos *Eclectic*   24 | 25 | 23 | $54

Warehouse | Graves 601 Hotel | 601 First Ave. N. (bet. 6th & 7th Sts.) | Minneapolis | 612-677-1100 | www.cosmosrestaurant.com

The "modern" decor is so "cool" it seems cut like an "Italian suit" quip backers of this Warehouse Eclectic set in the trendy Graves 601 Hotel; the digs are embellished by some "gems" on the menu and by "knowledgeable" service, so even "expensive" tabs don't deter the majority from this "best-kept secret."

Cue ⓜ *American*   20 | 26 | 20 | $49

Downtown | Guthrie Theater | 806 Second St. S. (Chicago Ave.) | Minneapolis | 612-225-6499 | www.cueatguthrie.com

Preen to "be seen" at this "pre-show hot" New American inside Downtown's new Guthrie Theater where "the view of the river" "makes it hard to leave to see the plays upstairs"; aside from agreement on the "fabulous" "big, splashy room", surveyors split on the food ("great" for some, "average" for others) and service ("efficient" vs. "slow").

Dakota Jazz Club & Restaurant *American*   21 | 22 | 20 | $40

Downtown | 1010 Nicollet Mall (10th St.) | Minneapolis | 612-332-1010 | www.dakotacooks.com

"Spot-on" food and "world-class jazz" strike a chord with guests of this Downtown American serving "comfort" fare and a "well-edited" drinks list too; the "swanky" site proves "a little dark and noisy (but that's the appeal)", so solace-seekers can always "request a table on the upper level" or seating on the sidewalk.

D'Amico Cucina ⓢ *Italian*   27 | 23 | 25 | $55

Warehouse | Butler Sq. | 100 N. Sixth St. (2nd Ave.) | Minneapolis | 612-338-2401 | www.damico.com

Still "top-notch" and still "a special-occasion" standby, this Warehouse Northern Italian tucked inside a "stylishly rehabbed" building "sets the bar" with "fabulous" food and an "understated", "classy" chandeliered setting; they've got service "down pat" too, so "if you have the money", treat yourself to this "ever-impressive" operation.

Fugaise ⓢ *French*   26 | 22 | 25 | $52

Northeast | 308 E. Hennepin Ave. (University Ave.) | Minneapolis | 612-436-0777 | www.fugaise.com

Behind a "narrow storefront" lies "dazzling" food say proponents of chef-owner Don Saunders' "minimalist" Northeast New French, a "rising star" on the scene; inside, expect "no windows", but just focus on the "phenomenal" quality and "enthusiastic" service.

Heartland ⓜ *American*   26 | 23 | 23 | $47

Groveland | 1806 St. Clair Ave. (Fairview Ave. S.) | St. Paul | 651-699-3536 | www.heartlandrestaurant.com

"Midwestern food will never be laughed at again" after you've sampled the "original" preparations created from "fantastically fresh", locally sourced ingredients at this Groveland American Regional whose cooking keeps "reviving comfort food"; "wonderful" service and the "Arts and Crafts" decor also please, and if it's all a "bit pricey for some", the adjacent wine bar is the answer.

ⓩ La Belle Vie *French/Mediterranean*   28 | 25 | 28 | $71

Loring Park | 510 Groveland Ave. (Hennepin Ave.) | Minneapolis | 612-874-6440 | www.labellevie.us

"Polish", "sophistication", "impeccable" service and "world-class" preparations that are truly "delicious balancing acts" (the "chef could make gruel taste great") are the hallmarks of this refined New French-Med (No. 1 for Food in the Twin Cities); the bill may require a "second mortgage" on your home, but you no doubt will "get what you pay for."

ⓩ Lucia's ⓜ *American*   27 | 21 | 25 | $38

Uptown | 1432 W. 31st St. (Hennepin Ave.) | Minneapolis | 612-825-1572 | www.lucias.com

"Talented" chef-owner Lucia Watson follows in the "Alice Waters tradition" of showcasing "fresh, local and organic" ingredients at her Uptown New American bistro, a 20+-year-old "standard bearer" whose "consistently good" servers deliver "interesting", "wonderful" creations to an "urbane" crowd in "spare" yet "smart" surroundings; P.S. pros propose both the "great" wine bar and bakery, both on-site.

ⓩ Manny's Steakhouse *Steak*   26 | 20 | 26 | $61

Downtown | Hyatt Regency | 1300 Nicollet Mall (Grant St.) | Minneapolis | 612-339-9900 | www.mannyssteakhouse.com

"Red meat" and "big red wines" come together at this quintessentially "clubby" Downtown steakhouse easily earning its rep as a "masculine" kind of eatery but also for its "fabulous" meats ferried by a "pro" staff; yes, "if the martinis don't knock you off your feet, the bill will", but nonetheless, cronies concur "this is the place for my last meal on earth."

ⓩ Oceanaire Seafood Room *Seafood*   26 | 23 | 25 | $55

Downtown | Hyatt Regency | 1300 Nicollet Mall (Grant St.) | Minneapolis | 612-333-2277 | www.theoceanaire.com

"So many delicious" fish dishes net lots of fans at this "upscale", "high-volume" (Most Popular) Downtown chain, a "peerless" performer with a "huge" menu, service that "sets the bar" and a "retro", "1940s-cruise-ship" design; come "on someone else's dime" or for "special occasions", for to "get such good" seafood "in the middle of a continent", you have to "pay a premium."

ⓩ 112 Eatery ◖ *Eclectic*   28 | 22 | 25 | $42

Warehouse | 112 N. Third St. (1st Ave. N.) | Minneapolis | 612-343-7696 | www.112eatery.com

"Eat where all the other chefs eat" and you'll know why they do after sitting down to "stellar" food at this Warehouse District Eclectic, where "taste takes center stage", the service is "excellent" and the atmosphere "immediately puts you at ease"; "fair" prices are the crowning touch at this winner dubbed the city's "toughest table" for good reason.

Solera *Spanish*
23 | 24 | 21 | $41

Downtown | 900 Hennepin Ave. (9th St.) | Minneapolis | 612-338-0062 | www.solera-restaurant.com

Say "hello Dali" when you enter the "surreal", "Gaudí"-esque decor at this "hip" Downtown Spaniard whose clientele feasts on a "cascade" of tapas (all of them "fantastic") while "people-watching"; "if you want to graze, there's no better place", and most maintain the "friendly" service and "fabulous" sherry list round out the appeal.

St. Paul Grill *American*
24 | 24 | 24 | $50

Downtown | St. Paul Hotel | 350 Market St. (5th St.) | St. Paul | 651-224-7455 | www.stpaulgrill.com

The "clubby" atmosphere, "attentive" service and menu of "well-executed" American food (pork chops, chocolate cake and such) sustains this "grand-old dame" Downtown; it's the official "19th hole for St. Paul movers and shakers", and a few note it's even "romantic to the nth degree"; P.S. snag one of the prized tables for a "great" view of Rice Park.

Town Talk Diner Ⓜ *American*
22 | 18 | 21 | $26

South Minneapolis | 2707 E. Lake St. (27th Ave.) | Minneapolis | 612-722-1312 | www.towntalkdiner.com

"Delicious" Americana, new and old, is the strength of this "upscale" yet "retro" South Minneapolis "foodies'" diner populated by "hip" customers feeding the "bustling" atmosphere; it's a "hidden nugget", plus the servers show lots of "hospitality."

20.21 *American*
26 | 24 | 23 | $49

Loring Park | Walker Art Ctr. | 1750 Hennepin Ave. (Vineland Pl.) | Minneapolis | 612-253-3410 | www.wolfgangpuck.com

"True consistency" across the board is what you'll hear from fans of Wolfgang Puck's Walker Art Center eatery, whose Asian-accented New American fare and "spiffy" setting are "hits"; no question, you'll have to deal with some "din", but few care since meals here are "unbeatable"; P.S. the window seats supply "terrific" city views.

☑ Vincent Ⓢ *French*
27 | 23 | 26 | $51

Downtown | 1100 Nicollet Mall (11th St.) | Minneapolis | 612-630-1189 | www.vincentarestaurant.com

"Outstanding" chef Vincent Francoual is "charming" and his food has the same effect on patrons of his Downtown New French bistro where the "impeccable" preparations are accompanied by "exceptional" service and an "excellent" 100-label wine selection; the "handsome", "simple" surroundings please as do all those windows and the "wonderful" views they provide.

New Jersey

TOP FOOD RANKING

Restaurant	Cuisine
29 Nicholas	American
28 DeLorenzo's	Pizza
Chef's Table	French
Cafe Panache	Eclectic
Bay Ave. Trattoria	American/Italian
27 André's	American
Saddle River Inn	American/French
Serenade	French
Whispers	American
Scalini Fedeli	Italian
Latour	French
Lorena's	French
David Drake	American
CulinAriane	American
Cafe Matisse	Eclectic
Blue Bottle	American
Ebbitt Room	American
Chez Catherine	French
26 David Burke	American
Sagami	Japanese

OTHER NOTEWORTHY PLACES

Amanda's	American
Anthony David's	Eclectic/Italian
Bernards Inn	American
Bistro Olé	Portuguese/Spanish
Cheesecake Factory	American
Copeland	American
Cucharamama	S American
Dining Room	American
Due Terre Enoteca	Italian
Fascino	Italian
Frog and the Peach	American
Hotoke	Pan-Asian
Legal Sea Foods	Seafood
Origin	French/Thai
Perryville Inn	American
Pluckemin Inn	American
Rat's	French
restaurant.mc	Eclectic
River Palm	Steak
Zoe's by the Lake	French

	FOOD	DECOR	SERVICE	COST

☑ Amanda's *American* — 26 | 25 | 25 | $45

Hoboken | 908 Washington St. (bet. 9th & 10th Sts.) | 201-798-0101 | www.amandasrestaurant.com

"After all these years", this "serene", "romantic" Hoboken New American in a "beautiful" brownstone still epitomizes "upscale", "classy" dining with its "impeccably" prepared cuisine, "extensive" wine list, "attentive" service and "lovely" decor; an "amazing" brunch and early-bird special – a "steal" at $14 per person – affirm this winning spot's seemingly everlasting appeal.

André's Ⓜ *American* — 27 | 22 | 26 | $53

Newton | 188 Spring St. (bet. Adams & Jefferson Sts.) | 973-300-4192 | www.andresrestaurant.com

This "friendly" BYO "behind a storefront" in Newton is "always a delight" given the "crafty creations" of "talented" chef-owner André de Waal, the man behind the "sublime" New American menu; if the "pricey" tabs prove a bit daunting, budget-conscious fans go for the "moderately" priced bistro menu on Sundays; N.B. wines may be purchased Wednesdays–Sundays at the on-site boutique.

Anthony David's *Eclectic/Italian* — 25 | 19 | 21 | $42

Hoboken | 953 Bloomfield St. (10th St.) | 201-222-8399 | www.anthonydavids.com

"Fantastic" fare emerges from the "tiny" kitchen within chef-owner Anthony Pino's pocket-size Hoboken BYO whose Eclectic–Northern Italian menu (along with "amazing" cheeses) is served in "low-key" quarters; what's more, the widely touted brunch is among the "best" in town; N.B. patrons can dine in the more casual, rustic front room, where prepared foods are sold.

☑ Bay Avenue Trattoria Ⓜ *American/Italian* — 28 | 11 | 21 | $38

Highlands | 122 Bay Ave. (Jackson St.) | 732-872-9800 | www.bayavetrattoria.com

"Back with a bang" are Joe Romanowski and Maggie Lubcke and their "friendly" Highlands BYO, where the "fantastic" American-Italian preparations are a cause for "rejoicing"; true, you "don't have to get dressed up" given the somewhat "lacking" ambiance, but the "top-quality" cooking trumps any decor issues.

Bernards Inn *American* — 26 | 25 | 25 | $65

Bernardsville | 27 Mine Brook Rd. (Quimby Ln.) | 908-766-0002 | www.bernardsinn.com

It's "high class all the way" at this "romantic", expense-account Bernardsville New American that keeps delivering "consistent excellence" from the kitchen of chef Corey Heyer, an "incredible" 750-label wine list and "professional" service; while the "well-groomed" interior is "wonderful" now, admirers expect the newly redecorated space (in the works) to be the icing on the cake; N.B. jacket required.

Bistro Olé *Portuguese/Spanish* — 25 | 18 | 23 | $39

Asbury Park | 230 Main St. (bet. Cookman & Mattison Aves.) | 732-897-0048 | www.bistroole.com

"Why go to Newark?" when you can step into this Asbury Park Iberian and experience "consistently delicious" cooking, not to mention "friendly" service and the "ebullience" of owner Rico Rivera, who showers diners with his well-known hospitality; BYO red wine, and watch how it somehow turns into "tasty" sangrias.

Blue Bottle Café 🅂🅼 *American*　27 | 18 | 22 | $43

Hopewell | 101 E. Broad St. (Elm St.) | 609-333-1710 | www.thebluebottlecafe.com

"Super-talented" husband-and-wife-team Aaron and Rory Philipson (chef and pastry chef, respectively) join forces at this "rural" Hopewell BYO "home run" serving "fantastic" New American cuisine in a "nondescript" building decked out in blue bottles; it's a "great addition" to the area claim correspondents who advise go and "see what all the fuss is about."

Cafe Matisse *Eclectic*　27 | 25 | 26 | $66

Rutherford | 167 Park Ave. (bet. E. Park Pl. & Highland Cross) | 201-935-2995 | www.cafematisse.com

This "artful find" in Rutherford is "as good as it gets" for "outstanding", "beautifully presented" Eclectic cuisine (with early-bird and prix fixe options) from "creative" chef-owner Peter Loria; though "pricey", this "special-occasion" experience comes complete with "superior service" and an "exceptional ambiance" that includes an "elegant dining room" with hand-blown glass chandeliers and "romantic" garden seating; P.S. it's BYO with a "lovely wine shop up front."

🄩 Cafe Panache 🅂 *Eclectic*　28 | 21 | 26 | $55

Ramsey | 130 E. Main St. (Franklin Tpke.) | 201-934-0030 | www.cafepanachenj.com

"From the minute you walk in until you leave", expect a "quality dining experience" at chef-owner Kevin Kohler's "gift to the palate", this "first-rate" "shining star" in Ramsey where an "always wonderful", "always changing" Eclectic menu is served by a "friendly", "knowledgeable" staff in a "charming" if "small" space; it's "expensive", but the BYO policy can "bring costs down"; P.S. be sure to make your reservation "well in advance."

🄩 Cheesecake Factory *American*　19 | 19 | 17 | $28

Hackensack | Riverside Square Mall | 197 Riverside Sq. (Hackensack Ave.) | 201-488-0330 ◑

Wayne | Willowbrook Mall | 1700 Willowbrook Blvd. (Rte. 46) | 973-890-1400

Edison | Menlo Park Mall | 455 Menlo Park Dr. (Rte. 1) | 732-494-7000

Cherry Hill | 931 Haddonfield Rd. (bet. Graham & Severn Aves.) | 856-665-7550

www.thecheesecakefactory.com

"There should be more of these places around" to feed the throngs marvel fans of these "overcrowded" Traditional American chain outlets famed for their "oversized" portions, "majestically" long menus and "dependably" good fare, not to mention "great" cheesecakes (with over 30 varieties); despite "crazy" waits, most leave these "cholesterol factories" "happy and well fed."

🄩 Chef's Table 🅼 *French*　28 | 18 | 25 | $49

Franklin Lakes | Franklin Square Shopping Ctr. | 754 Franklin Ave. (Pulis Ave.) | 201-891-6644

Everything that comes out of the kitchen is "*extraordinaire*" at this "fabulous" Classic French BYO in Franklin Lakes (the bailiwick of "pro" chef Claude Baills), a "little jewel" shoehorned into a "dowdy" strip mall; the setting's warmed by "knowledgeable" service, and regulars advise to just "sit back and let it all enchant you."

Chez Catherine 🗷 🅼 French
27 | 21 | 25 | $64

Westfield | 431 North Ave. (bet. E. Broad & Prospect Sts.) | 908-654-4011 | www.chezcatherine.com

A "top-drawer" experience is to be had at this "pretty" Provençal Westfield bistro where the bill of fare is "delectably" "expert" French cuisine backed by "excellent" wines and "polished" service, all presided over by proprietors Didier and Edith Jouvenet; try to imagine a "slice of France" to effectively shake off any thoughts about "steep prices."

Copeland Restaurant American
25 | 25 | 23 | $58

Morristown | Westin Governor Morris | 2 Whippany Rd. (Lyndsey Dr.) | 973-451-2619 | www.copelandrestaurant.com

For "NY style in NJ", those in-the-know go to this "outstanding" New American tucked inside Morristown's Westin Governor Morris to "marvel" at "talented" chef Thomas Ciszak's "truly distinguished" fare delivered by an "attentive" staff in a "luxurious", "tiered" setting; although it's "pricey", it'll be "the best money you've spent in a while"; P.S. spot cocktail connoisseurs at the "sophisticated" martini bar.

Cucharamama 🅼 S American
26 | 23 | 20 | $43

Hoboken | 233 Clinton St. (3rd St.) | 201-420-1700 | www.cucharamama.com

"Unique", "extraordinary" South American fare, a "beautiful" setting to match and "fantastic" drinks all greet those who visit what fans say is "the best of what Hoboken has to offer", celeb-chef Maricel Presilla's venue situated a block away from its counterpart, Zafra; P.S. insiders tout bar dining, which offers a perfect vantage point to "watch food being prepared in the wood-burning oven."

CulinAriane 🗷 🅼 American
27 | 18 | 22 | $50

Montclair | 33 Walnut St. (Pine St.) | 973-744-0533

It's "foodie heaven" at this modern New American BYO, a "great addition" to Montclair's dining scene thanks to the "stellar", "adventurous" cooking of husband-and-wife-team Michael and Ariane Duarte (pastry chef and executive chef, respectively), both ably backed by a "pleasant" staff; though it's hard to ignore the "tiny size and no waiting area", sidewalk seating almost doubles the capacity.

David Burke Fromagerie 🅼 American
26 | 25 | 24 | $67

Rumson | 26 Ridge Rd. (Ave. of Two Rivers) | 732-842-8088 | www.fromagerierestaurant.com

Culinary icon David Burke (of NYC renown) has "ratcheted things up" at this "great reincarnation" of a Rumson landmark that now sports new decor and, more importantly, "exciting", "unique presentations" of New American fare (like cheesecake lollipops) on which the toque's fame rests; "attentive" service rounds out an experience at "one of New Jersey's finest" – and priciest – restaurants.

David Drake, Restaurant 🗷 American
27 | 24 | 26 | $66

Rahway | 1449 Irving St. (Cherry St.) | 732-388-6677 | www.daviddrakes.com

A bona fide "destination for gourmets", David Drake's eponymous Rahway New American townhouse eatery is a "brilliant" "symphony of food, decor and service", with "fantastic" prix fixe meals and tasting menus ("order anything and be satisfied") and "attentive" servers who ably maneuver through a series of "intimate", "jewel"-like rooms; yes, it's "very expensive", but that's the price of "perfection."

☑ DeLorenzo's Tomato Pies ☑⃠ *Pizza* | 28 | 8 | 17 | $14 |

Trenton | 530 Hudson St. (bet. Mott & Swann Sts.) | 609-695-9534
"No salads, no appetizers, no ambiance", just "amazingly delicious", "brilliant" pizzas are served at this state "classic" in Trenton, the "best of the best" where "lines wrap around the block" and "house rules" are to be obeyed; all agree it's "worth the hype", "waits" and discomfort – there are no bathrooms, so "plan accordingly."

Dining Room ☑☑ *American* | 26 | 26 | 26 | $71 |

Short Hills | Hilton at Short Hills | 41 JFK Pkwy. (Rte. 24, exit 7C) | 973-379-0100 | www.hiltonshorthills.com
Be "pampered" by the "wonderful" New American cuisine and service at this Hilton Short Hills "special-occasion" destination that "sets the standard for luxury, style" and "romance"; yes, jackets are required and you'll have to "load your wallet in advance", but diners concede the reward is an "enchanted evening."

Due Terre Enoteca *Italian* | - | - | - | E |

Bernardsville | 107 Morristown Rd. (Finley Ave.) | 908-221-0040 | www.dueterre.com
Impeccable credentials (namely Michael White, ex chef of NYC's Fiamma Osteria, who's now leading the kitchens of the city's Alto and L'Impero) are behind this upscale Bernardsville arrival serving a modern Italian menu and wines that cover various price points; leather chairs and Craftsman touches are part of the decor's luxe profile.

Ebbitt Room *American* | 27 | 24 | 26 | $60 |

Cape May | Virginia Hotel | 25 Jackson St. (bet. Beach Dr. & Carpenter Ln.) | 609-884-5700 | www.virginiahotel.com
"Elegant, refined" atmosphere syncs up nicely with the "wonderful" food at this "romantic" Cape May New American, the epitome of "gourmet dining at its finest" thanks in no small part to the "great" service; a "charming" nightly jazz trio caps the "beautiful", "classy" scene.

Fascino ☑ *Italian* | 26 | 21 | 24 | $52 |

Montclair | 331 Bloomfield Ave. (bet. Grove & Willow Sts.) | 973-233-0350 | www.fascinorestaurant.com
"Fascinating" and "fantastic" are some of the superlatives used to describe this BYO "star" in Montclair, the home of the "incredible" DePersio family, and to the "superb" modern Italian of chef Ryan (and of "mom" Cynthia's "amazing" desserts); to get into the "place that has it all", fans are deterred by neither the "tough reservation" nor "pricey" tabs.

Frog and the Peach *American* | 26 | 23 | 24 | $57 |

New Brunswick | 29 Dennis St. (Hiram Sq.) | 732-846-3216 | www.frogandpeach.com
"Amazing in every respect", this multilevel New Brunswick New American "gastronomic paradise" is the home of Bruce Lefebvre's "flawless" cooking (with new lunch and dinner prix fixe options), "top-notch" service and wines, and an "extraordinary", "modern" ambiance

reflecting the building's industrial history; you may have to "mortgage a friend" for the experience, but then, what are friends for?

Hotoke *Pan-Asian*

— | — | — | E

New Brunswick | 350 George St. (Bayard St.) | 732-246-8999 | www.hotokerestaurant.com

Striking surroundings, including a giant golden Buddha, high ceilings and lava stone countertops, provide a dramatic backdrop for Edwyn Ferraris' Pan-Asian at this New Brunswick newcomer; prices are high-end, but $15 prix fixe lunches are one way to go.

Latour ⓜ *French*

27 | 21 | 25 | $52

Ridgewood | 6 E. Ridgewood Ave. (Broad St.) | 201-445-5056

"Warm greetings" from chef-owner Michael Latour enhance the "first-rate" repasts at his Ridgewood BYO, a standby and "standard-setter" for Classic French cookery, from savories to sweets; once you walk in, you're "instantly delighted to be here", with admirers affirming it's "adorable" – every inch of it; P.S. to "cut the expense", call ahead to check when they offer prix fixes.

ⓩ Legal Sea Foods *Seafood*

20 | 17 | 18 | $39

Short Hills | Short Hills Mall | 1200 Morris Tpke. (Rte. 24 W.) | 973-467-0089 | www.legalseafoods.com

Fish that's "good" and "fresh" is the hook at this nautical site in The Short Hills Mall that "upholds the chain's reputation", offering a "diverse" seafood selection that's appreciated by hordes of fans, including "kids"; hence, it's easy to fathom the appeal, and while "always crowded", "efficient" service keeps things flowing.

Lorena's ⓜ *French*

27 | 21 | 25 | $56

Maplewood | 168 Maplewood Ave. (off Valley St.) | 973-763-4460 | www.restaurantlorena.com

"Good things come in small packages" marvel fans of this super-"small" Maplewood French BYO where chef-owner Humberto Campos Jr. (ex Ryland Inn, Nicholas) uses "wonderful" ingredients to showcase his "stunning" preparations while his partner, Lorena Perez, presides over the "attentive" staff; the consensus: it's the town's "crown jewel."

ⓩ Nicholas ⓜ *American*

29 | 26 | 28 | $82

Middletown | 160 Rte. 35 S. (bet. Navesink River Rd. & Pine St.) | 732-345-9977 | www.restaurantnicholas.com

Epitomizing "ultrafine" dining, this "modern" Middletown New American "utopia of food and wine" near Red Bank is helmed by chef/co-owner (with wife Melissa) Nicholas Harary, whose "extraordinary" cuisine vaults this "amazing" restaurant to the top Food and Most Popular rankings in the state for the third straight year; add in "superlative" service (also No. 1), and even the "jaw-dropping" tabs don't deter devotees of the "absolute best" New Jersey has to offer; P.S. for more a casual experience, the bar/lounge is a "brilliant" alternative.

Origin ⓜ *French/Thai*

26 | 20 | 20 | $36

Morristown | 10 South St. (Morris St.) | 973-971-9933
Somerville | 25 Division St. (Main St.) | 908-685-1344
www.originthai.com

Whether you dine at the origin-al Somerville locale or the Morristown offshoot, these "bustling" BYO French-Thai fusionists are idolized for "spectacularly" conceived and executed preparations accompanied by "friendly", if "quick", service; at both expect to sit "in close proximity" to your neighbors and "deafening" acoustics, but meals at these "winners" are "worth anything."

Perryville Inn 🅼 *American*

26 | 24 | 22 | $56

Union Township | 167 Perryville Rd. (I-78, exit 12) | 908-730-9500 | www.theperryvilleinn.com

"Superlative experiences" are the norm at this Hunterdon County "class act" set in a historic Colonial tavern, where the "wonderful" Traditional American creations seem ideally suited to the "intimate" setting that comes complete with a number of fireplaces; overall, it all adds up to a "great destination at the end of a drive in the country"; N.B. jacket suggested.

Pluckemin Inn 🆉 *American*

25 | 26 | 24 | $68

Bedminster | 359 Rte. 202/206 S. (Pluckemin Way) | 908-658-9292 | www.pluckeminn.com

This Bedminster New American "covers all the bases" with a "gorgeous" modern-Colonial setting (evocative of a 19th-century farmhouse) that's centered by an "amazing" three-story wine tower and list (overseen by a "pro" sommelier), not to mention chef David C. Felton's "exceptional" dishes and "doting" service; you "won't regret emptying your wallet", since the "prices reflect the quality"; N.B. the adjacent Plucky Tavern offers quicker, more casual dining.

Rat's 🅼 *French*

24 | 28 | 24 | $63

Hamilton | Grounds for Sculpture | 16 Fairgrounds Rd. (Sculptors Way) | 609-584-7800 | www.ratsrestaurant.org

"Step into a Wonderland" of a setting when you visit this destination New French ranked NJ's No. 1 for Decor, where the "beautiful" Grounds for Sculpture (inspired by Monet's legendary Giverny) afford pre- or post-repast strolls; within the restaurant, "exciting" cuisine and "phenomenal" wines reign, both delivered by "excellent" servers; N.B. there's also a less formal cafe that accepts walk-ins.

restaurant.mc *Eclectic*

- | - | - | E

Millburn | 57 Main St. (Millburn Ave.) | 973-921-0888 | www.restaurantmc.com

This pricey Millburn Eclectic is already attracting attention for its globe-spanning ingredients and chic bar scene; at the helm of this hot newcomer is chef Steve Permaul, who regularly reinvents the menu to keep up with the town's sophisticated clientele.

🆉 River Palm Terrace *Steak*

25 | 19 | 20 | $58

Edgewater | 1416 River Rd. (Palisade Terr.) | 201-224-2013
Fair Lawn | 41-11 Rte. 4 W. (Plaza Rd.) | 201-703-3500
Mahwah | 209 Ramapo Valley Rd. (bet. W. Ramapo Ave. & Rte. 17) | 201-529-1111
www.riverpalmterrace.com

"If you love steak you can't miss" this triad of "classy", "very popular" North Jersey meat emporiums that also deliver "consistently good" Continental cuisine and seafood; expect to blow "lots of money", and note that many beef "reservations are meaningless", since you'll likely wind up waiting "too long a time" even if you have one.

	FOOD	DECOR	SERVICE	COST

Saddle River Inn 🗠 🅼 *American/French* — 27 | 25 | 26 | $62

Saddle River | 2 Barnstable Ct. (W. Saddle River Rd.) | 201-825-4016 |
www.saddleriverinn.com

"Top flight" is another name for this "rustic" yet "civilized" French–
New American near the Saddle River that's been dealing in delightful
dining for more than 25 years, serving "haute", "sublime" fare that
lends the "quaint" converted farmhouse setting an "elegant" touch;
blessedly, BYO helps suppress the cost.

Sagami 🅼 *Japanese* — 26 | 14 | 21 | $36

Collingswood | 37 Crescent Blvd. (bet. Haddon & Park Aves.) | 856-854-9773

The fish is "all it's cut up to be" at this Collingswood BYO, the birthplace of South Jersey's Japanese scene where the "best sushi around"
is still served in a "dark", "low-ceilinged" space; but since you can expect "heaven in the raw", "who cares how the place looks?"

Scalini Fedeli 🗠 *Italian* — 27 | 25 | 26 | $69

Chatham | 63 Main St. (bet. Parrott Mill Rd. & Tallmadge Ave.) |
973-701-9200 | www.scalinifedeli.com

"Prepare to be wowed" at top toque Michael Cetrulo's "magical"
Northern Italian "in the woods" of Chatham, where the "truly amazing" dining experience "from start to finish" consists of a "sublime"
prix fixe meal enhanced by "wonderful" wines, "superb" service and a
"lovely, intimate" setting; true, it's "expensive", but all agree it's
"worth every penny" you'll have to give up.

Serenade *French* — 27 | 26 | 26 | $70

Chatham | 6 Roosevelt Ave. (Main St.) | 973-701-0303 |
www.restaurantserenade.com

"Perfect in every way" is the refrain sung by fans of this "charming"
New French in Chatham, which hums with "delighted" diners who
"never tire" of the "impeccable" "fine dining", courtesy of husband-
wife team James Laird and Nancy Sheridan Laird (chef and manager,
respectively); the "superb" cuisine and wines, an "elegant" dining
room and an "excellent" staff all add up to make it like a "top NYC restaurant transplanted to the suburbs."

Whispers *American* — 27 | 23 | 25 | $56

Spring Lake | Hewitt Wellington Hotel | 200 Monmouth Ave. (2nd Ave.) |
732-974-9755 | www.whispersrestaurant.com

In a "fabulous" Victorian hotel near "beautiful" Spring Lake "lies a
mecca of gourmet treats" in the form of this "serene" New American
BYO, which specializes in "memorable" meals enhanced by "polished"
servers; devoted fans concur the positives easily outweigh any con-
cerns about the "expense" associated with this "oasis of elegance."

Zoe's by the Lake 🅼 *French* — 26 | 24 | 24 | $54

Sparta | 112 Tomahawk Trail (2 mi. east of Rte. 15) | 973-726-7226 |
www.zoesbythelake.com

"NYC and Paris" meet in Sussex County at this "out-of-the-way" Sparta
French, where the "exceptional" (and "expensive") fare is matched by
a "lovely, spacious" bi-level dining room and a "fantastic" lake setting
(not surprisingly, "sitting outside is best"); with a staff that "goes
above and beyond" to cater to the clientele, few hold no qualms about
calling this "jewel" "superb on all fronts."

New Orleans

TOP FOOD RANKING

Restaurant	Cuisine
28 August	Continental/French
Brigtsen's	Contemp. Louisiana
Bayona	American
Stella!	American
Alberta	French
Cuvée	Continental/Creole
27 La Provence	French
Mosca's	Italian
Vizard's on the Avenue*	Creole/Mediterranean
Jacques-Imo's Café	Creole/Soul Food
Clancy's	Creole
Dakota, The	American/Contemp. Louisiana
Galatoire's	Creole/French
K-Paul's	Cajun
Herbsaint	American/French
Dick & Jenny's	Creole/Eclectic
26 Upperline	Contemp. Louisiana
Dickie Brennan's	Steak
Irene's Cuisine	Italian
Lilette	French

OTHER NOTEWORTHY PLACES

Acme Oyster	Seafood
Antoine's	Creole
Arnaud's	Creole
Bistro at Maison de Ville	Creole/French
Brennan's	Creole
Cochon	Cajun
Commander's Palace	Creole
Eleven 79	Creole/Italian
Emeril's	Contemp. Louisiana
Gautreau's	American/French
La Petite Grocery	Contemp. Louisiana/French
Mandina's	Creole
Martinique Bistro	French
Mother's	Cajun
Mr. B's Bistro	Contemp. Louisiana
Muriel's Jackson Square	Creole
Napoleon House	Creole/Mediterranean
NOLA	Contemp. Louisiana
Pelican Club	American
Rib Room	Steak

* Indicates a tie with restaurant above

	FOOD	DECOR	SERVICE	COST

Acme Oyster House *Seafood*

22 | 13 | 17 | $21

French Quarter | 724 Iberville St. (bet. Bourbon & Royal Sts.) |
504-522-5973
Metairie | 3000 Veterans Memorial Blvd. (N. Causeway Blvd.) |
504-309-4056
www.acmeoyster.com

"Eat 'em as you shuck 'em" at this "old-school" seafood duo that's "bi-valve heaven" for lovers of "huge", "succulent" "fresh oysters" and "impossible-to-beat" po' boys paired with "local beers"; the lower-key Metairie locale just revamped its bar area, while the French Quarter's "checked-tablecloth" setting draws "long lines" of tourists and natives who dig into "cheap eats" and have a "raucous good time."

☑ Alberta 🅂🅼 *French*

28 | 21 | 24 | $54

Uptown | 5015 Magazine St. (Robert St.) | 504-891-3015
Regulars hope you "don't tell" about this unmarked Uptowner where fans are "floored" by chef Melody Pate's "intricate", "avant-garde" French bistro fare; though some say it's "pricey" for the neighborhood, most are "charmed" by the "kind, ebullient staff" and "hip", "jewel-box" setting featuring "honey-colored" lighting that flatters "everyone" – so naturally "reservations are a must"; N.B. after a brief closure, it was expected to reopen in September 2007 with a new partner on board.

Antoine's *Creole*

24 | 24 | 24 | $55

French Quarter | 713 St. Louis St. (bet. Bourbon & Royal Sts.) |
504-581-4422 | www.antoines.com
"You can feel the history" at this "beautiful", circa-1840 French Quarter "landmark", a Creole "grande dame" known for "classics" like oysters Rockefeller (which was invented here and "lives up to the hype"); it's long been a "special-occasion" destination for "old New Orleans society" and a tourist "must-do", but admirers report "new energy" post-Katrina, finding service "more attentive" and the Sunday jazz brunch "simply magical"; N.B. closed Tuesdays and Wednesdays.

Arnaud's *Creole*

26 | 25 | 26 | $50

French Quarter | 813 Bienville St. (bet. Bourbon & Dauphine Sts.) |
504-523-5433 | www.arnauds.com
"Old school . . . but wow" declare those dazzled by this "jewel of the Quarter", a "fabulous reminder of times that were", serving "remarkable", "traditional" Creole cuisine in an "elegant" tile-paved dining room (with the house Mardi Gras museum located upstairs); from its Sunday brunch – when the "jazz is fine and the milk punch potent" – to its "gracious" service, it remains a "quintessential", if somewhat "expensive", Crescent City "original."

☑ August *Continental/French*

28 | 28 | 27 | $58

CBD | 301 Tchoupitoulas St. (Gravier St.) | 504-299-9777 |
www.rest-august.com
"Spectacular" dishes blending "European style" with "a touch of the bayou" enchant guests at this "elegant" CBD Continental–New French, ranked No. 1 in New Orleans for Food, where chef/co-owner John Besh crafts a "daring" menu that showcases local ingredients; the "drop-dead gorgeous" setting (curving brick walls, lustrous chande-

	FOOD	DECOR	SERVICE	COST

liers), a "warm", "knowledgeable" staff and presentations "so beautiful you hesitate to mess up the plate" also impress, so if the tab's "pricey", you'll be "too blissed out to notice."

☑ Bayona ☒ American

| | 28 | 25 | 26 | $53 |

French Quarter | 430 Dauphine St. (bet. Conti & St. Louis Sts.) | 504-525-4455 | www.bayona.com

Admirers aver it "doesn't get any better" than this French Quarter "favorite" where "masterful" celebrity chef-owner Susan Spicer turns out "original", "peerless" New American cuisine with "global influences" in a Creole-cottage setting that features a "gracious", slightly "formal" interior and a "lovely patio"; the prix fixe options remain "a deal", and it's recently renovated its Katrina-damaged wine cellar and is building up an "amazing new wine list."

Bistro at Maison de Ville ☒Ⓜ Creole/French

| | – | – | – | E |

French Quarter | Maison de Ville | 733 Toulouse St. (bet. Bourbon & Royal Sts.) | 504-528-9206 | www.maisondeville.com

Quarterites and other chic gourmets think it's *fantastique* that this secluded jewel has reopened, and that chef-owner Greg Picolo is back in his tiny kitchen cooking up Creole and French creations; plus, the decor has a Parisian feel – dark-toned wooden walls, red leather banquettes and original artwork hanging on beveled glass mirrors – that makes it perfect for a romantic dinner or a leisurely lunch.

☑ Brennan's Creole

| | 25 | 24 | 24 | $51 |

French Quarter | 417 Royal St. (bet. Conti & St. Louis Sts.) | 504-525-9711 | www.brennansneworleans.com

"One of those places that defines old New Orleans", this Creole originator of "addictive bananas Foster" invites a "touristy" French Quarter crowd to "linger" over its "first-rate" dinners and "decadent" "three-hour breakfasts", which cost big bucks "if you do it right"; "Southern hospitality", "pleasant" if "dated" dining rooms and a "beautiful courtyard" are all pluses, and if opponents opine it's "overrated", more concur "you gotta go" "at least once."

☑ Brigtsen's ☒Ⓜ Contemp. Louisiana

| | 28 | 22 | 27 | $47 |

Riverbend | 723 Dante St. (Maple St.) | 504-861-7610 | www.brigtsens.com

"Genius" chef/co-owner Frank Brigtsen provides a "true NOLA experience" at this "charming Creole cottage" in Riverbend via "exquisite", "imaginative interpretations" of "Louisiana home cooking"; a staff that "treats you like family" while displaying "excellent attention to detail" combines with a blue-ribbon wine list and lively people-watching to round out a meal that's more than "worth the cab ride" and the need to make reservations early.

Clancy's ☒ Creole

| | 27 | 22 | 25 | $45 |

Uptown | 6100 Annunciation St. (Webster St.) | 504-895-1111

"Exquisite" dishes like "sublime smoked soft-shell crab" and "ooh-la-la" oysters with Brie tantalize a "tony", "table-hopping" "who's who" of "old New Orleans" at this "country club"–style Creole that some call the "Galatoire's of Uptown"; it can be "noisy and crowded" but "stands out as the quintessential locals' favorite", since it's "tucked away from all things touristy" and the "tuxedoed servers" have an "excellent rapport" with regulars.

	FOOD	DECOR	SERVICE	COST

Cochon ☒ *Cajun* | 25 | 22 | 23 | $35 |

Warehouse District | 930 Tchoupitoulas St. (bet. Andrew Higgins Dr. & S. Diamond St.) | 504-588-2123 | www.cochonrestaurant.com
Locals "pigging out" on "tapas-style plates" of "authentic" Cajun cuisine say "cheers for Donald Link" (also of Herbsaint) and Stephen Stryjewski, the chefs/co-owners who fire up "dynamite" Southern Louisiana cooking inside this Warehouse District "temple of swine"; the "fabulous" staff, open kitchen with wood-burning oven and "upscale-casual decor" guar-ontee its popularity.

Commander's Palace *Creole* | – | – | – | E |

Garden District | 1403 Washington Ave. (Coliseum St.) | 504-899-8221 | www.commanderspalace.com
Sumptuously redecorated with embroidered silk toile, leather banquettes and crystal chandeliers, this grand old Garden District star (rated the city's Most Popular restaurant from 1989 through 2005) has finally reopened after a $6 million post-Katrina makeover; its sophisticated Creole menu reflects the inventiveness of chef Tory McPhail, and its polished staff is guided by a new generation of Brennan ownership: cousins Lally Brennan and Ti Martin.

Cuvée ☒ *Continental/Creole* | 28 | 26 | 26 | $55 |

CBD | 322 Magazine St. (bet. Gravier & Poydras Sts.) | 504-587-9001 | www.restaurantcuvee.com
Even in "the darkest days" just after Katrina, this "shining light" in the CBD – a sibling of Dakota – maintained "exceptional" standards, starting with chef Bob Iacovone's "outstanding", "creative" Continental-Creole cuisine with rich touches (e.g. "last meal"–worthy duck confit); the "wonderful" "French-focused wine list", "polished service" and "warm, dark decor" also help make it a "special-occasion" "gem."

Dakota, The ☒ *American/Contemp. Louisiana* | 27 | 23 | 25 | $49 |

Covington | 629 N. Hwy. 190 (¼ mi. north of I-12) | 985-892-3712 | www.thedakotarestaurant.com
"Excellent game", "fabulous crab and Brie soup" and other "decadent, delicious" New American–Contemporary Louisiana dishes help this Covington classic win accolades as the "most accomplished restaurant on the Northshore"; factor in "awesome wines", "exceptional service" and a setting enriched by deep colors and "great art on the walls", and most agree it's "worth the drive across the Causeway."

Dick & Jenny's ☒Ⓜ *Creole/Eclectic* | 27 | 21 | 24 | $37 |

Uptown | 4501 Tchoupitoulas St. (Jena St.) | 504-894-9880
Following what many call a "seamless" change of owners post-Katrina, this clapboard-cottage bistro on a "working-class" Uptown block remains "beloved" by locals thanks to "sumptuous", "soulful" affordable Creole-Eclectic "comfort food"; with the same "friendly" servers and "laid-back", "folk-art" atmosphere, it continues to draw fans who roll with the no-reserving policy by "relaxing on the patio rockers."

Dickie Brennan's Steakhouse *Steak* | 26 | 25 | 25 | $53 |

French Quarter | 716 Iberville St. (bet. Bourbon & Royal Sts.) | 504-522-2467 | www.dickiebrennanssteakhouse.com
"Astounding steaks" "so tender they practically melt on the plate" wrangle French Quarter frequenters to this "beef eater's paradise"

from the Brennan clan; the menu comes through with "all the extras" plus a "superior" wine selection to boot, and the "clubby", "masculine" wood-paneled rooms, "well-trained" staff and hefty price tag are exactly what you'd expect "when you need that meat"; N.B. it's now open for lunch on weekdays.

Eleven 79 ☑ *Creole/Italian*
– | – | – | E

Warehouse District | 1179 Annunciation St. (Erato St.) | 504-299-1179

Having reopened its doors post-Katrina, this charming old cottage in the Warehouse District dishes up garlicky Creole-Italian pastas, veal and seafood from new chef James Sibal; even though it costs lots of lire to dine here, it fills up fast with patrons who appreciate warm decor and low lighting plus a trendy bar and spot-on service.

☑ Emeril's *Contemp. Louisiana*
25 | 24 | 25 | $59

Warehouse District | 800 Tchoupitoulas St. (Julia St.) | 504-528-9393 | www.emerils.com

"Don't let the celebrity-chef status hold you back" say a bevy of "bam!" believers who laud this Lagasse flagship in the Warehouse District for "robustly flavored", "earthy" eats that "capture the essence of New Orleans–style haute cuisine"; its "crisp" service, "sleek" looks and high energy ("the chef's bar is what I call 'dinner and a show'") please most, though some knock it as a "tourist mecca" that needs to kick the noise level and cost "down a notch."

☑ Galatoire's Ⓜ *Creole/French*
27 | 26 | 27 | $51

French Quarter | 209 Bourbon St. (Iberville St.) | 504-525-2021 | www.galatoires.com

"You could see Blanche DuBois sipping a Sazerac" at this "old-line", "almost cultish" French Quarter centenarian – the city's Most Popular restaurant – where "bigwigs" and "ladies in hats" find "gastronomic heaven" in a "classic" Creole-French cornucopia of "unbelievable seafood"; it's a "'dress up and live large' kinda place", so snag a table in the tiled downstairs ("where the action is"), "get to know your waiter" and don't be surprised if a leisurely lunch "turns into dinner"; N.B. jackets are required after 5 PM and on Sundays.

Gautreau's ☑Ⓜ *American/French*
– | – | – | E

Uptown | 1728 Soniat St. (Danneel St.) | 504-899-7397

Reopening an Uptown mainstay, owner Patrick Singley has brought chef Sue Zemanick back to the kitchen at this converted antique drugstore serving high-end New American–New French cuisine; its top-to-bottom renovation adds a sense of airiness to the space, but since it still fills up in a flash with longtime fans, reservations are a must.

Herbsaint ☑ *American/French*
27 | 22 | 25 | $45

Warehouse District | 701 St. Charles Ave. (Girod St.) | 504-524-4114 | www.herbsaint.com

In "top form" post-Katrina, the kitchen at this Warehouse District "winner" turns out "stellar" New American–New French fare with a "Southern twist" and a touch of "whimsy", thanks to "truly talented" chef Donald Link; energized by "enticing" cocktails, a "wonderful wine list" and "smart service", its "chic" dining room is both "casual" and "electric" – in sum, "another home run" from co-owner Susan Spicer.

Irene's Cuisine ⧄ *Italian*

26 | 22 | 23 | $41

French Quarter | 539 St. Philip St. (Chartres St.) | 504-529-8811
"Locals love" this "dark", "romantic" dinner-only trattoria that tourists seem to "find with their noses" as the scent of "delectable" Southern Italian food wafts from its French Quarter digs; inside, "cozy, quirky" dining rooms, a "delightful staff" and a "great piano bar" keep spirits soaring – but since limited reservations can mean "painful" waits, you'd best show up early, add your name to the list and "take the opportunity" to explore the neighborhood.

Jacques-Imo's Café ⧄ *Creole/Soul Food*

27 | 21 | 22 | $33

Carrollton | 8324 Oak St. (S. Carrollton Ave.) | 504-861-0886 | www.jacquesimoscafe.com
Fans of Jack Leonardi's "big-flavored", "down-home" Creole soul cooking insist you'll be "sighing in bliss and loosening your pants" before you can say "alligator cheesecake" (a "must-try") after chowing down at this dinner-only Carrollton "dive"; sure, many bemoan "insanely long" waits that can run over an hour, but most still consider this "funky", "boisterous" "Tulane students' favorite" "a blast" that "could only exist in New Orleans."

K-Paul's Louisiana Kitchen ⧄ *Cajun*

27 | 21 | 24 | $48

French Quarter | 416 Chartres St. (bet. Conti & St. Louis Sts.) | 504-596-2530 | www.kpauls.com
"Not the cliché you'd expect", the French Quarter birthplace of blackened redfish maintains high standards thanks to "flavor virtuoso" Paul Prudhomme and his "complex, sophisticated interpretations" of "robustly" spiced Cajun food; "long waits" are often a prelude to the "hot and pricey" fare, but "spirited" service and a "charming" vibe help pass the time.

La Petite Grocery ⧄Ⓜ *Contemp. Louisiana/French*

26 | 24 | 24 | $45

Uptown | 4238 Magazine St. (General Pershing St.) | 504-891-3377
Set in an Uptown space that once housed a corner grocery, this dinner destination serves up "sophisticated", "inventive" Contemporary Louisiana–French cuisine amid "understated" decor; fans find it a "perfect blend of special-occasion restaurant and neighborhood bistro", where "simple", "Parisian-style", "polished service" and "blissful" bites make you think "you're on the Left Bank."

La Provence Ⓜ *French*

27 | 26 | 26 | $46

Lacombe | 25020 Hwy. 190 (bet. Lacombe & Mandeville) | 985-626-7662 | www.laprovencerestaurant.com
John Besh (August) has revived this unexpected "bit of Provence" in rural Lacombe, where his culinary mentor, the late "treasured" toque Chris Kerageorgiou, turned out "superb" French fare for over three decades; while the "welcoming" service remains the same, recent renovations should heighten the already "romantic" ambiance (think "lovely hearth fires"); N.B. closed Mondays and Tuesdays.

Lilette ⧄Ⓜ *French*

26 | 23 | 23 | $46

Uptown | 3637 Magazine St. (Antonine St.) | 504-895-1636 | www.lileterestaurant.com
Whether for an "intimate dinner" or a "sybaritic lunch", this "top-tier" French bistro impresses Uptowners with "inventive combinations" of

"fresh seasonal ingredients" from "brilliant" chef-owner John Harris; "chic" yet "relaxed", it draws "young professionals" and other locals who "love the booths" as well as the "cool bar" (complete with "sexy drinks"), all tended to by a "friendly", "unrushed" staff.

Mandina's ⊄ *Creole* | – | – | – | I |
Mid-City | 3800 Canal St. (Cortez St.) | 504-482-9179 | www.mandinasrestaurant.com
Go early or late or be prepared to wait at this casual Mid-City shrine to overstuffed po' boys, fried seafood and other Creole delicacies; a post-Katrina redo has added some extra table space, but not nearly enough for all of the regulars – though the enduring crowds, noise and often pushy staff are all part of its quirky character; N.B. cash-only.

Martinique Bistro Ⓜ *French* | 25 | 22 | 22 | $40 |
Uptown | 5908 Magazine St. (bet. Eleonore & State Sts.) | 504-891-8495
Locals wax rhapsodic about the "exquisite" "seasonal" French cuisine with a seafood focus that's served at this "tiny", "intimate" Uptown "sleeper"; the staff is generally "attentive and unobtrusive", and meals run long with "romance" in the air (especially on the "transporting" garden patio); N.B. chef Eric Labouchere took over in late 2006.

Mosca's Ⓢ Ⓜ ⊄ *Italian* | 27 | 12 | 20 | $38 |
Avondale | 4137 Hwy. 90 W. (bet. Butler Dr. & Live Oak Blvd.) | 504-436-9942
"I'd do dishes to eat here!" exclaim enthusiasts about this hallowed "old roadhouse" in Avondale, where the "garlic-powered" menu of "in-spired" Italian like chicken à la grande and oysters Mosca is served "family-style" to a crowd that always includes a few fascinating "charac-ters"; insiders advise "call first to get directions", "bring at least six peo-ple so you can get everything on the menu" and always "take cash."

Mother's *Cajun* | 24 | 9 | 13 | $15 |
CBD | 401 Poydras St. (bet. Magazine & Tchoupitoulas Sts.) | 504-523-9656 | www.mothersrestaurant.net
"It would be a sin" to miss this "cafeteria-style" Cajun-American "dive", an ever-crowded CBD destination for "down-home" vittles like the 'debris' po' boy ("a thing of dripping beauty"), "out-of-this-world" étouffée and the "best damn ham", along with "hangover-curing" breakfasts; "tourist-trap" prices and "lines out the door" are draw-backs, but at least the "surly service" adds "character."

Mr. B's Bistro Ⓢ *Contemp. Louisiana* | – | – | – | E |
French Quarter | 201 Royal St. (Iberville St.) | 504-523-2078 | www.mrbsbistro.com
Reopened post-Katrina, this upscale French Quarter classic may evoke a Parisian bistro with its mirrored and wood-paneled walls, but dishes like the Gumbo Ya-Ya remind you that it's Contemporary Louisiana all the way; chef Michelle McRaney is back at the stove with managing partner Cindy Brennan in charge of the festive dining room.

Muriel's Jackson Square *Creole* | 23 | 26 | 22 | $42 |
French Quarter | Jackson Sq. | 801 Chartres St. (St. Ann St.) | 504-568-1885 | www.muriels.com
"Imaginatively decorated" rooms "ranging from haunting to haunted" beguile guests (and a few "resident ghosts") at this "festive", "romantic"

FOOD DECOR SERVICE COST

Creole "overlooking Jackson Square"; from its "rich and tasty creations" at a "fair price" to its "smiling service" and "historic charm" – particularly in the "decadent" Seance Lounge where you "feel like a sultan" – it's "what the French Quarter is all about."

Napoleon House   *Creole/Mediterranean*   19 | 24 | 17 | $21

French Quarter | 500 Chartres St. (St. Louis St.) | 504-524-9752 | www.napoleonhouse.com

"May it never close" pray worshipers of this "classic", "moody" French Quarter "hangout" (built in 1797), where Creole-Med dishes like jambalaya and warm muffalettas satisfy but it's "all about the atmosphere"; so savor a "wonderful" Pimm's Cup and some "classical music" in the "crumbling" interior that "oozes character" or out in the "blissful" courtyard – just don't be put off by the traditionally "grumpy", "bow-tied waiters"; N.B. it now serves dinner.

☑ NOLA   *Contemp. Louisiana*   26 | 23 | 24 | $51

French Quarter | 534 St. Louis St. (bet. Chartres & Decatur Sts.) | 504-522-6652 | www.emerils.com

"Delicious Creole-inspired" Contemporary Louisiana cuisine "served with style" draws the masses to Emeril Lagasse's "alternative" French Quarter outpost, which many find "hipper" and "more casual" than his namesake venue; most agree it's a "good value" and "runs like a clock", though the "touristy" crowd ups the "noise to stratospheric levels."

Pelican Club   *American*   26 | 24 | 23 | $48

French Quarter | 312 Exchange Pl. (Bienville St.) | 504-523-1504 | www.pelicanclub.com

"Cozy, clubby" and "off the beaten path in the French Quarter", this "upscale" New American set in a 19th-century townhouse is "worth seeking out" for "wonderful" seafood-centric meals; regulars recommend "dressing up", bringing a "large group" and starting with a cocktail at the "great bar with live piano" on the weekends.

Rib Room   *Steak*   25 | 25 | 25 | $50

French Quarter | Omni Royal Orleans | 621 St. Louis St. (Chartres St.) | 504-529-7046 | www.omnihotels.com

"A great place for beef in a seafood town", this "sophisticated" steakhouse is a "power-lunch" scene and a "longtime favorite of French Quarter residents" thanks to its "famous prime rib" among other cuts; warm "hospitality" and window seats for "watching people walk by" on Royal Street add to the allure, though opinions differ as to whether a recent redo is "reinvigorating" or has turned a "one-of-a-kind place" into a typical "nice hotel restaurant."

☑ Stella!   *American*   28 | 25 | 26 | $56

French Quarter | Hôtel Provincial | 1032 Chartres St. (bet. St. Philip & Ursuline Sts.) | 504-587-0091 | www.restaurantstella.com

At this "intimate" hotel dining room and patio "tucked away in the Quarter", "incredibly ambitious" chef-owner Scott Boswell crafts an "innovative" New American menu starring "experimental Creole fare" and "surprising flavor combinations", making it "worth the exclamation point"; if some cry "expensive", those who cherish their "memorable" meals are "shouting 'Stella!' all night."

	FOOD	DECOR	SERVICE	COST

Upperline Ⓜ *Contemp. Louisiana*   26 | 24 | 25 | $45

Uptown | 1413 Upperline St. (bet. Prytania St. & St. Charles Ave.) | 504-891-9822 | www.upperline.com

"Wonderful chef" Ken Smith and "consummate hostess" JoAnn Clevenger have "kept the torch lit" at this "quirky" Uptowner that offers "splendid", "inventive" Contemporary Louisiana cuisine with the option of an "excellent" seven-course 'Taste of New Orleans' menu; it's all served by a "fine", "cordial" staff and set in a lofty 1877 house featuring four dining rooms that are decorated with objects and paintings from Clevenger's personal art collection.

Vizard's on the Avenue ⓈⓂ *Creole/Mediterranean*   27 | 24 | 25 | $48

Garden District | Garden District Hotel | 2203 St. Charles Ave. (Jackson Ave.) | 504-529-9912 | www.vizardsontheavenue.com

Eager to tuck into chef-owner Kevin Vizard's "spellbinding" Creole-Mediterranean fare, the city's foodies, socialites, "movers and shakers" all head to this "lively" post-Katrina addition inside the Garden District Hotel; its "chic" ambiance and "pleasant" staff help to make it "worth" the expense – particularly if you nab "a table looking out onto the avenue"; N.B. reservations are suggested.

New York City

TOP FOOD RANKING

Restaurant	Cuisine
28 Daniel	French
Sushi Yasuda	Japanese
Le Bernardin	French/Seafood
Per Se	American/French
Peter Luger	Steak
Jean Georges	French
Bouley	French
27 Chanterelle	French
Sushi Seki	Japanese
L'Atelier de Joël Robuchon	French
Nobu	Japanese
Gotham B&G	American
Café Boulud	French
Gramercy Tavern	American
Di Fara	Pizza
La Grenouille	French
Babbo	Italian
Saul	American
Annisa	American
Il Mulino	Italian
Aureole	American
Masa	Japanese
Picholine	French/Mediterranean
Roberto	Italian
26 Union Square Cafe	American

OTHER NOTEWORTHY PLACES

Alto	Italian
Anthos	Greek
Balthazar	French
BLT Market	American
Blue Hill	American
Buddakan	Asian Fusion
Café des Artistes	French
Carnegie Deli	Deli
Cru	Modern European
Danube	Austrian
Del Posto	Italian
Eleven Madison Park	French
Four Seasons	Continental
Gordon Ramsay	French
Hill Country	BBQ
Milos	Greek/Seafood
Modern, The	American/French
Morimoto	Japanese
Oriental Garden	Chinese/Seafood

Palm	Steak
Rao's	Italian
River Café	American
Shun Lee Palace	Chinese
Spice Market	SE Asian
Tavern on the Green	American
Telepan	American
Tocqueville	American/French
21 Club	American
Wakiya	Chinese
Waverly Inn	American

Alto ⊠ *Italian*   26 | 25 | 25 | $81

E 50s | 11 E. 53rd St. (bet. 5th & Madison Aves.) | 212-308-1099 | www.altorestaurant.com

As chef Michael White picks up where Scott Conant left off, "power" patrons are watching to see how this "formal" East Side Italian evolves; known for its "fantastic", "intriguing" cuisine, "outstanding" wine list and "ultrachic", glass wine cellar–lined decor, all hope that everything stays the same, except maybe the "sky-high prices."

Annisa *American*   27 | 22 | 26 | $73

G Village | 13 Barrow St. (bet. 7th Ave. S. & W. 4th St.) | 212-741-6699 | www.annisarestaurant.com

"Top-tier chef" Anita Lo's Village oasis woos patrons with "refined, beautiful" New American cuisine, "impeccable service" and "stylish" "white-curtained" decor that add up to "magical experiences"; such a "superior" dining option doesn't come cheap, but for a relative bargain "go for the tasting menu" at $88.

Anthos ⊠ *Greek*   ▽ 25 | 21 | 24 | $66

W 50s | 36 W. 52nd St. (bet. 5th & 6th Aves.) | 212-582-6900

The "amazing" "haute Greek cuisine" based on the "finest fresh ingredients" and "fabulous service" provide the wow factor at this Midtown newcomer from Donatella Arpaia (davidburke & donatella) and rising toque Michael Psilakis (Kefi); the space is "pleasant" but on the plain side for such "top-of-the-line prices."

Aureole ⊠ *American*   27 | 25 | 26 | $105

E 60s | 34 E. 61st St. (bet. Madison & Park Aves.) | 212-319-1660 | www.charliepalmer.com

Excelling "in all categories", Charlie Palmer's "flower-filled" "celebratory dining spot" continues to delight with "outstanding" New American fare and "phenomenal service" that add up to a "royal experience" surely "worth the cost"; N.B. for an affordable introduction, try the $38 lunch prix fixe.

⊠ Babbo ● *Italian*   27 | 23 | 25 | $76

G Village | 110 Waverly Pl. (bet. MacDougal St. & 6th Ave.) | 212-777-0303 | www.babbonyc.com

"When it's this good" "it's not hype" is still the consensus as Mario Batali and Joe Bastianich celebrate the 10th anniversary of their "fabulously popular" Village "flagship" that's once again voted NYC's No. 1 Italian; given its "mind-blowing" cuisine, "epic wine list", "superlative" service and "cozy" bi-level carriage house setting, you'd better "keep their reservation number on redial"; sure, it's "expensive", but it's "worth every centesimo."

Balthazar ● *French*   23 | 23 | 20 | $53

SoHo | 80 Spring St. (bet. B'way & Crosby St.) | 212-965-1414 | www.balthazarny.com

Still "*très bon*" "after all these years", Keith McNally's exuberantly "chaotic" SoHo brasserie delivers "wonderful" French food in a "Parisian" setting; it successfully caters to everyone from sunglasses-sporting "celebs" and "socialites" to "tourists" and "B&T" types, all of whom pack in "elbow-to-elbow" for a taste of "big, brassy, fun."

BLT Market *American*   – | – | – | VE

W 50s | Ritz-Carlton | 1430 Sixth Ave. (CPS) | 212-521-6125 | www.bltmarket.com

Cross a farmer's market with the Ritz-Carlton and you get this pricey New American newcomer from Laurent Tourondel, where the focus is on seasonal, sometimes local ingredients that are the basis for its menus and weekly specials; in the reconfigured former Atelier space, it's now done up in cheery agrarian chic and lined with big windows looking out onto the street; N.B. there's sidewalk seating in summer.

Blue Hill *American*   26 | 22 | 25 | $73

G Village | 75 Washington Pl. (bet. MacDougal St. & 6th Ave.) | 212-539-1776 | www.bluehillnyc.com

"I found my thrill" declare disciples at Dan Barber's gastronomic "temple" near Washington Square, whose "delectable" yet "unfussy" New American cuisine lets "the freshest" "organic" ingredients "shine through"; served with "genuine care" in a "subtly elegant" setting with a "quaint garden", it's an "artful" experience "for grown-ups."

Bouley ● *French*   28 | 26 | 27 | $94

TriBeCa | 120 W. Broadway (Duane St.) | 212-964-2525 | www.davidbouley.com

David Bouley's TriBeCa "mecca" "never ceases to amaze", carrying "class" to an "exemplary level" with "stunning" New French cuisine and "dazzling" but "but unstuffy service"; the "opulent" space's "vaulted ceilings" and "soothing" lighting impart a "sense of contentment" that "memories are made of"; no, it's "not cheap."

Buddakan ● *Asian Fusion*   23 | 27 | 21 | $62

Chelsea | 75 Ninth Ave. (16th St.) | 212-989-6699 | www.buddakannyc.com

Stephen Starr's "awe-inspiring" Chelsea "spectacle" "lives up to the hype" with a "bold, beautiful" space "like a movie set" and an equally appealing "young, chic" customer base, and the "feast for the eyes" is nearly matched by the "delicious", "pricey" Asian fusion fare; as "everyone" wants to "eat here" it gets "way crowded" and "loud", so "go early" if you want to avoid the "zoo."

Café Boulud *French*   27 | 23 | 26 | $79

E 70s | Surrey Hotel | 20 E. 76th St. (bet. 5th & Madison Aves.) | 212-772-2600 | www.danielnyc.com

Dining is "bliss" at "Daniel's Uptown sibling", where the "superb experiences" are "less formal" and less costly (if still "not cheap") than at the flagship; a "chic" UES clientele "savors each bite" of its "innovative" French fare served in "simple, elegant" environs by "pampering" pro staffers; P.S. lunch is a particularly "good buy."

Café des Artistes ● *French* | 22 | 26 | 23 | $69 |

W 60s | 1 W. 67th St. (bet. Columbus Ave. & CPW) | 212-877-3500 | www.cafenyc.com

George and Jenifer Lang's "New York icon" near Lincoln Center is "still one of the most beautiful, romantic places to dine" thanks to an interior resplendent with "fresh flowers" and Howard Chandler Christy's "magical" "murals of nubile nymphs"; add "outstanding" French fare and "gracious" service, and it's "a superb evening every time" – "perfect for 'marry me' or "I'm sorry!'"; N.B. dinner only, except for brunch on weekends.

Carnegie Deli ●≠ *Deli* | 21 | 9 | 13 | $27 |

W 50s | 854 Seventh Ave. (55th St.) | 212-757-2245 | www.carnegiedeli.com

One sandwich could "feed an army" and the "classic" cheesecake "is the standard by which all others should be judged" at this Midtown "granddaddy of delis"; "true NYers" and "tourists" sit "shoulder-to-shoulder" in its "dumpy" quarters presided over by "fast", "surly servers" who've been on the job "since the beginning of time" – may this "quintessential NY" experience "never change."

Chanterelle *French* | 27 | 26 | 27 | $119 |

TriBeCa | 2 Harrison St. (Hudson St.) | 212-966-6960 | www.chanterellenyc.com

"Damn near perfect", David and Karen Waltuck's TriBeCa French "benchmark" keeps "getting better with age", providing a "regal dining experience" across "all categories"; "every bite of every course is heavenly", while the "elegant", "understated" interior is perfect for "special occasions" with "spot-on", "balletic" service to match; though dinner here is "worth every dollar", try the $42 lunch prix fixe if money is an object.

Cru ⧫ *European* | 26 | 23 | 26 | $108 |

G Village | 24 Fifth Ave. (9th St.) | 212-529-1700 | www.cru-nyc.com

It's the "right place for wine lovers", but don't let this Villager's "bible"-length list of *vins* overshadow Shea Gallante's "equally impressive" Modern European cuisine; yes, its prix fixe–only menus start at $78, but to most they're "worth the expense" considering the "five-star service" and "charming", "special occasion"–worthy decor; N.B. the casual no-reserving front room is à la carte.

⦿ Daniel ⧫ *French* | 28 | 28 | 28 | $132 |

E 60s | 60 E. 65th St. (bet. Madison & Park Aves.) | 212-288-0033 | www.danielnyc.com

An "unparalleled dining experience" awaits at Daniel Boulud's "impeccable" UES namesake, the "standard" for "luxe" New French fare and rated NYC's No. 1 for Food; add an "amazing" wine list, "breathtaking" decor and "flawless", "white-glove service" and it's easy to see why this is at the "top of the NY dining food chain"; of course, the tab is equal to a "mortgage payment", but "if you're going to splurge", splurge on "perfection."

Danube ●🅩 *Austrian*

26	27	26	$86

TriBeCa | 30 Hudson St. (bet. Duane & Reade Sts.) | 212-791-3771 |
www.davidbouley.com

At David Bouley's "transporting" "TriBeCa gem", the "Klimt"-inspired
dining room (among the "most beautiful in NYC") takes you back to "a
more elegant time", while "sensational" French-accented Viennese fare,
an "outstanding wine list" and "seamless", "pampering" service complete the "magical" experience; as one would expect, tabs also are "opulent"; P.S. for a "very special" private party, check out the downstairs.

Del Posto *Italian*

25	26	24	$88

Chelsea | 85 10th Ave. (16th St.) | 212-497-8090 | www.delposto.com

"Dazzled" disciples of the "dress-up dining" at this Batali-Bastianich
"instant classic" in Chelsea "come out reeling" after savoring its "sublime", "authentic" Italian cuisine, "phenomenal wine list" and service
as polished as the "beautiful marble floors" and dark-wood paneling in
its grand main dining room; yes, tabs here can "suck expense accounts
dry", but there's always the "less-formal", "less-expensive" enoteca.

Di Fara ⊄ *Pizza*

27	4	7	$13

Midwood | 1424 Ave. J (bet. 14th & 15th Sts.) | Brooklyn | 718-258-1367

It "looks like hell" and waits can be "timed with a calendar", but Dominic
De Marco's "legendary" circa-1963 Midwood "mecca of pizza" creates pies that are pure "heaven"; in sum, it's "all it's cracked up to be."

Eleven Madison Park *French*

26	26	26	$104

Gramercy | 11 Madison Ave. (24th St.) | 212-889-0905 |
www.elevenmadisonpark.com

Now with a "brilliant" New French menu from executive chef Daniel
Humm, Danny Meyer's "magical" Madison Square Park "triumph" is
"better than ever"; "it's posh", with "polished service" in a "huge",
"gorgeous", "vaulted room"; although the prix fixe "price tags equal"
its "high culinary" standard, and a few mutter about "midget portions", most "blather on" about "blissdom."

Four Seasons 🅩 *Continental*

25	27	26	$91

E 50s | 99 E. 52nd St. (bet. Lexington & Park Aves.) | 212-754-9494 |
www.fourseasonsrestaurant.com

Still a "stunner" after nearly 50 years, this "timeless" Midtown "classic" (led by suave host-owners Alex von Bidder and Julian Niccolini)
delivers "first-class" Continental cuisine to an "oh-so-urbane crowd"
that's practically a "who's who of the city"; service is "superior" and
the "NY landmark" surroundings famously "sleek and sumptuous",
whether among lunching "power players" in the Grill room or with
those who insist the "serene" "Pool Room is the cat's PJs"; naturally,
it's "expensive", but "if it's awesome you want, this is the place."

Gordon Ramsay *French*

25	24	25	$126

W 50s | The London NYC | 151 W. 54th St. (bet. 6th & 7th Aves.) |
212-468-8888 | www.gordonramsay.com

"Crusty" TV chef Gordon Ramsay "leaves the terror in the kitchen" at
this "sublime" New French arrival in Midtown's hotel London NYC, his
first U.S. foray, which "lives up to the hype" with "meticulously prepared", "exquisitely presented" cuisine full of "complex and layered"
flavors; service is "flawless without being stuffy", though the "mod-

ern", neutral-toned decor gets mixed reviews ("elegant" and "refined" vs. "bland" and "sterile"); naturally, all of this "understated" "excellence" is "not for the faint of pocketbook."

Gotham Bar & Grill *American*   27 | 25 | 26 | $72

G Village | 12 E. 12th St. (bet. 5th Ave. & University Pl.) | 212-620-4020 | www.gothambarandgrill.com

At this Village culinary "temple", "grand master" Alfred Portale continues to "excite" enthusiasts with his "soigné" "skyscrapers" of "spectacular" New American fare, while staffers "grant your wishes before you even know what to ask for" in a room that's "urbane" but "never pretentious"; a few fret it's "beginning to feel dated", but the majority declares this "quintessential NYC" experience is still "vibrant after all these years"; P.S. the $27 prix fixe lunch is "worth any detour."

☑ Gramercy Tavern *American*   27 | 25 | 27 | $92

Flatiron | 42 E. 20th St. (bet. B'way & Park Ave. S.) | 212-477-0777 | www.gramercytavern.com

Supporters of this "superb-in-all-respects" Flatiron New American hail the new chef – Michael Anthony, formerly of Blue Hill at Stone Barns – and salute his "spellbinding" market-centric cuisine, matched with an "extraordinary wine list"; the flower-filled, "rustic-yet-refined" main room "puts diners at ease", as does the "quicksilver" staff that's "on top of everything without being on top of you"; tabs are "costly" and reservations "tough" ("getting into Harvard is easier"), but there's always the "lower-priced", "more casual", "drop-in" front tavern.

Hill Country *BBQ*   – | – | – | M

Chelsea | 30 W. 26th St. (bet. B'way & 6th Ave.) | 212-255-4544 | www.hillcountryny.com

Taking you to Texas hill country by way of Chelsea, this big, boisterous, bi-level newcomer features three in-house smokers manned by a seasoned pit master (Robbie Richter) and decor right out of a back country roadhouse; the meats and sides are ordered from a counter, then carried on trays to long communal tables, and the result is a place that tastes, looks and smells as good as anything in the Lone Star state.

Il Mulino ☑ *Italian*   27 | 18 | 24 | $83

G Village | 86 W. Third St. (bet. Sullivan & Thompson Sts.) | 212-673-3783 | www.ilmulinonewyork.com

"Age has not diminished" the "one-of-a-kind" experience at this "outstanding", "crowded" Village Italian "classic", where nearly "every dish is a masterpiece", and the "white-glove" service has patrons feeling "like royalty"; while some insist "it's the best meal you'll ever have", it's also among "the hardest to book and the hardest to pay for" – to improve your chances in both respects, go for lunch.

☑ Jean Georges ☑ *French*   28 | 26 | 27 | $126

W 60s | Trump Int'l Hotel | 1 Central Park W. (bet. 60th & 61st Sts.) | 212-299-3900 | www.jean-georges.com

"From start to finish", expect "profound dining experiences" at Jean-Georges Vongerichten's "stunning" New French "temple to gastronomy" at Columbus Circle, where the frequently changing menus based on fresh seasonal ingredients are probably the "most creative" in town; add "flawless" formal service (supervised by the chef's brother,

Philippe), "elegant" high-ceilinged spaces overlooking Central Park and alfresco seating, and it's no wonder it's voted one of NY's most popular places; P.S. for a "bargain" alternative, the Nougatine Room offers "ethereal" repasts at "reasonable prices."

La Grenouille ☒ *French*   27 | 28 | 27 | $120

E 50s | 3 E. 52nd St. (bet. 5th & Madison Aves.) | 212-752-1495 | www.la-grenouille.com

NY's "last great haute French" restaurant, the Masson family's "timeless" Midtowner is "superlative" in every way, boasting "done-to-perfection" cuisine, "impeccable service" and an "enchanting" room filled with "flowers galore" (even the "diners exude class"); yes, you may need to "raid your piggy bank" to experience this *"magnifique* grande dame", but all concur it's "worth the splash"; P.S. the charming upstairs private party space is a "true find for a special occasion."

L'Atelier de Joël Robuchon *French*   27 | 24 | 26 | $131

E 50s | Four Seasons Hotel | 57 E. 57th St. (bet. Madison & Park Aves.) | 212-350-6658 | www.fourseasons.com

From the "brilliant" Robuchon comes this "off-the-charts" "consolidation of French technique and Japanese style", where "decadent" dishes in "tapas-style" portions come with a "perfectly designed wine list" and "impeccable service"; although there are comfortable tables, "counter seating is the way to go" in the "minimalist", "casually elegant" space, as the "theater of the open kitchen" is almost as "memorable" as the "eye-popping prices."

☒ Le Bernardin ☒ *French/Seafood*   28 | 27 | 28 | $129

W 50s | 155 W. 51st St. (bet. 6th & 7th Aves.) | 212-554-1515 | www.le-bernardin.com

All the "accolades are well deserved" at Maguy LeCoze's Midtown French "phenomenon" where "piscatorial fantasy" meets "culinary perfection" via chef Eric Ripert's "beyond sublime" seafood, abetted by "smooth-as-silk service" and a "quietly elegant" setting; to get around the "sky-high" prices, try the $64 prix fixe lunch, or go for broke and chalk it up as a "must-do experience."

Masa ☒ *Japanese*   27 | 24 | 26 | $485

W 60s | Time Warner Ctr. | 10 Columbus Circle, 4th fl. (60th St. at B'way) | 212-823-9800 | www.masanyc.com

At this Zen-like Time Warner Center Japanese, you can watch star chef Masayoshi Takayama's "exquisite" kaiseki technique yield an "unforgettable" "parade of perfection" for an "astronomical" $400 prix fixe that some consider a deal when compared to the cost of floor seats for the Knicks; the more "unassuming" Bar Masa next door is "not cheap", but still a "bargain compared to its big brother."

Milos, Estiatorio ● *Greek/Seafood*   26 | 23 | 22 | $73

W 50s | 125 W. 55th St. (bet. 6th & 7th Aves.) | 212-245-7400 | www.milos.ca

"Zeus couldn't eat better" than mere mortals do at this all-white, high-ceilinged Midtown Greek known for "pristine" seafood "grilled to perfection" (the "only way to get it fresher is to stick your head in the fish tank"); "smooth service" and "resortlike" decor add to the "quality" experience, but "bring the platinum card" to deal with the "Masa prices" – or stick to its less expensive, but equally delicious, appetizers.

	FOOD	DECOR	SERVICE	COST

Modern, The 🖼 *American/French* | 26 | 26 | 24 | $110

W 50s | Museum of Modern Art | 9 W. 53rd St. (bet. 5th & 6th Aves.) | 212-333-1220 | www.themodernnyc.com

Set in a "coolly elegant" room overlooking MoMA's sculpture garden, Danny Meyer's "splendid" French–New American is helmed by chef Gabriel Kreuther who "balances tradition with innovation" for prix fixe meals that are "as sophisticated as any Picasso" (and almost as expensive); a "thoroughly professional" staff adds to the "formal" scene, though the "livelier" adjacent bar with its gorgeous forest mural offers a "more flexible" small-plates menu at a "more reasonable" price.

Morimoto *Japanese* | 24 | 26 | 22 | $82

Chelsea | 88 10th Ave. (bet. 15th & 16th Sts.) | 212-989-8883 | www.morimotonyc.com

"It's showtime" at this "flashy" West Chelsea Japanese where Iron Chef Masaharu Morimoto's "mouthwatering delicacies" "vie for attention" with Tadao Ando's "spectacular", "ultramodern" interiors and the "futuristic loos"; even though it "costs a bundle", many urge you "splurge for omakase."

Nobu *Japanese* | 27 | 23 | 23 | $82

TriBeCa | 105 Hudson St. (Franklin St.) | 212-219-0500 | www.noburestaurants.com

"Exquisite", "palate-awakening" Japanese-Peruvian delicacies gratify gourmets at this ever-"buzzing" TriBeCan that hosts a "who's who" crowd right out of an "episode of *Entourage*"; constants include "informative" service and "one big bill" at meal's end, but "getting a table is a problem – unless you're Cameron Diaz"; its more "casual" Next Door sibling is "less expensive" and "every bit as delicious", "without the reservation fuss" since it only takes walk-ins.

Oriental Garden *Chinese/Seafood* | 24 | 12 | 16 | $30

Chinatown | 14 Elizabeth St. (bet. Bayard & Canal Sts.) | 212-619-0085

Setting the "standard for fresh-from-the-tank" seafood, this "dynamite" Chinatown Cantonese also rolls out "limitless dim sum varieties"; the "right price" makes the perpetual "noise", "inattention to decor" and "hurried but hilarious" service more palatable.

Palm *Steak* | 24 | 17 | 21 | $66

E 40s | 837 Second Ave. (bet. 44th & 45th Sts.) | 212-687-2953 🖼
E 40s | 840 Second Ave. (bet. 44th & 45th Sts.) | 212-697-5198
W 50s | 250 W. 50th St. (bet. B'way & 8th Ave.) | 212-333-7256 ◑
www.thepalm.com

"Masculine eating" is alive and well at these "boisterous" crosstown chophouses where a "gruff" crew dishes out "gargantuan steaks" and "colossal lobsters" in "macho" surroundings; purists prefer the original, circa-1926 west-side-of-Second-Avenue location, but wherever you wind up, you'd better "have plenty of money in your palm."

🔲 Per Se *American/French* | 28 | 28 | 28 | $301

W 60s | Time Warner Ctr. | 10 Columbus Circle, 4th fl. (60th St. at B'way) | 212-823-9335 | www.perseny.com

Like a "four-hour stroll through culinary paradise", Thomas Keller's French–New American offers "epic dining" in a "Zen-like space" featuring "drop-dead views" of Central Park and Columbus Circle; "tele-pathic service" (voted No. 1 in this Survey) adds to the overall "magic", so even if the reservations process can be "grueling" and the tariffs "stratospheric", this "once-in-a-blue-moon treat" is "everything it's cracked up to be" – "Per-Fect!"

◪ Peter Luger Steak House ⊅ *Steak*   28 | 14 | 20 | $71

Williamsburg | 178 Broadway (Driggs Ave.) | Brooklyn | 718-387-7400 | www.peterluger.com

The "holy grail of steakhouses", this Williamsburg "landmark" (NYC's No. 1 chop shop for the 24th year running) makes carnivores "salivate just hearing the name" that's synonymous with the "ultimate" in "suc-culent" beef, particularly those "buttery, perfectly marbled porter-houses"; "don't look for coddling" from the "brutally efficient" staff – just "consider them an amusement", like the "old-world" *brauhaus* atmo-spherics and that "outdated cash-only" policy.

Picholine   *French/Mediterranean*   27 | 24 | 25 | $87

W 60s | 35 W. 64th St. (bet. B'way & CPW) | 212-724-8585 | www.picholinenyc.com

"Celebrate", "pamper yourself" or just "swoon" at Terry Brennan's "better-than-ever" UWS French-Med where the "revamped" $65 prix fixe menu is "always excellent" and the "siren call of the cheese trol-ley" can be heard above the "raves" resounding through the "under-statedly elegant" room; "dignified" service and the "delectability factor" outweighs the "formal atmosphere", while "top-notch" private party rooms seal the deal.

Rao's   🖾⊅ *Italian*   22 | 16 | 21 | $61

Harlem | 455 E. 114th St. (Pleasant Ave.) | 212-722-6709 | www.raos.com

"Still the toughest reservation in town", Frank Pellegrino's "mystique"-laden East Harlem Southern Italian requires knowing a "friend with a table" for the chance to dine on "amazing" "old-world" dishes while rubbing elbows with the famous and the infamous; alternatives in-clude doing it yourself with a jar of their "supermarket sauce" or "fly-ing to Vegas to try the new one in Caesars Palace."

River Café   *American*   26 | 28 | 26 | $111

Dumbo | 1 Water St. (bet. Furman & Old Fulton Sts.) | Brooklyn | 718-522-5200 | www.rivercafe.com

"Sheer bliss from start to finish", Dumbo's "classic stunner" under the Brooklyn Bridge "wows visitors" with "top-notch" New American fare, a "flower-laden" interior and "glorious" river/skyline views (it's *the* place to propose – no matter what the proposition"); just remember to "dress sharp" (jackets required) and prepare for a "wallet busting" ($95 prix fixe-only dinner); P.S. they do spectacular parties.

Roberto   🖾 *Italian*   27 | 18 | 21 | $49

Bronx | 603 Crescent Ave. (Hughes Ave.) | 718-733-9503 | www.robertobronx.com

At this "neighborhood treasure" in the Bronx's version of Little Italy, Roberto Paciullo sends diners on "life-changing" tours of his native Salerno ("forget the menu", he'll "take good care of you"); still, that no-reservations policy makes for "looong" waits.

	FOOD	DECOR	SERVICE	COST

Saul *American*

27 | 19 | 24 | $57

Boerum Hill | 140 Smith St. (bet. Bergen & Dean Sts.) | Brooklyn | 718-935-9844 | www.saulrestaurant.com

Helmed by chef-owner Saul Bolton, this Boerum Hill New American "deserves all the raves" for its "sophisticated" yet "unpretentious" seasonal menu; a "remarkably helpful" staff, "civilized" setting and fair pricing add up to a "top-flight" experience.

Shun Lee Palace ❷ *Chinese*

24 | 20 | 22 | $55

E 50s | 155 E. 55th St. (bet. Lexington & 3rd Aves.) | 212-371-8844 | www.shunleepalace.com

The "emperor would be proud" of Michael Tong's "opulent" Midtown Chinese that makes a "lavish impression" with its "fusion-free", "museum-quality meals" and "second-to-none" service; if you "like to dress up" and are prepared to pay "premium prices", this "oldie but goodie" is certainly "worth the splurge."

Spice Market ❷ *SE Asian*

22 | 26 | 20 | $58

Meatpacking | 403 W. 13th St. (9th Ave.) | 212-675-2322 | www.jean-georges.com

Brace yourself for "visual overload" at Jean-Georges Vongerichten's "theatrical" Southeast Asian in the Meatpacking District, where transportingly "exotic" decor is matched by "intriguing" Thai-Malay-Vietnamese street food; the "maddening crowd" featuring lots of long legs and short skirts is supplemented by reasonable-for-the-quality prices and servers wearing "sexy" uniforms; P.S. the "basement catacombs" are a "great place to throw an intimate party."

Sushi Seki ❷🄯 *Japanese*

27 | 13 | 21 | $66

E 60s | 1143 First Ave. (bet. 62nd & 63rd Sts.) | 212-371-0238

You can "put your trust in chef Seki" and he'll lead the way to "omakase heaven" at this "cult-ish" Upper East Side Japanese where the "faultless" sushi easily out-"sparkles" the dull decor; even better, you can "keep it coming" (while "spending a small fortune") since it's open until 3 AM.

🄯 Sushi Yasuda 🄯 *Japanese*

28 | 22 | 24 | $78

E 40s | 204 E. 43rd St. (bet. 2nd & 3rd Aves.) | 212-972-1001 | www.sushiyasuda.com

Sushi verges on the "spiritual" at this Grand Central–area "pinnacle" once again voted NYC's No. 1 Japanese, where chef Naomichi Yasuda provides raw fish "bliss" via "celestial" morsels that "span the seven seas" ("bring a snorkel if you want it fresher"); service is "knowledgeable", the decor "simple" but elegant and the overall vibe "calm" – at least until the bill arrives.

Tavern on the Green *American*

15 | 24 | 17 | $64

W 60s | Central Park W. (bet. 66th & 67th Sts.) | 212-873-3200 | www.tavernonthegreen.com

"More spectacle than restaurant", this "over-the-top wonderland" in Central Park is best celebrated for its gorgeous garden and "kitschy", "fairy-tale" ambiance by way of "Liberace", not the only "adequate" American eats, "gaping tourists" and "rushed" service; nonetheless, it's capable of doing great parties, and on the right "spring evening", it still may render you "starry-eyed."

Telepan *American*

25 | 20 | 23 | $69

W 60s | 72 W. 69th St. (bet. Columbus Ave. & CPW) | 212-580-4300 | www.telepan-ny.com

Bill Telepan is the mastermind behind this "brilliant" New American near Lincoln Center, where they "hit the ground running and have just kept going" thanks to an "exceptional", "market-driven menu", "highly professional" service and a "grown-up, non-sceney" setting; more debatable are the "pasture"-colored walls and unneighborly tabs, but many feel this "triumph" verges on the "transcendent."

Tocqueville *American/French*

26 | 24 | 25 | $73

Union Sq | 1 E. 15th St. (bet. 5th Ave. & Union Sq. W.) | 212-647-1515 | www.tocquevillerestaurant.com

"Civilized dining for adults" is on the docket at this "oasis of calm" off Union Square where chef Marco Moreira demonstrates his "dexterity" with "serious" French-American cooking yielding "sublime" results; granted, the "minuscule portions" arrive at "major prices", but in return the place "purrs like a luxury automobile."

21 Club *American*

22 | 23 | 24 | $71

W 50s | 21 W. 52nd St. (bet. 5th & 6th Aves.) | 212-582-7200 | www.21club.com

This "venerable" onetime speakeasy, a "formidable fixture" in Midtown, delivers "satisfying" Traditional American fare to a "virtual who's who" of "high rollers" in "clubby", "quintessential NY" quarters manned by a "solicitous yet unobtrusive" "formal" crew; to avoid a "shocker" of a tab "check out the $40 pre-theater prix fixe"; P.S. party-throwers should note there are 10 "lovely" private rooms.

☑ Union Square Cafe *American*

26 | 22 | 26 | $65

Union Sq | 21 E. 16th St. (bet. 5th Ave. & Union Sq. W.) | 212-243-4020 | www.unionsquarecafe.com

Once again voted Most Popular in this Survey, Danny Meyer's New American off Union Square "proves its reputation every time", thanks to Michael Romano's "artfully executed" cuisine, a choice of "well-appointed" spaces and "friendly" service that "never wavers"; true, a reservation can be "problematic", but the walk-in bar area is always available to experience this "definition of comfortable dining."

Wakiya ● *Chinese*

– | – | – | E

Gramercy | Gramercy Park Hotel | 2 Lexington Ave. (21st St.) | 212-995-1330 | www.gramercyparkhotel.com

Ian Schrager's trendy Gramercy Park Hotel is the setting for this nouveau Chinese named after its Japanese chef, Yuji Wakiya, who offers a 'sharing menu' of hot and cold items as well as dim sum; the long, slender space, done up in red and black, exudes a James Bond vibe (i.e. *Diamonds are Forever*), though pricing is far more modern.

Waverly Inn and Garden ● *American*

18 | 21 | 17 | $57

W Village | 16 Bank St. (Waverly Pl.) | 212-243-7900

This remake of a circa-1920 West Village tavern produces "reliable", tasty Americana in a "cozy" setting featuring a "celeb" crowd that is mostly friends of owner/*Vanity Fair* editor Graydon Carter; it's virtually "impossible to get in" without connections, but walk-ins are allowed in the charming front bar, sidewalk tables and back 'garden room.'

Orange County, CA

TOP FOOD RANKING

	Restaurant	Cuisine
28	Basilic	French/Swiss
	Stonehill Tavern	American
27	Tradition by Pascal	French
	Napa Rose	Californian
	Hobbit, The	Continental/French
	Studio	Californian/French
26	Tabu Grill	Seafood/Steak
	Cafe Zoolu	Californian
	Golden Truffle	Caribbean/French
	Ramos House	American

OTHER NOTEWORTHY PLACES

Bayside	American
Bluefin	Japanese
Fleming's Prime	Steak
French 75	French
Marche Modern	French
Mastro's Steak	Steak
Onotria	Eclectic
Pinot Provence	French
Roy's	Hawaiian
Sage	American

Z Basilic ⊠M *French/Swiss* | 28 | 20 | 25 | $53 |

Newport Beach | 217 Marine Ave. (Park Ave.) | 949-673-0570 |
www.basilicrestaurant.com

Francophile fans "don't want to share the secret" of this "cute, minute" Newport Beach bistro, voted No. 1 for Food in Orange County, but word's out that chef-owner Bernard Althaus "is a master" of "delicately prepared" French-Swiss dishes backed by "five-star" service; despite "decidedly high prices", this *très romantique* spot "just gets better and better"; P.S. there's "limited seating" (24 maximum).

Bayside *American* | 25 | 23 | 23 | $50 |

Newport Beach | 900 Bayside Dr. (Jamboree Rd.) | 949-721-1222 |
www.baysiderestaurant.com

"Nothing on the menu fails to please" at this Newport "upscale" New American "favorite" where "imaginative" dishes are served in a sleek setting with bay views, rotating art exhibits, a "great patio" and a "scene at the bar"; usually "attentive" service "can be spotty" on "busy weekends" when the "elite" "over-40 OC crowd" holds court.

Bluefin *Japanese* | 25 | 20 | 21 | $57 |

Newport Coast | Crystal Cove Promenade | 7952 E. PCH (Crystal Heights Dr.) | 949-715-7373 | www.bluefinbyabe.com

Connoisseurs call the "cutting-edge" sushi and other Japanese creations from "master" chef-owner Takashi Abe "a marvel" at Crystal

Cove's "sleek" spot for "world-class" feasts aided by "exquisite sakes" and a "slight view" of the Pacific; while guests can expect to "pay dearly" for the "unforgettable experience", insiders know the "lunch omakase" is a "gourmet bargain"; P.S. reservations are a "must" on weekends.

Cafe Zoolu Ⓜ Californian
26 | 13 | 20 | $40

Laguna Beach | 860 Glenneyre St. (bet. St. Anne's Dr. & Thalia St.) | 949-494-6825 | www.cafezoolu.com

"One of Laguna's few remaining old funky spots", this "tiny, out-of-the-way" Californian "sleeper" earns raves for "flavors that demand attention" in dishes such as the "unbelievably thick" charbroiled swordfish, which "reigns supreme here"; along with an "eclectic" staff, the "terrific" mom-and-pop owners make sure that their "in-the-know" diners are "happy as clams", but since the "campy", Polynesian-themed "bungalow" seats only 33, "don't try it without a reservation."

☑ Fleming's Prime Steakhouse & Wine Bar Steak
25 | 23 | 23 | $55

Newport Beach | Fashion Island | 455 Newport Center Dr. (San Miguel Dr.) | 949-720-9633 | www.flemingssteakhouse.com

"Get your red meat groove on" at this "impressive", "posh" chain steakhouse that "gets everything right" from the "perfectly cooked" beef down to the "huge variety of wines by the glass" and "wonderful martinis" all served by a staff that "treats you like a king"; considering this "high-energy" spot gets "noisy" ("what did the waiter say?") and the "bill can add up fast", you might consider "earplugs" an essential addition along with a fat wallet.

☑ French 75 French
21 | 23 | 20 | $45

Laguna Beach | 1464 S. PCH (bet. Calliope St. & Mountain Rd.) | 949-494-8444
Newport Beach | Fashion Island | 327 Newport Center Dr. (Atrium Ct.) | 949-640-2700

☑ French 75 Brasserie French

Irvine | 13290 Jamboree Rd. (bet. Bryan Ave. & Irvine Blvd.) | 714-573-7600
www.culinaryadventures.com

David Wilhelm's expanding "empire" of "non-intimidating" "Parisian" bistros offers "excellent", "consistent" fare served by a "warmly professional" staff in settings that might "impress your date", even if some deem them "baroque" and "French at its fauxest"; perhaps it's "a bit ersatz, but that's part of the charm" say voters willing to pay "pricey" tabs for "live jazz", "champagne cocktails" and the "best onion soup this side of the Eiffel Tower."

Golden Truffle, The ☒Ⓜ Caribbean/French
26 | 11 | 21 | $45

Costa Mesa | 1767 Newport Blvd. (bet. 17th & 18th Sts.) | 949-645-9858

"Ask what chef Greeley recommends" as "Alan always finds the high note" assure enthusiasts of the "inventive", "subtle" and seasonal Caribbean-French "concoctions" matched with a "superb wine list" at this Costa Mesa "strip-mall" scrapper; despite somewhat uneven service and a room that "needs refurbishing", what it "lacks in style" is compensated for by "one of OC's best chefs" (just be sure to go "when he's there").

ORANGE COUNTY, CA

	FOOD	DECOR	SERVICE	COST

☒ Hobbit, The Ⓜ *Continental/French* — 27 | 25 | 28 | $87

Orange | 2932 E. Chapman Ave. (Malena St.) | 714-997-1972 |
www.hobbitrestaurant.com

"Prepare to spend hours" on this "unique" seven-course "adventure"
where French-Continental feasts unfold "like posh private dinner parties" fit for "Gatsby", with chef Michael Philippi's "superb" "culinary
delights" delivered by an "outstanding" staff that earns it the No. 1
score for Service in Orange County; the "warm" 1930s Spanish house,
complete with a "theatrical" wine cellar, provides an "elegant" backdrop for "costly" meals that most find "unforgettable"; P.S. there's
only one seating each night (Wednesday–Sunday), which must be "reserved well in advance."

Marché Moderne *French* — – | – | – | E

Costa Mesa | South Coast Plaza | 3333 Bristol St. (Anton Blvd.) |
714-434-7900

Esteemed OC chef Florent Marneau (ex Pinot Provence) breaks out on
his own at this luxe Costa Mesa mall site (last home to Troquet) that's
been handsomely remade to suit his assured, market-inspired French
cuisine; expect pricey seasonal fare informed by local and artisan producers plus graceful desserts by his pastry chef wife, Amelia.

Mastro's Steakhouse *Steak* — 25 | 22 | 23 | $70

Costa Mesa | 633 Anton Blvd. (Park Center Dr.) | 714-546-7405 |
www.mastrosoceanclub.com

"Welcome to the high rollers' steakhouse" in Costa Mesa where "over-
doing it is a must", as the "first-rate" "bone-in filet" is "T. rex" size, the
"seafood tower is extraordinary" and the "drinks are colossal"; its "glam"
location is staffed by "courteous" servers, though some surveyors balk
at the "steep prices" and all the "businessmen with blonds" at the bar.

☒ Napa Rose *Californian* — 27 | 26 | 27 | $62

Anaheim | Grand Californian Hotel | 1600 S. Disneyland Dr. (Katella Ave.) |
714-300-7170 | www.disneyland.com

"This is no Mickey Mouse operation" claim those captivated by
this Anaheim "foodie mecca", voted Orange County's Most Popular
restaurant, where "inspired" chef Andrew Sutton's "adventurous" and
"masterfully executed" "wine-country" cuisine is bolstered by a "cellar that satisfies even the fussiest lush", and served by a "five-star"
staff; the "elegant" dining room has a "rustic, Napa" feel, and while
most appreciate the "family-friendly" vibe, a few quibble that "sweat-
shirts" and "kids on portable DVD players" have no place in such a
"first-rate" establishment.

Onotria Wine Country Cuisine ☒ *Eclectic* — ▽ 24 | 19 | 20 | $47

Costa Mesa | 2831 Bristol St. (Bear St.) | 714-641-5952 |
www.onotria.com

A "creative", "wine-friendly" menu distinguishes this midpriced Costa
Mesa charmer where chef-owner Massimo Navarretta turns out "seasonal" Eclectic creations with an "emphasis on game meats" that pair
with vintages from the 500-label cellar; the spacious, "rustic" digs
with high beamed ceilings are deemed "too loud" by some, but the
majority of reviewers raves this "gem" is "one of Orange County's
best new additions."

	FOOD	DECOR	SERVICE	COST

Pinot Provence *French*
25 | 24 | 23 | $57

Costa Mesa | Westin South Coast Plaza Hotel | 686 Anton Blvd.
(Bristol St.) | 714-444-5900 | www.patinagroup.com

"Admirably French through and through", this "sophisticated" Patina Group effort set in the Westin South Coast Plaza is the place "to impress" with "divine", "delicately prepared" Gallic-Med cuisine that's "impeccably served" in a "romantic" space that evokes "the other Provence"; tabs can be "a little pricey", so those in-the-know suggest you take advantage of the "prix fixe lunch deals" and "free corkage policy" to keep the damage minimal; N.B. the Food score may not fully reflect a December 2006 chef change.

Ramos House Café 🅜 *American*
26 | 20 | 21 | $31

San Juan Capistrano | 31752 Los Rios St. (Ramos St.) | 949-443-1342 |
www.ramoshouse.com

"Steps from the San Juan Capistrano mission", this "historic" abode (built in 1881) wows with chef-owner John Q. Humphreys' "phenomenal" Southern-accented New American dishes that bring out the "natural flavors of the ingredients"; a denim-donning staff ups the "character" of the "rustic", "garden-patio" setting where the somewhat "pricey" brunches kick off with a "famous" soju Bloody Mary and finish with "fighting over the last slice of buttermilk pie"; N.B. open until 3 PM, Tuesday–Sunday.

🆉 Roy's *Hawaiian*
24 | 22 | 22 | $47

Newport Beach | Fashion Island | 453 Newport Center Dr. (San Miguel Dr.) |
949-640-7697 | www.roysrestaurant.com

"The best Hawaiian export since Don Ho" claim those "wowed" by the "imaginative" and "beautifully presented" fusion dishes at Roy Yamaguchi's "pricey" SoCal spin-off of his Honolulu original; though the "well-trained staff" strikes many as "exceptional", a rising minority complains it's left "disappointed" by "unfulfilled expectations" and "too-sweet" fare, leading some to wonder if this chain is "just getting too big."

🆉 Sage *American*
24 | 22 | 22 | $47

Newport Beach | Eastbluff Shopping Ctr. | 2531 Eastbluff Dr. (Vista del Sol) |
949-718-9650 | www.sagerestaurant.com

🆉 Sage on the Coast *American*

Newport Beach | Crystal Cove Promenade | 7862 E. PCH
(Crystal Heights Dr.) | 949-715-7243 | www.sagerestaurant.com

"Creative" chef-owner Rich Mead "never ceases to amaze" report advocates of his "fresh", "imaginative" New American fare offered at dual Newport Beach locales that cater to a "well-heeled" "local contingent" seeking a "relaxing" vibe that's "hip yet not snobbish"; the "chic" Crystal Cove site boasts a "covered patio with roaring fireplace" while Eastbluff's "original charmer" has a heated "garden setting" (and some say stronger service), but it's "hard to go wrong" at either one.

🆉 Stonehill Tavern 🅜 *American*
28 | 27 | 26 | $79

Dana Point | St. Regis Resort, Monarch Bch. | 1 Monarch Beach Resort
(Niguel Rd.) | 949-234-3318 | www.michaelmina.net

"Star" chef Michael Mina's "smash hit" at the luxe St. Regis Resort "embodies OC chic" with a "phenomenal" take on New American dishes, highlighted in "artfully presented tastings" that are even "more beautiful" than the "endless parade of pretty people"; along with a "swanky" design by Tony Chi, patrons are impressed by the "first-class service" – just expect a little "noise" and some "prohibitive" costs, especially on the wine list.

Studio *Californian/French*   27 | 27 | 26 | $84

Laguna Beach | St. Regis Resort, Monarch Bch. | 30801 S. PCH (Montage Dr.) | 949-715-6420 | www.studiolagunabeach.com
Smitten surveyors say "you don't want to leave, ever" after "sublime" dining in this Laguna resort destination "on a bluff" that "may be the most beautiful spot on the entire SoCal coast", flaunting wraparound vistas of "breaking Pacific waves" that buoy it to No. 1 for Decor in Orange County; the "top-notch" Cal-New French fare from chef James Boyce is equally "stunning", and "impeccable" service adds to an experience that feels like "no expense has been spared", so "forget what it costs" and "don't miss the sunset" (as there's less to see "after dark").

Tabu Grill *Seafood/Steak*   26 | 21 | 24 | $55

Laguna Beach | 2892 S. PCH (Nyes Pl.) | 949-494-7743 | www.tabugrill.com
"Utterly amazing" "big flavors" of surf 'n' turf cooking with a Pacific Rim touch distinguish Nancy Wilhelm's "shining star" where the "closely packed" "Lilliputian tables" benefit from "beautiful" Polynesian-inspired surroundings; the servers are "courteous" and "know their wines", so once guests get past the Laguna site's "limited parking" and "PCH traffic roaring outside the front door" ("where you sit can make a difference") to the "palate-pleasing meal", "everything else is forgotten"; P.S. "make reservations."

∑ Tradition by Pascal *French*   27 | 21 | 25 | $59
(aka Pascal)

Newport Beach | 1000 N. Bristol St. (Jamboree Rd.) | 949-263-9400 | www.pascalnewportbeach.com
Chef-owner Pascal Olhats "continues to dazzle" "Newport foodies" with "classical", "unpretentious" French cookery (he "excels with fish dishes") that's "still the best" for "wooing someone special"; loyalists "overlook" the "strip-mall location" because the interior "oozes understated elegance" and the service is "first-class", making a trip to this "high altar" of Gallic gastronomy a "worthwhile treat."

Orlando

	Restaurant	Cuisine
27	Le Coq au Vin	French
	Victoria & Albert's	American
	Chatham's Place	Continental
	Del Frisco's	Steak
	Taquitos Jalisco	Mexican
26	Primo	Italian
	Norman's	New World
	California Grill	Californian
	Amura	Japanese
25	K Restaurant	Eclectic
	Jiko	African
	Ruth's Chris	Steak
	Seasons 52	American
	Thai House	Thai
	Roy's	Hawaiian
	Enzo's	Italian
	Antonio's	Italian
	Vito's Chop House	Steak
24	Boma	African
	Palm	Steak

OTHER NOTEWORTHY PLACES

Beacon, The	American
Beluga	Seafood
Blue Bistro	Eclectic
Boheme, The	American
Chez Vincent	French
Christini's	Italian
Emeril's Orlando	Contemp. Louisiana
Emeril's Tchoup Chop	Asian/Polynesian
Fifi's	Mediterranean
Fleming's Prime	Steak
HUE	American
Kres	Steak
Ming's Bistro	Chinese
MoonFish	Seafood/Steak
Shari Sushi	Japanese
Thai Thani	Thai
Todd English's bluezoo	Seafood
Venetian Room	Continental
Wazzabi	Japanese
Wolfgang Puck Café	Californian

ORLANDO

	FOOD	DECOR	SERVICE	COST

Amura *Japanese* — 26 | 20 | 19 | $33

Bay Hill/Dr. Phillips | Plaza Venezia | 7786 W. Sand Lake Rd. (bet. Della Dr. & Dr. Phillips Blvd.) | 407-370-0007
Downtown Orlando | 55 W. Church St. (bet. S. Garland & S. Orange Aves.) | 407-316-8500
Lake Mary | Colonial Town Ctr. | 950 Market Promenade Plaza (Townpark Ave.) | 407-936-6001

"Sushi lovers will be delighted" by this "trendy" trio's "King Kong portions" of "super-fresh seafood" and "inventive rolls" "with an edge" selected from a "seemingly endless list of options"; a few frown on service that "could be quicker", but most find them "funky, vibrant" and "aglow with ambiance"; N.B. the locations in Dr. Phillips and Lake Mary also offer teppanyaki.

Antonio's La Fiamma Ristorante *Italian* — 25 | 22 | 23 | $42

Maitland | 611 S. Orlando Ave. (Maitland Ave.) | 407-645-1035

Antonio's Sand Lake 🗷 *Italian*

Bay Hill/Dr. Phillips | The Fountains | 7559 W. Sand Lake Rd. (bet. Dr. Phillips Blvd. & Turkey Lake Rd.) | 407-363-9191
www.antoniosonline.com

For what some claim is the "best Italian food outside of Italy", head to this "popular" Maitland mainstay owned by local legend Greg Gentile, where "wonderful, authentic", "zesty dishes like mama made" are accompanied by a "can't-beat" wine list; "though sometimes noisy", it has a "lovely atmosphere" courtesy of servers who "treat you like a family member" and a dining room with "romantic lake views"; N.B. the Sand Lake Road location opened post-Survey.

Beacon, The ● *American* — - | - | - | M

Thornton Park | The Sanctuary | 100 S. Eola Dr. (E. Pine St.) | 407-841-5444 | www.beaconorlando.com

A beacon for the city's sophisticates, this Thornton Park New American serves up serious suppers and equally interesting weekend brunches; a bold red-and-gold interior with a leather-topped bar and a shaded patio with sofas are enough to incite martini madness as the chic clientele ends their evening with the sounds of acid jazz.

Beluga 🗷 *Seafood* — - | - | - | E

Winter Park | Winter Park Vill. | 460 N. Orlando Ave. (Gay Rd.) | 407-644-2962 | www.beluga-restaurant.com

At this whale of an addition to Winter Park's open-air mall, trendy types enjoy fresh fish and other globally tinged seafood dishes in a big-budget dining room; live entertainment at a Plexiglas-topped piano adds élan, while five enticing indoor and outdoor bars help to keep things spirited, drawing a young crowd that appreciates the combination of captivating cocktails and an appetizer-heavy menu.

Blue Bistro & Grill 🗷 *Eclectic* — 24 | 17 | 21 | $43

ViMi District | 815 N. Mills Ave. (E. Park Lake St.) | 407-898-5660

"You simply cannot beat the value" at this "Asian-influenced" Eclectic "secret" that offers up "edgy", "NYC-quality food at Orlando prices" in the form of an "always delicious", ever-changing menu served with "personal attention" amid "technopop" decor; it's "small" and located "on an otherwise gritty stretch" of the ViMi District, but its supporters advise "go for the food – it's worth it."

	FOOD	DECOR	SERVICE	COST

Boheme, The *American*   `23` `25` `22` `$53`

Downtown Orlando | Grand Bohemian Hotel | 325 S. Orange Ave.
(bet. Jackson & South Sts.) | 407-581-4700 | www.grandbohemianhotel.com
"It's like eating in an art gallery" observe ardent admirers of this
"elegant" destination in the Grand Bohemian Hotel, where "beautiful-
looking" New American "creations" and "incredible service" are complemented by "cosmopolitan", "Klimt-meets-Dietrich" decor and
nightly live piano in the lounge; it's "big-city food at big-city prices",
but "worth it" "for a special occasion", "business lunch" or "quality-
over-quantity" Sunday jazz brunch.

Boma – Flavors of Africa *African*   `24` `24` `22` `$33`

Animal Kingdom Area | Disney's Animal Kingdom Lodge | 2901
Osceola Pkwy. (Sherbert Rd.) | Lake Buena Vista | 407-938-4722 |
www.disneyworld.com
"Take a safari and never leave your table" at this "unique" buffet in
Disney's Animal Kingdom Lodge, where "an excellent spread" mingles
"exotic African preparations" for "adventurous palates" with "common but well-prepared American dishes" for kids and "picky eaters";
the "amazing variety of flavors" extends to "mouthwatering desserts"
and a small but "fantastic South African wine list", all served in a
themed setting that's "done remarkably well, without being campy."

☒ California Grill *Californian*   `26` `25` `24` `$50`

Magic Kingdom Area | Disney's Contemporary Resort | 4600 N. World Dr.,
15th fl. (Contemporary Resort Access Rd.) | Lake Buena Vista |
407-939-3463 | www.disneyworld.com
Located on the 15th floor of Disney's Contemporary Resort, the Orlando
area's Most Popular restaurant is an "unparalleled" "retreat", from its
"inventive" if "expensive" Californian dinner menu and "exemplary
staff" to its "upscale" ambiance and a "wine list that's second to
none"; but "make your reservations ahead of time" and "request a
window seat" in order to catch the "spectacular" view of the nightly
"fireworks exploding over the Magic Kingdom."

☒ Chatham's Place *Continental*   `27` `19` `26` `$53`

Bay Hill/Dr. Phillips | 7575 Dr. Phillips Blvd. (Sand Lake Rd.) |
407-345-2992 | www.chathamsplace.com
At this "heavenly" "local favorite" in Dr. Phillips, "a serious kitchen"
spins out "pricey but excellent" and "creative" Florida-tinged
Continental cuisine that's served by "attentive and gracious" "professionals"; it's "small" and located "out of the way" "in an office building", but it offers an "intimate", "old-world ambiance" complete with
"romantic" nightly guitar music.

Chez Vincent *French*   `23` `17` `24` `$42`

Winter Park | 533 W. New England Ave. (Pennsylvania Ave.) |
407-599-2929 | www.chezvincent.com
A "most hospitable chef-owner" and a "friendly", "highly trained" staff
are just the beginning at this "small", "charming" French bistro in
Winter Park "that's big on service" and even more focused on turning
out "wonderful" Gallic fare; still, a few fickle types find the cuisine to
be "a noble attempt" that's "hit-or-miss", while others claim the
"cramped" setting offers "little privacy" and "no ambiance."

	FOOD	DECOR	SERVICE	COST

Christini's Ristorante Italiano ● *Italian* | 24 | 21 | 24 | $59 |

Bay Hill/Dr. Phillips | The Marketplace | 7600 Dr. Phillips Blvd.
(Sand Lake Rd.) | 407-345-8770 | www.christinis.com
At this "warm", "intimate", "old-world Italian" in Dr. Phillips, you'll get
everything you expect from a "New York–style" restaurant – "epicurean
delights", a "romantic" ambiance, "top-notch service" – "delivered in
an endearing way" ("a rose is given to the ladies" as they are seated);
surveyors say this "standard-bearer" is "suited to special occasions",
although they admit the prices may be designed for "expense-
account" and "tourist budgets only."

☑ Del Frisco's Prime Steak & Lobster ⑤ *Steak* | 27 | 18 | 25 | $58 |

Winter Park | 729 Lee Rd. (I-4) | 407-645-4443 | www.delfriscosorlando.com
"Don't change a thing!" cry carnivores captivated by this Winter Park
chophouse "for a man to love", where what some believe is "the best
steak at any restaurant, in any city, at any price" (plus "lobsters better
than in Maine") is served in "huge portions" by an "excellent", "old-
school" staff; a "very good wine list", nightly live music and "typical",
"dark-wood and leather" decor rounds out the "expense-account" experience; N.B. reservations are recommended.

☑ Emeril's Orlando *Contemp. Louisiana* | 24 | 22 | 23 | $52 |

Universal Orlando | Universal Studios CityWalk | 6000 Universal Blvd.
(Vineland Rd.) | 407-224-2424 | www.emerils.com
This culinary "island of adventure" in Universal Studios CityWalk provides a "sophisticated break from the theme parks" via Emeril
Lagasse's "delicious", "memorable" Contemporary Louisiana cuisine –
"close your eyes and you're in NOLA" – plus "friendly service" and
"great wines"; it's "pricey", however, and can get "packed" with "tourists" "in tank tops and shorts", leading some to suggest "a novel idea:
a dress code"; P.S. "make reservations in advance."

Emeril's Tchoup Chop *Asian/Polynesian* | 23 | 26 | 23 | $53 |

Universal Orlando | Royal Pacific Hotel & Resort | 6300 Hollywood Way
(Universal Blvd.) | 407-503-2467 | www.emerils.com
Über-chef Emeril Lagasse "outdid himself" with this "visually stunning" Asian-Polynesian restaurant in Universal's Royal Pacific Hotel, a
"jaw-dropping" David Rockwell–designed "feast for the eyes" and the
palate with its "interesting mix" of "creative and delicious" dishes that
wield "the wow factor in spades"; "attentive but not intrusive" service
adds to an "unbelievable experience" that's maximized by sitting "at
the food bar to watch the kitchen" at work – it's "a must."

Enzo's Restaurant on the Lake ⑤Ⓜ *Italian* | 25 | 22 | 22 | $51 |

Longwood | 1130 S. Hwy. 17-92 (Wildmere Ave.) | 407-834-9872 |
www.enzos.com
"A big-city-quality restaurant in a small suburb", this "Italian delight"
in Longwood "has been cranking out first-rate meals forever", from an
"amazing antipasti table" to "authentic", "fresh, flavorful, fabulous"
classics that are "worth the splurge" – "you can taste the love in the
handmade pasta"; it's the "perfect blend of true hospitality" and "lovely"
lakeside setting, and it has a "buzz" that "keeps 'em coming back";
N.B. lunch is served on Fridays only.

Fifi's *Mediterranean*   – | – | – | M

Thornton Park | The Sanctuary | 100 S. Eola Dr. (E. Pine St.) | 407-481-2250 | www.fifisorlando.com

A casual cafe for the urban-chic set, this Thornton Park eatery dishes out Mediterranean fare – including savory crêpes – plus an array of pastries and desserts in a simple but colorful space; a solid selection of European beers and a martini menu up the ante, while sidewalk seating is a people-watching paradise during the weekend brunch.

Fleming's Prime Steakhouse & Wine Bar *Steak*   23 | 23 | 22 | $53

Winter Park | 933 N. Orlando Ave. (Rte. 423) | 407-699-9463 | www.flemingssteakhouse.com

"Definitely a cut above the rest", this Winter Park link in a national chophouse chain is a "consistently excellent" choice for "large portions" of "fabulous steak and perfect side dishes", enhanced by "attentive service", "warm decor" and a "fantastic wine list" that includes over 100 selections by the glass; though foes find it "misses the mark for the prices", more insist you're "in for a lovely evening."

HUE – A Restaurant *American*   24 | 23 | 21 | $44

Thornton Park | 629 E. Central Blvd. (Summerlin Ave.) | 407-849-1800 | www.huerestaurant.com

"Wear all black and you'll be fine" as you dine at this "avant-garde" Thornton Park bistro where a "splash of South Beach style" plus Asian-influenced New American cooking make it "the coolest place to eat"; a few fuss about "inconsistent service", but all in all it's a "lively scene" with outdoor seating "for watching the world go by" and an "awesome disco brunch" on the third Sunday of every month.

Jiko – The Cooking Place *African*   25 | 25 | 25 | $48

Animal Kingdom Area | Disney's Animal Kingdom Lodge | 2901 Osceola Pkwy. (Hwy. 192) | Lake Buena Vista | 407-938-4733 | www.disneyworld.com

"Let your taste buds be adventurous" counsel safari-seekers who trek to this "sleek", "serene" spot in Disney's Animal Kingdom Lodge for "sumptuous", "African-inspired cuisine" featuring sub-Saharan spices on foods from an array of cultures; the "exotic tastes" are complemented by "tantalizing" South African wines and "helpful" service.

Kres Chophouse ●🖂 *Steak*   22 | 24 | 22 | $49

Downtown Orlando | 17 W. Church St. (S. Orange Ave.) | 407-447-7950 | www.kresrestaurant.com

Sporting "ultraswanky", "classical-meets-Asian decor", this "elegant, urban" Downtown chophouse is "a certified hit" with "beautiful people" who champion its "awesome" but "expensive" menu and "great steaks" as well as its "see-and-be-seen bar", an ideal spot "for after-work drinks"; but a few chide the food and service as "not always consistent", hinting that this may be "a triumph of style over substance."

K Restaurant Wine Bar 🖂 *Eclectic*   25 | 20 | 22 | $46

College Park | 2401 Edgewater Dr. (Vassar St.) | 407-872-2332 | www.krestaurantwinebar.com

Owned by "talented" chef Kevin Fonzo, this "bustling" "culinary prize" in Orlando's College Park delivers "to-die-for" "food art" in the form of a "pricey", "ever-changing menu" chock-full of "scrumdiddlyumptious" Eclectic eats that are served by a "charming, down-to-earth staff"; it also boasts a "solid wine list" and "yummy desserts", and the "pleasant", "casual" setting is enhanced by local artwork, leading many to give this K an "A++."

☑ Le Coq au Vin 🅼 *French*
27 | 19 | 25 | $46

South Orlando | 4800 S. Orange Ave. (Holden Ave.) | 407-851-6980 | www.lecoqauvinrestaurant.com

"Julia Child would be proud" of this "longtime favorite" "hidden" away in an unlikely South Orlando locale, because this "petite" "farm-style French" is the area's No. 1 for Food "year after year" courtesy of chef-owner Louis Perrotte's "unpretentious yet spectacular" seasonal dinner menu; "quaint", "country-style decor", "professional service" and "decent prices" all make it "a pleasure to eat" here, leading patrons to plead: "shhh! don't tell anyone"; P.S. there are now half-portions, meaning you'll "have room for the spectacular soufflé."

Ming's Bistro *Chinese*
- | - | - | I

ViMi District | 1212 Woodward St. (N. Mills Ave.) | 407-898-9672

Hidden away in an easy-to-miss ViMi District location, this tiny restaurant draws the city's Chinese-American contingent for authentic Hong Kong–style dishes and all-day dim sum; a simple interior with high ceilings and a few small accents (framed pictures, a fish tank) make it clear that the emphasis is on the wallet-friendly cuisine.

MoonFish *Seafood/Steak*
23 | 23 | 21 | $47

Bay Hill/Dr. Phillips | The Fountains | 7525 W. Sand Lake Rd. (International Dr.) | 407-363-7262 | www.fishfusion.com

Regulars rave about this "lively" Dr. Phillips surf 'n' turfer that turns out "excellent sushi" ("anything raw that's legal!") plus "mammoth portions" of "awesome" seafood and steaks; it can get "loud", but respondents report that its "entertaining", "inviting decor" – including "restrooms that defy description" – helps to make it "a great place to bring out-of-towners"; nevertheless, a few find it "sometimes good, sometimes average" and make note of the "big prices."

Norman's *New World*
26 | 26 | 26 | $72

South Orlando | Ritz-Carlton Orlando, Grande Lakes | 4012 Central Florida Pkwy. (John Young Pkwy.) | 407-393-4333 | www.normans.com

"South Florida's best chef rocks Orlando!" declare devotees "in love with New World cuisine" thanks to the Ritz-Carlton's "superb" dinner destination from chef-owner Norman Van Aken, whose original Coral Gables eatery closed in June 2007; the tasting menu is "the way to go" and "worth the price" (four courses for $80), while a "gorgeous room" and "terrific service" make for "elegant dining on all levels"; in short, "on a scale of one to five, it's a 10!"

Palm *Steak*
24 | 21 | 24 | $56

Universal Orlando | Hard Rock Hotel | 5800 Universal Blvd. (Vineland St.) | 407-503-7256 | www.thepalm.com

"An oasis of attentive service", this chophouse in Universal's Hard Rock Hotel "is where you go for beef if you're on the attractions side of Orlando", offering "enormous portions" of "always consistent" steaks and lobster, plus desserts for which you'll want to "save room"; dissenters deem it "middle of the pack", but most declare that this "satisfying" chain link is "as good as the ones in NYC without the attitude", i.e. "don't expect power brokers."

Primo *Italian*   26 | 26 | 24 | $58

South Orlando | JW Marriott Orlando Grande Lakes |
4040 Central Florida Pkwy. (John Young Pkwy.) | 407-393-4444 |
www.grandelakes.com
At this "primo experience" in South Orlando's JW Marriott Grande
Lakes, "foodies will not be disappointed" by the "glorious" Italian "surprises" from "amazing" Maine-based maestro Melissa Kelly, whose
menu includes organic touches and "fresh, local produce (often from
the chef's own garden)"; the same "exquisite care given" to the "intriguing pastas" and seafood can also be seen in the "attentive service" and "casual but elegant setting."

Roy's *Hawaiian*   25 | 23 | 22 | $49

Bay Hill/Dr. Phillips | Plaza Venezia | 7760 W. Sand Lake Rd.
(Dr. Phillips Blvd.) | 407-352-4844 | www.roysrestaurant.com
Roy Yamaguchi "is king of Hawaiian [fusion] cooking, even in
Orlando" aver admirers of this chain outpost in Dr. Phillips that "will
stun you" with its "creative preparations" of "exotic", "swooningly delicious" "twists on seafood" and "aloha hospitality"; the "busy", "happening scene makes it a winner" for some, although sensitive sorts
insist "the acoustics could use a bit of tuning . . . down."

Ruth's Chris Steak House *Steak*   25 | 22 | 24 | $58

Bay Hill/Dr. Phillips | 7501 W. Sand Lake Rd. (Turkey Lake Rd.) |
407-226-3900
Lake Mary | 80 Colonial Center Pkwy. (Village Oak Ln.) | 407-804-8220
Winter Park | Winter Park Village | 610 N. Orlando Ave. (Webster Ave.) |
407-622-2444
www.ruthschris.com
"Bring a big appetite and a bigger wallet" to these "class acts" that offer
"the juiciest cuts of beef", tableside service and "quiet, subdued" decor; while a few feel they've "seen one, seen 'em all", most think these
steakhouse "havens" "have got it down to a science", although they
view the Sand Lake Road venue as "vulnerable to Mouseketeers in flipflops"; N.B. Lake Mary and Winter Park both serve lunch on Fridays.

☑ Seasons 52 *American*   25 | 26 | 25 | $39

Altamonte Springs | The Altamonte Mall | 463 E. Altamonte Dr.
(Palm Springs Dr.) | 407-767-1252
Bay Hill/Dr. Phillips | Plaza Venezia | 7700 W. Sand Lake Rd. (bet. Della Dr. &
Dr. Phillips Blvd.) | 407-354-5212
www.seasons52.com
"You'll feel positively angelic as you devour" the "light, flavorful" seasonal cuisine at these "sophisticated yet comfortable" "formula restaurants that finally get the equation right": "creative", "guilt-free"
New American entrees "each under 475 calories" that are complemented by a "wonderful wine list", topped off with "amazing", "shot
glass–sized desserts" and served by a "well-trained staff"; but since
both the Dr. Phillips and Altamonte Springs locations are "always
packed", "good luck getting in (or even near) them."

	FOOD	DECOR	SERVICE	COST

Shari Sushi Lounge *Japanese*

22 | 22 | 17 | $40

Thornton Park | 621 E. Central Blvd. (bet. Eola Dr. & Summerlin Ave.) | 407-420-9420 | www.sharisushilounge.com

Swimming off with "the 'Most Sophisticated Sushi' award" is this "small" but chic Thornton Park restaurant that raises raw fin fare "to the next level" with its menu of "creative rolls" and sashimi, plus Asian-influenced grill and tempura specialties; surveyors also stop in "for the eye-candy" crowd and the "great-looking, trendy decor."

☑ Taquitos Jalisco *Mexican*

27 | 17 | 22 | $19

MetroWest | MetroWest Village Shopping Ctr. | 2419 S. Hiawassee Rd. (Westpointe Blvd.) | 407-296-0626
Winter Garden | Tri-City Shopping Ctr. | 1041 S. Dillard St. (W. Colonial Dr.) | 407-654-0363

At these twin "family restaurants" in MetroWest and Winter Garden, you'll "feel like you're on vacation in Mexico" as you down *"delicioso"* south-of-the-border eats that are "consistent, authentic" and served with "big smiles"; live mariachi bands play Thursday–Sunday at both locations, so "sip a cold Corona" (or a "great margarita") and enjoy the "comfortable decor", "fun" ambiance and low tabs.

Thai House ☒ *Thai*

25 | 15 | 22 | $21

East Orlando | 2117 E. Colonial Dr. (N. Hillside Ave.) | 407-898-0820

Satisfied surveyors "can't wait to get back" to this "consistent" east-of-Downtown "favorite" for "delicious" Thai food made with the "freshest ingredients"; despite unassuming decor, this "not-to-be-missed restaurant" "exceeds expectations by far" right down to the "professional" service and "downright cheap" charges.

Thai Thani *Thai*

24 | 21 | 20 | $26

International Drive | International Plaza | 11025 S. International Dr. (Central Florida Pkwy.) | 407-239-9733 | www.thaithani.net

"Thai me up and let me stay here" demand devotees who appreciate this sprawling Siamese's "vast selection" of "authentic", "flavorful and bountiful" edibles at "very reasonable" prices; though this "treat" is located "in a strip-mall setting" near the convention center, it's "smartly decorated" with "wonderful, traditional" trimmings that are so elaborate, it's like "walking through the door into a different land."

Todd English's bluezoo *Seafood*

24 | 26 | 23 | $53

Epcot Area | Walt Disney World Dolphin Hotel | 1500 Epcot Resort Blvd. (World Dr.) | Lake Buena Vista | 407-934-1111 | www.thebluezoo.com

"Todd English outdid himself" with this "classy" seafooder in the Dolphin Hotel, where a "funky but elegant", "under-the-sea" setting that's "more aquarium than zoo" is the backdrop for "artistic", "out-of-this-world dishes with prices to match"; most find it a "wonderful experience", with a "knowledgeable staff" and "fabulous wines", but a "disappointed" few deem the scene "more show than substance."

Venetian Room, The ☒Ⓜ *Continental*

24 | 22 | 24 | $66

Downtown Orlando | Caribe Royale Orlando | 8101 World Center Dr. (bet. International Dr. & S. Apopka Vineland Rd.) | 407-238-8060 | www.thevenetianroom.com

"Miss Manners would be at home" at this "fine-dining establishment", a "posh", "classy" Continental "hidden" in Lake Buena Vista's unassuming Caribe Royale resort and convention center; it's a copper-domed den of "elegance and decadence", with "lavish cuisine" and "smart service" that's "second to none", which makes it some savvy surveyors' culinary equivalent of a "get out of jail free card", i.e. a "destination to get me out of trouble with the Mrs.!"

☑ Victoria & Albert's American   27 | 27 | 27 | $89

Magic Kingdom Area | Disney's Grand Floridian Resort & Spa | 4401 Grand Floridian Way (bet. Maple Rd. & W. Seven Seas Dr.) | Lake Buena Vista | 407-939-3463 | www.disneyworld.com

This jacket-required "oasis of civility" in Disney's Grand Floridian Resort "really does [try] to spoil you", offering "pricey" six-course New American dinners from "culinary god" Scott Hunnel that can be "exquisitely matched" with wines or enjoyed at the "coveted chef's table" (reservable six months in advance); if a few find it "overhyped", more consider it a "once-in-a-lifetime experience" complete with nightly harp music and "superb service" from a Victorian-garbed staff.

Vito's Chop House Steak   25 | 21 | 24 | $50

International Drive | 8633 International Dr. (bet. Austrian Row & Via Mercado) | 407-354-2467 | www.vitoschophouse.com

An old-timer "in the heart of tourist land" near the convention center, this Italian-style chophouse "blows away the other big-name" beef purveyors by "doing the classics well", offering "succulent" aged steaks and seafood plus an "amazingly long", "nicely priced" wine list to "make any connoisseur quiver"; although a handful of surveyors suggest it's "solid, but not overly memorable", meat mavens maintain that "attentive", "professional" service and a "cozy" setting are just two more reasons that "Vito's has it all."

Wazzabi Japanese   - | - | - | E

Winter Park | 1408 Gay Rd. (N. Orlando Ave.) | 407-647-8744 | www.wazzabisushi.com

Add some pizzazz to your wasabi at this Winter Park sushi stop where an enormous selection of specialty rolls takes pride of place on a pricey menu that also offers appetizers and entrees; well-heeled thirty-somethings appreciate the long martini list and colorful indoor and outdoor dining areas, while family types head to the teppanyaki room for a bit of culinary entertainment.

☑ Wolfgang Puck Café California   21 | 19 | 18 | $34

Downtown Disney Area | 1482 E. Buena Vista Dr. (Hotel Plaza Blvd.) | Lake Buena Vista | 407-938-9653 | www.wolfgangpuckorlando.com

If you "want variety and quality", "the Puck stops here" praise pals of this Downtown Disney Californian, a "bright, breezy" culinary oasis encompassing a "fun downstairs" cafe and sushi bar, a "more refined" upstairs dining room ("i.e. a thousand fewer kids"), plus a quick-service section; still, opponents point to "long lines", "shaky service" and a "noisy atmosphere" as proof that Wolfgang's "well-known name is pretty much all he brought to this place."

Palm Beach

TOP FOOD RANKING

Restaurant	Cuisine
27 Chez Jean-Pierre	French
Marcello's La Sirena	Italian
L'Escalier	French
Four Seasons	Floridian
Little Moirs	Seafood
26 Café Chardonnay	American
11 Maple Street	American
Café Boulud	French
Chops Lobster Bar	Seafood/Steak
Kathy's Gazebo	Continental

OTHER NOTEWORTHY PLACES

Abe & Louie's	Steak
Bonefish Grill	Seafood
Cafe L'Europe	Continental
Cheesecake Factory	American
Houston's	American
Kee Grill	Seafood
New York Prime	Steak
Seasons 52	American
Sushi Jo's	Japanese
32 East	American
Trattoria Romana	Italian

Z Abe & Louie's *Steak* — 25 | 24 | 23 | $63

Boca Raton | 2200 W. Glades Rd. (Renaissance Way) | 561-447-0024 | www.bbrginc.com

"Attractive" and "old school"–looking (though it opened in 2005), this Boston-based steakhouse beckons "Boca's rich and beautiful" with "yum-o" filets, "superlative service" and "a fine wine list with fair prices"; but the "decibel level is like being on the Florida turnpike" and even with "huge portions", "prices are crazy", so it's "worth paying the hefty sharing charge" or to "skip the dinner scene" altogether (some feel it's "best for lunch or brunch", anyway).

Bonefish Grill *Seafood* — 22 | 19 | 21 | $35

Stuart | Stuart Ctr. | 2283 S. Federal Hwy. (SE Monterey Rd.) | 772-288-4388
Palm Beach Gardens | 11650 US Hwy. 1 (PGA Blvd.) | 561-799-2965 www.bonefishgrill.com

Make "no bones about it" – there's "nothing on the menu you'll throw back" at these "casual, comfortable" seafooders; converts "can't believe it's a chain", given the "intimate" atmosphere and "pleasant" servers who "know their fish"; perhaps it's a bit "predictable", but the principal problem with these "popular" *poissoneries* is, you gotta "go early or late or expect a wait."

⊠ Café Boulud *French*

| 26 | 27 | 25 | $77 |

Palm Beach | Brazilian Court Hotel | 301 Australian Ave. (Hibiscus Ave.) |
561-655-6060 | www.danielnyc.com

Almost "as good as its NYC sister" declare devotees of Daniel Boulud's
Brazilian Court Hotel bistro, a "beautifully serene" site with the "best
courtyard dining room"; the food is a "French event" – "delicious
and beautiful" – and service is "smooth as old silk", particularly the
"pleasant" sommeliers; it's a "very 'old money' PB atmosphere", but
many say "it's a pleasure to see men wearing jackets", and even those
who "had to hock some jewelry" to pay the "astronomical prices" find
"it's worth it."

Cafe Chardonnay *American*

| 26 | 22 | 24 | $57 |

Palm Beach Gardens | Garden Square Shoppes | 4533 PGA Blvd.
(Military Trail) | 561-627-2662 | www.cafechardonnay.com

"Don't be put off by the shopping center" locale of this Palm Beach
Gardens New American – still a "standout" after 25+ years – where a
"dynamite wine list" ("by the glass too!") and "well-trained staff"
complement the "creative", "consistently excellent" food in a "beautiful setting"; it's "like New York in Florida" – read: "crowded in
season" – so "reservations in advance are a must."

Café L'Europe *Continental*

| 25 | 26 | 24 | $77 |

Palm Beach | 331 S. County Rd. (bet. Australian & Brazilian Aves.) |
561-655-4020 | www.cafeleurope.com

"The wealth of Palm Beach dines here" at the town's "most glamorous
and well-decorated" place; "an oasis of flowers" sets the scene for
"divine, luscious" Continental cuisine that "balances between old
standbys and creative new dishes", backed by an "extensive" wine
list and "genteel" service; the sensitive sense a "somewhat haughty"
attitude toward non-regulars, but "if your budget can handle it", "this
is the place to splurge"; P.S. for a "better deal", try the "midweek
lunch" prix fixe.

Cheesecake Factory ● *American*

| 20 | 19 | 19 | $28 |

West Palm Beach | CityPlace | 701 S. Rosemary Ave. (Okeechobee Blvd.) |
561-802-3838
Palm Beach Gardens | Downtown at the Gardens |
11800 Lake Victoria Gardens Ave. (Gardens Blvd.) | 561-776-3711
Boca Raton | 5530 Glades Rd. (Butts Rd.) | 561-393-0344
www.thecheesecakefactory.com

"It's a chain but a great one" is the verdict of a veritable factory of fans
who delight in this American's "phonebooklike", region-ranging menu
offering "huge portions" of "something for everyone, from tacos to
tuna", plus "reliable" service and "incredibly good prices"; it's "always
crowded" – but "always a crowd-pleaser" – so "be prepared for roaring
noise levels" and to "wait for hours for a table."

⊠ Chez Jean-Pierre Bistro ⊠ *French*

| 27 | 22 | 25 | $75 |

Palm Beach | 132 N. County Rd. (bet. Sunrise & Sunset Aves.) |
561-833-1171

"Simply the best in PB" (with the No. 1 Food rating to prove it), this
"family-owned and -run jewel" of a Classic French furnishes a "fantasy
dining experience" for the flush, with "fun", diversely decorated
rooms and "professional" but "not stuffy" service to complement chef

Jean-Pierre Leverrier's "fahbulous" fare; "reservations can be difficult, but persevere – you won't regret it."

Chops Lobster Bar *Seafood/Steak*
26 | 27 | 24 | $73

Boca Raton | Royal Palm Plaza | 101 Plaza Real (SE Mizner Blvd.) | 561-395-2675 | www.chopslobsterbar.com

"Brand-new in Boca Raton", this "beautiful" "addition from Atlanta" has surveyors licking their chops over the "incredible steaks" – even "the smallest are huge" – and "to-die-for fried lobster" fetched from the "cool, open kitchen" by an "obliging staff"; yes, you better "bring bags of bucks" and be braced for a highly "noisy" scene, but "fortunately the food is so good, that conversation is not necessary anyway."

11 Maple Street M *American*
26 | 24 | 25 | $56

Jensen Beach | 3224 NE Maple Ave. (11th Ave.) | 772-334-7714

"Drive an hour each way if you have to" for the "sublime dining experience" of this veteran in Jensen Beach ("Mapquest it if you're not familiar with the area"); converts "can't get enough" of chef-owner Mike Perrin's "towering edible constructions" – "imaginative" New American fare offered amid the "charming Old Florida" setting of an "antiques-adorned house", along with an "amazing rare wine list and amazing servers too (a rarity!)."

⧩ Four Seasons – The Restaurant M *American*
27 | 27 | 27 | $78

Palm Beach | Four Seasons Resort | 2800 S. Ocean Blvd. (Lake Ave.) | 561-533-3750 | www.fourseasons.com

Exuding "the quality the wannabes should strive for", this "beautiful oasis" perched oceanside boasts "the best service" in Palm Beach (voted No. 1), as exhibited by a staff that'll "spoil you rotten", "even matching the napkins to your outfit"; while Hubert Des Marais, "the orignal chef, has left" (not fully reflected in the Food score), the kitchen is still turning out "imaginative" Floridian favorites "layered with so many exquisite flavors" that "even if you go broke, you must eat here once in your lifetime – this is heaven."

Houston's *American*
21 | 20 | 21 | $37

Boca Raton | 1900 NW Executive Center Circle (Glades Rd.) | 561-998-0550 | www.hillstone.com

"Yes, it's a chain" but it "doesn't feel like a chain" at this Boca Raton American, thanks to the "low lighting", "personable" "tag-team service" and "hearty" fare ("don't miss the spinach dip"); alas, "long waits" for a table are as "consistent" as the food, but it's a "great date spot, even if you're married", and there's a "happening bar" "packed" with singles if you're not.

Kathy's Gazebo Café ⧩ *Continental*
26 | 22 | 24 | $63

Boca Raton | 4199 N. Federal Hwy. (Spanish River Blvd.) | 561-395-6033 | www.kathysgazebo.com

"Jackets are not required, but everyone wears one" at this "romantic" "classic" Continental in Boca, where an "older crowd" delights in "Dover sole as it should be" and "old-fashioned European service"; it all may be "too traditional" for trendsetters, especially given the "tight quarters", but most enjoy this "elegant" experience.

	FOOD	DECOR	SERVICE	COST

☑ Kee Grill *Seafood* → 24 | 21 | 21 | $46

Juno Beach | 14020 US Hwy. 1 (Donald Ross Rd.) | 561-776-1167
Boca Raton | 17940 N. Military Trail (bet. Champion Blvd. & Clint Moore Rd.) |
561-995-5044

Though they're technically surf 'n' turfers, the "seafood is king" at this
(Most Popular) Palm Beach County pair popular with a "more mature
crowd" (or anyone who appreciates a "really good deal for early-birds");
true, there's "too long a wait for a table" – reservations are taken only
at the Boca branch – and some protest "your plate's cleared before the
fork hits the china", but most concentrate on the "always fresh fish",
"awesome spinach side" and bamboo-walled "Florida atmosphere."

☑ L'Escalier ☒Ⓜ *French* → 27 | 28 | 26 | $87

Palm Beach | The Breakers | 1 S. County Rd. (Breakers Row) | 561-655-6611 |
www.thebreakers.com

The "breathtaking", "grand atmosphere of The Breakers is the setting"
for the "finest" "flawlessly executed" French cuisine and "excellent
wines", backed by "solicitous but discreet service"; "elegant" and "extraordinary", it's "expensive" of course – but also a "unique experience", so "bring out the jewels and sell some to eat here."

☑ Little Moirs Food Shack ☒ *Seafood* → 27 | 12 | 22 | $31

Jupiter | Jupiter Sq. | 103 US Hwy. 1 (E. Indiantown Rd.) | 561-741-3626

"It's all about the food" at this "kooky", "ultracasual" pescatorial
place, since the decor's pure beach "shack-y", the wine "severely lacking" and the "fast service" ensures "no lingering" at table (though you
"wait" to get in); but oh, those "so-fresh" and "fantastic" fish choices
with "unusual" coatings – they cause even the intially skeptic to say
"don't walk, run" to this Jupiter joint.

☑ Marcello's La Sirena ☒ *Italian* → 27 | 19 | 23 | $57

West Palm Beach | 6316 S. Dixie Hwy. (Forest Hill Blvd.) | 561-585-3128 |
www.lasirenaonline.com

An "old-timer" "off the beaten path" in West Palm Beach, this Italian
has a "chef-owner who can cook with the country's best", and backs
up his *cucina* with a "great cellar of fine wines" from around the globe;
the service is "refined", and though they do "need to spruce the place
up a little", fans implore "don't tell too many people about this gem."

☑ New York Prime *Steak* → 25 | 21 | 21 | $68

Boca Raton | 2350 Executive Center Dr. NW (Glades Rd.) | 561-998-3881 |
www.newyorkprime.com

Expect "prime food" at "prime prices" at this "loud" "very Boca" meatery where "many celebs" and other "with-it" types nosh on the "top
quality" filets after quaffing a few at the "old-world Euro bar"; if the
bellicose beef there's "attitude everywhere", and you "have to wait
even with a reservation", advocates argue it's "annoying but worth it."

☑ Seasons 52 *American* → 23 | 24 | 23 | $40

Palm Beach Gardens | 11611 Ellison Wilson Rd. (PGA Blvd.) | 561-625-5852
Boca Raton | 2300 NW Executive Center Dr. (NW Executive Center Circle) |
561-998-9952
www.seasons52.com

"Everything's under 475 calories and it tastes fantastic" proclaim
"pleasantly surprised" surveyors captivated by the "clever concept" of

this "always busy" New American chain; staffers who can describe the ingredients and calorie counts of any dish serve "small portions" of grilled "seasonal veggies, lean meats and whole grains" "without trans fats", a "terrific wine-by-the-glass" selection and "delicious desserts" "in shot glasses" ("just a tiny sin").

Sushi Jo's *Japanese*
`25` `17` `21` `$39`

West Palm Beach | 319 Belvedere Rd. (S. Olive Ave.) | 561-868-7893
Boynton Beach | Ocean Plaza | 640 E. Ocean Ave. (SE 6th Ct.) | 561-737-0606
www.sushijo.com

"Go for the food, stay for the hip scene" at this West Palm Beach and Ocean Plaza duo where "top-notch" "insanely fresh" sushi and a "fantastic selection of cold sake" are served in a "dim" "lounge-type atmosphere"; raw fish fans rave this is "not your typical 'clinical' Japanese restaurant", even if the "hip music" can be "too loud" and the prices – "well, just don't look."

32 East *American*
`25` `19` `22` `$54`

Delray Beach | 32 E. Atlantic Ave. (bet. SE 1st & Swinton Aves.) | 561-276-7868 | www.32east.com

A "scene-o-rama" with "sexy atmosphere", this Delray Beach New American is where "the who's who of Palm Beach County hang", sampling "market-fresh cuisine" from "wildly creative chef" Nick Morfogen, who "changes the menu at whim" (and "depending on what he finds" that day); while "knowledgeable", the staff can be "distracted – perhaps by the eardrum-splitting volume of the room", but when this "cosmopolitan" place "is on, it's all the way."

Trattoria Romana *Italian*
`25` `17` `20` `$54`

Boca Raton | 499 E. Palmetto Park Rd. (NE 5th Ave.) | 561 393-6715

"They take care of the regulars" at this "dependable" "old-time Italian" where the "spare-nothing" menu includes a "humongous veal chop" and "b-i-ggg" drinks; there's "not much atmosphere" and it gets quite "loud" (tip: the back room "has a lot less noise"), but believers bellow *"buonissimo!"* for this East Boca bit of The Boot.

Philadelphia

TOP FOOD RANKING

	Restaurant	Cuisine
28	Fountain	Continental/French
	Le Bar Lyonnais	French
	Birchrunville Store	French/Italian
	Le Bec-Fin	French
	Vetri	Italian
27	Lacroix/Rittenhouse	French
	Gilmore's	French
	Morimoto	Japanese
	Savona	French/Italian
	Amada	Spanish
	Buddakan	Asian
	Bluefin	Japanese
26	Paloma	French/Mexican
	Gayle	American
	Mainland Inn	American
	Striped Bass	Seafood
	Blue Sage	Vegetarian
	La Bonne Auberge	French
	Swann Lounge	American/French
	Alison/Blue Bell	American

OTHER NOTEWORTHY PLACES

Restaurant	Cuisine
Blackfish	Seafood
Brasserie Perrier	French
Dmitri's	Greek
Jake's	American
James	American
L'Angolo	Italian
Marigold Kitchen	American
Melograno	Italian
Nan	French/Thai
Osteria	Italian
Overtures	French/Mediterranean
Prime Rib	Steak
Rae	American
Shiao Lan Kung	Chinese
Southwark	American
Sovalo	Californian/Italian
Susanna Foo	Chinese/French
Tinto	Spanish
Twenty Manning	American
Xochitl	Mexican

	FOOD	DECOR	SERVICE	COST

Alison at Blue Bell 🗷Ⓜ⇗ American   26 | 16 | 22 | $44

Blue Bell | 721 Skippack Pike (Penllyn-Blue Bell Pike) | 215-641-2660 |
www.alisonatbluebell.com

There's "no need to schlep to Center City" since "skilled" chef-owner
Alison Barshak is "on top of every detail" at her cash-only New
American in the Montco 'burbs; her fan club calls it a "foodie's delight" with "innovative", "Manhattan-quality" eats served in a "warm",
"simple" space – just don't mind "being squashed" ("get used to sitting in your neighbor's lap").

Amada Spanish   27 | 25 | 23 | $47

Old City | 217 Chestnut St. (bet. 2nd & 3rd Sts.) | 215-625-2450 |
www.amadarestaurant.com

Spanish-loving surveyors dip into their bag of superlatives over Jose
Garces' Old City venue, where "magical" justly describes the tapas
that are accompanied by "fantastic" sangria, "phenomenal" flamenco
dancers (some nights) and "attentive" service; it's the "best thing to
happen to Philadelphia in a long time", but it's advisable to go early
before the "noise" rises "above the pain threshold."

🗷 Birchrunville Store   28 | 23 | 26 | $50
Cafe 🗷Ⓜ⇗ French/Italian

Birchrunville | 1403 Hollow Rd. (Flowing Springs Rd.) | 610-827-9002 |
www.birchrunvillestorecafe.com

Bring cash along with your GPS to Francis Trzeciak's "remote", "bare-
bones" BYO in an old Chester County "country" store; diehards know
to "reserve" a spot "well in advance" for the "sophisticated" Franco-
Italian cuisine prepared with "thought and care", "romantic" atmosphere and servers so "gracious" you "want them as your friends";
N.B. closed Sundays–Tuesdays.

Blackfish 🗷 Seafood   – | – | – | E

Conshohocken | 119 Fayette St. (bet. 1st & 2nd Aves.) | 610-397-0888 |
www.blackfishrestaurant.com

The New American–influenced, seafood-heavy menu at this BYO
Conshy entry reflects chef-owner Chip Roman's background (Le Bec-Fin
and Vetri); the decor's bright and comfy, and the prices fitting for the
food and main-drag location.

Bluefin 🗷 Japanese   27 | 14 | 20 | $34

Plymouth Meeting | 1017 Germantown Pike (Virginia Rd.) | 610-277-3917 |
www.sushibluefin.com

Sushi-philes swear "if you aren't going to Morimoto", this "tiny"
Japanese BYO in a "slightly dated" Plymouth Meeting strip center is an
"excellent" alternative, where the "phenomenal", "amazingly fresh"
fare includes rolls that are a "treat for the eyes and taste buds"; a
"pleasant" staff helps make up for the "modest" decor.

Blue Sage Vegetarian Grille 🗷Ⓜ Vegetarian   26 | 14 | 22 | $26

Southampton | 772 Second St. Pike (Street Rd.) | 215-942-8888 |
www.bluesagegrille.com

Come "prepared to wait" – even with "reservations" – for the "ridiculously good" fare at Mike and Holly Jackson's "tiny", Bucks strip-mall
vegetarian BYO, where fans forget about "mock" ingredients, "substi-
tutes" and meat, since what they taste is an "amazing creativity with

veggies"; who cares if the setting "isn't fancy-schmancy" when "huge" portions can supply you with a "tantalizing" meal the next day?

⊿ Brasserie Perrier *French* 26 | 24 | 24 | $57
Center City West | 1619 Walnut St. (bet. 16th & 17th Sts.) | 215-568-3000 | www.brasserieperrier.com

Philly's "established boomer crowd" keeps "coming back" to Le Bec-Fin's nearby, "scaled-down" Center City brother "for the rest of us", an art deco–designed destination where Georges Perrier and Chris Scarduzio deliver "divine" New French cuisine; though the fare's "not cheap", a "professional" staff helps – overall, this one "hits all the right notes"; insider's dish: check out the bar area before "a night on the town."

⊿ Buddakan *Asian* 27 | 27 | 23 | $53
Old City | 325 Chestnut St. (bet. 3rd & 4th Sts.) | 215-574-9440 | www.buddakan.com

If you want to "impress someone" who's "hard to impress", join the "wait list" for Stephen Starr's "swank", "theatrical" Asian in Old City, a fave of "fashionistas" and "celebs"; it's Philly's Most Popular restaurant thanks to "memorable", "groundbreaking" food served by "solicitous" servers and a "gorgeous" setting that "makes you feel beautiful, even if you think you're not"; as far as scoring a reservation in prime time, try rubbing the "giant" Buddha's belly inside.

Dmitri's *Greek* 24 | 13 | 18 | $30
Center City West | 2227 Pine St. (23rd St.) | 215-985-3680
Queen Village | 795 S. Third St. (Catharine St.) | 215-625-0556 ⊅

"A shark couldn't get better seafood" than at Dmitri Chimes' "bustling", "no-frills" Greek twins serving the "freshest" grilled calamari, octopus and other bounty of the sea there is; the Queen Village BYO isn't for "claustrophobes", and if you want to "hear your companion" or avoid the "crush", arrive early at both locations.

⊿ Fountain Restaurant *Continental/French* 28 | 28 | 29 | $82
Center City West | Four Seasons Hotel | 1 Logan Sq.
(Benjamin Franklin Pkwy.) | 215-963-1500 | www.fourseasons.com

"As good as it gets" sizes up the Philly Survey's winner of the triple crown (No. 1 for Food, Decor and Service) in the Four Seasons Hotel; Philly's "elite" "live it up" and find "a treat for all the senses" in an "opulent" setting that showcases Martin Hamann's "divine" New French-Continental cuisine and "formal", yet "low-key" service that gives you the "royal treatment" ("they could serve me Cheerios and I'd think it was the best meal I ever had"); yes, the "shockingly high" tabs may be hard to absorb, but they're easily justified, especially for "expense-account" or "special-occasion" visits; N.B. jacket required.

Gayle 🅂🅼 *American* 26 | 19 | 24 | $58
South St. | 617 S. Third St. (bet. Bainbridge & South Sts.) | 215-922-3850 | www.gaylephiladelphia.com

"Go and be adventurous" at former Le Bec-Fin executive chef Daniel Stern's "little" New American off South Street, a "casual" though still upscale venue blowing away fans with "knowledgeable" service and "well-executed", "complex" fare that deftly combines the "experimental" and "classic"; N.B. it's à la carte Tuesdays, Wednesdays and Thursdays, but prix fixe only Fridays and Saturdays.

PHILADELPHIA

	FOOD	DECOR	SERVICE	COST

Gilmore's 🅱️Ⓜ️ *French* — 27 | 23 | 27 | $55
West Chester | 133 E. Gay St. (bet. Matlack & Walnut Sts.) | 610-431-2800 | www.gilmoresrestaurant.com
Peter Gilmore (an alum of Le Bec-Fin) "amazes" with his Classic French West Chester BYO widely regarded as the "Le Bec of the 'burbs" for its "fantastic" "special-occasion" cuisine served by an "attitude-free" staff; at 35 seats, scoring a reservation in the snug, "intimate" quarters means either many redials or divine intervention.

Jake's *American* — 25 | 21 | 23 | $51
Manayunk | 4365 Main St. (bet. Grape & Levering Sts.) | 215-483-0444 | www.jakesrestaurant.com
"Main Line yuppies" are still happily "slumming it" at Bruce Cooper's "sophisticated" Manayunk New American; it maintains its rep as "the grande dame" of Main Street with "skillfully prepared", "splurge"-worthy food and "impeccable" service; the seating's "tight", especially at peak times, so expect to almost "sit in your neighbor's lap."

James 🅱️ *American* — - | - | - | E
South Philly | 824 S. Eighth St. (bet. Catharine & Christian Sts.) | 215-629-4980 | www.jameson8th.com
Fine dining hits South Philly in the form of this ambitious Italian-influenced New American from exec chef Jim Burke (ex Angelina) and his wife, Kristina, the general manager; the food, which embodies a philosophy of humanely raised/sustainable agriculture, is ably complemented by a warm, modern setting.

La Bonne Auberge Ⓜ️ *French* — 26 | 27 | 26 | $75
New Hope | Village 2 Apartment Complex | 1 Rittenhouse Circle (River Rd.) | 215-862-2462 | www.bonneauberge.com
An auberge to remember is Gerard Caronello's "formal", "precious" French serving up a "romantic" ambiance, "super" food and "super" service to "special-occasion" seekers; the 18th-century farmhouse setting (within a New Hope apartment complex) evokes the French "countryside", though "stratospheric" prices bring everyone back to reality; N.B. dinner only, Thursdays–Sundays.

🅉 Lacroix at The Rittenhouse *French* — 27 | 27 | 27 | $79
Center City West | Rittenhouse Hotel | 210 W. Rittenhouse Sq. (bet. Locust & Walnut Sts.) | 215-790-2533 | www.lacroixrestaurant.com
For a taste of what "the gods on Olympus eat", there's no better example than Jean-Marie Lacroix's "dreamy" New French extravaganza in the Rittenhouse Hotel; count on "culinary mastery", with a menu devised of three-, four- and five-course "artfully presented" small plates, a "modern", "tranquil" room overlooking the Square and "sublime" service; true, you'll have to dip heavily into your piggy bank, but it's sure to impress; N.B. post-Survey, Lacroix has yielded the reins to new executive chef Matt Levin; jacket and tie preferred.

L'Angolo Ⓜ️ *Italian* — 26 | 15 | 22 | $35
South Philly | 1415 W. Porter St. (Broad St.) | 215-389-4252
It's "well worth" braving South Philly's "double-parking traps" and bringing your "best Barolo" to pair with Davide Faenza's "outstanding" Southern Italian cooking at this "upbeat" BYO trattoria, where the chef's wife, Kathryn, oversees a "charming" floor crew who "aim to

please"; keep in mind, "you may need a shoehorn to get in", but after all the "amazing" food, "you'll need a wheelbarrow to get out."

☑ Le Bar Lyonnais ☑ French | 28 | 23 | 25 | $58 |

Center City West | 1523 Walnut St. (bet. 15th & 16th Sts.) | 215-567-1000 | www.lebecfin.com

Georges Perrier's Center City "gem" beneath Le Bec-Fin continues to impress gourmets who crave an "intimate" meal with "spectacular" French bistro food and "fantastic" service but can't fork over a "whole paycheck" at the mother ship upstairs; it's even better when you can visit the bar at peak times and gaze at the "impressive examples of plastic surgery."

☑ Le Bec-Fin ☑ French | 28 | 27 | 27 | $120 |

Center City West | 1523 Walnut St. (bet. 15th & 16th Sts.) | 215-567-1000 | www.lebecfin.com

Still "the pinnacle" of Philly restaurants is Georges Perrier's "big-bucks" haute Center City French institution that "bows to no other" in its class and is a "must-see", "must-experience" "masterpiece"; indeed, the "magnificent" food (including the "unbelievable" dessert cart), ornate, "beautiful Parisian" setting and "perfect" service from a "fleet" of waiters all leave you as "breathless" as the "sticker-shock"-inducing bill, but it's all worth the admission to "one of the best ever"; N.B. jacket recommended at dinner.

Mainland Inn American | 26 | 23 | 25 | $48 |

Mainland | 17 Main St. (Sumneytown Pike) | 215-256-8500 | www.themainlandinn.com

"Understated" is another name for this central Montco "secret" decorated in "18th-century Americana" that "lives up to its rep" as "one of the best" in the 'burbs with "sublime" New American food and service that makes you "forget about traveling to Center City"; insiders advise you check out the $21.95 Sunday brunch.

Marigold Kitchen Ⓜ American | 25 | 18 | 22 | $45 |

University City | 501 S. 45th St. (Larchwood Ave.) | 215-222-3699 | www.marigoldkitchenbyob.com

Acolytes of "culinary artistry" are all over this "hidden" New American BYO in a touched-up West Philly Victorian, the showcase for chef Michael Solomonov who twirls his "magic wand" over "eccentric", yet "excellent" dishes; many also endorse the service, which is "well-informed" considering what's on the plate "ain't mama's cooking."

Melograno Ⓜ Italian | 25 | 16 | 20 | $37 |

Center City West | 2201 Spruce St. (22nd St.) | 215-875-8116

"Pure joy" sums up this "minimally" decorated yet "inviting" (and "tiny") Tuscan BYO corner bistro, a Fitler Square "treasure" where you must "arrive as soon as it opens" to avoid the crowds that await Gianluca Demontis' "simple" and "beautifully prepared" fare served in a "deafening" room; now, if only they "took reservations" more often.

Morimoto Japanese | 27 | 27 | 25 | $72 |

Washington Square | 723 Chestnut St. (bet. 7th & 8th Sts.) | 215-413-9070 | www.morimotorestaurant.com

Even with 'Iron Chef' Masaharu Morimoto spending time in the new namesake NYC offshoot, Stephen Starr's "trendy" "neo"-Japanese "masterpiece" in Center City is still a "must visit" for "sublime", "Tokyo-quality" sushi and "exciting" fusion fare in a "surreal" and "seriously sexy" setting complete with "changing mood lights"; "flawless" service is part of an overall experience that feels like "winning the lottery", so it's advised to "splurge" to take advantage of what will be a "memorable" meal ("you won't be sorry, even when you get the bill").

Nan ☒ French/Thai   26 | 16 | 21 | $38

University City | 4000 Chestnut St. (40th St.) | 215-382-0818 | www.nanrestaurant.com

Word is "from the outside, you'd never guess that you're in for one of the best meals" around at "talented" chef-owner Kamol Phutlek's French-Thai BYO, a "jewel" in University City's "lower rent district"; they "get all the courses right" say the amazed when describing the "exceptional" fare, though it also helps when service is this "good."

Osteria *Italian*   - | - | - | E

North Philly | 640 N. Broad St. (Wallace St.) | 215-763-0920 | www.osteriaphilly.com

Marc Vetri and Jeff Benjamin (of Vetri fame) have ventured just north of Center City to this warm, spacious room where the roaring brick oven (used to produce the house specialty thin-crust pizzas topped with porchetta) is the centerpiece of the open kitchen; if you can't get a reservation, belly up to the counter or the bar for some seductive pastas.

Overtures ⓜ *French/Mediterranean*   24 | 23 | 23 | $50

South St. | 609-611 E. Passyunk Ave. (bet. Bainbridge & South Sts.) | 215-627-3455

Peter LamLein continues to create "lovely" music in the kitchen of his "romantic" French-Med BYO off South Street, arguably "Philly's best-kept secret" for "terrific" midweek prix fixes "worthy of your finest wines"; it's all complemented by "excellent" service in a "jewel box" of a setting featuring trompe l'oeil paintings and "beautiful" flower arrangements; in other words, "bravo!"

Paloma ☒ⓜ *French/Mexican*   26 | 18 | 25 | $49

Northeast Philly | 6516 Castor Ave. (bet. Hellerman St. & Magee Ave.) | 215-533-0356 | www.palomafinedining.com

In a "food-starved", "down-at-the-heels" Northeast Philly area resides this "haute" French-Mexican "standout" wowing those who've been to its "relaxing" space for Adan Saavedra's "artistic" presentations backed by "reasonably" priced wines and "excellent" service; for some who're thinking twice about making the trip, consider that food "doesn't get any better than this."

Prime Rib *Steak*   25 | 25 | 24 | $63

Center City West | Radisson Plaza Warwick Hotel | 1701 Locust St. (17th St.) | 215-772-1701 | www.theprimerib.com

Tame the "carnivore in you" at this "old-school" Warwick steakhouse supplying "top-of-the-line" steaks to a well-heeled crowd that digs the "quiet" "Rat Pack"-esque setting and "amazing" piano music (the "crowning touch"); you'll feel like a "royal" sitting in the "cushy", "thronelike chairs" while "attentive" servers pamper you – even though your "budget will be eaten up quickly" here; N.B. jackets required in the main dining room, but upstairs is more casual.

Rae *American*   - | - | - | VE
University City | Cira Ctr. | 2929 Arch St. (30th St.) | 215-922-3839 | www.raerestaurant.com

Gayle chef-owner Daniel Stern's New American in a gorgeous, ultramodern setting next to Amtrak's 30th Street Station is on track to become the season's glitziest (and most expensive) newcomer; from the open kitchen comes classic meat and fish preparations as well as more adventurous entrees; N.B. vino fans are already booking the six-seat wine room.

Savona *French/Italian*   27 | 26 | 25 | $69
Gulph Mills | 100 Old Gulph Rd. (Rte. 320) | 610-520-1200 | www.savonarestaurant.com

For a "special occasion" (like "winning the lottery") Main Liners "heartily recommend" this "formal" yet "convivial" "winner" in Gulph Mills for Andrew Masciangelo's "glorious" French-Italian menu, an "incredible" 1,000-label wine list and "romantic" Riviera-style setting; "mind-reading" servers tend to a well-heeled crowd so enthralled they thought they "owned the place."

Shiao Lan Kung ●Ⓜ *Chinese*   25 | 9 | 18 | $22
Chinatown | 930 Race St. (bet. 9th & 10th Sts.) | 215-928-0282

The salt-baked shrimp is the stuff of "dreams" at this "small" Chinese Chinatown BYO whose looks may be "lacking" but where the "excellent" quality of all the dishes "speaks for itself"; you may have to "wait or share a table with strangers", but most maintain it's worth it since "this is the only place" you need to go when in the neighborhood.

Southwark Ⓜ *American*   24 | 20 | 21 | $42
South St. | 701 S. Fourth St. (Bainbridge St.) | 215-238-1888

Sheri Waide's takes on New American at this "warm" Queen Villager "put many NYC restaurants to shame", while the ambiance (abetted by a "beautiful" mahogany bar) satisfies as a "fine-dining" destination or a "neighborhood haunt"; it also gets points for "helpful" servers and an "affordable" wine list – in other words, it's "super in every way."

Sovalo Ⓢ *Californian/Italian*   25 | 22 | 23 | $43
Northern Liberties | 702 N. Second St. (bet. Brown St. & Fairmount Ave.) | 215-413-7770 | www.sovalo.com

Northern Liberties bursts with pride over this "chic" and "charming" Napa-meets-Italy "up-and-comer" on the Second Street strip; it's hard not to "come back" considering the "intensely flavorful" dishes (Italian food has "never been better") under the hand of Joseph Scarpone, and factor in "excellent" service and this "bright spot" is likely to stick around awhile.

Striped Bass *Seafood*   26 | 26 | 24 | $72
Center City West | 1500 Walnut St. (15th St.) | 215-732-4444 | www.stripedbassrestaurant.com

A "Starr's shining" on this "reincarnated" Center City seafooder, Stephen Starr's "grand" yet "sexy", high-ceilinged "triumph" where the "extraordinary creativity" shows in every one of the "cleverly presented", "intensely flavorful" dishes supported by "crisp" service; it's no surprise then that the room swarms with a "contented", "beautiful" crowd that willingly pays "top dollar" for the experience.

Susanna Foo *Chinese/French* 25 24 25 $59
Center City West | 1512 Walnut St. (bet. 15th & 16th Sts.) | 215-545-2666 | www.susannafoo.com
"Food is art" at Philly's best-known and best-"loved" French-Chinese "Foo-sion" spot, the "calm and classy" Center City salon of celeb chef Susanna Foo, who turns "any ingredient into a masterpiece" on the plate; the staff specializes in "pampering" (perhaps making it easier to swallow the "exorbitant" prices), and while some "aren't sure what all the hype is about", legions of loyalists say this "gold standard for Chinese food" remains "one of the city's treasures."

Swann Lounge ● *American/French* 26 27 27 $55
Center City West | Four Seasons Hotel | 1 Logan Sq. (Benjamin Franklin Pkwy.) | 215-963-1500 | www.fourseasons.com
"All the best for a little less" than the Fountain, and "less formal" (but still a picture of "luxury"), this New American–New French at the Four Seasons offers "spectacular" food, whether in the cafe, the "great" bar, or at the "amazing" brunch and buffets or during afternoon tea; P.S. some should go here for a "primer" on service, for "every restaurant should treat its customers this well."

Tinto ● *Spanish* - - - M
Center City West | 114 S. 20th St. (Sansom St.) | 215-665-9150 | www.tintorestaurant.com
Jose Garces, whose Old City entry, Amada, is still all the rage, has ventured off Rittenhouse Square with this warm, woodsy Basque bistro specializing in small plates (pintxos) paired with Spanish and French wines; reservations are a must, except for the bar, which is now first-come, first-served.

Twenty Manning *American* 21 22 19 $43
Center City West | 261 S. 20th St. (bet. Locust & Spruce Sts.) | 215-731-0900 | www.twentymanning.com
Audrey Claire's "snazzy" relative near Rittenhouse Square is as "trendy" as ever; you'll still find Kiong Banh's "artfully prepared" Asian-inflected New American cuisine, "exciting" drinks in the lounge and "plenty of window coverage for the outdoor parade"; in all, it's easy to "impress a date" here even if the bill is more accessible for "BMW" owners.

Z Vetri Ⓢ *Italian* 28 22 27 $78
Avenue of the Arts | 1312 Spruce St. (bet. Broad & 13th Sts.) | 215-732-3478 | www.vetriristorante.com
"I thought I'd died and gone to Italy" is a common refrain when speaking of "genius" chef Marc Vetri's "rustic" 35-seat Italian in an Avenue of the Arts brownstone; "become the guest who doesn't want to leave" after you sample "wondrous" fare that's the "essence of pleasure" served without "pomp" by the "expert" staff; you'll need to use "speed-dial" on your phone to land a reservation, and sure, it's "costly", but

then again, it's a "great use for a home equity loan" since it may be the "best restaurant of its kind in America."

Xochitl Ⓜ *Mexican* — — — M

Society Hill | 408 S. Second St. (Pine St.) | 215-238-7280 | www.xochitlphilly.com

From the owners of Marigold Kitchen comes this handsome, mid-priced Mexican across from Head House Square; Philly's hipsters pack the tiny dining room, as well as the downstairs lounge, which serves plenty of tequilas to wash down the interesting late-night menu; N.B. the restaurant name is pronounced 'SO-cheat.'

Phoenix/Scottsdale

Asia de Cuba *Asian/Cuban*

– | – | – | E

Old Town | Mondrian Scottsdale | 7353 E. Indian School Rd. (bet. N. Drinkwater Blvd. & N. Scottsdale Rd.) | Scottsdale | 480-308-1100 | www.chinagrillmanagement.com

The latest link in Jeffrey Chodorow's popular chain of Asian-Cuban restaurants, this sleek Old Town hot spot is done up in an icy, cool-white motif featuring a large mural of a rooster inside and an eight-ft.-tall egg sculpture on the patio; festive mojitos and a communal table make it perfect for dining alone or with friends.

☑ Barrio Cafe Ⓜ *Mexican*

27 | 17 | 22 | $29

Phoenix | 2814 N. 16th St. (Thomas Rd.) | 602-636-0240 | www.barriocafe.com

"Come early or late" or "bet on a wait" at this "small", "popular" "gem" in Phoenix dishing out "exciting" renditions of southern Mexican cuisine; it draws crowds unafraid to venture "beyond the burrito", and if the "amazing guacamole" and "scrumptious churros" aren't enough, you can take the edge off by sipping "sangria with a hit of Jack Daniels."

☑ Binkley's Restaurant Ⓜ *American*

27 | 20 | 25 | $54

Cave Creek | 6920 E. Cave Creek Rd. (½ mile west of Tom Darlington Dr.) | 480-437-1072 | www.binkleysrestaurant.com

"Fresh", "fabulous" and "fastidiously prepared" New American cuisine comes to Cave Creek thanks to the "Gary Danko of the desert", "rising

FOOD DECOR SERVICE COST

culinary star" Kevin Binkley (ex French Laundry in Napa and Inn at Little Washington in VA), who revises the dinner menu daily, inventing "splendid tasting menus" to sate the appetites of "serious foodies"; it's all set in a "sophisticated", "art-filled" space that's managed by wife, partner and maitre d' Ann Binkley; N.B. closed Sundays from May till September.

Christopher's Fermier Brasserie *French* 24 | 20 | 23 | $44

Phoenix | Biltmore Fashion Park | 2584 E. Camelback Rd. (N. 24th St.) | 602-522-2344 | www.fermier.com

Paris meets Phoenix at Christopher Gross' "casual" *maison* offering "fancy yet accessible" and "consistently terrific" French fare; besides offering the "best lunch deal in the city" (prompted by its mall location, no doubt), this "gem" also shines with an "excellent cheese plate", an "outstanding wine selection" and a "great late-night" menu available at "easy-to-swallow" prices; N.B. oenophiles can also indulge at Paola's, the next-door wine bar.

Cyclo 🅢 Ⓜ *Vietnamese* 26 | 15 | 20 | $18

Chandler | 1919 W. Chandler Blvd. (Dobson Rd.) | 480-963-4490 | www.cycloaz.com

Expect "plenty of sass" and "charm" from "fashionable" proprietor/menu designer/server Justina Duong, who "makes everyone feel like a lifelong friend" at her "casual" BYO Vietnamese in a Chandler strip mall; since the "amazing" food is as "fresh" and "lovely" as its creator, this "small" "piece of Saigon" is always "worth the wait."

Eddie V's Edgewater Grille *Seafood/Steak* 26 | 25 | 24 | $47

North Scottsdale | 20715 N. Pima Rd. (E. Thompson Peak Pkwy.) | Scottsdale | 480-538-8468 | www.eddiev.com

Find some surf on desert turf at this "large", "clubby" eatery in North Scottsdale serving "fresh", "fantastic" seafood plus "excellent" steaks and chops for red-meat mavens; budget-seekers baited by the "amazing 50-cent oysters" and select half-price happy-hour appetizers forsake the "vibrant dining room" for the "happening" jazz lounge.

elements *American* 25 | 27 | 24 | $52

Paradise Valley | Sanctuary on Camelback Mountain | 5700 E. McDonald Dr. (bet. Scottsdale Rd. & Tatum Blvd.) | 480-607-2300 | www.elementsrestaurant.com

"Request a window table at sunset" and treat yourself to a "breathtaking view" at this "stunning", "romantic" New American tucked away on the northern slope of Camelback Mountain; the "spectacular architecture" and "contemporary", "Zen-like" decor echo the Asian-influenced menu, which offers "divine", "healthy" cuisine in "artful", "minimalist" presentations; all things considered, it's a "perfect" choice for a "special occasion."

Lon's at the Hermosa *American* 24 | 26 | 23 | $51

Paradise Valley | Hermosa Inn | 5532 N. Palo Cristi Rd. (E. Stanford Dr.) | 602-955-7878 | www.lons.com

Combining a "Southwestern atmosphere with cosmopolitan flair", this "spectacular" retreat (once belonging to cowboy artist Lon Megargee) in Paradise Valley's "romantic" Hermosa Inn showcases "dynamic" SW-inspired New American food in a "beautiful" adobe ranch house surrounded by "wonderful flowering gardens"; so "dine under the stars" with a "fabulous" view of Camelback Mountain and experience a "memorable" "slice of the Old West."

Z Mary Elaine's M *French*   27 | 28 | 27 | $82

Scottsdale | The Phoenician | 6000 E. Camelback Rd. (N. 60th St.) | 480-423-2530 | www.thephoenician.com

Setting the standard for a "special-occasion" experience, this "elegant", "ultrafancy" dining room at The Phoenician features "exquisite" New French cuisine complemented by an "extraordinary" wine list and "heavenly" city views; the "unparalleled" service "anticipates every desire", so even though you'll need to dress up – jackets are suggested – and bring "buckets of cash", it's "more than worth it"; N.B. a new lounge with nightly jazz offers a more casual alternative.

Mastro's City Hall Steakhouse *Steak*   27 | 24 | 25 | $54
(fka Drinkwater's City Hall Steakhouse)

Scottsdale | 6991 E. Camelback Rd. (Goldwater Blvd.) | 480-941-4700 | www.mastrosoceanclub.com

Soak up the "dark", "sexy" atmosphere at this Scottsdale beefery crowned "king of AZ's steakhouses" for "unbeatable" chops that are as "juicy" as the scene – think "great martinis", live music and a "terrific bar area" where a "spunky" crowd dances off the "huge portions" of meat; in short, "if you have to go somewhere, make this the place."

Z Mastro's Steakhouse *Steak*   26 | 24 | 24 | $59

North Scottsdale | La Mirada | 8852 E. Pinnacle Peak Rd. (N. Pima Rd.) | Scottsdale | 480-585-9500 | www.mastrosoceanclub.com

Meat mavens give this North Scottsdale "paradise" an "A+" for serving up "mouthwatering" steaks along with "excellent sides" plus a "seafood tower that's not to be missed"; scene-seekers say the "lively" piano bar ("eye candy" included) amps up both the "East Coast vibe" and the "noise levels", so even though "high rollers" concede it's "expensive", the majority just can't help "loving it."

Z P.F. Chang's China Bistro *Chinese*   21 | 20 | 20 | $29

Chandler | Chandler Fashion Ctr. | 3255 W. Chandler Blvd. (bet. Chandler Village Dr. & Rte. 101) | 480-899-0472
Fashion Square | The Waterfront | 7135 E. Camelback Rd. (Scottsdale Rd.) | Scottsdale | 480-949-2610
Mesa | 6610 E. Superstition Springs Blvd. (Power Rd.) | 480-218-4900
Peoria | 16170 N. 83rd Ave. (E. Alameda St.) | 623-412-3335
Scottsdale | Kierland Commons | 7132 E. Greenway Pkwy. (N. Scottsdale Rd.) | 480-367-2999
Tempe | 740 S. Mill Ave. (E. University Dr.) | 480-731-4600
www.pfchangs.com

"Wear comfortable shoes" to help cushion the invariably "unbearable waits" at these "busy" outposts of a national chain; while purists pan the provisions as "Americanized Chinese", partisans praise the "dependably delicious" fare, singling out the "fabulous lettuce wraps."

Z Pizzeria Bianco S M *Pizza*   28 | 20 | 21 | $25

Phoenix | Heritage Sq. | 623 E. Adams St. (N. 7th St.) | 602-258-8300 | www.pizzeriabianco.com

"Believe the hype": chef/co-owner Chris Bianco's "pizza temple" cops the No. 1 rating for Food in the Phoenix/Scottsdale area for "outstand-

FOOD DECOR SERVICE COST

"ing" pies ("they make life worth living") deemed "the best in the country"; expect "mind-numbing waits", but insiders suggest stopping for a pre-meal drink at the adjacent Bar Bianco; N.B. no lunch.

Postino Winecafé *Italian* | 24 | 25 | 22 | $25 |

Central Phoenix | 3939 E. Campbell Ave. (40th St.) | Phoenix | 602-852-3939 | www.postinowinecafe.com

Once a humble post office and now a "so-trendy-it-hurts" wine bar, this "stylish" "favorite" in Central Phoenix packs in "couples and groups" who graze on "light", "tasty" Italian fare (including "amazing bruschetta") served by a "courteous staff"; "be prepared for a wait", and if you can't get a table, try to snag a seat on one of the sofas.

Rancho Pinot 🖪 🕅 *American* | 25 | 20 | 24 | $47 |

Scottsdale | Lincoln Vill. | 6208 N. Scottsdale Rd. (E. Lincoln Dr.) | 480-367-8030 | www.ranchopinot.com

"Creative" "comfort food" abetted by a "comfortable", "rustic" ranch setting turns this "low-key" New American into an "all-around winner"; it's located in a Scottsdale strip mall, but chef Chrysa Kaufman's "excellent" cooking and partner Tom Kaufman's "fantastic wine list" have supporters saying "you owe it to yourself" to eat here.

⚡ Roy's *Hawaiian* | 24 | 22 | 22 | $44 |

Chandler | 7151 W. Ray Rd. (bet. N. 54th & 55th Sts.) | 480-705-7697

Phoenix | JW Marriott Desert Ridge Resort & Spa | 5350 E. Marriott Dr. (bet. Deer Valley Rd. & Tatum Blvd.) | 480-419-7697

Scottsdale | Scottsdale Seville | 7001 N. Scottsdale Rd. (Indian Bend Rd.) | 480-905-1155

www.roysrestaurant.com

"Magical", "cutting-edge" Hawaiian fusion fare lands in the desert at these "gorgeous" links in Roy Yamaguchi's international chain; though some find they "don't compare" to the original island locations, most swim with the tide, insisting the "beautifully prepared fish" and downright "sinful desserts" "meet the highest standards."

⚡ Sea Saw *Japanese* | 28 | 18 | 25 | $61 |

Old Town | 7133 E. Stetson Dr. (E. 6th Ave.) | Scottsdale | 480-481-9463 | www.seasaw.net

"Take out a loan" if necessary before visiting this spartan, 28-seat "foodie destination" in Old Town Scottsdale, where "astonishing" Japanese tapas and "unsurpassed sushi" (courtesy of "genius" chef Nobuo Fukuda) are prepared in "ways you never thought possible"; an "incredible" 2,800-plus-label wine list and the "best sake selection in town" also help put it into the "inspirational" category.

Sol y Sombra 🕅 *Spanish* | - | - | - | M |

North Scottsdale | 20707 N. Pima Rd. | Scottsdale | 480-443-5399 | www.solysombraaz.com

At this sophisticated kitchen in North Scottsdale, chef-owner Aaron May serves up traditional Spanish tapas as well as small plates with a more modern sensibility; a parade of beautiful people can be found at the communal table or out on the colorful patio, but local foodies prefer to focus on the ever-changing menu, the Basque-centric wine and sherry selection and the popular Sunday brunch.

	FOOD	DECOR	SERVICE	COST

☑ **T. Cook's** *Mediterranean* | 27 | 28 | 26 | $56 |

Phoenix | Royal Palms Resort and Spa | 5200 E. Camelback Rd.
(bet. N. Arcadia Dr. & N. 56th St.) | 602-808-0766 |
www.royalpalmshotel.com

"All around", it "doesn't get better" than this "romantic" retreat in the
Royal Palms – the Most Popular place in the Phoenix/Scottsdale area –
that "blows away" admirers with its "beautiful hacienda-style" setting
and "luxurious" atmosphere; it's also impossible to overlook the "marvelous" Mediterranean creations and the "professional staff", making
a trip here "a must for out-of-town guests" and "lots of locals" alike.

Vincent's on Camelback ☒ *French* | 26 | 22 | 24 | $58 |

Phoenix | 3930 E. Camelback Rd. (N. 40th St.) | 602-224-0225 |
www.vincentsoncamelback.com

Considered a "classic" by its fans, this "elegant" Camelback Corridor
stalwart still "charms" via Vincent Guerithault's "terrific", "innovative" Gallic interpretation of Southwestern fare and "elegant" country
French decor; if it's "tired" to a few, this piece of "gastronomic heaven"
in the desert remains "at the top" for most.

Portland, OR

TOP FOOD RANKING

	Restaurant	Cuisine
27	Paley's Place	French/Pacific NW
	Genoa	Italian
	Apizza Scholls	Pizza
26	Higgins	Pacific NW
	Heathman	French/Pacific NW
	Joel Palmer House	Pacific NW
	Alberta St. Oyster B&G	Pacific NW
	Tabla	Mediterranean
	Caffe Mingo	Italian
	Nuestra Cocina	Mexican

OTHER NOTEWORTHY PLACES

Alba	Italian
Andina	Peruvian
Bluehour	American/Mediterranean
Hiroshi	Japanese
Hurley's	American/French
Le Pigeon	French
Park Kitchen	Pacific NW
Pok Pok	Thai
Toro Bravo	Spanish
Wildwood	Pacific NW

Alba Osteria & Enoteca Ⓜ *Italian*   24 | 19 | 22 | $39

Southwest Portland | 6440 SW Capitol Hwy. (Bertha Blvd.) |
503-977-3045 | www.albaosteria.com

Set in an old train depot, this "hidden" SW Portland Northern Italian
"bastion" hosts aficionados of Barolos and Barbarescos who swear by
the "authentic" (if somewhat obscure in the United States) Piedmontese
dishes offered on the "killer" roster, especially the "fantastic" pastas
and the "best" sweetbreads; "spot-on" service and a "darling" setting
play a large role in the restaurant's winning formula.

Alberta Street Oyster Bar & Grill *Pacific NW*   26 | 21 | 24 | $38

Alberta | 2926 NE Alberta St. (29th Ave.) | 503-284-9600 |
www.albertaoyster.com

It may have a plain-Jane name, but this rising "star" is shining in "funky"
NE Alberta; beyond the "outstanding variety" of "fresh" oysters is
"dangerously delicious" and moderately "pricey" Pacific Northwest
creations served by "polished" staffers in a "warm", "stylish" setting,
all serving to make this spot a "wonderful addition" to the scene.

Ⓩ Andina *Peruvian*   25 | 24 | 22 | $38

Pearl District | Pennington Bldg. | 1314 NW Glisan St. (13th Ave.) |
503-228-9535 | www.andinarestaurant.com

"Imaginative" modern Peruvian cuisine that scales uncharted "culinary heights" distinguishes this "chic", "high-energy", high-ceilinged

FOOD	DECOR	SERVICE	COST

Pearl District venue; the "extensive" small-plate options make sampling the "sexy" offerings easy, and "pro" service and "fabulous" drinks should help give everyone a reason to come and experience a "hedonistic feast for the senses."

☒ Apizza Scholls ⑤Ⓜ *Pizza* | 27 | 13 | 18 | $20 |
| --- | --- | --- | --- |

Hawthorne | 4741 SE Hawthorne Blvd. (bet. 47th & 48th Aves.) | 503-233-1286 | www.apizzascholls.com

Depending on who's talking (or eating), the "best pizza this side of the Mississippi" – or perhaps "this side of Italy" – can be found at this "cramped" Hawthorne pizzeria whose pies leave even a "New Yorker happy"; aside from "long lines", "spacey" service and "strict limitations on the number of toppings" (there are "more regulations than the nastiest divorce settlement"), few dispute there's "sublime" 'za here that's "more for foodies than fratties."

☒ Bluehour *American/Mediterranean* | 23 | 25 | 22 | $46 |
| --- | --- | --- | --- |

Pearl District | Wieden & Kennedy Headquarters | 250 NW 13th Ave. (Everett St.) | 503-226-3394 | www.bluehouronline.com

Wear your "Helmut Langs" to this "swanky" Pearl District Med–New American, the "hang of P-Town's who's who" where the "dramatic" interior (complete with soaring drapery) matches the "glam" crowd; it's no surprise that happy hour here is the "best" around, and as far as the food, it's "good", but since the staff supplies as much "eye candy" as the patrons, does it really matter?

Caffe Mingo *Italian* | 26 | 20 | 23 | $33 |
| --- | --- | --- | --- |

Nob Hill | 807 NW 21st Ave. (Johnson St.) | 503-226-4646

Devotees line NW 21st for this "lively" Nob Hill eatery cranking out "fantastic" "farmhouse" Italian specialties enhanced by a staff that "couldn't be friendlier"; you'll feel like you're eating "in someone's home", especially if you dine at the communal "chef's table" that boasts prime kitchen viewing.

☒ Genoa ◗Ⓜ *Italian* | 27 | 19 | 27 | $74 |
| --- | --- | --- | --- |

NE/SE 28th | 2832 SE Belmont St. (bet. 28th & 29th Aves.) | 503-238-1464 | www.genoarestaurant.com

"Fulfill all your palate's dreams" at this 35-year-old Portland "institution" in Belmont where the "incredible hospitality" complements the "formal" ambiance and "lovingly prepared" Italian fare consisting of three, four or seven course meals; even though it's known as the city's "most expensive" restaurant, it's still, for many, "the most special" and "worth every penny."

☒ Heathman Restaurant, The *French/Pacific NW* | 26 | 22 | 24 | $46 |
| --- | --- | --- | --- |

Downtown | The Heathman Hotel | 1001 SW Broadway (Salmon St.) | 503-790-7752 | www.heathmanhotel.com

"One dines, not eats" at this Downtown Heathman Hotel stalwart for "special occasions" that's perfect either for a "power lunch" or "dress-up dinner"; chef Philippe Boulot's kitchen sends out "superlative" Pacific NW fare infused with "Gallic savoir-faire" while "helpful" service ensures such a smooth ride that any thoughts of "high costs" are quickly erased from memory; P.S. a "great" high tea is served in the adjacent lounge.

	FOOD	DECOR	SERVICE	COST

☑ Higgins Restaurant & Bar *Pacific NW* — 26 | 22 | 25 | $44

Downtown | 1239 SW Broadway (Jefferson St.) | 503-222-9070
The bona fide "temple" of Pacific Northwest fare is this Downtown
mainstay (Portland's Most Popular) where chef Greg Higgins, an
early champion of organic, seasonal and sustainable agriculture,
has a knack for turning the "simple things into something extraordinary"; more kudos go to the "laid-back" ambiance, "excellent"
service and "impressive" beer and wine lists; P.S. bargain-hunters
applaud the "affordable" menu (and the "best" burgers in town") at
the adjoining bar.

Hiroshi 🅼 *Japanese* — - | - | - | E

Pearl District | 926 NW 10th Ave. (bet. Lovejoy & NW Johnson Sts.) |
503-619-0580
After a stint in Lake Oswego, sushi master Hiroshi Ikegaya has turned
up in the glitzy Pearl District with his eponymous, smartly decorated
white-tablecloth Japanese; no surprise, the rolls are meticulously as-
sembled, be it a simple California version with real King Crab or one
prepared with monkfish liver pâté.

Hurley's 🅼 *American/French* — 25 | 20 | 22 | $56

Nob Hill | 1987 NW Kearney St. (bet. 19th & 20th Aves.) | 503-295-6487 |
www.hurleys-restaurant.com
Enthusiasts aver "no restaurant in Portland can hold a candle" to this
"posh", "first-rate" French–New American on a side street in Nob Hill;
Tom Hurley's small-plates (albeit "microscopic") slate may translate
into "high" prices, but the payoff is "memorable" food that shows an "attention to detail"; in short, all of the above add up to a "rich" experience.

Joel Palmer House 🅱🅼 *Pacific NW* — 26 | 23 | 24 | $50

Dayton | 600 Ferry St. (6th St.) | 503-864-2995 |
www.joelpalmerhouse.com
"Mushroom maniacs" clear a path to Dayton and end up at this "historic" house in the "country", the showcase of chef Jack Czarnecki,
who uses 'shrooms – from matsutakes to morels – and "lovingly
weaves" them into Pacific NW dishes; the consensus: for "fun and
fungi in the middle of nowhere", it's "fabulous."

Le Pigeon *French* — - | - | - | E

E. Burnside | 738 E. Burnside St. (bet. 7th & 8th Aves. NE) | 503-546-8796 |
www.lepigeon.com
Rising star chef Gabriel Rucker may only be 26 years old, but the food
at this Eastside French eatery is for mature, adventurous palates attuned to the glories of pig's trotters, beef cheek bourguignon and, as
advertised, pigeon that are features of the menu; mismatched china
and chipped teacups add funky notes to the farmhouse-style setting.

Nuestra Cocina 🅱🅼 *Mexican* — 26 | 20 | 22 | $28

Southeast Portland | 2135 SE Division St. (bet. 21st & 22nd Aves.) |
503-232-2135 | www.nuestra-cocina.com
When it comes to "fabulous" food to lift you up when the "city's grays"
are getting you down, this SE Portland Mexican favorite "takes the
cake" ("or rather, the flan"); while the "long waits" can grate, the "colorful" mosaic-tiled setting and an "authentic", "no-burrito" Oaxacan-
influenced menu compensate.

	FOOD	DECOR	SERVICE	COST

☑ Paley's Place
Bistro & Bar ☒ *French/Pacific NW* — 27 | 22 | 26 | $50

Nob Hill | 1204 NW 21st Ave. (Northrup St.) | 503-243-2403 |
www.paleysplace.net

At this "intimate" "upscale bistro" in Nob Hill, "consummate hostess" Kimberly Paley oversees a staff that makes you "feel like you have just arrived at their home", while husband and chef Vitaly puts a French spin on "superb" Pacific NW food (No. 1 in Portland); it seems everyone here has the "perfect touch", so it's no surprise that its reputation "still holds."

Park Kitchen ☒ *Pacific NW* — 25 | 19 | 23 | $39

Pearl District | 422 NW Eighth Ave. (Flanders St.) | 503-223-7275 |
www.parkkitchen.com

Enthusiasts eagerly await whatever surprises chef Scott Dolich has up his sleeve at this "low-key" bistro in the Pearl District; the "intriguing", "clever" New American–Pacific NW food is ably matched by "engaging" service, and the whole package is made even more enticing with "cool" decor and sidewalk seating that "looks out onto the bocce" action.

Pok Pok/Whiskey Soda Lounge ☒ *Thai* — - | - | - | M

Southeast Portland | 3226 SE Division St. (SE 32nd Ave.) | 503-232-1387 |
www.pokpokpdx.com

Inspired by the markets of Chiang Mai, this arrival in Southeast serves addictive, modestly priced Siamese street fare that's hard to find in most Thai restaurants here; started by Portland native Andy Ricker as a tiny to-go cart, the site now encompasses an outdoor patio and a moody, slightly retro basement room where items such as lemongrass-stuffed game hen help bring in night owls.

Tabla ⓜ *Mediterranean* — 26 | 21 | 24 | $35

NE/SE 28th | 200 NE 28th Ave. (Davis St.) | 503-238-3777 |
www.tabla-restaurant.com

Fans invariably "end up falling in love" with this "hip" Med small-plates specialist that "stands apart" from the other restaurants lining NE 28th Street; the fare is "worth repeat visits", as are the three-course tasting menu (aka "the best deal in Portland"), "comfortable" casual vibe and the back bar, where patrons can watch the drama unfold in the kitchen.

Toro Bravo *Spanish* — - | - | - | M

Northeast Portland | 120 NE Russell St. (NE Rodney Ave.) | 503-281-4464 |
www.torobravopdx.com

Heading up the latest culinary expansion into Northeast Portland, this new Spanish haunt next to the Wonder Ballroom highlights tapas in many forms; communal tables, stand-up bars, a chef's counter and private nooks complete the Galician scene.

☑ Wildwood *Pacific NW* — 25 | 23 | 23 | $44

Nob Hill | 1221 NW 21st Ave. (Northrup St.) | 503-248-9663 |
www.wildwoodrestaurant.com

Serving "true" Pacific NW fare, this Nob Hill mainstay, the domain of celebrity chef Corey Schreiber (one of the founding fathers of the local-sustainable-organic movement), is where the "divine" food still "shines" and where sitting at the "chef's table" by the wood-burning oven or in the "casual" dining room is a treat; overall, it's a "must" for anyone wanting to experience one of the Northwest's gastronomic "treasures."

Salt Lake City & Mountain Resorts

TOP FOOD RANKING

	Restaurant	Cuisine
_27_	Takashi	Japanese
	Mariposa, The	American
_26_	Red Iguana	Mexican
	Shabu	Asian
	Mazza	Mideastern
	Cucina Toscana	Italian
_25_	Metropolitan	American
	Seafood Buffet	Seafood
	Tree Room	American
	Glitretind	American

OTHER NOTEWORTHY PLACES

Restaurant	Cuisine
Bambara	American
Chez Betty	Continental
Franck's	American/French
Jean Louis	Eclectic
Log Haven	American
Lugano	Italian
Market Street	Seafood
Martine	Mediterranean
New Yorker Club	American
Wahso	Asian Fusion

☑ Bambara *American* 24 | 24 | 23 | $44

Downtown | Hotel Monaco | 202 S. Main St. (200 South) | Salt Lake City |
801-363-5454 | www.bambara-slc.com
The scene's "pretty hip" inside this "lively", airy Downtown New
American (a resident of the Hotel Monaco) whose origins as a
former bank explain the "wonderful" marble-accented decor; "good
vibes" and looks aside, the open kitchen creates "delicious" food
that's delivered by a "sharp" staff; N.B. the Food score may not reflect
a recent chef change.

Chez Betty *American/Continental* 25 | 18 | 25 | $50

Park City | Copper Bottom Inn | 1637 Short Line Rd. (Deer Valley Dr.) |
435-649-8181 | www.chezbetty.com
Although "hard to find" and somewhat of a "hike to get to when you're
tired from skiing", this "unassuming" eatery has devotees relying on
the "consistent" Continental-American cuisine that's immensely "enjoyable"; some even say although it's "pricey", it's still a "value" by
Park City standards.

☑ Cucina Toscana 🗗 *Italian* 26 | 22 | 23 | $42

Downtown | 307 W. Pierpont Ave. (S. 300 West) | Salt Lake City |
801-328-3463 | www.cucina-toscana.com
Diners extend rounds of *"bravissimos!"* to the housemade pastas that
are among the "sublime" offerings at this Downtown Northern Italian

whose staff "expertly guides you through the comprehensive menu"; Valter Nassi, a "whirlwind" of a host, "makes the meal an experience" to remember, and you "can't help but make friends" with diners next to you – the "tables are so close together."

Franck's 🅱 American/French
24 | 23 | 22 | $44

Cottonwood | 6263 S. Holladay Blvd. (bet. Holladay Blvd. & 6200 South) | Salt Lake City | 801-274-6264 | www.francksfood.com

"Inspired", "interesting" cooking from the hands of chef Franck Peissel guides this Cottonwood French-American situated in a "lovely" cottage "tucked under" towering trees; they seem to "get it all right", right down to the "personable" service; N.B. gawkers can check out the workings of the kitchen, thanks to the plasma screen in the dining room.

Glitretind Restaurant American
25 | 25 | 26 | $64

Deer Valley | Stein Eriksen Lodge | 7700 Stein Way (Royal St.) | 435-645-6455 | www.steinlodge.com

Chef Zane Holmquist's "sophisticated" New American cooking complements a "great" wine list at this "pricey", "top" dining destination in Deer Valley whose blonde-wood, Alpine decor is "mountain lavish" yet "relaxing"; "impeccable" service at dinner and "obscenely good" lunch and brunch buffets help give the restaurant its "first-class" standing.

Jean Louis Eclectic
21 | 19 | 23 | $49

Park City | 136 Heber Ave., Ste. 107 (bet. Main St. & Park Ave.) | 435-200-0260 | www.jeanlouisrestaurant.com

After more than a decade at the helm of various Park City restaurants, chef Jean-Louis Montecot is now laying down "quite-good" Eclectic cuisine in his Lower Main eatery where the "sophisticated" crowd mingles with a "genial" staff; "request a banquette" or choose the "buzzing" bar and enjoy the scene as the toque "makes the rounds."

Log Haven American
24 | 27 | 24 | $49

Eastside | 6451 E. Millcreek Canyon Rd. (Wasatch Blvd.) | Salt Lake City | 801-272-8255 | www.log-haven.com

"It's worth the ride" up Salt Lake's Millcreek Canyon to reach this "picture-perfect" cabin, a New American proffering "splendid" food amid a "magical setting"; "go to impress clients" but also remember it's a "cozy", "romantic" spot where the "cheery" staff offers "excellent" service.

Lugano Italian
24 | 17 | 22 | $34

Holladay | 3364 S. 2300 East (3300 South) | Salt Lake City | 801-412-9994 | www.luganorestaurant.com

"Thoughtfully" prepared Northern Italian specialties keep "winning over local hearts and stomachs" at this Holladay "hit" with acoustics on the "noisy" side; the "welcoming" ambiance is abetted by a chef-owner whose frequent visits to tables "make people feel important."

⛰ Mariposa, The Ⓜ American
27 | 26 | 27 | $70

Deer Valley | Silver Lake Lodge, Deer Valley Resort | 7600 Royal St. (Rte. 224) | 435-645-6715 | www.deervalley.com

"Magnificent" New American food "in a magnificent mountain setting" keeps this Deer Valley Resort site on the map as a "ski country dining" destination where the "exquisite" food and "fantastic" desserts (such as the 'chocolate snowball') are matched by the "excellent" floor crew; the "romantic" wood-paneled room and those "roaring" fireplaces lure loyals back to this "great splurge"; N.B. open December through mid-April.

☑ Market Street Grill *Seafood* — 23 | 21 | 21 | $36

Downtown | 48 W. Market St. (W. Temple St., bet. 300 South & 400 South) | Salt Lake City | 801-322-4668
Holladay | 2985 E. Cottonwood Pkwy. (S. 3000 East) | Salt Lake City | 801-942-8860
South Jordan | 10702 S. River Front Pkwy. (W. South Jordan Pkwy.) | 801-302-2262

☑ Market Street Oyster Bar *Seafood*

Downtown | 54 W. Market St. (W. Temple St., bet. 300 South & 400 South) | Salt Lake City | 801-531-6044
Holladay | 2985 E. Cottonwood Pkwy. (S. 3000 E.) | Salt Lake City | 801-942-8870
South Jordan | 10702 S. River Front Pkwy. (W. South Jordan Pkwy.) | 801-302-2264
www.gastronomyinc.com

The "legendary" clam chowder is "second to none" at Salt Lake's Most Popular restaurants dishing menus that consistently "excel" in all locations (not to mention the "incredibly fresh" oysters, the specialty of the new South Jordan spin-off); "nobody does it better" when it comes to fish, say fans, who keep the affordable trio "bustling."

Martine ☒ *Mediterranean* — 25 | 23 | 22 | $36

Downtown | 22 E. 100 South (bet. Main & State Sts.) | Salt Lake City | 801-363-9328

"Imaginative combinations" of "unexpected textures and flavors" put this "great little find" for midpriced Mediterranean-Modern European preparations (featuring "fantastic" tapas) on the Downtown map; the brownstone space, with its "dark woods" and "candlelit" atmosphere, breathes "romance."

☑ Mazza ☒ *Mideastern* — 26 | 18 | 21 | $25

Downtown | 912 E. 900 South (S. 900 East) | Salt Lake City | 801-521-4572
Eastside | 1515 S. 1500 East (bet. Emerson & Kensington Aves.) | Salt Lake City | 801-484-9259
www.mazzacafe.com

Fans simply "can't go without" the "tasty" cooking offered at this affordable Lebanese pair, one the "tiny" original storefront on Salt Lake's Eastside, and the other a new "chicly designed" Downtown spin-off; at both restaurants, the "best baba ghanoush in the history of time" joins "fantastic" Lebanese wines, plus, the staff sets an "inviting" tone.

Metropolitan ☒ *American* — 25 | 25 | 24 | $56

Downtown | 173 W. Broadway (300 South, bet. 200 West & W. Temple St.) | Salt Lake City | 801-364-3472 | www.themetropolitan.com

"New York style" and an "eclectic", "high-quality" menu draw discriminating diners to this "cosmopolitan" Downtown New American where "modern" decor meets "choreographed" service and "excellent" wines; the tabs are on the "high end", so insiders advise to capitalize on the "sophisticated", lower-priced bites at the bar where you can comfortably "eat solo."

☑ New Yorker Club ⑤ American 24 | 23 | 24 | $51

Downtown | 60 W. Market St. (W. Temple St., bet. 300 South & 400 South) | Salt Lake City | 801-363-0166 | www.gastronomyinc.com

The "old guard" and "power brokers" keep this "venerable" Downtown "classic" serving "consistently good" steaks and Traditional American items humming after 30 years; to reinforce its "clubby" bona fides, potential patrons have to fork over a guest membership fee to "become part of the scene."

☑ Red Iguana Mexican 26 | 14 | 21 | $19

Downtown | 736 W. North Temple St. (800 West) | Salt Lake City | 801-322-1489 | www.rediguana.com

Boosters still brand this "homey" Downtown "institution" the "gold standard" for its "authentic" Mexican menu and "outstanding" moles; ok, it's constantly "crowded" and there's "no waiting area, except on the sidewalk of a busy street", but who cares with all that "stellar" food and "cheap" prices?

Seafood Buffet ⑤ Seafood 25 | 17 | 19 | $65

Deer Valley | Snow Park Lodge | 2250 Deer Valley Dr. (Mellow Mountain Rd.) | 435-645-6632 | www.deervalley.com

Even "before booking a condo" at Deer Valley, savvy skiers make reservations to and wind up "making laps" back to the "fantastic feast" of a buffet that's the hallmark of this "high-class" Snow Park Lodge seafood specialist that "puts taste above volume"; even if you have to "save up" to pay, all agree that eating here makes you "happy as a blue whale cruising through a field of krill."

☑ Shabu Asian 26 | 21 | 23 | $52

Park City | 333 Main St. (bet. 4th St. & King Rd.) | 435-645-7253 | www.shabupc.com

Although the "odd" second-floor mall location may put it out of sight, this Park City Asian on "historic" Main Street is readily sought after by fans sweet on the "delightful" fare that packs "dynamic flavors"; "chic" decor draws an "upbeat" crowd that would happily "go every day", "pricey" tabs notwithstanding.

☑ Takashi ⑤ Japanese 27 | 23 | 22 | $38

Downtown | 18 W. Market St. (W. Temple St., bet. 300 South & 400 South) | Salt Lake City | 801-519-9595

"Watch out, Nobu!" aver raw-fare fanatics who've delved into Takashi Gibo's "creative", "incredible" preparations with "Peruvian flair" that arrive via "attentive" servers at this "exciting" Downtown Japanese (No. 1 for Food in Salt Lake) sporting a "modern" look; the "terrific" sake selection fuels the "noise", while simultaneously sating "the who's who" crowd.

Tree Room American 25 | 27 | 25 | $53

Sundance | Sundance Resort | Scenic Rte. 92 (Hwy. 189) | 801-223-4200 | www.sundanceresort.com

Within its elegantly rustic, "simply amazing" dining room built around a tree (and also featuring Native American art), this "blissful" Regional American in the Sundance Resort serves a "well-prepared"

	FOOD	DECOR	SERVICE	COST

seasonal menu (including game) drawn from local resources; beyond contemplating the "impossibly beautiful" surroundings, there's always the possibility of catching the sight of its owner, Robert Redford.

Wahso *Asian Fusion* | 25 | 26 | 24 | $64 |

Park City | 577 Main St. (Heber Ave.) | 435-615-0300 |
www.wahso.com

"Am I still in Utah?" is the first thing you'll ask after entering chef-impresario Bill White's Park City Asian fusion complete with a "drop-dead" beautiful, Far-East interior (including "secluded", curtained booths) like a "movie set"; if some ask "Wahso expensive?", the "magnificent" menu and all the "delicious" food on it compensate.

San Antonio

TOP FOOD RANKING

	Restaurant	Cuisine
28	Le Rêve	French
27	Lodge Rest.	American
26	Korean B.B.Q. House	Korean
	Biga on the Banks	American
	Bistro Vatel	French
	L'Etoile	French
25	Las Canarias	French/Mediterranean
	Francesca's at Sunset	Southwestern
	Fleming's Prime	Steak
	Frederick's	Asian Fusion/French
	Silo*	American

OTHER NOTEWORTHY PLACES

Ácenar	Tex-Mex
Bin 555	American
Boudro's/Riverwalk	Seafood/Steak
Cafe Paladar	Pan-Latin
Grill at Leon Springs	Eclectic
La Frite	Belgian
Liberty Bar	Eclectic
Paesanos	Italian
Pesca on the River	Seafood
P.F. Chang's	Chinese

Ácenar *Tex-Mex* | 22 | 24 | 20 | $27 |

Downtown | 146 E. Houston St. (N. St. Mary's St.) | 210-222-2362 | www.acenar.com

With "groovy" decor and a "fab outdoor patio", this River Walk Downtowner provides a "swinging atmosphere" to go with its "va-va-voom" "nuevo Tex-Mex" fare and "killer margaritas"; show-goers suggest stopping in "before or after the theater", though some warn of "long waits" and "uneven service" in the "sometimes noisy" dining area; N.B. its bar, Átomar, is open till 2 AM Thursday–Saturday.

☑ Biga on the Banks *American* | 26 | 25 | 26 | $48 |

Downtown | 203 S. St. Mary's St. (W. Market St.) | 210-225-0722 | www.biga.com

Foodies are "big on" this "urbane" Downtown dining room, a "modern" space recently updated (post-Survey) in darker tones and shorn of tablecloths, where "culinary magician" Bruce Auden conjures "bold", "luscious" Asian-inflected New American cuisine to go with his "excellent" wine list; meanwhile, the "knowledgeable, attentive" servers enable diners to "relax" and enjoy the "fantastic River Walk views"; sure, it's "expensive", but for an evening in "heaven", most

---

* Indicates tie with restaurant above

maintain the cost is "worth it" – despite the recent removal of foie gras from the menu.

Bin 555 ●☑ *American* | - | - | - | M |

Hill County Village | Shops at Artisans Alley | 555 W. Bitters Rd.
(bet. Blanco Rd. & West Ave.) | 210-496-0555 | www.bin555.com
This New American in Hill County Village from chef Jason Dady and
his brother, Jake, is a more casual version of their first restaurant, The
Lodge; here they serve tapas, wood-oven offerings, larger plates with
a Med cast and affordable vintages – all in a sunny yellow setting tucked
away in an eclectic shopping center; N.B. in a nod to the restaurant's
name, the wine list offers 55 choices priced at $55 each.

☑ Bistro Vatel ☒Ⓜ *French* | 26 | 18 | 23 | $44 |

Olmos Park | 218 E. Olmos Dr. (El Prado Dr. W.) | 210-828-3141 |
www.bistrovatel.com
Chef-owner Damien Watel's "delicately delectable", "perfectly prepared French classics" ("outstanding foie gras", "exquisite" seafood)
and "great" wine list have elevated his Olmos Park strip-center bistro
to "gourmet-haven" status; "twice-a-week" regulars rhapsodize over
its "intimate", "truly European" vibe – complete with "flea-market-
chic" styling – and a "gracious" staff that's "diligent but not overwhelming"; in short, an "unexpected" "gem"; P.S. three-course, $34
prix fixe dinners are such a "bargain" they're practically a "gift."

☑ Boudro's on the Riverwalk *Seafood/Steak* | 24 | 20 | 21 | $33 |

River Walk | 421 E. Commerce St. (N. Presa St.) | 210-224-8484 |
www.boudros.com
"One of the few" River Walk restaurants lauded by locals, this "much-
talked-about" "haven" "continues to succeed" because of its "excellent regional" (read: Louisianan-Texan) seafood and steaks, bolstered
by "awesome guacamole" and "addictive" cactus-pear margaritas;
"knowledgeable" staffers can "manage groups big or small", but since
there may be "lots of noise" and "very little elbow room" inside, "snag
an outdoor table" if weather permits; P.S. "dinner on one of the barges
as you float" downstream "is a blast."

Cafe Paladar Ⓜ *Pan-Latin* | - | - | - | M |
(fka Cafe Mariposa)

Stone Oak | 18322 Sonterra Pl. (Stone Oak Pkwy.) | 210-771-6961 |
www.cafepaladar.com
Tony tapas are the starters of choice for flush Outer-Looplanders at this
snazzy, Stone Oak Pan-Latin lair whose compact, art-accented space is
appealingly colorful and contemporary; it leans toward Mexico with offerings like lusty beef tinga on plantain chips, barbecued lamb quesadil-
las and Baja ceviche, while desserts such as a Mexican chocolate cake
made macho by ancho chiles make the trip even from the deepest
Southside worth contemplating, as does the sumptuous Sunday brunch.

Fleming's Prime Steakhouse & Wine Bar *Steak* | 25 | 23 | 23 | $50 |

Quarry | Alamo Quarry Mkt. | 255 E. Basse Rd. (Hwy. 281) | 210-824-9463 |
www.flemingssteakhouse.com
Carnivores have no beef with this "upscale" Quarry steakhouse, claiming
it "does everything well": the "high-quality" rib-eyes are "delicious"

and the wine list "extensive", all backed by a "cheerful" staff; if some say it's "overpriced", most consider this chain a "can't-miss" choice.

Francesca's at Sunset 🅱 🅼 *Southwestern* | 25 | 27 | 27 | $48

La Cantera | Westin La Cantera Resort | 16441 La Cantera Pkwy. (Fiesta Texas Dr.) | 210-558-2442 | www.westinlacantera.com
Appropriately "breathtaking" sunset views make this upscale address in the Westin La Cantera SA's No. 1 for Decor – but surveyors are also gasping over the "spectacular" pro service and Southwestern-slanted cuisine (à la Santa Fe's Mark Miller); those who "want to live large" and explore the "extensive" wine list can put off the "long drive home" by staying overnight at the resort; N.B. a post-Survey chef change may outdate the above Food score.

Frederick's 🅱 *Asian Fusion/French* | 25 | 15 | 23 | $44

Alamo Heights | 7701 Broadway St. (W. Nottingham Pl.) | 210-828-9050 | www.fredericksa.com
"Amazing" and "always reliable" French–Asian fusion fare "bursting with flavor" (especially the "extremely well-done" seafood) is the forte of this Alamo Heights "fave", "hidden in the back" of a strip center; owner Frederick Costa, who's "always present to ensure things run smoothly", and his "friendly, attentive" staff foster a "pleasant ambiance" despite the place's "cramped" confines and "less-than-inspirational", apparently "improvised" decor.

Grill at Leon Springs, The *Eclectic* | - | - | - | M

Leon Springs | 24116 I-10 W. (Boerne Stage Rd.) | 210-698-8797
There's an Eclectic-French bent to the menu at this Leon Springs counterpart to its more formal relative, L'Etoile; here, wood-fired pizzas and steaks turn up, the prices are moderate and the setting equally exhibits modern and country touches.

🅉 Korean B.B.Q. House 🅱 🅼 *Korean* | 26 | 13 | 19 | $22
(aka Go Hyang Jib)

San Antonio East | 4400 Rittiman Rd. (Melton Dr.) | 210-822-8846
"You want ethnic in SA? this is it" assert admirers who adore the "very authentic" Korean barbecue and "excellent bulgoki and bibimbop" at this far Eastside eatery, complete with exotic indoor waterfall; the "wonderful owners" and "helpful staffers" help neophytes out with "knowledgeable explanations" of unfamiliar fare; N.B. owner Young Casey's offspring are now in charge here.

La Frite 🅱 🅼 *Belgian* | - | - | - | M

Downtown | 728 S. Alamo St. (S. Presa St.) | 210-224-7555
Multilingual chef Damien Watel's latest endeavor is this Belgian eatery in a Downtown storefront, which joins his French (Bistro Vatel) and Italian (Ciao Lavanderia) entries; fries, as the name implies, are front and center, as, of course, are the marvelous moules, all served in a shoestring setting.

Las Canarias *French/Mediterranean* | 25 | 25 | 25 | $48

River Walk | Omni La Mansión del Rio Hotel | 112 College St. (bet. Navarro & N. St. Mary's Sts.) | 210-518-1063 | www.lamansion.com
Chef Scott Cohen has turned this "spacious, gracious" venue in the "elegant" La Mansión del Rio Hotel into a "tremendous" dining

destination replete with "class and taste"; his "polished", "imaginative" French-Mediterranean cuisine, drawing on local ingredients, "lives up to the hype" (the Sunday brunch buffet, in particular, is "unbeatable"), while a crew of "true professionals" helps create a "romantic" ambiance via "impeccable" service and "lovely", "gentle" guitar music on weekends.

☑ Le Rêve 🅂🅜 French   28 | 24 | 27 | $81

Downtown | Historic Exchange Bldg. | 152 E. Pecan St. (N. St. Mary's St.) | 210-212-2221 | www.restaurantlereve.com

Now that smitten surveyors have voted it SA's No. 1 for Food and Service, Andrew Weissman's "romantic" Downtown "gem" might as well be renamed Le Rave; this petite New French exhibits its chef-owner's "amazing attention to detail" throughout each "three-hour" dinner – "excellent" prix fixe and tasting menus with "superb" wine pairings are "impeccably" served by a "pampering" staff in a modern room adorned with "lovely, fresh floral arrangements"; a vocal minority sniffs the scene is "beyond snooty", but most find it "the epitome of elegant dining"; N.B. jacket and reservations required.

L'Etoile French/Seafood   26 | 19 | 24 | $43

Alamo Heights | 6106 Broadway St. (Albany St.) | 210-826-4551 | www.letoilesa.com

"It's not called the star for nothing" beam Lone Star Staters who are high on this "comfortable", "quiet and relaxing" Alamo Heights "favorite"; they report its "classic" French seafood is "perfectly prepared" and "artistically presented" by "careful" servers; trendier types declare "it's time for some new recipes" at this "dowdy" spot and detect a soupçon of Gallic "attitude"; P.S. shellfish lovers laud the "wonderful" summer lobster festival.

Liberty Bar Eclectic   23 | 20 | 21 | $23

North Central | 328 E. Josephine St. (Ave. A) | 210-227-1187 | www.liberty-bar.com

Located in North Central SA, the building housing this "funky" "classic" "leans noticeably" to the left, just like much of its "arty" "hipster" clientele; its similarly "unique" Eclectic menu lets you "mix and match" an array of "strictly gourmet" noshes with "awesome housemade bread", "great desserts" and esoteric wines and beers; the "friendly" servers can be "quirky", but this "pure Texas" "charmer" is often "the first place" locals take "visiting foodies."

☑ Lodge Restaurant   27 | 26 | 24 | $51
of Castle Hills, The 🅂 American

Castle Hills | 1746 Lockhill Selma Rd. (West Ave.) | 210-349-8466 | www.thelodgerestaurant.com

It feels like you're spending the evening "at a rich friend's house" when you settle in at this 1929 Castle Hills "converted mansion" where "inventive" chef-owner Jason Dady turns out "expertly prepared" New American dishes you can savor à la carte or in various prix fixe configurations, cared for by staffers who manage to be "knowledgeable and attentive" without "smothering"; plan to occupy one of the "quaint", "romantic" small rooms "for hours" enjoying this "pricey" but "fabulous" experience.

	FOOD	DECOR	SERVICE	COST

Ⓩ Paesanos *Italian* **22 | 21 | 20 | $31**

Quarry | Alamo Quarry Mkt. | 555 E. Basse Rd. (Treeline Park) | 210-828-5191

Ⓩ Paesanos Riverwalk *Italian*

River Walk | 111 W. Crockett St. (Presa St.) | 210-227-2782
www.paesanos.com

Thanks to its "transcendent" Shrimp Paesano, these "lively" Italian "institutions" remain "family favorites" – indeed, they're voted SA's Most Popular; "better service" and a "fun ambiance" impel locals toward the Alamo Quarry Market location – where "boldface" types mingle at the city's "largest sit-down cocktail party" – rather than the "contemporary", "tourist-destination" River Walk outpost; still, a sizable minority charges the "decent" but "dull" fare "has been declining."

Pesca on the River *Seafood* **22 | 22 | 20 | $45**

River Walk | Watermark Hotel & Spa | 212 W. Crockett St. (N. St. Mary's St.) | 210-396-5817 | www.watermarkhotel.com

"Refined", "spacious" and handsome, this seafooder at the Watermark Hotel "has the potential for excellence"; pescavores who feel "the best seat is at the raw bar" can slurp "excellent" oysters and sample any of the 75-plus tequilas on hand, while mellower sorts prefer dining outdoors "along the River Walk" with a glass of wine; surveyors are split on service, though ("lively, young and attentive" vs. "poorly trained" and "slow").

Ⓩ P.F. Chang's China Bistro *Chinese* **22 | 21 | 20 | $25**

Quarry | Alamo Quarry Mkt. | 255 E. Basse Rd. (Hwy. 281) | 210-507-1000 | www.pfchangs.com

"Always crowded" and "consistent", this "ubiquitous" chain keeps its clientele coming back with "generous portions" of "tasty", "upscale" (if "Americanized") Chinese food and "great wine by the glass", served amid "distinctive" decor; still, even fans grumble about waiting "too long" in "too-noisy" environs for "too-pricey" cuisine that sometimes seems "too formulaic."

Silo *American* **25 | 23 | 23 | $43**

Terrell Heights | 1133 Austin Hwy. (Mt. Calvary Dr.) | 210-824-8686 | www.siloelevatedcuisine.com

This "hip", "minimalist" Terrell Heights showplace provides an "elevated experience" in more ways than one; the dining mezzanine overlooks a "fabulous", "wild and fun" first-floor bar, and the New American fare "hits great heights" as well with "imaginative", "beautifully presented" dishes (e.g. the "trademark" chicken-fried oysters) complemented by "astonishing" wines and served "attentively"; though a few sigh the food's "static" and "pricey", most maintain this eatery is "as close to a sure thing as you can get"; N.B. a branch near Sonterra is set to open in spring 2007.

San Diego

TOP FOOD RANKING

	Restaurant	Cuisine
27	WineSellar & Brasserie	French
	Sushi Ota	Japanese
	Pamplemousse Grille	American/French
	Arterra	American
	A.R. Valentien	Californian
26	Tapenade	French
	Oceanaire	Seafood
	El Bizcocho	French
	Donovan's	Steak
	Rama	Thai

OTHER NOTEWORTHY PLACES

Restaurant	Cuisine
Blue Coral	Seafood
George's Cal. Modern	Californian
Grant Grill	Californian
Laurel	French/Mediterranean
Marine Room	French
Mille Fleurs	French
Ortega's	Mexican
Quarter Kitchen	Californian
Roppongi	Asian Fusion
Ruth's Chris	Steak

⧖ Arterra *American* | 27 | 23 | 24 | $53 |

Del Mar | San Diego Marriott Del Mar | 11966 El Camino Real
(Carmel Valley Rd.) | 858-369-6032 | www.arterrarestaurant.com
Fans "love Bradley Ogden in any city", and his "not-your-average"
Marriott destination near Del Mar confirms it; though gourmets need
look no further than the "sublime" New American dishes, most also
consider the "excellent" service by "waiters, not surfers", "buzzy" ambiance and "cool, modern" decor to all factor in the success of this
"outstanding" venue from one of the West's more prominent chefs.

⧖ A.R. Valentien *Californian* | 27 | 27 | 26 | $61 |

La Jolla | The Lodge at Torrey Pines | 11480 N. Torrey Pines Rd.
(Torrey Pines Golf Course) | 858-777-6635 | www.lodgetorreypines.com
A "genteel" getaway on the Torrey Pines golf course, this Californian
benefits from a "gorgeous" setting, namely the "classic" Craftsman-
designed space with "beautiful" views of the pines and the ocean, all
supplying an ideal stage for "superb" cuisine and "attentive" service;
even after the "expensive" tabs arrive, this place is still easy to "love."

Blue Coral *Seafood* | - | - | - | E |

Golden Triangle | The Aventine Ctr. | 8990 University Center Ln.
(La Jolla Village Dr.) | 858-453-2583 | www.bluecoralseafood.com
This vast expense-accounter in the Golden Triangle rests in a cool dining
room bracketed by a wall-spanning display kitchen and a bar flanked

by waterfalls that flow over big-screen TV monitors; chef William Gnam orchestrates a seafood menu that emphasizes luxurious shellfish presentations such as lobsters *en fuego,* while servers present a bar list that offers 60 different vodkas and assorted creative cocktails.

Donovan's Steak & Chop House ☒ *Steak* | 26 | 23 | 25 | $60 |

Golden Triangle | 4340 La Jolla Village Dr. (Genesee Ave.) | 877-611-6688 | www.donovanssteakhouse.com

"Get your money's worth" of meat and plentiful portions of "testoster-one" at this "old-school" chophouse in the Golden Triangle; "if you crave outstanding, top-quality beef, this is your place" confirm carni-vores who also aver the "extensive" (if "expensive") wine list and "de-tail"-oriented service make it "the best of the steakhouses" in town.

El Bizcocho *French* | 26 | 25 | 25 | $62 |

Rancho Bernardo | Rancho Bernardo Inn | 17550 Bernardo Oaks Dr. (Francisco Dr.) | 858-675-8550 | www.ranchobernardoinn.com

Still as "sturdy" as ever, this Rancho Bernardo mainstay of "special-occasion" dining unites chef Gavin Kaysen's "sumptuous" French fare with "impeccable" service, an "excellent" 1,600 label wine list and an "old-money" formality that has sustained its appeal over the years; the standards here are perhaps as "high" as the bill when it comes, so be sure to bring "someone else to pay"; N.B. the restau-rant no longer requires jackets.

☑ George's California Modern *Californian* | 25 | - | 24 | $53 |
(aka The Fine Dining Room at George's at the Cove)

La Jolla | 1250 Prospect St. (Ivanhoe Ave.) | 858-454-4244 | www.georgesatthecove.com

Owners have overhauled this Californian mainstay (San Diego's Most Popular restaurant), giving it a modern look to go along not only with its million-dollar views of the Pacific, but with the cute young things and wallet-heavy conventioneers who show up; the new relaxed mood is ac-companied by "dignified" service and by long-running chef Trey Foshee's "take-your-breath-away" food (crafted from the area's exquisite pro-duce and rich seafood resources) that's, as always, "not to be missed."

Grant Grill *Californian* | - | - | - | E |

Downtown | U.S. Grant Hotel | 326 Broadway (bet. 3rd & 4th Aves.) | 619-744-2077 | www.grantgrill.com

This celebrated San Diego dining room reopened in late 2006 after it and the 1909 U.S. Grant Hotel underwent extensive renovations; the new, sophisticated decor (once a dark wood–lined den perfect for deal making) underscores the creations of chef Andreas Nieto, who brews a Californian roster including Pacific bouillabaisse, and lavender and maple-glazed pork chops; local high society and well-off hotel guests don't worry much about up-there tabs.

Laurel *French/Mediterranean* | 24 | 24 | 23 | $55 |

Banker's Hill | 505 Laurel St. (5th Ave.) | 619-239-2222 | www.laurelrestaurant.com

Stylish sorts show up at this "trendy" Banker's Hill venue near Balboa Park serving "sophisticated", "interesting" French-Mediterranean fare along with an "incomparable" wine list; decorwise, the "hip" *Alice In Wonderland*-like setting is either "brilliant" or somewhat "overdone."

☑ Marine Room *French*

24 | 25 | 24 | $60

La Jolla | 2000 Spindrift Dr. (off Torrey Pines Rd.) | 858-459-7222 | www.marineroom.com

"The ocean seems to roll right into the dining room" at this "breathtaking" La Jolla Shores landmark that some say is the "best place to take guests from out of town"; chef Bernard Guillas' New French cuisine deftly employs "classic techniques" with "inventive" results, while the "attentive" service makes the clientele feel "pampered"; tip: it's so "romantic" you can "take your date and you're sure to get another one."

Mille Fleurs *French*

25 | 25 | 25 | $70

Rancho Santa Fe | Country Squire Courtyard | 6009 Paseo Delicias (Avenida De Acacias) | 858-756-3085 | www.millefleurs.com

"Top host" Bertrand Hug's ab-"fab" New French salon in posh Rancho Santa Fe offers an "elegant" stage for "superb" fare (thanks to chef Martin Woesle) and for the "professional" servers who attend to the "old-money" clientele; sure, the prices are "high" and flip-flop fans find fault in the setting ("stuffy"), but supporters say "if you want to treat yourself right", go here.

Oceanaire Seafood Room *Seafood*

26 | 25 | 24 | $55

Gaslamp Quarter | 400 J St. (4th Ave.) | 619-858-2277 | www.theoceanaire.com

"What a place for a date" avow advocates of this "winning" Minneapolis-based seafood chain link in San Diego's Gaslamp Quarter; "bring a life vest because the food will blow you away" say enthusiasts also baited by "exceptional" service and "great" decor done up like a "'30s ocean liner"; ok, it's "pricey", but overall, things are shipshape here.

Ortega's, A Mexican Bistro ● *Mexican*

24 | 20 | 21 | $28

Hillcrest | 141 University Ave. (bet. 1st & 3rd Aves.) | 619-692-4200 | www.ortegasbistro.com

"*Muy delicioso*" dishes mark the menu of this "gourmet" Hillcrest Mexican celebrated for serving the same "incredible" Baja Cal–style lobsters and flour tortillas popularized by the original namesake in Puerto Nuevo, Mexico; "exceptionally warm", "rustic" decor lends a welcome "neighborhood" vibe.

☑ Pamplemousse Grille *American/French*

27 | 22 | 25 | $61

Solana Beach | 514 Via de la Valle (Hialeah Circle) | 858-792-9090 | www.pgrille.com

The "gastronomical equivalent of a Panerai watch" is this Solana Beach "staple for gourmands" opposite the Del Mar Racetrack; there's "no horsing around" though, since chef-owner Jeffrey Strauss' French–New American preparations are "lovingly transformed into art" and partnered with "knowledgeable" service and an "endless" wine list amid an "entertaining", "provincial-France" setting; overall, it's "extra special."

Quarter Kitchen *Californian*

- | - | - | E

Downtown | Ivy Hotel | 600 F St. (bet 6th & 7th Aves.) | 619-814-1000 | www.quarterkitchen.com

Inside the luxe Ivy Hotel, perhaps the most noteworthy of its kind to open in Downtown San Diego in memory, this newcomer targets a well-heeled audience with Damon Gordon's dramatic Cal dishes (such as caviar 'tacos'), and with the whimsical, modern surroundings.

	FOOD	DECOR	SERVICE	COST

Rama *Thai* `26` `27` `23` `$33`

Gaslamp Quarter | 327 Fourth Ave. (bet. J & K Sts.) | 619-501-8424 |
www.ramarestaurant.com

Like its "trendy, sexy" clientele, this "transporting" Gaslamp Quarter
Thai is a "beauty" to behold and features a floor-to-ceiling water wall and
"willowy" fabrics – in all a "heavenly" setting for "fresh", "incredibly"
good dishes; what's more, you'll be treated like a "special guest" of the
staff, which helps you feel as if "you're on the other side of the Pacific."

☒ Roppongi *Asian Fusion* `24` `22` `21` `$45`

La Jolla | 875 Prospect St. (Fay Ave.) | 858-551-5252 | www.roppongiusa.com
Asian fusion fans frequent this Downtown La Jolla "favorite" offering
"fabulous" selections on an "interesting" slate; "order several dishes
and share" with "friends", hit the "sake sampler" or just take in the
"trendy" types who simultaneously provide "eye appeal" and blend
right in to the "terrific" feng shui–inspired space.

☒ Ruth's Chris Steak House *Steak* `25` `22` `24` `$59`

Del Mar | 11582 El Camino Real (Carmel Valley Rd.) | 858-755-1454
Downtown | 1355 N. Harbor Dr. (Ash St.) | 619-233-1422
www.ruthschris.com

"Nothing beats the sizzling sound" when steak arrives at these chain
chophouses, aka "the kings of coronary clogging" whose "attentive"
staff serves "butterific" beef and "yummy" sides; Downtown's got the
"picture-perfect" view of San Diego Bay while Del Mar boasts a
"sleek" interior; either way, both are "worth the spike in your cholesterol count" and dent in your wallet.

☒ Sushi Ota *Japanese* `27` `12` `19` `$40`

Pacific Beach | 4529 Mission Bay Dr. (Grand Ave.) | 858-270-5670
"You know it has to be good when you need a reservation" for a "storefront" aver amazed fans of this "legendary" Japanese – what its Pacific
Beach "strip-mall" locale lacks in charm is more than made up for by
"incomparable" sushi from "genius" chef-owner Yukito Ota; it's widely
known as "heaven" for raw-fish purists and "businessmen from
Japan", so expect "waits."

Tapenade *French* `26` `20` `23` `$58`

La Jolla | 7612 Fay Ave. (bet. Kline & Pearl Sts.) | 858-551-7500 |
www.tapenaderestaurant.com

"Bravo to Jean-Michel Diot" and company for the "excellent" New
French cooking and overall "high standards" at his "upscale" bistro
that's La Jolla's answer to "Paris or New York"; it's "always a treat –
and a splurge" coming here, though most maintain it's also a "deal"
considering the quality of the food – besides, you can always capitalize
on the pre-theater or lunch prix fixes.

☒ WineSellar & Brasserie ☒ Ⓜ *French* `27` `19` `26` `$59`

Golden Triangle | 9550 Waples St. (off Mira Mesa Blvd.) | 858-450-9557 |
www.winesellar.com

It's "tough to find, but find it" insist oenophiles and gourmets of this retail
store/French brasserie (No. 1 for Food in SD) in an industrial area of
Sorrento Mesa; true, neither the "exceptionally" good food (served on
the second floor) nor "smooth" service is a surprise, but it's the wine
that "shines" say those who "explore the shop" pre- or post-dinner.

San Francisco Bay Area

	Restaurant	Cuisine
<u>29</u>	Gary Danko	American
	French Laundry	American/French
<u>28</u>	Cyrus	French
	Erna's Elderberry	Californian/French
	Fleur de Lys	Californian/French
	Sushi Ran	Japanese
	Kaygetsu	Japanese
	Michael Mina	American
<u>27</u>	Chez Panisse	Californian/Mediterranean
	Le Papillon	French
	Ritz-Carlton Din. Rm.	French
	Manresa	American
	Chez Panisse Café	Californian/Mediterranean
	La Folie	French
	Acquerello	Italian
	Chapeau!	French
	Masa's	French
	Rivoli	Californian/Mediterranean
	Boulevard	American
	Farmhouse Inn	Californian

OTHER NOTEWORTHY PLACES

Restaurant	Cuisine
ad hoc	American
Ame	American
Aqua	Californian/Seafood
Bistro Jeanty	French
Canteen	Californian
Coi	Californian/French
Delfina	Italian
Greens	Vegetarian
Jardinière	Californian/French
Lark Creek Inn	American
La Toque	French
Myth	American
NoPa	Californian
Oliveto	Italian
Perbacco	Italian
Quince	French/Italian
Range	American
Redd	Californian
Slanted Door	Vietnamese
Zuni Café	Mediterranean

	FOOD	DECOR	SERVICE	COST

Acquerello 🔳🔳 *Italian* 　　27 | 24 | 27 | $74

Polk Gulch | 1722 Sacramento St. (bet. Polk St. & Van Ness Ave.) | San Francisco | 415-567-5432 | www.acquerello.com

One of SF's "rare quiet", "formal" Italian restaurants with "old-world sophistication", this "intimate" Polk Gulch "foodie delight" ("no noisy young 'uns here") set in a converted church is "the absolutely perfect setting" for a "fantastic celebratory experience"; "raid your piggy bank", order the chef's "sublime" wine-inclusive tasting menu ("each table gets their own decanter") and "ride it all the way", letting the "remarkable staff cater to your every need"; N.B. a recent remodel may not be reflected in the Decor score.

ad hoc *American* 　　26 | 19 | 24 | $58

Yountville | 6476 Washington St. (bet. California Dr. & Oak Circle) | 707-944-2487

Thomas Keller's now-permanent "version of a family-style home cookin' eatery" is "the yang to the French Laundry's yin", presenting "superb" four-course prix fixe Traditional "Americana" dinners in a Yountville diner "without the muss or fuss" of a "two month waiting list" and at prices that "won't take you to the cleaners"; "you're s.o.l." if you don't fancy the nightly selection, but "rest assured", the "generously portioned" chow is "always magnificent", as are the "spot-on wine pairings" made by the "friendly, friendly" staff clothed in gear reminiscent of "old-fashioned service-station" uniforms.

Ame *American* 　　26 | 25 | 25 | $69

SoMa | St. Regis Hotel | 689 Mission St. (3rd St.) | San Francisco | 415-284-4040 | www.amerestaurant.com

"Hiro is my hero!" exclaim "real foodies" who "feel fortunate to sample" "genius" chef Sone's wildly "unexpected", "sublime" "exotic" New American creations "with subtle Asian and Euro accents" at Terra's "serene", "sophisticated" "big-city" SoMa outpost, a "real looker" set in the "luxe" St. Regis Hotel; the "tasting menu truly showcases his talents and the wine pairings are not to be missed", plus the "sake sommelier is invaluable"; P.S. for a "refreshing" change try the "adventurous" crudo at the custom-made marble sushi bar.

Aqua *Californian/Seafood* 　　26 | 25 | 25 | $72

Downtown | 252 California St. (bet. Battery & Front Sts.) | San Francisco | 415-956-9662 | www.aqua-sf.com

"Posh", "packed" to the gills and "still swimming strong" under chef Laurent Manrique's stewardship, this Downtown "power-lunch institution" remains a "shrine to seafood", wowing fans with "fantastic" Cal-French "flavor combinations"; "wine and dine your client or stuffy in-laws" with "inventive, unexpected" fare and "incredible wines" "artfully presented" by a "superlative" staff in a "chic" setting accented with "gorgeous flower arrangements fit for the glamorous" VIP crowd; "if you have to look at the prices . . . well you know the rest."

Bistro Jeanty *French* 　　25 | 21 | 22 | $50

Yountville | 6510 Washington St. (Mulberry St.) | 707-944-0103 | www.bistrojeanty.com

"Another winner" "in the middle of fine-dining central", Philippe Jeanty's convivial Yountville bistro "induces easy spirits" where regulars indulge in "soul food" "like *grand-mère* use to make" in a "*très* authentic", "get-to-know-your-neighbors" setting (plus a pooch-friendly patio); best of all, this bargain boîte is open all day (should "you lose yourself in the wineries") and "walk-ins" can "wait for seating at the bar", where vintners and other locals often "linger" over "their own wines."

☑ Boulevard *American*
27 | 25 | 25 | $64

Embarcadero | Audiffred Bldg. | 1 Mission St. (Steuart St.) | San Francisco | 415-543-6084 | www.boulevardrestaurant.com

This "sizzling" belle epoque brasserie on the Embarcadero with "breathtaking views of the Bay" may be a "wallet flattener", but remains the "consummate" "go-as-you-are" San Francisco hot spot delivering "unforgettable food" "without the 'tude"; "suits", "tourists and locals" "sit elbow to elbow" soaking up the "party" vibe and Nancy Oakes' French-influenced New American fare that's "inventive without being fussy", while the "sensational" staff "goes above and beyond the call of duty" and "never fails to provide the perfect" wine match.

Canteen *Californian*
25 | 14 | 20 | $44

Downtown | Commodore Hotel | 817 Sutter St. (Jones St.) | San Francisco | 415-928-8870 | www.sfcanteen.com

Dennis Leary's "micro restaurant" Downtown offers a "one-of-a-kind" experience: patrons "wait in the dreary lobby" of the Commodore Hotel for set seating times only to be "rushed" by a "perfunctory" staff in and out of the "cramped", "drab" "old" "luncheonette"; luckily, the "cuisine does not match the decor", as the "master" prepares "absolutely remarkable" Californian fare that "never fails" to "astound"; P.S. the "short but well-structured menu" "changes daily", but "the vanilla soufflé is always served, and you'd be insane not to have it."

Chapeau! ☑ *French*
27 | 18 | 26 | $47

Outer Richmond | 1408 Clement St. (15th Ave.) | San Francisco | 415-750-9787

"Budget-minded foodies" "make the trek" to this "quaint" – alright, "cramped" – bistro so "religiously", they "should move" to the Outer Richmond, because the "extraordinary" French cuisine is "better than restaurants [that charge] twice the price" (the "early-bird prix fixe is a steal"); the pièce de résistance is Philippe Gardelle, the "charming" chef-owner who "personally greets everyone" as well as "seats, cuts meats and pecks cheeks", transforming every meal into "a special experience"; N.B. an ongoing renovation may impact the Decor score.

Chez Panisse ☑ *Californian/Mediterranean*
27 | 23 | 26 | $80

Berkeley | 1517 Shattuck Ave. (bet. Cedar & Vine Sts.) | 510-548-5525 | www.chezpanisse.com

"Don't know whether to dine or bow" quip "those lucky enough" to savor the "sublime simplicity" of Berkeley "pioneer" Alice Waters' Cal-Med "culinary delights" that "celebrate what's at the peak of the season"; expect "no frills" at this "modest" Craftsman-style "mother ship", "just thrills, naturally" – "every foodie must go to complete their Bingo card" and "partake" of the "divine" daily prix fixe menu that spotlights the "clear, crisp" "essence" of local ingredients; the "combinations make you sigh with delight", the staff is "enthusiastic" and the wine list is a "knockout" – it's "all it's cracked up to be."

	FOOD	DECOR	SERVICE	COST

Chez Panisse Café ⑤ *Californian/Mediterranean*   27 | 22 | 25 | $50

Berkeley | 1517 Shattuck Ave. (bet. Cedar & Vine Sts.) | 510-548-5049 | www.chezpanisse.com

A "near mystical experience" – yes, "upstairs is the place for me" exclaim budget-conscious Berkeleyites who sample the "pure flavors" of "Alice Waters' culinary frontier" "without spending half the month's rent" at this "wonderfully relaxed" "Paradise Lite" cafe above the "legendary" original staffed with "attentive", not "smothering" servers; she may be "the Queen" but the organic, sustainable ingredients are "king", resulting in "dreamy pizzas" and "truly delectable", "straightforward" à la carte Cal-Med dishes that "reflect both the seasons and the incredible abundance" of local purveyors.

Coi ⑤Ⓜ *Californian/French*   25 | 25 | 25 | $94

North Beach | 373 Broadway (Montgomery St.) | San Francisco | 415-393-9000 | www.coirestaurant.com

"This bloke is seriously talented" marvel "adventurous" eaters agog over "rogue chef" Daniel Patterson's "esoteric", "cutting-edge" "El Bulli–style" Californian-French four-course prix fixe and "11 bites" tasting menus; although the scent-illating meals "theatrically" presented with a "dab of perfume alongside" in this minuscule, "minimalist" "tranquil sanctuary amid the strip clubs on Broadway" are "not for everyone", the less formal, late-night lounge offering an additional à la carte menu sans the "big league" prices is a "real boon."

ⓩ Cyrus *French*   28 | 27 | 28 | $110

Healdsburg | Les Mars Hotel | 29 North St. (Healdsburg Ave.) | 707-433-3311 | www.cyrusrestaurant.com

"Who needs Napa?" quip fans "blown away" by this "pull-out-the-stops" lair of "luxury", a "gorgeous" "budget-breaker" in Healdsburg's Les Mars Hotel; "no detail is overlooked", from the "caviar cart where the pricey eggs are weighed on a scale with a real gold bullion" to the "decadent" New French "mix-and-match" prix fixe menus "beautifully presented" by staffers that move like a "well-choreographed ballet"; there are no "absurd reservation hoops" to jump through, plus "everyone is treated" "like the leader of a small country."

Delfina *Italian*   26 | 19 | 23 | $45

Mission | 3621 18th St. (bet. Dolores & Guerrero Sts.) | San Francisco | 415-552-4055 | www.delfinasf.com

"You won't find tomato sauce" at this "go-to" "Mission treasure" with a "cool, comfy neighborhood vibe", but you will find "exquisitely prepared", "tasty modern" Northern Italian dishes "bursting with flavor" accompanied by an "approachable wine list", all delivered by a "scantily dressed" staff; the "divine", "deceptively simple menu" is so in demand that "it's brutal getting a reservation", so "try waiting for a seat at the bar" – it's even worth enduring the "ridiculous noise factor."

ⓩ Erna's Elderberry House *Californian/French*   28 | 26 | 28 | $84

Oakhurst | Château du Sureau | 48688 Victoria Ln. (Hwy. 41) | 559-683-6800 | www.elderberryhouse.com

Yosemite-bound adventurers "strike gourmet gold just south of the Gold Country" at this "quaint Europe-in-America setting" on the grounds of the Château du Sureau hotel in Oakhurst, basically the "middle of nowhere"; "what an amazing" "symphony" of flavors – every "breath-takingly beautiful" Californian-French dish on the prix fixe menus is "different and unexpected" – and coupled with "fine" wine pairings and "attentive service" that's rated No. 1 in the SF Survey, it's a "delightful dining experience" that will "put you in a high state."

Farmhouse Inn & Restaurant *Californian* 27 | 25 | 25 | $64
Forestville | Farmhouse Inn | 7871 River Rd. (bet. Trenton & Wohler Rds.) | 707-887-3300 | www.farmhouseinn.com

"Put on your best duds", grab "your most significant other" and "hop over" to this "charming" "old" clapboard farmhouse in "lovely" Forestville hidden "away from the Napa crowds" for the "fabulous" signature rabbit dish; add in a "cheese course that would tempt a Frenchman" and other "wonderfully prepared" Californian fare made with bounty from the family ranch and an "extensive wine list", all "served with a deft hand", and it's plain to see why this "sparkling gem" is on a par with the "biggies."

Z Fleur de Lys Ⓢ *Californian/French* 28 | 27 | 26 | $94
Nob Hill | 777 Sutter St. (bet. Jones & Taylor Sts.) | San Francisco | 415-673-7779 | www.fleurdelyssf.com

"Can you improve on fabulous?" ask the starstruck who spend a "magical evening of luxury" at Nob Hill's "ultraromantic" Cal-New French "oasis of calm and civility" where "even the menu is pretty", the decor is *très* "Moulin Rouge" and the "bright servers suggest, deliver and describe" the "culinary delights"; longtime chef Hubert Keller keeps everything "fresh and exciting", crafting "decadent" prix fixe options (including an "exquisite" vegetarian choice) with "whimsical touches"; *oui*, prices are "princely", but the "outstanding" wine list alone "seduces you back."

Z French Laundry, The *American/French* 29 | 26 | 28 | $291
Yountville | 6640 Washington St. (Creek St.) | 707-944-2380 | www.frenchlaundry.com

"Thomas Keller's magnum opus" in Yountville may be "famous for being famous but consider yourself royalty if you land a table" at this "haute" French-New American "gastronomic experience" that's "expensive" enough "for three lifetimes" and "fantastic" enough to "halt all conversation"; "foodies with four hours on their hands" know the drill: "stroll through the gardens", then let the "gracious", "mind-reading" staff handle the "spot-on wine pairings" and "prepare for orbit" as each "wildly imaginative" course in the tasting menus arrives; P.S. it's "better than ever" with new chef de cuisine Corey Lee onboard.

Z Gary Danko *American* 29 | 26 | 28 | $104
Fisherman's Wharf | 800 N. Point St. (Hyde St.) | San Francisco | 415-749-2060 | www.garydanko.com

"Gary Swanko" "fully merits its superb reputation" gush "flush" "foodies" who vote the "celebrity" chef-owner's "sleek" New American "temple of gastronomy" in Fisherman's Wharf No. 1 in the SF Survey for Food and Popularity; it's an "epicurean extravaganza" from the glass of champagne when you sit down to the "impeccable" "build-your-own" "haute" tasting menus and "perfect wine pairings" you'll "talk about for weeks, months and years" to the "simply amazing

| | FOOD | DECOR | SERVICE | COST |

cheese course"; add in a "surprisingly unstuffy", "synchronized" staff that "treats customers like VIPs" and it's little wonder devotees declare it's the "epitome of fine dining, San Francisco–style."

Greens *Vegetarian* | 24 | 23 | 22 | $40 |

Marina | Bldg. A, Fort Mason Ctr. (Buchanan St.) | San Francisco | 415-771-6222 | www.greensrestaurant.com

"Nonvegetarians find plenty to love" at Annie Somerville's "grande old dame" of "haute Zen cuisine", a veritable "Garden of Eden" that presents "amazingly fresh", "artfully prepared" fare made from "ingredients grown on its own farm" and complemented by "fabulous" biodynamic wines; the "overwhelming" views of the Marina, Bay and Golden Gate make the "simple" "warehouse" setting "sublime."

Jardinière *Californian/French* | 26 | 26 | 25 | $69 |

Hayes Valley | 300 Grove St. (Franklin St.) | San Francisco | 415-861-5555 | www.jardiniere.com

Even "when the opera is having a bad night, you know" that Traci Des Jardins' "posh", "pricey", pre- and post-performance "enchanter" in Hayes Valley "will still be hitting all the right notes", belting out "exceptional" Cal-French fare in a "sexy" setting; *oui*, the "pitch-perfect service" gets the "well-heeled" habitués to their "limos" on time, but what a "waste" to be in haste when the "gorgeous bar" below is such a "sparkling" spot "to engage in a cocktail or get engaged."

Kaygetsu Ⓜ *Japanese* | 28 | 18 | 25 | $80 |

Menlo Park | Sharon Heights Shopping Ctr. | 325 Sharon Park Dr. (Sand Hill Rd.) | 650-234-1084 | www.kaygetsu.com

"You'll be hard-pressed to find Japanese food made with more care" without "getting on a jet to Tokyo" attest admirers who say get thee to this "spartan" yet "transcendent" "power dining spot for VCs" in a Menlo Park strip mall; the fish is "über-fresh" and the seasonal kaiseki dinners are "extraordinary", from the "beautiful presentation" that's like "art on a plate" to the "melt-in-your-mouth creations" that taste like "heaven"; the "drawback: you must offer your paycheck to the sushi gods" ("genius chef"/owner Toshi) but it's "worth every penny."

La Folie Ⓩ *French* | 27 | 23 | 26 | $87 |

Russian Hill | 2316 Polk St. (bet. Green & Union Sts.) | San Francisco | 415-776-5577 | www.lafolie.com

Oui, "'twould be a folly to miss" this "haute French" "culinary experience" on Russian Hill where "masterful chef" "Monsieur Passot cooks his heart out" crafting "perfection on a plate" à la carte dishes and "artfully displayed" prix fixe menus "well worth the special-occasion prices"; it's "*magnifique* in every way", from the "amazing wine" list and "grand", "intimate environment" to the "dazzling" staff that exudes a "touch of Gallic humor"; P.S. if the "elbow-to-elbow seating" in the main room "crimps your privacy", the back room provides "an elegant alternative."

Lark Creek Inn *American* | 23 | 25 | 22 | $55 |

Larkspur | 234 Magnolia Ave. (Madrone Ave.) | 415-924-7766 | www.larkcreek.com

Bradley Ogden's "enchanted hideaway" located in a "beautiful Victorian next to a creek" in an "idyllic" Larkspur locale is "still Marin's most romantic", "grand old friend"; even with a "revolving door" of chefs, it's a "consistently memorable" "special-occasion splurge" thanks to the "hearty, high-end" Traditional American comfort food, "elegantly spacious dining room" replete with a "lovely view" of the redwoods and "outdoor dining in the back garden in the summer."

La Toque Ⓜ *French*   26 23 26 $105

Rutherford | 1140 Rutherford Rd. (east of Hwy. 29) | 707-963-9770 | www.latoque.com

"Toques off" to "incredible" chef Ken Frank – he "continues to wow" purr patrons "impressed by" the "attention to detail" from the "superior" service to the "rustic setting" in Rutherford; "sit by the fire and swoon" over the "always-evolving", "over-the-top" French prix fixe menu – you feel so "pampered" – and "for an extra treat", get the "superb" wine pairings as "excellent" sommelier Scott Tracy's "insights" may be the "best part of the night"; "yes, you need a special occasion to justify the expense, but that's what celebrating is for, right?"

Le Papillon *French*   27 24 27 $67

San Jose | 410 Saratoga Ave. (Kiely Blvd.) | 408-296-3730 | www.lepapillon.com

Escape the "hustle and bustle of Silicon Valley" at this "hidden gem" in San Jose that feels like a "little bit of France"; the "classy" environment means you can "speak quietly to your tablemates" – it's enough to make you "stand and cheer" – the staff that's "second to none" extends the "elegant treatment" and the "over-the-top", "outstanding" wine and food pairings on the New French tasting menu offer "interesting twists" that "leave you floating like the proverbial butterfly."

Manresa Ⓜ *American*   27 24 25 $108

Los Gatos | 320 Village Ln. (bet. N. Santa Cruz & University Aves.) | 408-354-4330 | www.manresarestaurant.com

"Worth the detour" to Los Gatos, David Kinch's "celestial" New American "foodie paradise" serves meals so wildly "inventive" that some wonder if the chef's "creative genius" is tinged with "a touch of insanity"; for best results, "bring an open mind" and splurge on the "three-hour-long" tasting menu, which "surprises with every course"; sure, a few find the service and "casually elegant" setting less wow-worthy than the food, but overall most predict this "will easily be your dinner of the year."

Masa's 🖼Ⓜ *French*   27 24 26 $93

Downtown | Hotel Vintage Ct. | 648 Bush St. (bet. Powell & Stockton Sts.) | San Francisco | 415-989-7154 | www.masasrestaurant.com

Bring "your quiet voice" and "a few credit cards" to Downtown's "high-end bastion" of "old-boy network" fine dining that's "settled into a rhythm" since chef "Gregory Short was poached from French Laundry" to oversee the "haute" New French tasting menus; the "taupe everything" digs are "understated", but the "*gastronomique*" "theatrics" are definitely not "for a simple steak-and-potatoes eater", while the "wine list is thicker than the Bible."

Ⓩ Michael Mina *American*   28 24 27 $108

Downtown | Westin St. Francis | 335 Powell St. (bet. Geary & Post Sts.) | San Francisco | 415-397-9222 | www.michaelmina.net

"Mmmmichael Mmmmmina's" Downtown "hi-style, hi-concept, hi-priced" temple to "food wizardry" (where "everything comes in three different preparations") is a "triple treat" attest "foodies" who enjoy the "sublime experience of being coveted, cosseted and pampered"; the "delectable" New American tasting menus and "mind-boggling" wine list are served in a "stunning" setting, plus you can order "classics" à la carte at the bar – what a "marvelous" way to "spend all your money"; if some shout "you need a semaphore to talk" over the Westin lobby din, others retort "there's a lovely energy, but it's never raucous."

Myth ⊠ Ⓜ American   26 | 25 | 24 | $57

Downtown | 470 Pacific Ave. (bet. Montgomery & Sansome Sts.) | San Francisco | 415-677-8986 | www.mythsf.com

"Believe the hype": this "sexy", "sophisticated" "'in' place" Downtown packed with "pretty people" provides an "unforgettable experience" that "never fails to dazzle" – and that's "no myth"; "Gary Danko grad" Sean O'Brien "hits it out of the park", conjuring up "divine" New American "creations" that "shine" ("love the half-portion alternative") accompanied by a "stellar" wine list, all served by an "attentive" staff; P.S. Cafe Myth next door purveys "elegant bag lunches at bargain prices."

NoPa ⬤ Californian   23 | 21 | 21 | $41

Western Addition | 560 Divisadero St. (bet. Fell & Hayes Sts.) | San Francisco | 415-864-8643 | www.nopasf.com

So "hot" it single-handedly "redefined an entire neighborhood" declare denizens who descend on the Western Addition's "crazy loud" "food lovers' mecca" "of the moment", a "huge but still cozy" "former Laundromat" boasting "funky wall murals", an open kitchen and a communal table that "totally works"; ex- Chow and Chez Nous chef Laurence Jessel "does his magic" "conjuring up" "heavenly" "rustic" Cal "comfort food" "brilliantly matched" with a "well-chosen" wine list, and it's all served by a staff that thankfully lacks "SUV-size egos"; P.S. the "lively" bar serves "sublime" drinks.

Oliveto Restaurant Italian   25 | 22 | 23 | $56

Oakland | 5655 College Ave. (Keith St.) | 510-547-5356 | www.oliveto.com

Oakland's "serene" "mecca for Italian food" on "fashionable College Avenue" "continues to shine" assert "epicureans", Europhiles and the area's "upper crust" who "splurge" on "memorable", "superbly cooked" "exquisitely luxurious" meals boasting "artisanal" "favorites" like "wonderful housemade charcuterie" and rotisserie meats delivered by an "unobtrusive" staff; "nothing beats" "incredible" theme nights like February's Whole Hog dinner that spotlight chef Paul Canales' "signature rustic yet refined style", plus the "dishes you dream about" even "trickle out of the everyday menus" making us "squeal with delight!"

Perbacco ⊠ Italian   24 | 21 | 21 | $50

Downtown | 230 California St. (bet. Battery & Front Sts.) | San Francisco | 415-955-0663 | www.perbaccosf.com

Downtown's year-old "power-lunch spot" and "showy date place" lures in "young trendies, old lawyers" and "celebs" with chef Staffan Terje's (ex Scala's Bistro) "incredibly good" Piedmonte and Ligurian specialties including "scrumptious pasta" and "salumi made on-site"; the "split-level", "modern" Milan-meets-"old Gold Coast" decor is a refreshing (if "noisy") "alternative" to "seafood row", so though the staff seems overwhelmed "with the popularity", concensus is that it's "one of the best newcomers of the year."

Quince *French/Italian* | 26 | 23 | 25 | $68 |
Pacific Heights | 1701 Octavia St. (bet. Bush & Pine Sts.) | San Francisco | 415-775-8500 | www.quincerestaurant.com

A "definite 'must' on the foodie circuit" when you want a "dining extravaganza" but don't "want to eat in a theater" this "quinti-sensual", "fancy with a curlicue 'f'" Pac Heights "delight" is "like being in a fine home with a private waiter and chef"; the "dazzling", "one-of-a-kind" New French–Italian creations are fashioned from "pure", "pedigreed ingredients" ("handmade" "luscious pastas" "should be mandatory") while the "excellent" staff is "beyond reproach"; if a few wince it's "a bit prissy", for most it's "lovely in all respects."

Range *American* | 26 | 20 | 23 | $46 |
Mission | 842 Valencia St. (20th St.) | San Francisco | 415-282-8283 | www.rangesf.com

"I want to be home on this Range nightly" agree urban cowboys who cool their heels at this "awesome-all-around" stomping ground that's bringing "sexy" – and "tasty" – "back to the Mission"; yeah, "parking is impossible" and the "cool" bar "gets very crowded, but nothing can take away from the inventive and often brilliant" New American fare that's "priced right"; add in "super-friendly" staffers and a "hip environment" and it's plain to see it "deserves the buzz."

Redd Restaurant *Californian* | 26 | 22 | 23 | $70 |
Yountville | 6480 Washington St. (California Dr.) | 707-944-2222 | www.reddnapavalley.com

"We're always 'reddy' for our next visit" to chef Richard Reddington's "astonishingly good", "much-heralded" Californian "gem" in "glorious", "foodie-filled Yountville"; "prices soar" but so do the "dazzling" à la carte and tasting menus "starring" "fabulous" ingredients "gathered from local farms" and served by an "attentive" staff in "modern, minimalist" digs with a "pretty patio" ("think Finland meets Amish Country") that dispense with that "tired rustic-wine-country cliché"; N.B. the bar has its own "unique menu."

Ritz-Carlton Dining Room 🅂🅼 *French* | 27 | 26 | 28 | $96 |
Nob Hill | Ritz-Carlton Hotel | 600 Stockton St. (bet. California & Pine Sts.) | San Francisco | 415-773-6198 | www.ritzcarltondiningroom.com

"For that special occasion when a little formality (some would call stuffiness) is called for" ("tux optional"), Ritz it up at this "pampering" Nob Hill dining room; you can almost "hear an orchestra warming up" before embarking on chef Ron Siegel's prix fixe or tasting menu and wine pairings showcasing "unimaginable", "untraditional" New French creations "with Japanese touches"; it's akin to an operatic "performance", "from the first amuse"-bouche down to the "candy cart", with "lots of 'eye-closing' moments" in between.

Rivoli *Californian/Mediterranean* | 27 | 23 | 25 | $47 |
Berkeley | 1539 Solano Ave. (bet. Neilson St. & Peralta Ave.) | 510-526-2542 | www.rivolirestaurant.com

We "can't stop ooohing and ahing" about Wendy and Roscoe's "lovely, tranquil" Berkeley "treasure" exclaim hometown "foodies" and "even the fussiest oenophiles"; the "imaginative" and "soul-satisfying" California-Mediterranean cuisine is "comparable to anyplace in the City", plus it's all ferried to table by a staff that "seems to have PhDs in the art of making a meal enjoyable"; yes, you can expect "snug quarters", nevertheless it's still a "real treat" to look out at the "illuminated garden" filled with "a wildlife menagerie snacking" on their own food.

☒ Slanted Door, The *Vietnamese*   26 | 22 | 21 | $46

Embarcadero | 1 Ferry Bldg. (Market St.) | San Francisco | 415-861-8032 | www.slanteddoor.com

"Local celebs", "adventurous" tourists and Missionites who visited the old site "back in the day" all "fight for a table" at Charles Phan's "straight-up" "phantastic" Vietnamese "empire", a "jam-packed" waterfront-wonder deemed the "crown jewel" of the Embarcadero's Ferry Building; the "industrial" digs are as "noisy as a Hanoi street corner" and not everyone's cup of "blossoming tea" but the "high-end" Saigon specialties served "speedily" and enhanced by "insightful" wine pairings "shine brighter than the Bay Bridge" outside the "expansive windows"; N.B. for takeout pop into Out the Door next door.

Sushi Ran *Japanese*   28 | 20 | 22 | $50

Sausalito | 107 Caledonia St. (bet. Pine & Turney Sts.) | 415-332-3620 | www.sushiran.com

"If there's a better" place to shed your "disposable income" than Sausalito's fin-fare "mecca" that "takes Japanese food to a totally different solar system", "I haven't found it" report gaga "gaijins" and "true aficionados"; whether you "splurge" on rolls that "rival sushi temples in Tokyo" or "innovative", "top-notch cooked entrees", "every meal here" ends with "a sigh of profound pleasure"; P.S. it's "hard to hook a reservation", but remember the adjacent "sake bar has blossomed with its own identity"

Zuni Café ● Ⓜ *Mediterranean*   25 | 20 | 21 | $47

Hayes Valley | 1658 Market St. (bet. Franklin & Gough Sts.) | San Francisco | 415-552-2522 | www.zunicafe.com

"Before the fame, before the cookbooks" and before "Hayes Valley was invaded by hipsters", Judy Rodgers "worked her magic" – and continues to – "drawing crowds" of opera buffs and the "hoi polloi", "rain or shine", "day or night" to her "delicious, de-lovely" "iconic" "triangular" corner cafe/oyster bar; the "champagne flows and so does the evening", with devotees feasting on "heavenly", "deceptively simple" Mediterranean "comfort food" and "late-night burgers"; "even the 'attitudinal' service" and "one-hour wait" for "custom-roasted chicken" are "part of the charm."

Seattle

TOP FOOD RANKING

Restaurant	Cuisine
28 Herbfarm, The	Pacific NW
Nishino	Japanese
Lampreia	Pacific NW
Rover's	French
Mistral	American/French
Cafe Juanita	Italian/Sandwiches
Lark	American
Armandino's Salumi	Italian/Sandwiches
27 Le Gourmand	French
Shiro's Sushi	Japanese
Harvest Vine	Spanish
Canlis	Pacific NW/Seafood
26 Campagne	French
Metropolitan Grill	Steak
Il Terrazzo Carmine	Italian
JaK's Grill	Steak
Seastar	Seafood
La Carta de Oaxaca	Mexican
Dahlia Lounge	Pacific NW
Georgian, The	French/Pacific NW

OTHER NOTEWORTHY PLACES

Bakery Nouveau	Bakery/French
Boat Street Cafe	French/Italian
Carmelita	Mediterranean/Vegetarian
Cascadia	American
Chiso	Japanese
Crush	American
Earth & Ocean	American
El Gaucho	Steak
Green Leaf	Vietnamese
Inn at Langley	Pacific NW
Macrina	Bakery/Dessert
Monsoon	Vietnamese
Nell's	Pacific NW
Paseo	Caribbean
Sitka & Spruce	Eclectic
Tavolàta	Italian
Toyoda	Japanese
Union	American
Volterra	Italian
Wild Ginger	Pacific Rim

	FOOD	DECOR	SERVICE	COST

Armandino's Salumi 🅂 Ⓜ *Italian/Sandwiches* — 28 | 10 | 17 | $16

Pioneer Square | 309 Third Ave. S. (bet. Jackson & Main Sts.) | 206-621-8772 | www.salumicuredmeats.com

"Shoehorn your way in" to this "warm", "authentic" 24-seat salumeria in Pioneer Square, Armandino Batali's (Mario's father) veritable "wonderland" for pleasure-seekers on the hunt for "incomparable" examples of "Italian charcuterie" and the "best sandwiches in Seattle"; expect "slabs of cured meat" for decor and "long lines" – both part of the one-of-a-kind experience you'll have here.

Bakery Nouveau *Bakery/French* — – | – | – | I

West Seattle | 4737 California Ave. SW (Alaska St.) | 206-923-0534 | www.bakerynouveau.com

Flaky French pastries, handmade chocolates and gourmet sandwiches (like its hot muffaletta and pressed artisanal cheese) at easy-on-the-wallet prices attract West Seattle foodies to this charming bakery/cafe with a chic striped awning; owner William Leaman led the U.S. team to the gold in the 2005 World Cup of Baking, and it shows.

Boat Street Cafe Ⓜ *French/Italian* — ▽ 26 | 22 | 24 | $36

Queen Anne | 3131 Western Ave. (Denny Way) | 206-632-4602 | www.boatstreetkitchen.com

Pâtés and poussins rule the roost at this French-Italian bistro at the bottom of Queen Anne Hill; the "delicious", "beautifully" conceived fare comes courtesy of chef-owner Renee Erickson and provides a fitting match for the reasonably priced wines and "sweetly understated" decor that's ripe for "intimacy."

☑ Cafe Juanita *Italian/Sandwiches* — 28 | 23 | 27 | $56

Kirkland | 9702 NE 120th Pl. (97th St.) | 425-823-1505 | www.cafejuanita.com

Habitués say chef-owner Holly Smith's Kirkland Northern Italian hideaway operating in an "intimate" yet "chic" midcentury house serves up "what manna must taste like" considering the "brilliant combinations" of ingredients shown on "meticulously prepared" dishes that use locally grown produce and meats; the "impeccable" service is part of a package that "regardless of the price" has everyone waiting to "go back."

Campagne *French* — 26 | 23 | 24 | $55

Pike Place Market | Pike Place Mkt. | 86 Pine St. (1st Ave.) | 206-728-2800 | www.campagnerestaurant.com

The "crème de la crème of market fresh haute cuisine" laud loyal francophiles about this "serene" enclave in the bustling Pike Place Market; chef Daisley Gordon conjures up "magical" country French food while "gracious, unobtrusive" servers glide between the "refined" dining room overlooking the market and the "romantic" summer patio; P.S. potential penny-pinchers look out for the "amazing" prix fixe deals along with the less expensive downstairs cafe.

☑ Canlis 🅂 *Pacific NW/Seafood* — 27 | 27 | 28 | $69

Lake Union | 2576 Aurora Ave. N. (Halladay St., south of Aurora Bridge) | 206-283-3313 | www.canlis.com

"When only the best will do", movers and shakers head for this "old-money" family-owned 56-year-old "classic" with "spectacular views" of Lake Union, "phenomenal", "haute-modern" Pacific NW cuisine, a serene, "modern" space and a "deep" wine list (abetted by a crew of sommeliers) that keeps winning "every award in the book"; the staff is "discrete" yet "attuned to your every need" – and helps neutralize any thoughts about prices here.

Carmelita Ⓜ Mediterranean/Vegetarian

25 | 20 | 21 | $35

Greenwood | 7314 Greenwood Ave. N. (bet. 73rd & 74th Sts.) | 206-706-7703 | www.carmelita.net

"Vegetables have never tasted as good" as they do at this Greenwood Med-vegetarian offering a boldly accented, stylish setting to showcase "complex" dishes that reveal an "attention to flavor and color"; for "some of the tastiest eats" around, even those who "love meat would return in a heartbeat."

Cascadia Ⓩ American

25 | 26 | 25 | $55

Belltown | 2328 First Ave. (bet. Battery & Bell Sts.) | 206-448-8884 | www.cascadiarestaurant.com

Kerry Sear's "uptempo" Belltown New American garners accolades for its "exquisite attention to detail" that's evident on all fronts, from the "out-of-this-world" dishes, "well-chosen" Pacific NW–focused wine list, "attractive" decor featuring a water wall and "top-notch" staff; the $40 prix fixe and vegetarian tasting menus are "dreams come true."

Chiso Restaurant Japanese

▽ 27 | 21 | 23 | $33

Fremont | 3520 Fremont Ave. N. (36th St.) | 206-632-3430 | www.chisoseattle.com

"The enjoyment here is only limited by my budget" confess admirers of this Fremont Japanese where the "quality, freshness and presentation of sushi is high" while the "excellent" cooked fare puts a twist in classic dishes; the "addition of a liquor license" has helped pump up the "noise" and made it all the more "fun."

Crush ⓏⓂ American

25 | 22 | 21 | $56

Capitol Hill | 2319 E. Madison St. (23rd Ave.) | 206-302-7874 | www.crushonmadison.com

"Serious food lovers" descend on this "super-hot" Capitol Hill New American boasting a "terrific" mix of a "quaint" yet "modern" converted-house setting and "carefully crafted" comestibles that "delight the palate" (thanks to chef Jason Wilson, an alum of Jeremiah Tower's Stars in Seattle) and "take advantage of fresh, local ingredients."

Ⓩ Dahlia Lounge Pacific NW

26 | 23 | 24 | $47

Downtown | 2001 Fourth Ave. (Virginia St.) | 206-682-4142 | www.tomdouglas.com

"A jewel in Tom Douglas' crown" and the flagship of the chef's mini-empire is this Downtown Pacific Northwest "favorite" of locals and tourists that "shoots and scores" with "zippy", "artful food in an arty" crimson-toned space complete with Chinese lanterns, and "attentive, not cloying" service; as everyone can see, there's "a lively buzz in the air" along with an abundance of "deliciousness" at the attached bakery.

Earth & Ocean American

22 | 22 | 21 | $48

Downtown | W Hotel | 1112 Fourth Ave. (Seneca St.) | 206-264-6060 | www.earthocean.net

This "pricey" Downtown New American in the W Hotel captivates an "achingly hip" audience with a "Zen-like" setting that suits the "fresh", "innovative" cooking that, along with "excellent" service, helps the restaurant "rise above mere trendiness"; N.B. the Food score may not reflect post-Survey chef changes.

El Gaucho ● Steak
25 | 24 | 25 | $65

Belltown | 2505 First Ave. (Wall St.) | 206-728-1337 | www.elgaucho.com
"Dining is theater" and "swank" is standard at this "retro" steakhouse whose plush booths and banquettes complete the overall "Rat-Pack"-y vibe and ensure a "fabulously decadent" time; the "pro" crew serves up "melt-in-your-mouth" beef and some old-school flourishes – "tableside" Caesars and bananas Foster – all for tabs tailored to expense accounts, while the nightly piano provides the crowning touch.

Georgian, The French/Pacific NW
26 | 28 | 27 | $67

Downtown | Fairmont Olympic Hotel | 411 University St. (bet. 4th & 5th Aves.) | 206-621-7889 | www.fairmont.com
Epitomizing "timeless beauty" is this Downtown Pacific NW hotel "class" act, where "generations of Seattleites" have gathered for "special occasions" or an "upper-class dining fix" amid a chandeliered space framed by the signature butter-yellow walls; the "wonderful" food at breakfast, lunch and dinner delights, as does the "exceptional" service.

Green Leaf Vietnamese
▽ 24 | 16 | 21 | $15

International District | 418 Eighth Ave S. (Jackson St.) | 206-340-1388
"Authentic, delicious" food and the magic combination of "large portions and small prices" have conspired to transform this "small" bamboo-decorated International District Vietnamese into a popular choice for local foodies; hence, it's often "crowded", so it's smart to get there early.

Harvest Vine, The Spanish
27 | 20 | 22 | $46

Madison Park | 2701 E. Madison St. (27th Ave.) | 206-320-9771 | www.harvestvine.com
Lovers of high-end Basque cuisine swoon over the "fresh, intense, complex" creations at chef/co-owner Joseba Jimenez de Jimenez's Madison Park "gastronomic" destination where you can nab a chair at the copper dining bar, swap tapas tips with fellow diners and watch "great dinner theater" while "down-to-earth" staffers cater to you; note this "taste of San Sebastian" seats only 40.

☑ Herbfarm, The Ⓜ Pacific NW
28 | 26 | 28 | $153

Woodinville | Willows Lodge | 14590 NE 145th St. (Woodinville-Redmond Rd.) | 206-784-2222 | www.theherbfarm.com
"Mecca" for "serious diners" from all over the world is this Pacific NW extravaganza (Seattle's No. 1 for Food) in Woodinville that seamlessly "weaves herbs" into a "beautiful symphony" – nine courses of "resoundingly excellent" food paired with wines and served by a "terrific" staff in a "precious" setting; true, given the "amazing expense", this "event" may need to be reserved for a "financial windfall", but go if you can, for it's likely to be the best four or five hours of your life.

Il Terrazzo Carmine ☒ Italian
26 | 24 | 26 | $48

Pioneer Square | 411 First Ave. S. (bet. Jackson & King Sts.) | 206-467-7797 | www.ilterrazzocarmine.com
Just "wonderful" is what you'll hear from fans who describe this popular Pioneer Square "treasure" of an Italian still "charming" comers after

23 years; you can taste the "care in every bite" of the "superb" food brought to table by a "top-notch" staff in a space that exudes "warmth": "is it possible to be in love with a restaurant?"

Inn at Langley M *Pacific NW* ∇ 27 | 25 | 27 | $75

Langley | Inn at Langley | 400 First St. (Anthes Ave.) | 360-221-3033 | www.innatlangley.com

"A wonderful part of a great getaway" in Langley, this "grand" multi-hour event involves Matt Costello's "inventive", "unforgettable" Pacific NW six-course tasting menus bolstered by "local delicacies" – all prepared in the gleaming, stainless-steel kitchen right before the patrons' eyes; Japanese antiquities and a river rock fireplace add to the "deluxe" experience, but book ahead – it's only open Thursdays–Sundays in the summer, and Fridays–Sundays the rest of the year.

JaK's Grill *Steak* 26 | 17 | 21 | $39

Issaquah | 14 Front St. N. (Sunset Way) | 425-837-8834
Laurelhurst | 3701 NE 45th St. (37th Ave.) | 206-985-8545
West Seattle | 4548 California Ave. SW (bet. Alaska & Oregon Sts.) | 206-937-7809
www.jaksgrill.com

It's all about the "high-quality" beef that's "seared to mouthwatering perfection" at this steakhouse trio where service is "fast and pleasant" and the rooms "noisy"; the combination of the "bang-for-the-buck" appeal ("your pocketbook doesn't get à la carte-d to death") and no reservations suggests you should go "early or really late" or expect a wait akin to "an endurance event."

La Carta de Oaxaca Ⓢ *Mexican* 26 | 19 | 19 | $22

Ballard | 5431 Ballard Ave. NW (22nd Ave.) | 206-782-8722 | www.lacartadeoaxaca.com

"Like *abuela's* kitchen" is this "small" Mexican eatery in quaint Ballard packing in enthusiasts eager to indulge in "heavenly", "authentic" Oaxacan fare; while the "good" servers seem practiced in the art of "crowd control", the "super-friendly bartenders" do their bit too, and help make "the long waits fly by" with "great" margaritas.

Ⓩ Lampreia Ⓢ M *Pacific NW* 28 | 23 | 25 | $68

Belltown | 2400 First Ave. (Battery St.) | 206-443-3301 | www.lampreiarestaurant.com

An "amazing dining experience", this "extraordinary" Belltown Pacific NW–New American is "a place for foodies" to sample "sublime" and "visually stunning" small plates of "art" (conceived and executed by chef Scott Carsberg, an "uncompromising genius") while being attended to by "excellent" servers within a "soothing" room; naturally, it's a "bit pricey", but few mind given a meal here "is one you'll never forget."

Lark M *American* 28 | 23 | 25 | $49

Capitol Hill | 926 12th Ave. (bet. E. Marion & E. Spring Sts.) | 206-323-5275 | www.larkseattle.com

"Seductive" small plates steer devotees to Capitol Hill for this "temple" of seasonal, "extraordinary" New American preparations from chef John Sundstrom; the menu mirrors the rusticated "elegance" expressed in the small room, where the "good" service influences the overall effect: "you feel like you're eating in a friend's house, albeit a friend with amazing talent"; N.B. reservations taken only for parties of six or more.

Le Gourmand 🛎 Ⓜ *French* | 27 | 24 | 27 | $63 |

Ballard | 425 NW Market St. (6th Ave.) | 206-784-3463

Bruce Naftaly's "fabulous" French food – and fresh ingredients sourced from his garden – make "dreamy dinners" happen at this "overlooked" Ballard "hideaway" that keeps gourmands dazzled with a "jewel-box" setting and "sweet" service; P.S. grab an "incredible drink" and some "fancy snacks" at the modern, *très hip* Sambar cocktail bar next door.

Macrina Bakery & Cafe *Bakery/Dessert* | 25 | 15 | 16 | $17 |

Belltown | 2408 First Ave. (Battery St.) | 206-448-4032
Queen Anne | 615 W. McGraw St. (6th Ave.) | 206-283-5900
www.macrinabakery.com

These "essential" "artisan" bakeries supply not only "amazing" baked goods (including the "best breads in town"), but also entice as "tasty" stops for breakfast, brunch and lunch; "expect a line whenever you go", and note that while the settings are "hip", the spaces seem no bigger than a "closet"; N.B. McGraw Street is counter service only.

Ⓩ Metropolitan Grill *Steak* | 26 | 23 | 25 | $57 |

Downtown | 820 Second Ave. (Marion St.) | 206-624-3287 | www.themetropolitangrill.com

"They know how to take care of you" at this "big" and "bustling" Downtown "epitome of a classic steakhouse", "one of the greats" synonymous with "manly" steaks (the "kids' portions are fit for adults"), "classy", "clubby" wine-hued and wood-appointed quarters, a "superb" wine list and martinis, and, of course, "pricey" tabs; it all "sits well with the sports and business set", who help keep the place booked solid.

Ⓩ Mistral 🛎 Ⓜ *American/French* | 28 | 20 | 26 | $109 |

Belltown | 113 Blanchard St. (bet. 1st & 2nd Aves.) | 206-770-7799 | www.mistralseattle.com

This "star" would shine everywhere – "even in NYC" is the refrain at William Belickis' Belltown New American–New French, where the "austere" setting provides contrast for the "visual and gustatory" "brilliance" of the dishes along with "warm" service from a staff that seems to move around "effortlessly"; just know you may have to "blow your bank account" for the privilege of dining at "one that's not to be missed."

Monsoon *Vietnamese* | 25 | 20 | 21 | $37 |

Capitol Hill | 615 19th Ave. E. (bet. Mercer & Roy Sts.) | 206-325-2111 | www.monsoonseattle.com

Woks and grills turn out "amazing" upscale Vietnamese cuisine that's ingeniously paired with fine wines at this Capitol Hill staple helmed by siblings Eric and Sophie Banh; the "innovative" menu changes daily, which helps explain why fans swarm the "stark", modern dining room in droves.

Nell's *Pacific NW* | 26 | 19 | 24 | $46 |

Green Lake | 6804 E. Green Lake Way N. (bet. 2nd & 4th Aves.) | 206-524-4044 | www.nellsrestaurant.com

"Why would anyone live far from Green Lake" when there's this New American around, the domain of chef-owner Philip Mihalski, who brings an "innovative" awareness to his menu, one from which you can "order anything and it will be excellent"; though perhaps "nondescript", the setting seems suited to "relaxing" repasts.

☑ Nishino *Japanese*
28 | 21 | 25 | $47

Madison Park | 3130 E. Madison St. (Lake Washington Blvd.) | 206-322-5800 | www.nishinorestaurant.com

The fare's so "creative" you'd think "Armani was designing" it at Nobu protégé Tatsu Nishino's "minimalist", "ever-popular" Madison Park Japanese proffering the chefs' "fabulous" handiwork, whether it's "sublime" sushi or "wonderful" cooked dishes; after eating all the "amazing" goods, you're bound to walk out "weak in the knees"; P.S. "take advantage of the omakase option."

Paseo ☒ Ⓜ ⇆ *Caribbean*
▽ 28 | 8 | 15 | $12

Fremont | 4225 Fremont Ave. N. (bet. 42nd & 43rd Sts.) | 206-545-7440

"Castro would embrace capitalism if he tasted the pork sandwich" at this "funky" Fremonter proffering "fabulous" Caribbean comestibles; some say service is sometimes "brusque", others that it comes with a "smile", but everyone agrees that "takeout is the best plan" given the "quintessentially hole-in-the-wall" digs.

☑ Rover's ☒ Ⓜ *French*
28 | 25 | 28 | $95

Madison Valley | 2808 E. Madison St. (28th Ave.) | 206-325-7442 | www.rovers-seattle.com

"Superlative" sums up the workings of "Seattle icon" Thierry Rautereau and his Madison Valley cottage where the "incomparable" staff serves New French dishes fit for the most discerning "foodie" (the "vegetarian menu is a testament to excellent eating without meat") and where the "intimate" quarters delight; go "if you can afford it", or at least capitalize on the offerings at the Friday lunch.

Seastar Restaurant & Raw Bar *Seafood*
26 | 24 | 24 | $49

Bellevue | Civica Office Commons | 205 108th Ave. NE (2nd St.) | 425-456-0010 | www.seastarrestaurant.com

If ever there was "a reason to go to the Eastside", this "trendy" Bellevue fisherie provides it on account of "utterly sumptuous" seafood that's "right-off-the-boat fresh" dispensed by an open kitchen, with chef John Howie at the helm; sommelier Erik Liedholm's "excellent" wine selections are oenophile-friendly, and "professional" service keeps the ship steady.

Shiro's Sushi *Japanese*
27 | 15 | 22 | $42

Belltown | 2401 Second Ave. (Battery St.) | 206-443-9844 | www.shiros.com

Despite "minimal" decor, "heaven on earth" can still be found in this Japanese Belltown, the domain of "star"-chef Shiro Kashiba, whose sushi expresses "pristine" "simplicity"; for a "wonderful" experience, fans sit at the bar and let the "personable" servers "take care of you" – but arrive early since it fills up fast.

Sitka & Spruce Ⓜ *Eclectic*
- | - | - | M

Eastlake | 2238 Eastlake Ave. E. (bet. Boston & E. Lynn Sts.) | 206-324-0662 | www.sitkaandspruce.com

Seattleites have quickly taken to this Eastlake Eclectic that uses wholesome, hand-raised organic ingredients and coaxes them into

	FOOD	DECOR	SERVICE	COST

dishes fit for gourmets; a communal table dominates the tiny, quirky space, whose strip-mall surroundings supply an interesting contrast to the vibe inside.

Tavolàta ● *Italian*

| | – | – | – | I |

Belltown | 2323 Second Ave. (bet. Battery & Bell Sts.) | 206-838-8008 | www.tavolata.com

Belltown hails the arrival of this *nuovo* Italian from wonder-chef Ethan Stowell (Union), with its wallet-friendly menu of housemade mozzarella and unique handmade pastas; its industrial decor is softened by a communal table that stretches through the center of the room, glowing with dozens of candles and perfect for late-night suppers.

Toyoda Sushi *Japanese*

| | ▽ 27 | 14 | 21 | $28 |

Lake City | 12543 Lake City Way NE (bet. 125th & 127th Sts.) | 206-367-7972

"Looks can be deceiving" say sushi sharks about this Lake City Japanese where the setting belies the "incredible" raw fare, the handiwork of chef Natsuyoshi Toyoda ("you're in good hands when he's behind the counter"); "true believers" in this spot also vouch for the "friendly" service and "reasonable" prices.

Union *American*

| | 25 | 21 | 23 | $56 |

Downtown | 1400 First Ave. (Union St.) | 206-838-8000 | www.unionseattle.com

"Blissful" dining defines this Downtown New American whose chef sources his ingredients locally (and daily) and transforms them into "delicious" dishes geared to palates that pick up on "delicate, subtle" flavors; the modern space seems in union with the food and mood here.

Volterra ● *Italian*

| | 26 | 22 | 23 | $42 |

Ballard | 5411 Ballard Ave. NW (22nd Ave.) | 206-789-5100 | www.volterrarestaurant.com

"*Cucina fantastico*" is another name for chef Don Curtiss' "bold" and "comforting" Northern Italian cooking at this "inviting" room on Ballard's hippest street; the service is "good", and thanks perhaps to the tiled floor, the din from happy gourmets is high ("I can't hear you, but this pasta is amazing!").

☒ Wild Ginger *Pacific Rim*

| | 25 | 23 | 22 | $41 |

Downtown | 1401 Third Ave. (Union St.) | 206-623-4450 | www.wildginger.net

"Wildly popular" (in fact, Seattle's Most Popular restaurant), this "cavernous", colorful Downtown "landmark" is an "obligatory destination for out-of-towners" and locals, where the "excellent" staff serves "clever" Pacific Rim preparations bound to "tickle the taste buds" amid a (not surprisingly) "noisy" setting; P.S. savvy diners say the "satay bar is the place to be."

St. Louis

TOP FOOD RANKING

	Restaurant	Cuisine
28	Sidney St. Cafe	American
	Paul Manno's	Italian
27	Tony's	Italian
	Trattoria Marcella	Italian
	Niche	American
	Al's Restaurant	Seafood/Steak
	Dominic's	Italian
	Pomme	American/French
26	Crossing, The	American
	Annie Gunn's	American

OTHER NOTEWORTHY PLACES

Acero	Italian
An American Place	American
Atlas	French/Italian
Cardwell's/Plaza	American
Chez Leon	French
1111 Mississippi	Californian/Italian
Frazer's	American
Harvest	American
Truffles	American
Zinnia	American

Acero ☒ Italian

| – | – | – | E |

Maplewood | 7266 Manchester Rd. (Southwest Ave.) | 314-644-1790
Jim Fiala offers a twist on traditional dining with this Italian Maplewood newcomer where dishes are known to come served on marble and there's a salumeria selection second to none; the rustic atmosphere stands in direct contrast to Crossing, the chef's elegant flagship.

Al's Restaurant ☒Ⓜ Seafood/Steak

| 27 | 18 | 26 | $55 |

Downtown | 1200 N. First St. (Biddle St.) | 314-421-6399 | www.alsrestaurant.net
Although longtime owner Al Baroni has passed away, this "true St. Louis landmark" ("since 1925") remains "a trip back in time", an Italian-style chophouse featuring "fabulous steaks, veal" and seafood that are "worth" both "the dress code" (jackets required in fall and winter) and the "expense-account" prices; sure, the "tired but nostalgic" Downtown digs "could use some dusting", but given the "fantastic" food and service, most "don't even remember the decor."

American Place, An ☒Ⓜ American

| 25 | 27 | 23 | $53 |

Downtown | 822 Washington Ave. (bet. 8th & 9th Sts.) | 314-418-5800 | www.aapstl.com
Rated No. 1 for Decor in St. Louis, this Downtown Traditional American located "in the former lobby of a historic hotel" boasts a space whose

soaring, 40-ft. ceilings, "marble columns and rich colors" are "so beautiful, you'll want to eat" the setting, although diners may wish to nibble instead on chef-owner Larry Forgione's "even more delicious" dishes; hearty eaters pout about "portions too small for the prices", but admirers insist this "special-occasion place is worth the money."

☑ Annie Gunn's ☑ *American*   26 | 21 | 23 | $44

Chesterfield | 16806 Chesterfield Airport Rd. (Baxter Rd.) | 636-532-7684 | www.anniegunns.com

One of "the best West County has to offer" is this Traditional American that's "worth the trip" to Chesterfield for "superb steaks" and "top-notch seafood" from chef "Lou Rook, the genius in the kitchen"; it's "pricey but you get what you pay for" – "terrific service", a "casual atmosphere" and a "fantastic wine list" – although a few warn that it's also "crowded", making reservations "a must"; P.S. don't forget to "fill your car up with goodies" from the attached Smoke House Market.

Atlas Restaurant ☒☑ *French/Italian*   26 | 20 | 25 | $35

Midtown | 5513 Pershing Ave. (bet. De Baliviere Ave. & Union Blvd.) | 314-367-6800 | www.atlasrestaurantstl.com

Regulars "hope nobody ever finds out about" Midtown's "true Paris bistro without the jet lag", where the "honest, uncontrived, classic" French and Italian dishes are both "toe-curlingly good" and "a great value"; the seasonal fare (plus a "nice late-night dessert and coffee menu") is enhanced by "warm", "attentive owners", a "thoughtful" staff and a "simple", recently "redesigned interior that's wonderful" and "much more roomy."

Cardwell's at the Plaza *American*   25 | 22 | 22 | $38

Frontenac | 94 Plaza Frontenac (Clayton Rd. & Lindbergh Blvd.) | 314-997-8885 | www.cardwellsattheplaza.com

"Don't let the mall location fool you": this Plaza Frontenac New American offers "some of St. Louis' finest cooking" in the form of an "exceptionally delicious", "daily changing menu" with "something for everyone", including "amazing vegetarian dishes"; so "dress up" and "stop in after a day of shopping", because given the "beautiful", "well-heeled crowd", there's "no better place to people-watch"; P.S. there's also a "relaxing outdoor area."

Chez Leon ☑ *French*   26 | 24 | 24 | $43

Central West End | 4580 Laclede Ave. (Euclid Ave.) | 314-361-1589 | www.chezleon.com

"There's something about it that makes me happy" smile supporters of this "authentic" Central West End bistro where a "skillfully executed menu" is paired with "faithfully French decor" that's "so charming, you feel like you're in Paris"; the "lively, inviting atmosphere" comes complete with "fantastic service", sidewalk seating and a pianist on Fridays and Sundays, so "order the Grand Marnier soufflé" and "settle in for the evening"; P.S. the prix fixe menu is a "great value."

Crossing, The ☒ *American*   26 | 20 | 24 | $47

Clayton | 7823 Forsyth Blvd. (Central Ave.) | 314-721-7375 | www.thecrossingstl.com

Chef-owner Jim Fiala delivers one of "the finest dining experiences in St. Louis" at this Clayton New American offering a "continually updated" selection of "innovative, delicious" dishes "with French and Italian influences" ("the tasting menu with wine flights is the way to go"); "unmemorable decor" gives nitpickers pause, but most agree it's an "intimate", "charming environment" with "seamless" "service to match", hence fans "never come away with anything but a giant smile."

Dominic's ☒ Italian
27 | 23 | 26 | $52

The Hill | 5101 Wilson Ave. (Hereford St.) | 314-771-1632

"Old-world charm meets fine Italian cuisine" at this "all-around wonderful", family-owned "classic" that's "a must on the Hill" for its "outstanding, authentic" fare and "extremely attentive", "personal tableside service"; entering the "dimly lit, romantic" space is "like stepping back in time", and its "elegant", "classy" decor makes it a "favorite" "for special occasions and business dinners."

Frazer's ☒ American
24 | 19 | 22 | $30

Benton Park | 1811 Pestalozzi St. (Lemp Ave.) | 314-773-8646 | www.frazergoodeats.com

"Continuing to subtly impress, year after year", this "funky" New American in Benton Park (just west of Anheuser-Busch) is "considered a local treasure" for its pairing of "refined" New Orleans-influenced cuisine with a "casual atmosphere" whose "warmth sets it apart"; it's the type of "sophisticated yet comfortable" spot "where you can take a first date", and outdoor seating plus a "striking new bar/lounge" "add a level of interest."

Harvest Ⓜ American
25 | 23 | 24 | $45

Richmond Heights | 1059 S. Big Bend Blvd. (Clayton Rd.) | 314-645-3522 | www.harveststlouis.com

This "fabulous" Richmond Heights restaurant is "worth checking out every few months" for some of "the most creative cooking in St. Louis" courtesy of a "seasonally changing menu" that "incorporates regional, market-ready ingredients" into "adventurous takes on [New] American cuisine"; the "cozy", "rustic atmosphere" and "wonderful service" are "exceeded only by the wine list", although a few sweet tooths find "the bread pudding alone" reason enough to go.

☑ Niche Ⓜ American
27 | 25 | 24 | $40

Benton Park | 1831 Sidney St. (I-55) | 314-773-7755 | www.nichestlouis.com

"Bringing great food and an enjoyable ambiance together", this "welcome newcomer" in Benton Park offers a "short" "but top-notch" menu of "flawless", "cutting-edge" New American cuisine in a "sleek, modern" setting that "makes you feel chic"; meanwhile, "outstanding service" and a "fabulous value" of a three-course $30 prix fixe meal "makes it a delight on every visit"; N.B. a late-night dessert and wine menu is served until 1:30 AM on Fridays and Saturdays.

☑ 1111 Mississippi ☒ Californian/Italian
25 | 25 | 23 | $37

Lafayette Square | 1111 Mississippi Ave. (Chouteau Ave.) | 314-241-9999 | www.1111-m.com

"A cornerstone in the Lafayette Square revival", this "trendy" spot set in a "renovated warehouse" offers an "interesting menu" of Tuscan-Californian cuisine "with an emphasis on fresh provisions", "variety and quality" but "without pretension"; the "multilevel interior" can get "noisy, but who cares" counter fans who focus instead on the "meticulous service", "superbly cultivated wine list" and patio seating; P.S. the "gooey butter cake is a must-try!"

☑ Paul Manno's Ⓢ Italian   28 | 18 | 24 | $39

Chesterfield | 75 Forum Shopping Ctr. (Woods Mill Rd.) | 314-878-1274
"Skip the Hill" and head to this veteran Italian "hidden" in a Chesterfield strip mall, where the "marvelous", "authentic" Sicilian fare is "just like mama used to make, because mama is still in the kitchen"; an "attentive staff" provides "impeccable service", while owner Paul Manno "loves to make his customers happy"; but a "small" dining room means you "sometimes have to wait" and then "eat elbow-to-elbow" – so do yourself a favor and "don't tell anyone."

Pomme ⓈⓂ American/French   27 | 22 | 25 | $44

Clayton | 40 N. Central Ave. (bet. Forsyth Blvd. & Maryland Ave.) | 314-727-4141 | www.pommerestaurant.com
For "inventive cuisine that's always satisfying" and "executed with care", take a detour to this "intimate" Clayton venue where chef-owner Bryan Carr delivers "big flavor" via "fresh, innovative, seasonal" New French-New American cuisine that "uses only the best ingredients"; it's "great for a date or quiet dinner", with a "comfortable atmosphere" that's enhanced by "attentive service" and a "thoughtful wine list"; nevertheless, a handful harrumph about portions that are "modest given the prices."

☑ Sidney Street Cafe ⓈⓂ American   28 | 23 | 26 | $43

Benton Park | 2000 Sidney St. (Salena St.) | 314-771-5777 | www.sidneystreetcafe.com
Rated No. 1 for Food and Popularity in St. Louis, this Benton Park "standard for others to follow" is a "perennial favorite" proffering a "superb", "inventive" array of "universally wonderful" New American cuisine; the "friendly", "knowledgeable" servers recite "from chalkboard menus" "with appetizing flair", while the "inviting" and "romantic atmosphere" proves "perfect for business, dates or special occasions"; nevertheless, "for such fine dining", regulars recommend "calling weeks in advance for a reservation."

☑ Tony's Ⓢ Italian   27 | 24 | 27 | $62

Downtown | 410 Market St. (B'way St.) | 314-231-7007 | www.tonysstlouis.com
It's "still the best special-occasion restaurant in St. Louis" sigh supporters of this Downtown "treasure" that "lives up to its reputation" via "impeccable" Italian cuisine and "professional servers" who "anticipate your every need"; an "elegant ambiance" and "attention to detail" make this "a class act" for most, although modernists maintain it can be "a bit old-fashioned" (jackets are required) and cite "high prices."

☑ Trattoria Marcella ⓈⓂ Italian   27 | 20 | 25 | $36

South City | 3600 Watson Rd. (Pernod Ave.) | 314-352-7706 | www.trattoriamarcella.com
"Sometimes the labor of love that goes into a restaurant is so palpable you can taste it in the food" fawn fans of this "vibrant", "convivial" South Side Italian where "always remarkable", "reasonably priced" fare ("risotto to dream about") is served by a "friendly, gracious staff"; "now that they've expanded, you can get a seat" in the still-"cramped"

space, although a nostalgic few feel it "lost a little of its ambiance" in the process.

Truffles 🛇 *American*   23 | 22 | 23 | $46

Ladue | 9202 Clayton Rd. (Price Rd.) | 314-567-9100 |
www.trufflesinladue.com

Since chef Mark Serice (ex Brennan's in New Orleans) "relocated here post-Katrina", things "have gotten really interesting" at this Ladue standby: the new toque "has breathed life into the kitchen", "adding Cajun flair" to an already "inspiring" New American menu; the "exceptional wine list" and "warm", "personable service" have stayed the same, however, as has a "lovely", "classy atmosphere" that seems "a little stodgy" to some.

Zinnia Ⓜ *American*   24 | 18 | 23 | $38

Webster Groves | 7491 Big Bend Blvd. (Shrewsbury Ave.) | 314-962-0572 |
www.zinnia-stl.com

"The purple exterior may have you wondering what you're getting yourself into", but this "favorite" set in a "charming converted gas station" is "a Webster Groves gem" whose chef-owner "David Guempel has it and has had it for years", whipping up "creative, seasonal" New American meals; and whether you're relaxing in the "intimate" dining room or out on the "fabulous" patio, you'll find the same "attentive staff" and "welcoming" ambiance.

Tampa/Sarasota

TOP FOOD RANKING

	Restaurant	Cuisine
28	Cafe Ponte	American
27	Restaurant B.T.	French/Vietnamese
	Beach Bistro	American
	SideBern's	American
26	Mise en Place	American
	Black Pearl	American
	Pane Rustica	Pizza
	Roy's	Seafood
	Bern's Steak	Steak
	Armani's	Italian

OTHER NOTEWORTHY PLACES

Americano	Italian
Bijou Café	Continental
Columbia	Caribbean
Euphemia Haye	Eclectic
Fly Bar	Eclectic
Marchand's	Mediterranean
Marlin Darlin' Grill	American
Michael's On East	American
Savant	Eclectic
Table, The	Seafood

Americano *American/Italian* — | — | — | M

Sarasota | 1409 Main St. (N. Pineapple Ave.) | 941-365-1026
This Sarasota entry cooks up a straightforward American-Italian slate, with omelets, frittatas and sandwiches the focus at lunch, and rotisserie meats the emphasis come dinner time; decorwise, silver-toned walls help place it in the sleek category.

Armani's *Italian* 26 | 26 | 26 | $62

Tampa | Grand Hyatt Tampa Bay | 2900 Bayport Dr., 14th fl. (Hwy. 60) | 813-207-6800 | www.armanisrestaurant.com
"High-end and high up" on the 14th floor of the Grand Hyatt, Tampa's "venerable" "special-occasion place" pairs a "killer view" of the bay ("Giorgio would totally appreciate" it) with "consistent", "top-notch" Northern Italian cuisine, including a "fabulous antipasti bar" and a "tasting menu that shouldn't be missed"; it "drips with romance" and enough "suave sophistication" to satisfy even those who grumble about "pricey tabs" and "snooty" servers.

Z Beach Bistro *American* 27 | 22 | 27 | $63

Holmes Beach | 6600 Gulf Dr. (66th St.) | 941-778-6444 | www.beachbistro.com
"Setting the standard for fine dining on Florida's west coast" – it's rated No. 1 in the area for Service – is this "consistent" Anna Maria

	FOOD	DECOR	SERVICE	COST

Island "winner", a "beautiful little gem" that "foodies love" for its "knowledgeable staff" ("a well-oiled machine"), "pricey", "world-class" Floridian cuisine and "awesome wine selections"; although some make note of the "tight quarters", it's located "literally on the beach" with "magnificent views of the sunset."

☑ Bern's Steak House *Steak*   26 | 20 | 26 | $63

Tampa | 1208 S. Howard Ave. (bet. Marjory Ave. & Watrous St.) | 813-251-2421 | www.bernssteakhouse.com

"Take your chains, I'll take Bern's" aver acolytes of this "independent, locally owned" "Tampa landmark" (voted Most Popular on the Gulf Coast) that pairs its "pricey" "melt-in-your-mouth steaks" and vegetables "straight from their own farm" with an "encyclopedic wine list"; although nitpickers insist the "gaudy" "bordello decor" "needs a revamp", an "exceptional" staff and a "unique", "don't-miss" upstairs dessert room compensate; P.S. "insider tip: the kitchen/wine cellar tour is amazing."

☑ Bijou Café *Continental*   25 | 23 | 25 | $50

Sarasota | 1287 First St. (Pineapple Ave.) | 941-366-8111 | www.bijoucafe.net

"As the name suggests, this is Sarasota's jewel", a "classy" Downtown "standby" that's "beloved by gourmets" for its "consistent" if "costly" Continental cuisine; the recently expanded setting in a "former gas station" now has a "warm", "dignified ambiance" that's matched by a "professional staff" that quipsters say wins "top service in a service station" honors, especially for its ability to get "opera buffs" "out in time for the curtain"; P.S. the "valet makes parking easy."

Black Pearl *American*   26 | 21 | 26 | $49

Dunedin | 315 Main St. (Broadway St.) | 727-734-3463 | www.theblackpearlofdunedin.com

This "wonderful" "surprise" in "charming", small-town Dunedin is "worth driving to" for its "satisfying" menu of "inventive" New American dishes "cooked to perfection"; the "quiet, dark, intimate setting" is "very romantic" and enhanced by "attentive" servers who "could not be better", leading regulars to recommend you "make a reservation" in advance, since it's as "popular" as it is "small."

☑ Cafe Ponte 🅂🅜 *American*   28 | 23 | 25 | $47

Clearwater | Icot Ctr. | 13505 Icot Blvd. (Ulmerton Rd.) | 727-538-5768 | www.cafeponte.com

Rated No. 1 for Food on the Gulf Coast, this "smart, stylish" gastronomic "gem" in Clearwater has foodies singing the praises of "gifted" chef-owner Christopher Ponte, who delivers "quality for the price" via "playful presentations" of "exquisite" New American cuisine; "don't be fooled" by the "strip-mall setting" – "everything is top-notch" here, including the "attentive" staff – but do keep in mind that "reservations are a must" to experience one of these "magical, memorable meals."

☑ Columbia *Caribbean*   20 | 21 | 20 | $35

Sarasota | 411 St. Armands Circle (Blvd. of the Presidents) | 941-388-3987
Clearwater | 1241 Gulf Blvd. (½ mi. south of Sand Key Bridge) | 727-596-8400
St. Petersburg | St. Petersburg Pier | 800 Second Ave. NE (Beach Dr.) | 727-822-8000

(continued)

Columbia

Ybor City | 2117 E. Seventh Ave. (bet. 21st & 22nd Sts.) | 813-248-4961
www.columbiarestaurant.com

"One of Florida's oldest and finest", this "enormous" Ybor City Caribbean ("the original" in a statewide chain) is "a real classic" that gets the nod as a "great place to take visitors" for "authentic food", "ambrosial sangria" and "flamenco dancers that stomp it up inches from your table"; the signature "1905 salad is worth the trip" to any of the four locations, but the patio at the Sarasota branch is an added treat "for watching the shoppers" "on beautiful St. Armands Circle."

Euphemia Haye *Eclectic* | 26 | 22 | 23 | $56 |

Longboat Key | 5540 Gulf of Mexico Dr. (Gulf Bay Rd.) | 941-383-3633 |
www.euphemiahaye.com

A "romantic atmosphere and superb service contribute to the longevity" of Longboat Key's 26-year-old "favorite" for "gourmet, Southern-influenced" Eclectic fare that's "pricey" but "consistently excellent"; "few first-time visitors can find" this "charming", "out-of-the-way place", but once they do, they agree that a post-meal trip upstairs to The HayeLoft is "a must" "for outstanding and very generous" "desserts, coffee and jazz."

Fly Bar & Restaurant ●⑤ *Eclectic* | – | – | – | M |

Tampa | 1202 Franklin St. (E. Royal St.) | 813-275-5000 |
www.flybarandrestaurant.com

Leslie Shirah has brought her chic supper-club concept (in San Francisco) to Downtown Tampa, transforming a small 1920s brick storefront into a hip, industrial-glam live-music venue and restaurant; the fairly priced, small-plates Eclectic menu wanders through a number of countries (think Kobe sliders and lemongrass-glazed ribs), while the rooftop patio is swarmed late night with young professionals enjoying expertly prepared cocktails.

Marchand's Bar & Grill *Mediterranean* | 24 | 25 | 25 | $47 |

St. Petersburg | Renaissance Vinoy Resort & Golf Club | 501 Fifth Ave. NE (Beach Dr.) | 727-824-8072 | www.vinoyrenaissanceresort.com

"You can feel the excitement of the Roaring '20s" as you sample Med dishes "prepared with skill" at this "elegant", "historically preserved" restaurant in the Renaissance Vinoy Resort; the "swanky atmosphere" is "perfect for breakfast with clients, lunch with colleagues or drinks with old friends", and given a "most accommodating staff", live jazz and a "legendary Sunday brunch", some even go so far as to call it "the premier dining experience in St. Pete."

Marlin Darlin' Grill *American* | – | – | – | E |

Bellaire Bluffs | 2819 W. Bay Dr. (S. Indian Rocks Rd.) |
727-584-1700

From the team that brought us Island Way Grill and Salt Rock Grill comes this Bellaire Bluffs newcomer designed like a salon on a luxury sport-fishing boat: fiberglass trophy fish and nautical touches provide a sleek backdrop for a seafood-focused, moderately pricey Traditional American menu that isn't without playful touches, such as crab corndogs and a range of ceviche offered in ceramic tasting spoons.

Michael's On East ☒ *American* 24 | 24 | 23 | $55

Sarasota | 1212 East Ave. S. (Bahia Vista St.) | 941-366-0007 | www.bestfood.com

Suitable for either "a very special occasion" or a "power lunch", Sarasota's "feast at East" is a "consistent leader", proffering "gourmet" New American fare that remains "heavenly" despite a "revolving door for chefs in recent years"; though it's "a bit pricey" to some, acolytes aver you'll be as "pleased" as the "local dignitaries" and "beautiful people" who come here for "well-versed" service, a "clubby atmosphere" and a 350-bottle "wine cellar that's tops in the area."

☑ Mise en Place ☒Ⓜ *American* 26 | 22 | 24 | $49

Tampa | 442 W. Kennedy Blvd. (Grand Central Pl.) | 813-254-5373 | www.miseonline.com

For over two decades, this "gem" blessed with "beautiful views of the University of Tampa" has been the stage on which chef/co-owner Marty Blitz "shines as always", "dazzling the palates" of area foodies with a "creative, changing menu" of New American cuisine that utilizes "fresh, local ingredients" in "unexpected" "flavor combinations"; "understated", "modern" decor and "friendly" service add to the "spectacular" experience.

Pane Rustica Ⓜ *Eclectic/Pizza* 26 | 18 | 18 | $22

Tampa | 3225 S. MacDill Ave. (Bay to Bay Blvd.) | 813-902-8828

Long known as a "delightful", counter-service spot "packed at lunchtime" with fans of its "delicious sandwiches", "great bread and pastries" made on-site and "crisp", wood-fired pizza ("a religious experience"), this "old standby" in South Tampa "has now added a casual fine-dining menu" featuring Italian-tinged Eclectic fare; with a "warm, inviting" setting and "aim-to-please owners" and staff, devotees decree that, "dollar for dollar, it's the best meal in town."

☑ Restaurant B.T. ☒ *French/Vietnamese* 27 | 24 | 24 | $44

Tampa | 1633 W. Snow Ave. (S. Rome Ave.) | 813-258-1916 | www.restaurantbt.com

At this ambitious "oasis" in the middle of "trendy" Old Hyde Park Village, "incredibly talented" and "demanding chef-owner" B.T. Nguyen "expects only the best", and her "continually innovative" French-Vietnamese fusion fare has "an uncanny flair for pleasing both the taste buds and the eyes"; "sophisticated", "minimalist decor" and a "hip staff" draw "a well-groomed South Tampa clientele", as does a "hot bar scene" fueled by "amazing", "exotic drinks."

☑ Roy's *Hawaiian* 26 | 23 | 24 | $51

Bonita Springs | Promenade at Bonita Bay | 26831 S. Bay Dr. (Tamiami Trail S.) | 239-498-7697
Tampa | 4342 W. Boy Scout Blvd. (bet. Lois Ave. & Westshore Blvd.) | 813-873-7697
www.roysrestaurant.com

They "may be part of a chain, but don't tell that to the food" at Roy Yamaguchi's "lively", "loud" links in Bonita Springs and Tampa, where "presentation and inventive sauces are the hallmarks" of the "exotic", "unbelievably delicious" Hawaii seafood dishes that can be followed up with "don't-miss" desserts like the signature "luscious lava cake";

the "pricey" duo proves equally "great for family and business" occasions with its "eager servers" and "fantastic wine selection"; N.B. a Sarasota offshoot is set to open soon.

Savant Fine Dining *Eclectic*

- | - | - | VE

Clearwater | 2551 Drew St. (off Rte. 19) | 727-421-9975 | www.savantfinedining.com

The intimacy of someone's private dining room and the sophistication of a big-city restaurant are part of the charm of this tiny labor of love, chef David Miller's Clearwater Eclectic that's making waves with its fanciful desserts and savory menu, the latter harboring intriguing items such as a citrus-curry boar tenderloin and miso-brined escolar; chocolate sculptures adorn the room, suggesting the toque's professional background in the pastry arts.

☑ SideBern's ☒ *American*

27 | 25 | 24 | $53

Tampa | 2208 W. Morrison Ave. (S. Howard Ave.) | 813-258-2233 | www.bernssteakhouse.com

At "stately" Bern's Steak House's "trendy", "energetic" little sister, "young Tampa flirts and feeds" on chef-partner Jeannie Pierola's "must-try" dim sum and "pricey", "inventive" New American entrees and desserts that "combine the best of the old world with new-world sensibilities" and "international ingredients"; meanwhile, "top-notch service" and an attached wine store (sample from the "excellent choices" for a small corkage fee) make it even more of "a joy to visit."

Table, The ☒ *Seafood*

- | - | - | M

Sarasota | 1934 Hillview St. (bet. Osprey Ave. & Tamiami Trail) | 941-365-4558 | www.thetablesarasota.com

Anchoring the sophisticated Southside Village restaurant corridor, this affordable seafooder gets its inspiration from the cuisines of the so-called 'Atlantic Rim', notably the Caribbean, South America and Spain; braised short ribs and other slow-cooked specialties have made the restaurant a comfort-food destination for Sarasota's food cognoscenti; N.B. plans are underway to open a St. Petersburg location.

		FOOD	DECOR	SERVICE	COST

TOP FOOD RANKING

	Restaurant	Cuisine
28	Dish, The	American
26	Vivace	Italian
	Grill at Hacienda del Sol	American
	Le Rendez-Vous	French
	Cafe Poca Cosa	Mexican
25	Ventana Room	American
	Feast	Eclectic
	Janos	Southwestern
	Tavolino	Italian
24	Beyond Bread	Sandwiches

OTHER NOTEWORTHY PLACES

Restaurant	Cuisine
Blanco Tacos + Tequila	Mexican
Cuvée World Bistro	Eclectic
J Bar	Nuevo Latino
Kingfisher Bar & Grill	American
McMahon's Prime	Steak
Montana Avenue	American
Neo of Melaka	Malaysian
Terra Cotta	Southwestern
Vintabla	American
Wildflower	American

Beyond Bread 🅢 *Sandwiches* — 24 | 15 | 19 | $11

Midtown | 3026 N. Campbell Ave. (Blacklidge Dr.) | 520-322-9965
Midtown | Monterey Vill. | 6260 E. Speedway Blvd. (Wilmot Rd.) |
520-747-7477
www.beyondbread.com

"Knead we say more?" for "fabulous", "freshly baked" goods, these Midtown Tucson bakery/cafes go "above and beyond" the call of duty by purveying "amazing" breads, sandwiches and pastries to those who "plan their day around" visits there.

Blanco Tacos + Tequila *Mexican* — - | - | - | M

Foothills | La Encantada | 2905 E. Skyline Dr. (N. Campbell Ave.) |
520-232-1007 | www.foxrc.com

Credit Sam Fox of Montana Avenue and Wildflower fame for the early success of his new La Encantada mall Mexican drawing diverse diners with a chic, light-filled setting that frames offerings (e.g. crab-roasted poblano enchiladas); no surprise, as far as libations, it's all about tequilas such as the kumquat-cucumber fresco.

🅩 Cafe Poca Cosa 🅢 *Mexican* — 26 | - | 22 | $28

Downtown | 100 E. Pennington St. (Scott Ave.) | 520-622-6400 |
www.pocacosatucson.com

"Bring an open mind and empty stomach" to Suzana Davila's "frantically" paced Downtown "must-visit" Mexican (Tucson's Most Popular restaurant) where the "exciting" food blends the "homestyle" with the "innovative"; the daily changing menu showcasing a slew of "interesting moles" helps make a meal here "magical"; N.B. they are now in sleeker digs featuring an appropriately swanky bar area.

Cuvée World Bistro 🗷 *Eclectic*   23 | 21 | 21 | $34
Midtown | Rancho Ctr. | 3352 E. Speedway Blvd. (bet. Alvernon Way & Country Club Blvd.) | 520-881-7577 | www.cuveebistro.com
"A real find", this "trendy" Midtown bistro from chef-owner Mitch Levy lures locals with "terrific" temptations in the way of "artistically presented" Eclectic eats and a "friendly staff" that makes everyone "feel at home" – even those who "dine alone"; the "great wine list" (and wine pairings with each course) makes it a "treat."

☑ Dish, The 🗷🅼 *American*   28 | 20 | 26 | $44
Midtown | 3131 E. First St. (E. Speedway Blvd.) | 520-326-1714 | www.dishbistro.com
"Reservations are a must" at this "tiny", "romantic" mainstay in Midtown that's ranked No. 1 for Food in Tucson – no surprise, considering each "fabulous" course on its New American menu is a "treasure"; a "discreet" atmosphere enhanced by a "wonderful staff" helps ensure an "exceptional evening"; N.B. the restaurant has moved to East First Street.

Feast 🅼 *Eclectic*   25 | 16 | 20 | $24
Midtown | 4122 E. Speedway Blvd. (bet. Alvernon Way & Columbus Blvd.) | 520-326-9363 | www.eatatfeast.com
Although slightly roomier, it's still tough to get a seat at Midtown's revered, no-reservations take-out destination, a "festive" Eclectic Tucson bistro perpetually "packed" with loyalists who can't get enough of "happy chef" Doug Levy's "inventive", "vegetarian-friendly" food that's "heaven on a plate"; the "fantastic wine wall" and "casual" atmosphere complete with communal table make it feel like you're in "San Fran."

☑ Grill at Hacienda del Sol *American*   26 | 27 | 25 | $55
Foothills | Hacienda del Sol | 5601 N. Hacienda del Sol (bet. E. River Rd. & E. Sunrise Dr.) | 520-529-3500 | www.haciendadelsol.com
A "romantic" representative of "quintessential old Arizona", this perennially popular Foothills New American, situated in a "historic" "resort to the golden-age Hollywood crowd", cops the top Decor rating in Tucson for its "beautiful" interior and "stunning" setting that boasts "magnificent city views" and an enviable perch for catching a "great sunset"; if the "divine" food appears a little "pricey", save this "star in the desert" for "those special nights when only the best will do."

☑ Janos 🗷 *Southwestern*   25 | 25 | 25 | $63
Foothills | Westin La Paloma | 3770 E. Sunrise Dr. (bet. N. Campbell Ave. & N. Swan Rd.) | 520-615-6100 | www.janos.com
Dinner at this "top-notch" hotel restaurant in the Foothills is always "an event", thanks to its "guru", chef-owner Janos Wilder, whose "superb", "cutting-edge" French-inspired Southwestern cooking gets "extra points" for using "local ingredients"; although a few lament prices "in orbit", most insist that the "wild man" and his "special-occasion" place deserve their reputation as one of the "Southwest's best"; P.S. the wine list is "a feast in itself."

	FOOD	DECOR	SERVICE	COST

J Bar ⊠ *Nuevo Latino*
23 | 21 | 21 | $34

Foothills | Westin La Paloma | 3770 E. Sunrise Dr. (bet. N. Campbell Ave. & N. Swan Rd.) | 520-615-6100 | www.janos.com

"Can't afford Janos?" try its "trendy" "little brother" next door, a "lively" Nuevo Latino offshoot in the Foothills where "every bite" from the open kitchen "amazes", making it for some "as good as its relative" at a "fraction of the cost"; supporters who "love that happy hour" rave about "out-of-sight" margaritas and add that the "cool view" from the balcony makes this "hipster" a "wonderful place to hang."

Kingfisher Bar & Grill ● *American*
22 | 17 | 21 | $36

Midtown | 2564 E. Grant Rd. (N. Tucson Blvd.) | 520-323-7739 | www.kingfisherbarandgrill.com

"Even coastal seafood snobs would be impressed" with the "imaginatively prepared" fish at this "funky" Midtown New American; although surveyors split on the decor ("dark and dreary" vs. "swanky and cool"), there's no argument about the "exceptional wine list" and "wonderful late-night menu" for post-theater eaters.

⊠ Le Rendez-Vous Ⓜ *French*
26 | 17 | 20 | $45

Midtown | 3844 E. Fort Lowell Rd. (N. Alvernon Way) | 520-323-7373 | www.lerendez-vous.com

"By all means the place to go" for the closest thing to a "trip to France", this Midtown "favorite" offers "delicious", "rich", "old-time" Gallic classics; while a finicky faction suggests the decor "needs a face-lift", fawning Francophiles shrug *c'est la vie* and testify that "amazing sauces" and a "to-die-for Grand Marnier soufflé" help turn this place into "a must."

McMahon's Prime Steakhouse *Steak*
23 | 24 | 22 | $51

Midtown | 2959 N. Swan Rd. (bet. E. Fort Lowell Rd. & E. Glenn St.) | 520-327-7463 | www.metrorestaurants.com

This "clubby", "traditional" Midtown steakhouse turns out "fabulous" "melt-in-your-mouth" meat in portions so "overly generous" that they give new meaning to "diet-busting" fare; it's a "budget breaker", but most say the "fantastic wine selection" and "top-notch cigar bar" make it perfect for "expense-account dining."

Montana Avenue *American*
– | – | – | M

Midtown | 6390 E. Grant Rd. (Wilmot Rd.) | 520-298-2020 | www.foxrc.com

Sam Fox, the restaurateur of Bistro Zin and Wildflower, has opened this trendy Midtown New American whose open kitchen turns out Californian-Southwest preparations, while the muted tones of the space (graced with wooden beams) supply a thoroughly chic, Zen-like air; the buzz (and noise) is noticeable here, as evidenced by the trendy types who swarm.

Neo of Melaka *Malaysian*
– | – | – | M

Midtown | 1765 E. River Rd. (Campbell Ave.) | 520-299-7815 | www.neomelaka.com

It's a tossup which gets more notice at this Midtown Malaysian neophyte: the exposed ductwork and antique wood carvings of the modern decor, or the fare, which melds flavors from China, India and the Middle East; count on the staff to explain unfamiliar dishes, and if there's a wait to get a table, pass your time by checking out all the duded-up local foodies.

	FOOD	DECOR	SERVICE	COST

Tavolino Ⓢ *Italian* ▽ 25 | 16 | 23 | $33

Northwest | Safeway Shopping Ctr. | 7090 N. Oracle Rd. (Ina Rd.) | 520-531-1913

Chef-owner Massimo Tenino and wife Deborah have "their act together" at their "small" Northwest Northern Italian where each dish is "inventive without being contrived"; cognoscenti caution "Italophonies" to take heed, since the menu is "scampi"-free and "sophisticated" enough to remind some of "an upscale restaurant in Italy."

Z **Terra Cotta** *Southwestern* 22 | 23 | 21 | $37

Foothills | 3500 E. Sunrise Dr. (Campo Abierto) | 520-577-8100 | www.dineterracotta.com

This Southwestern "mainstay" in the Foothills is "better than ever", still serving up a combo of "fantastic" standards (the garlic custard appetizer is "sensuous") and newer items in a dramatic Southwestern-style building; if the disaffected denounce "uneven" food and service, others are glad to have this place around.

Ventana Room Ⓢ Ⓜ *American* 25 | 26 | 25 | $65

Foothills | Loews Ventana Canyon Resort | 7000 N. Resort Dr. (N. Kolb Rd.) | 520-615-5494 | www.ventanaroom.com

It's "no contest" crow cognoscenti who put this "spectacular" New American hotel restaurant in the Foothills at the "top of the heap" for its "breathtaking views", "impeccable service" and "artful presentations" of "fabulous" food; sure, it may be a little "stodgy" (and "expensive"), but that's part and parcel of a "first-class" experience; N.B. jackets required.

Vintabla *American* - | - | - | M

Foothills | Plaza Colonial | 2890 E. Skyline Dr. (N. Campbell Ave.) | 520-577-6210 | www.vintabla.com

For wine lovers, this stylish New American in the Foothills is a paradise, thanks to co-owner Laura Williamson (one of only 16 female Master Sommeliers in the world) and her well-edited, global inventory; naturally, the *vins* sync up with the New American fare, which is offered in a small-plates format; N.B. there's a retail and cheese market on-site.

Z **Vivace** Ⓢ *Italian* 26 | 23 | 24 | $41

Midtown | St. Philip's Plaza | 4310 N. Campbell Ave. (River Rd.) | 520-795-7221

This "charming" Midtown Northern Italian is considered an "all-around" winner by locals who point to chef-owner Daniel Scordato's "creative cooking" driven by the "finest", "freshest" ingredients; indeed, many marvel at "reasonable prices" given the "excellent quality" of the dishes (served by the "responsive staff"); P.S. alfresco dining in the "pretty courtyard" complete with fountain is "a plus."

Z **Wildflower** *American* 24 | 21 | 22 | $33

Northwest | Casas Adobes Plaza | 7037 N. Oracle Rd. (W. Ina Rd.) | 520-219-4230 | www.foxrc.com

Not just "yuppies" fly to this perennially "popular", "ultratrendy" Northwest New American, which "overcomes its strip-mall locale" with an "unbeatable combination" of "excellent", "unique" food and a "snappy", "modern" setting that features a "relaxing patio"; insiders insist it's "especially good for lunch" when the "energetic staff" may have a better chance of becoming less "flustered."

Washington, DC

	Restaurant	Cuisine
29	Inn at Little Washington	American
28	Makoto	Japanese
	Citronelle	French
	Marcel's	Belgian/French
27	Eve	American
	2941 Restaurant	American
	Ray's The Steaks	Steak
	L'Auberge Chez François	French
	Obelisk	Italian
	Le Paradou	French
	Prime Rib	Steak
	Seasons	American
26	CityZen	American
	Kinkead's	Seafood
	Palena	American
	Tosca	Italian
	Thai Square	Thai
	La Bergerie	French
	Vidalia	American
	BlackSalt	American/Seafood

OTHER NOTEWORTHY PLACES

Restaurant	Cuisine
Bebo Trattoria	Italian
Bis	French
Black's Bar & Kitchen	American
Blue Duck Tavern	American
Brasserie Beck	Belgian/French
Bread Line	Bakery
Café Atlántico	Nuevo Latino
Café du Parc	French
Central Michel Richard	American/French
Equinox	American
Farrah Olivia	American
Hook	American
Jaleo	Spanish
Johnny's Half Shell	American/Seafood
Komi	American
Pizzeria Paradiso	Pizza
Rasika	Indian
1789	American
Taberna del Alabardero	Spanish
TenPenh	Pan-Asian
Zaytinya	Mediterranean/Mideastern

	FOOD	DECOR	SERVICE	COST

Bebo Trattoria *Italian* | - | - | - | M |

Crystal City | 2250B Crystal Dr. (23rd St. S.) | Arlington | 703-412-5076 | www.robertodonna.com

With DC's Galileo closed for renovations, chef-owner Roberto Donna has set up shop in Arlington's Crystal City with this midpriced Italian located in the airy, orange-hued space that Oyamel once occupied; also making the trip are a full menu of trattoria favorites and a chic bar scene; N.B. there's a four-course, family-style brunch on Sundays.

Bis *French* | 24 | 22 | 22 | $51 |

Capitol Hill | Hotel George | 15 E St. NW (bet. New Jersey Ave. & N. Capitol St.) | Washington | 202-661-2700 | www.bistrobis.com

"All the cosmos align" at this "minimalist" Capitol Hill New French bistro with "subdued lighting, plenty of Olympians lobbying Congress", an "inventive, comforting" menu and "primo" wines; then there's the "happening" bar, "efficient service" and the anticipation that "you never know who you'll see" during any given "power lunch" or "pricey" dinner.

BlackSalt Ⓜ *American/Seafood* | 26 | 20 | 21 | $53 |

Palisades | 4883 MacArthur Blvd. NW (U St.) | Washington | 202-342-9101 | www.blacksaltrestaurant.com

The Black restaurant family's latest "winner", a fin-fare-focused New American in the Palisades, earns praise for "sophisticated and assured" creations that "explode with taste", along with a wine list of "exceptionally well-valued gems"; if you can't snag a table in the "minimalist", "noisy" dining room or the unreserved cafe, go for a "drink at the great bar", down a couple of the "freshest" oysters you've ever tasted and then pick up some "pristine" fish to cook at home.

Black's Bar & Kitchen *American* | 23 | - | 20 | $43 |

Bethesda | 7750 Woodmont Ave. (bet. Cheltenham Dr. & Old Georgetown Rd.) | 301-652-5525 | www.blacksbarandkitchen.com

Recently reopened after a floor-to-ceiling renovation, this New American from the family behind Addie's, Black Market and BlackSalt is Bethesda's "go-to place" for "terrific seafood", a "fantastic raw bar" and "plenty of choices for meat eaters"; the setting now offers lots of light, a red-tiled open kitchen, glass bifold doors and a black pebble patio with reflecting pool.

Blue Duck Tavern *American* | ▽ 26 | 25 | 21 | $63 |

West End | Park Hyatt Hotel | 1201 24th St. NW (M St.) | Washington | 202-419-6755 | www.parkwashington.hyatt.com

Every "outstandingly original" dish is "a winner" declare early fans of this "wonderful" Park Hyatt Hotel restaurant that showcases regional New American cuisine crafted by chef Brian McBride (ex Melrose); the "chic" Tony Chi–designed space boasts a "stunning" open kitchen with a cobalt-blue, state-of-the-art, wood-burning Molteni range, but the "slow" service leaves a few diners "cold."

Brasserie Beck Ⓩ *Belgian/French* | - | - | - | M |

Downtown | JBG Bldg. | 1101 K St. NW (11th St.) | Washington | 202-408-1717 | www.beckdc.com

Inspired by vintage railroad stations and his North European culinary roots, chef-owner Robert Wiedmaier's Downtown French-Belgian brasserie is done up in dark wood, white tiles and lots of mirrors; a

FOOD | DECOR | SERVICE | COST

trendy, casual alternative to sibling Marcel's, it offers a midpriced menu of steamed mussels (in multiple preparations) and hearty stews; N.B. patrons can wash it all down with some 50 wines under $50.

Bread Line ⬛ *Bakery*

| 24 | 10 | 15 | $13 |

World Bank | 1751 Pennsylvania Ave. NW (bet. 17th & 18th Sts.) | Washington | 202-822-8900

"Absolutely the best" "bread-based lunch" in town keeps this "wonderful" weekday-only bakery/cafe, "just steps from the White House", jammed; luckily, the "long lines move quickly", and loyalists, including the WH press corps, are "rewarded with the freshest, most flavorful sandwiches" on "terrific, crunchy" artesian bread (it "bites back"), "inventive" soups, "amazing salads" and "don't-miss" fries "worth every penny"; N.B. sit outside in nice weather.

Café Atlántico/Minibar *Nuevo Latino*

| 25 | 22 | 22 | $49 |

Penn Quarter | 405 Eighth St. NW (bet. D & E Sts.) | Washington | 202-393-0812 | www.cafeatlantico.com

"Phenomenal" mojitos and "mouthwatering" guacamole made tableside kick start a "mini-vacation" on this Penn Quarterite's "three levels of Caribbean fun"; its Nuevo Latino kitchen "makes cutting-edge food deliciously edible", while "terrific" pre-theater and weekend Latin dim sum keep it "affordable"; at its six-seat, reservations-only Minibar – a $120-per-person "carnival" of "art and chemistry" – "daring types" test their "bravado" on 30-plus bite-size "creations."

Café du Parc *French*

| - | - | - | M |

Downtown | Willard InterContinental Washington | 1401 Pennsylvania Ave. NW (bet. 14th & 15th Sts.) | Washington | 202-942-7000 | www.cafeduparc.com

The White House is just a bonbon's toss away from the Willard InterContinental's handsome double-decker French bistro, where the menus were designed by one of France's top toques, consulting chef Antoine Westermann; its cafe tables, overlooking Pennsylvania Avenue's Pershing Park, are an ideal perch for people-watching.

Central Michel Richard ⬛ *American/French*

| ▽ 26 | 24 | 24 | $58 |

Penn Quarter | 1001 Pennsylvania Ave. NW (11th St.) | Washington | 202-626-0015 | www.centralmichelrichard.com

At this "sleek" French–New American bistro in Penn Quarter, patrons can "experience Michel Richard's talents at a fraction [of the cost] of his more formal flagship, Citronelle", via "delicious", "interesting takes on everyday dishes" – including an "indulgent" lobster burger – along with selections from a "well-priced" wine list; although a few find it "noisy" (expect a "hot bar scene"), most praise an "attention to detail" that extends to "friendly, informed" service.

⬛ Citronelle *French*

| 28 | 25 | 26 | $88 |

(aka Michel Richard's Citronelle)

Georgetown | Latham Hotel | 3000 M St. NW (30th St.) | Washington | 202-625-2150 | www.citronelledc.com

Georgetown's "Washington monument" for "visiting dignitaries" is chef-owner Michel Richard's "extraordinary" New French, where "sterling ingredients, a sure hand and a dollop of whimsy" (try the "breakfast" dessert, a "masterwork of trompe l'oeil") make it "the best

DC has to offer"; get a table near the see-in kitchen to watch the "fun", then relax in the "lovely" modern space and be "spoiled" by an "impeccable" staff; P.S. the lofty prices match the "high caliber", but both the bar/lounge and terrace offer a more casual menu.

CityZen ⌘Ⓜ *American*   26 | 26 | 25 | $100

SW | Mandarin Oriental | 1330 Maryland Ave. SW (12th St. SW) | Washington | 202-787-6006 | www.cityzenrestaurant.com

For "New York chic" in a "government town" head to this New American "extravaganza" in the "plush" Mandarin Oriental in SW; its "sleek" look, with an open kitchen, a wall of flames in the bar and lots of steel, leather and wood, suits the "fashionable" enthusiasts of its "glorious" tasting menus, "attractive wine list" and "creative" details like the "fantastic mini–Parker House rolls"; add in a "personable" staff and you might want to remember this "flawless operation" "for birthdays and anniversaries."

Equinox *American*   25 | 20 | 23 | $63

Golden Triangle | 818 Connecticut Ave. NW (bet. H & I Sts.) | Washington | 202-331-8118 | www.equinoxrestaurant.com

Todd and Ellen Gray's "wonderful" Golden Triangle New American near the Oval Office rings "superb" to its many fans who fawn over the "highly innovative" tasting menus full of "exquisite delights" and "local flavors" paired with "tastefully chosen" wines (there are à la carte selections as well); the service is "attentive without being intrusive", and even if a few faultfinders want an "update" of the "subdued" decor, others find it amenable for "quiet" conversation.

🔤 Eve, Restaurant ⌘ *American*   27 | 24 | 25 | $71

Old Town | 110 S. Pitt St. (bet. King & Prince Sts.) | Alexandria | 703-706-0450 | www.restauranteve.com

"Save the superlatives" for this Old Town Alexandria New American "foodie paradise", where Irish-born chef-owner Cathal Armstrong's "creative insights into flavors" transform "interesting ingredients" (tripe as well as foie gras) into "mind-blowing" meals with "memorable" matches of wine; "knowledgeable" staffers "treat you like VIPs", and you can choose among its "romantic bistro", "happening bar" or tasting room where the "beautiful dance of waiters" is "worth every penny"; since "none of the many faces of Eve disappoint", she's a "tough" reservation.

Farrah Olivia Ⓜ *American*   - | - | - | E

Old Town | 600 Franklin St. (S. Washington St.) | Alexandria | 703-778-2233 | www.farraholiviarestaurant.com

This elegant Old Town Alexandria destination provides a white-tablecloth setting for distinctive New American cuisine that features influences from France and from chef-owner Morou Ouattara's native Ivory Coast; coconut-shell rings that hang from the ceiling enliven the sophisticated, neutral-toned room.

Hook *American*   - | - | - | M

Georgetown | 3241 M St. NW (bet. 33rd St. & Wisconsin Ave.) | Washington | 202-625-4488 | www.hookdc.com

Rising star chef Barton Seaver, formerly of Café Saint-Ex, has moored this midpriced New American in Cilantro's old Georgetown berth; a

| | FOOD | DECOR | SERVICE | COST |

cerulean blue space with chrome and dark-wood accents sets the stage for a menu focused on sustainable seafood and local produce, while eye candy perched along the roomy bar is yet another lure.

☑ Inn at Little Washington *American*

| 29 | 28 | 28 | $141 |

Washington | The Inn at Little Washington | 309 Middle St. (Warren Ave.), VA | 540-675-3800 | www.theinnatlittlewashington.com

"Heaven on earth" is found in the VA countryside at this "romantic" "mecca of fine dining" that scores a triple: a No. 1 rating for Food, Decor and Service; its loyalists find a "gourmand's paradise" that features the "best" New American cuisine, a setting that's a "treat for the eyes" and "choreographed" "masterful service" that makes you "feel coddled from the moment" you pull in; everything from the "exquisite" amuse-bouche to the "hilarious" "cow-shaped mooing cheese cart" "exceeds expectations" – but, of course, "perfection doesn't come cheap"; N.B. try to get a room for the night.

☑ Jaleo *Spanish*

| 23 | 20 | 19 | $33 |

Penn Quarter | 480 Seventh St. NW (E St.) | Washington | 202-628-7949 ◐
Bethesda | 7271 Woodmont Ave. (Elm St.) | 301-913-0003
Crystal City | 2250A Crystal Dr. (23rd St. S.) | Arlington | 703-413-8181
www.jaleo.com

Invite your amigos to "nibble the evening away" on "tantalizing", "imaginative" yet "authentic" Spanish tapas with "never-ending sangria to wash it all down" at this trio of "crowd-pleasers"; they're a "loud", "chaotic" "fiesta", especially if there's flamenco dancing, and they're among the "few places where 'small plate' does not equal 'large bill'"; P.S. beware of "long waits", as they take only a limited number of reservations.

Johnny's Half Shell ☒ *American/Seafood*

| – | – | – | M |

Capitol Hill | 400 N. Capitol St. NW (D St.) | Washington | 202-737-0400 | www.johnnyshalfshell.net

Having shucked its "cramped" Dupont Circle digs in favor of a spacious Capitol Hill setting, this "terrific" New American seafood bistro – now serving steaks in addition to "Gulf classics" – evokes a San Francisco oyster house with its tiled floor, marble-topped bar and wood-and-etched-glass booths; there's a see-and-be-seen terrace too, and you can expect the same "hospitable" staff; N.B. its new take-out taqueria serves up breakfast, inexpensive tacos and daily specials.

☑ Kinkead's *Seafood*

| 26 | 21 | 24 | $59 |

Foggy Bottom | 2000 Pennsylvania Ave. NW (I St.) | Washington | 202-296-7700 | www.kinkead.com

"The perfect catch" for "seafood-inside-the-Beltway power dining", Bob Kinkead's Foggy Bottom "classic", rated the DC Survey's Most Popular, "easily holds its own with newer pretenders to the throne", serving "glistening" fin fare "inventively prepared" in "classy" quarters filled with "celebs and politicos"; it has a "can't-miss location" – a "short walk from the White House" and an "easy trip" to the Kennedy Center – and while the service is generally "meticulous", it's probably "best enjoyed in the company of a VIP."

	FOOD	DECOR	SERVICE	COST

Komi ⊠Ⓜ *American* `26` `18` `24` `$53`
Dupont Circle | 1509 17th St. NW (P St.) | Washington | 202-332-9200

"So much talent in such a small place" is the story at this Dupont Circle New American where "talented" chef-owner Johnny Monis "thrills" with "fresh combinations" and "surprising ingredients" and his crew "explains each dish with such fervor that you want to try" them all; the "stylish" spot also offers a "bargain" weeknight fixed-price menu format with à la carte choices; P.S. don't skip the cheese course that offers "the stinky, the ripe and the crumbly."

La Bergerie *French* `26` `22` `25` `$55`
Old Town | 218 N. Lee St. (bet. Cameron & Queen Sts.) | Alexandria | 703-683-1007 | www.labergerie.com

"*C'est magnifique*" declare devotees of this "charming" Old Town Alexandria boîte serving "classic" French fare in a "splendid" setting with "fresh flowers and cozy banquettes" that's perfect for a "long romantic lunch"; it's "worth every penny of the bankroll you'll need" – from the "amazing Caesar salad, prepared tableside" to the "must-order" quenelles to the "best dessert soufflé in town", all served by a "solicitous staff"; P.S. don't miss the "bargain" prix fixe lunch.

L'Auberge Chez François Ⓜ *French* `27` `26` `27` `$75`
Great Falls | 332 Springvale Rd. (Beach Mill Rd.) | 703-759-3800 | www.laubergechezfrancois.com

"Special occasions" are made "memorable" at this "universally beloved" "rustic" Alsatian in a "magical" country setting in Great Falls that takes you to "pastoral" France; the "excellent" French fare is served by a staff that makes you "feel loved and taken care of" whether you're enjoying the "fireplace warmth" in winter or the garden "on a lovely summer night", so overall many find it a "top value."

Le Paradou 🅢 *French* `27` `25` `24` `$89`
Penn Quarter | 678 Indiana Ave. NW (bet. 6th & 7th Sts.) | Washington | 202-347-6780 | www.leparadou.net

"Brilliant" chef Yannick Cam "has done it again" at this "unique and exquisite" New French Penn Quarter eatery that's risen to DC's "top echelon"; the "out-of-this-world" tasting menu can be paired with bottles from an "amazing wine bible" in a "sublime setting", presided over by "professional" (if sometimes "haughty") help; devotees are surprised it's "easy to get into", but that's probably because a meal here could cost "more than your mortgage payment"; N.B. prix fixe lunch and dinner options make its luxury more affordable.

🆉 Makoto Ⓜ *Japanese* `28` `21` `27` `$65`
Palisades | 4822 MacArthur Blvd. NW (U St.) | Washington | 202-298-6866

"Take off your shoes" and time travel "back to the 19th century" when you enter this "shoebox"-size Palisades eatery, reminiscent of a Kyoto "*ryokan*" (rustic inn) that feels "more Japanese than today's Japan"; its highlights include "exquisite", "authentic" omakase meals that are "almost too pretty to eat" and "witty sushi chefs" who create "a wonderful meal at the bar"; it's just the "horrendously uncomfortable" box seats that annoy.

☑ Marcel's *Belgian/French*
28 | 24 | 27 | $73

West End | 2401 Pennsylvania Ave. NW (24th St.) | Washington | 202-296-1166 | www.marcelsdc.com

"A class act" from the "exquisitely prepared" Belgian-French fare to the "first-rate" staff to the "door-to-door" sedan service to the Kennedy Center, this West End fine-dining venue oozes ambiance; chef-owner Robert Wiedmaier's cooking, including a "wonderful" pre-theater prix fixe, "makes your heart sing" (and the cash register ring) with selections like the "best boudin blanc (sausage) in the city"; but lovers beware, when it gets "loud" it's "not the place for intimacy."

Obelisk ☑Ⓜ *Italian*
27 | 20 | 25 | $73

Dupont Circle | 2029 P St. NW (bet. 20th & 21st Sts.) | Washington | 202-872-1180

"Fanatic" chef-owner Peter Pastan "keeps you focused on the finest Italian in the city" at his "intimate" Dupont Circle space; connoisseurs swear his daily changing prix fixe menu "could pass a blind taste test" with Italy's "best", and the "unique" dishes are "prepared and served by people who clearly respect food" and want to "take very good care of you"; just remember to reserve "well in advance" if you want to "spend an evening with your true love" in this 30-seat room.

Palena ☑Ⓜ *American*
26 | 22 | 22 | $57

Cleveland Park | 3529 Connecticut Ave. NW (bet. Ordway & Porter Sts.) | Washington | 202-537-9250 | www.palenarestaurant.com

Have "a night to remember" with "all-around excellence in food, wine and service" at this "casual" Cleveland Park New American, "whether supping in the bar"/cafe or dining in the "quieter and more romantic" formal space in back; "if you can get reservations", you'll be amazed at chef-owner Frank Ruta's "superbly prepared" "twists on classics" and his "ambitious" "attention to detail" from the "house-cured" charcuterie to the "produce from his garden."

Pizzeria Paradiso *Pizza*
24 | 15 | 18 | $23

Dupont Circle | 2029 P St. NW (bet. 20th & 21st Sts.) | Washington | 202-223-1245

Georgetown | 3282 M St. NW (bet. 32nd & 33rd Sts.) | Washington | 202-337-1245

www.eatyourpizza.com

It's "pizza nirvana" at these "dressed-down" Dupont Circle and Georgetown eateries where the "slightly chewy" yet "crisp" wood-oven-baked pies come topped with the "very freshest ingredients", accompanied by "wonderful salads" and "rustic wines by the tumbler"; since they're "always bustling" with a "lock on fun with style", you should "get there early and be prepared to wait"; N.B. the Georgetown branch's cozy basement is now a birreria boasting 90-plus brews from around the world.

Prime Rib ☑ *Steak*
27 | 24 | 26 | $62

Golden Triangle | 2020 K St. NW (bet. 20th & 21st Sts.) | Washington | 202-466-8811 | www.theprimerib.com

"Classy, swanky and all dressed up", this black-lacquered "old-fashioned supper club" in Golden Triangle is the quintessential spot to celebrate anniversaries or the "close of a big deal" over "massive cuts of buttery, beefy, masculine prime rib", the "most succulent" crab and "perfect" martinis brought to table by "impeccable" tuxedoed waiters; it's still a "powerhouse scene" where "high-profile politicians" "wine and dine", but even sentimentalists think the leopard-print rug should "be retired to a '70s time capsule."

Rasika ⑤ *Indian*   26 | 26 | 23 | $46

Penn Quarter | 633 D St. NW (bet. 6th & 7th Sts.) | Washington | 202-637-1222 | www.rasikarestaurant.com

Here's a "hip" Penn Quarter Indian that's in a "class by itself" say its sophisticated fans; expect a "sexy" setting, "exemplary service", "unique" tapas influenced by street cooking (you "must have" the "crispy" deep-fried spinach appetizer) and "innovative and thoughtful wine pairings that work well with the dynamic range" of "fabulous flavors"; indeed, from the "killer" cocktails to the "delectable dishes fit for the maharajah", they "seem to be doing everything right."

Ray's The Steaks Ⓜ *Steak*   27 | 10 | 22 | $43

Courthouse | Colonial Vill. | 1725 Wilson Blvd. (bet. Quinn & Rhodes Sts.) | Arlington | 703-841-7297

Chef-owner/butcher Mike 'Ray' Landrum is "a genius with a side of cow" – and the "no-frills ambiance" at his "bare-bones" meatery in an Arlington strip mall near the Courthouse metro "keeps the price down" for "some of the best red meat you'll eat anywhere", "cooked to perfection" and complemented by a "thoughtful, gently priced wine list"; still, "come early", as they don't take reservations; N.B. expect a move to more spacious quarters in Clarendon by the end of 2007.

Seasons *American*   27 | 25 | 27 | $64

Georgetown | Four Seasons Hotel | 2800 Pennsylvania Ave. NW (28th St.) | Washington | 202-944-2000 | www.fourseasons.com

The Georgetown Four Seasons' "elegant" "high standards pay off" at its New American restaurant where the "out-of-this-world" fare, "quiet ambiance, terrific service and tables spaced so that you're not afraid to tell the person you're with what you're thinking about" draw a "diplomatic and senior policy crowd"; it's *the* business hotel in DC, so "having breakfast anywhere else before you've been elected is just plain silly", plus there's a "mind-boggling" weekend brunch.

1789 *American*   26 | 25 | 25 | $61

Georgetown | 1226 36th St. NW (Prospect St.) | Washington | 202-965-1789 | www.1789restaurant.com

"Everything" about this "elegant" Georgetowner "screams quality and class": the "excellent" seasonal New American fare, the "impeccable" service and the "classic" Federal period dining rooms favored for "romance" "by the fireplace"; the 2006 departure of longtime chef Ris Lacoste concerned loyalists, but early reports say her replacement, Nathan Beauchamp (ex Eve), has been able to "liven up the menu while still keeping true to the standards."

Taberna del Alabardero ⑤ *Spanish*   24 | 24 | 23 | $59

World Bank | 1776 I St. NW (18th St.) | Washington | 202-429-2200 | www.alabardero.com

You'll "feel like you're blocks from the Puerta del Sol, rather than the White House" at this "sumptuously decorated" bastion of "old-world

	FOOD	DECOR	SERVICE	COST

Madrid" near the World Bank, where the "excellent", "authentic" blend of "modern cuisine with Spanish tradition" means there are even some "Ferran Adrià–like" items (i.e. frozen olive oil) to try; "dress well" and experience "wonderfully civilized" cosseting that makes "special occasions" "*muy romantico*", or for a "far less expensive evening out", try the bar's half-price happy-hour tapas.

☑ TenPenh ⑤ *Pan-Asian*

24	24	23	$48

Downtown | 1001 Pennsylvania Ave. NW (10th St.) | Washington | 202-393-4500 | www.tenpenh.com

"Everyone looks beautiful" at this Downtowner and "the food is just as pretty": a "killer menu of tongue-tingling favorites" from chef Jeff Tunks "pushes the Pan-Asian envelope without straying into truly rebellious territory", and the "dramatic, colorful atmosphere" is as "stylish" as its crowd; even though pensive types pout it "gets really loud" and the "tables are too close together", seasoned vets say the "biggest problem will be getting past the appetizers" – they're the "winners."

Thai Square *Thai*

26	10	18	$22

Arlington | 3217 Columbia Pike (S. Highland St.) | 703-685-7040

"Hot means hot for a change" at this "authentic" Arlington "hole-in-the-wall" "where Thais go for Thai food"; it "doesn't put on airs, decorwise" – the "space is cramped" and service can be "surly" – but "in terms of pricing and quality" "no other place can match" the "exciting blend of texture and flavors" in the "simply wonderful" dishes.

Tosca ⑤ *Italian*

26	23	25	$59

Penn Quarter | 1112 F St. NW (bet. 11th & 12th Sts.) | Washington | 202-367-1990 | www.toscadc.com

Celebrated for "inventive modern interpretations of Northern Italian", this "understated and elegant" Penn Quarterite is set in a "serene, monochromatic" space that's usually "buzzing with 'heavy hitters'"; it "always lives up" to "expectations of the highest quality in food and service" with "amazing dishes and beautiful presentations", but it can be a "somewhat expensive date" unless you opt for the "absolute steal" $35 pre-theater three-course dinner.

2941 Restaurant *American*

27	28	25	$77

Falls Church | 2941 Fairview Park Dr. (Arlington Blvd.) | 703-270-1500 | www.2941.com

"Manhattan meets the Beltway in this surprisingly sophisticated suburban enclave" set in a Falls Church office park, where "wonderful" French-inflected New American is served in "gorgeous" tall-windowed dining rooms overlooking koi ponds and waterfalls; chef-owner Jonathan Krinn "architects flavors masterfully", pairs them "excellently" with wines and has them served by a "gracious, pampering" staff; but with all those "generous" end-of-meal goodies (chocolates, cotton candy), you'll wonder "does 2941 refer to the bill or the calories from the extra desserts?"

Vidalia *American*

26	22	24	$58

Golden Triangle | 1990 M St. NW (bet. 19th & 20th Sts.) | Washington | 202-659-1990 | www.vidaliadc.com

"It has its off nights, but when it's 'on'", this Golden Triangle "destination" "really delivers" via a "delicious, innovative" New American menu with "an upscale Southern touch"; the "ambrosial fare" is served by a "gracious" staff that provides "VIP treatment" and "excellent wine matches" in a "lovely" underground setting "made brighter" by a "beautiful remodeling"; there's also a "stylish bar" suitable for sampling small plates or one of the 40 "well-researched" vinos by the glass.

☑ Zaytinya ◑ *Mediterranean/Mideastern*   25 | 25 | 20 | $39

Penn Quarter | Pepco Bldg. | 701 Ninth St. NW (G St.) | Washington | 202-638-0800 | www.zaytinya.com

"Stunning, sleek white walls provide a dramatic background for a buzzing crowd" at this "fabulous" "fast-paced" Penn Quarter "meze heaven" where an "epic menu" of Med–Middle Eastern (Turkish, Greek and Lebanese) "unique" small plates encourages "sharing", and a "knowledgeable staff keeps it from being overwhelming"; its "divine" "big-city atmosphere" (one of the "best-looking restaurants in town"), "excellent" prices and limited reservations can make "tables hard to come by."

Westchester/Hudson Valley

Restaurant	Cuisine
29] Xaviar's at Piermont	American
28] Freelance Café	American
27] Blue Hill/Stone Barns	American
Rest. X/Bully	American
Aroma Osteria	Italian
Ocean House	New England/Seafood
La Panetière	French
La Crémaillère	French
Iron Horse Grill	American
Le Pavillon	French
Il Cenàcolo	Italian
Azuma Sushi	Japanese
Wasabi	Japanese
26] Caterina de Medici	Italian
Il Barilotto	Italian
American Bounty	American
Coromandel	Indian
Equus	American/French
Escoffier, The	French
Busy Bee	American

OTHER NOTEWORTHY PLACES

Arch	Eclectic
Beso	Eclectic
Bloom	American
Buffet de la Gare	French
Crabtree's	American
DePuy Canal House	American
French Corner	French
Harvest on Hudson	Mediterranean
Mulino's	Italian
One	American
Plates	American
Relish	American/Eclectic
Sabroso	Nuevo Latino/Spanish
Serevan	Mediterranean
Sonora	Nuevo Latino
Sushi Nanase	Japanese
Swoon Kitchenbar	American
Terrapin	American
Twist	American
X2O Xaviars/Hudson	American/Seafood

	FOOD	DECOR	SERVICE	COST

American Bounty
Restaurant 🗷Ⓜ *American*   26 | 24 | 23 | $48

Hyde Park | Culinary Institute of America | 1946 Campus Dr. (Rte. 9) |
845-471-6608 | www.ciachef.edu

A "superb" menu of "delicious" New American fare featuring "high-quality local ingredients" is "tuned in" rather than "trendy" say fans of this Hyde Park cooking school restaurant, where the "blossoming chefs" earn top marks; the "elegant", "peaceful" room exudes a "lovely ambiance", and if service is "a bit bumpy", be patient, it might be "a student's first day" – "they're really out to please"; "all in all, it's a bargain" for such "outstanding" "four-star quality."

Arch Ⓜ *Eclectic*   25 | 24 | 25 | $69

Brewster | 1296 Rte. 22 (end of I-684) | 845-279-5011 |
www.archrestaurant.com

"Top-notch" Eclectic fare and "sublime desserts" served by a "caring" staff in "romantic", "gorgeous surroundings" add up to "elegant country hospitality" at this venerable, tucked-away Brewster "treasure"; yes, it's "expensive" (though "not too pricey for brunch") but it's a "wonderful special-occasion" spot "worth traveling for"; N.B. jackets required at dinner.

🗷 Aroma Osteria Ⓜ *Italian*   27 | 25 | 24 | $46

Wappingers Falls | 114 Old Post Rd. (Rte. 9) | 845-298-6790 |
www.aromaosteriarestaurant.com

"Fantastic" Italian food and a "top-notch" wine list featuring "some small vineyards" add up to "fine dining at its best" proclaim patrons of chef-owner Eduardo Lauria's Wappingers Falls "gem"; spacious Tuscan-style digs featuring textured walls, wrought-iron accents and a waterfall are deemed "classy yet warm" and service "attentive", so "the only drawback" "could be the noise level" when things get "hectic" – just "bring earplugs" along with "a hearty appetite."

Azuma Sushi Ⓜ *Japanese*   27 | 14 | 21 | $44

Hartsdale | 219 E. Hartsdale Ave. (bet. Bronx River Pkwy. &
Central Park Ave.) | 914-725-0660

"Impeccable" "Tokyo-style sushi" for the "serious" "purist" is what you'll find at this "costly" Hartsdale Japanese where "nothing is cooked" and "they do one thing, and they do it great"; "don't bring the kids" as there are "no crazy rolls or funny chefs", and while a few surveyors carp about the "boring" "all-white" decor, "cramped tables" and occasional "attitude" from the staff, it's a restaurant that "separates itself from the pack" and is a "legit" contender for the "best" raw fish in Westchester.

Beso *Eclectic*   25 | 20 | 21 | $46

New Paltz | 46 Main St. (Chestnut St.) | 845-255-1426

At this "terrific" two-year-old New Paltz Eclectic, chef Chad Greer's "excellent", "sophisticated" dishes, prepared with an emphasis on "local ingredients", are bested only by wife Tammy Ogletree's "decadent desserts"; seating in the "pleasant" two-story skylit space may be a little "cramped" but the "atmosphere's relaxing", and if tabs are a touch "expensive for the area", that (and "professional service") just adds to the "Manhattan feel."

FOOD   DECOR   SERVICE   COST

Bloom *American* ▽ 21 | 21 | 20 | $51

Hastings-on-Hudson | 19 Main St. (Warburton Ave.) | 914-478-3250 |
www.bloom-restaurant.com

Eco-happy eaters flock to this "promising" Hastings newcomer where
the "creative" New American menu is prepared with organic ingredients
and complemented by a selection of biodynamic wines; "quiet" and
"comfortable" earth-toned digs and a staff that "tries hard" smooth
the sting of "high" prices.

🅉 Blue Hill at Stone Barns 🅜 *American* 27 | 28 | 27 | $84

Pocantico Hills | Stone Barns Ctr. | 630 Bedford Rd. (Lake Rd.) |
914-366-9600 | www.bluehillfarm.com

A "stunning" "conduit from earth to table", Dan Barber's Pocantico
Hills New American (ranked No. 1 for Popularity in Westchester/HV)
showcases "ultrafresh" ingredients grown "on a former Rockefeller es-
tate" in "heavenly" (and "pricey") prix fixe meals "creatively" served
in a converted barn that's the picture of "unstuffy elegance"; though
"hard to get" a reservation, most urge "go at least once" to experience
"what food is meant to be."

Buffet de la Gare 🅜 *French* 26 | 21 | 24 | $61

Hastings-on-Hudson | 155 Southside Ave. (Spring St.) | 914-478-1671 |
www.buffetdelagare.us

"Homesick French gourmets" head to this Hastings "jewel" where
"charming" new owners Luc and Nicole Dimnet "are upholding the tradition" of "consistently sublime" "classic bistro fare" including "magnificent cassoulet" and escargots; decor is "quaint" and "warm" as ever with
a pressed tin ceiling and 100-year-old oak bar, and if prices are a bit
"haute" for some, it's "worth every penny."

Busy Bee Cafe 🅔 *American* 26 | 17 | 23 | $36

Poughkeepsie | 138 South Ave. (Reade Pl.) | 845-452-6800

Buzz has it that "wonderful", "always delicious" New American food
has patrons "licking the plate clean" at this Poughkeepsie cafe set in a
modest residential area; it's sometimes "tough to get a table" in the
"tiny" "cute" room that, despite a remodel, doesn't quite disguise "the
deli it used to be", although "welcoming service" more than makes up
for that, as do monthly "supper club"-style jazz nights.

Caterina de Medici 🅔 *Italian* 26 | 25 | 24 | $49

Hyde Park | Culinary Institute of America | 1946 Campus Dr. (Rte. 9) |
845-471-6608 | www.ciachef.edu

Budding chefs and "adorable" "student personnel" deliver a "phenomenal experience" at this "preeminent" Hyde Park cooking school restaurant, turning out "fabulous" "Italian classics that acknowledge the
change of seasons", "elegantly presented" in a "very pretty" chandeliered "Tuscanesque" space where "no decorative cliché is left out"; as
for service, you'll get the "royal treatment" even if you opt for more casual dining in the Al Forno room overlooking the kitchen.

Coromandel *Indian* 26 | 17 | 21 | $33

New Rochelle | 30 Division St. (bet. Huguenot & Main Sts.) | 914-235-8390 |
www.coromandelcuisine.com

"Bring on the heat!" boast boosters of this "top-rated" subcontinental
in New Rochelle offering "wonderful regional selections" that appeal

to "both Indian émigrés and the hair-band set"; the "outstanding cuisine and impeccable service are marred only by decor that seems not to have changed since the Moghuls ruled Delhi"; N.B. proponents particularly praise the all-you-can-eat lunch buffets.

☑ Crabtree's Kittle House *American* | 24 | 23 | 23 | $60 |

Chappaqua | Crabtree's Kittle House Inn | 11 Kittle Rd. (Rte. 117) | 914-666-8044 | www.kittlehouse.com

For "special occasions" or a "secret rendezvous", you can't go wrong at this "sophisticated" Chappaqua country inn where "delectable", if not "overly exciting", New American cuisine is served by a "gracious" staff and "knowledgeable sommeliers" guide you through a "world-class" wine list the size of "a phone book"; "bucolic views" of "beautiful trees" and an English garden enhance the experience, and while a few detractors say service is "sometimes off" and find the 19th-century-style decor "dowdy", most agree it's worth the "splurge."

DePuy Canal House ☒ *American* | 25 | 25 | 22 | $62 |

High Falls | 1315 Rte. 213 (Lucas Tpke.) | 845-687-7700 | www.depuycanalhouse.net

"Still the grand old lady of Hudson Valley dining", this High Falls New American set in a "charming" stone Colonial house "retains the cuisine of high camp it grew famous for", with chef-owner John Novi's "original, creative" dishes declared "delectable" as ever; yes, it's "extravagant", but "unobtrusive service" and "ridiculously romantic" rooms furnished in period style make it perfect "to celebrate a red-letter occasion."

Equus *American/French* | 26 | 28 | 25 | $78 |

Tarrytown | Castle on the Hudson | 400 Benedict Ave. (bet. Maple St. & Martling Ave.) | 914-631-3646 | www.castleonthehudson.com

It's no surprise surveyors vote this "posh" New American–French restaurant in Tarrytown No. 1 for Decor this year considering the "otherworldly" setting within a "beautiful" 1897 stone castle on a hill with "gorgeous sweeping views" of the Hudson River and three dining rooms (Garden Room, Oak Room, Tapestry Room), each "elegant" in its own way; the cuisine is "divine" as well, so "don a jacket", "bring a fat wallet" and prepare to be "meticulously doted upon" and made to feel "like a baron" in some "fairy tale."

Escoffier, The ☒☒ *French* | 26 | 24 | 25 | $56 |

Hyde Park | Culinary Institute of America | 1946 Campus Dr. (Rte. 9) | 845-471-6608 | www.ciachef.edu

"Escoffier must be proud" of the chefs-to-be "trying hard to live up to the name" at this Hyde Park culinary school's "bastion of French haute cuisine"; "delicious" fare, a "beautiful", "sedate" setting and "classical service" delivered with an "abundance of grace and enthusiasm" all elicit "one word: superb", and though "booking ahead is a pain" and "prices high", "a table near the kitchen" is as good as "dinner theater"; "the Washington CIA should do as well."

☑ Freelance Café & Wine Bar ☒ *American* | 28 | 21 | 26 | $50 |

Piermont | 506 Piermont Ave. (Gerhardt Strasse St.) | 845-365-3250 | www.xaviars.com

"Heavenly" New American dishes "graciously served despite all the hustle and bustle" make this Piermont "lower-cost sister" to "tonier

Xavier's next door" "simply outstanding" sigh the smitten; thanks to "extraordinarily pleasant" "host Ned Kelly", it "feels like family, only cooler" in the "upscale yet casual" "closet of a bistro", but no reservations mean the "challenge is getting in", so "go early" or "during the week"; "you won't be disappointed" – "hip food, hip wine, hip people, hip-hip hooray!"

French Corner 🅼 French
25 | 21 | 22 | $46

Stone Ridge | 3407 Cooper St./Rte. 213 W. (Rte. 209) | 845-687-0810 | www.frcorner.com

"Adventurous" chef Jacques Qualin and front-of-house spouse Leslie Flam "run a smooth operation" at this Stone Ridge boîte, delivering "wonderful", "genuine" French dishes you can "select with a blindfold and not go wrong"; all come "served politely" in a "delightful" room with "lovely lighting", so even though it's "upscale for the nabe", it's "worth the money", especially if you go for the $28 prix fixe.

🆉 Harvest on Hudson Mediterranean
22 | 26 | 21 | $52

Hastings-on-Hudson | 1 River St. (W. Main St. off Southside Ave.) | 914-478-2800 | www.harvest2000.com

A "rare combination" of "spectacular" setting and "culinary excellence", this "enchanting" Hastings Med overlooking the Hudson turns out a "consistently delicious" "harvest of flavors" thanks to "fresh-picked" herbs and vegetables "grown on the property"; a few insist the fare and service can be "inconsistent", but most devotees declare the "transporting" Tuscan feel in the high-ceilinged interior works for "group" dinners or "romantic" escapades alike.

Il Barilotto 🆉 Italian
26 | 23 | 23 | $43

Fishkill | 1113 Main St. (North St.) | 845-897-4300 | www.ilbarilottorestaurant.com

"Don't go expecting" "typical" Italian food at Fishkill's "outstanding" sister to Aroma Osteria, because "innovative" is the word, with a "top-quality" "rustic" menu "surpassed" only by "fantastic" specials – and there's an "extensive list" of vinos "to boot"; "large, well-spaced tables" help create a "contemporary wine bar look" in the "intimate" space, and "professional" "service is always there when needed", so apart from "deafening acoustics", it's "a hit" all around.

Il Cenàcolo Italian
27 | 22 | 23 | $56

Newburgh | 228 S. Plank Rd./Rte. 52 (bet. I-87 & Rte. 300) | 845-564-4494 | www.ilcenacolorestaurant.com

"Sublime" swoon fans at this "middle-of-nowhere" Newburgh Northern Italian that "lives up to its reputation" with "unbelievable" dishes, a "zillion specials, each better than the next", and an "amazing wine list"; it "looks like an abandoned bowling alley", but inside, "softly lit", Tuscan-style decor (complete with hanging copper pots and temptingly laid-out antipasti) is enhanced by "gracious" service, so though tabs may trigger "sticker shock", it's "fabulous", and "well worth it."

Iron Horse Grill 🆉🅼 American
27 | 22 | 25 | $56

Pleasantville | 20 Wheeler Ave. (Manville Rd.) | 914-741-0717 | www.ironhorsegrill.com

"Gracious" as both a host and a chef, Philip McGrath "pampers" his customers with "memorable", "beautifully presented" New American

FOOD DECOR SERVICE COST

cuisine at his "elegant" Pleasantville "destination" set in a converted 1904 railway station where "attentive service" "makes everyone feel special"; the "small", high-ceilinged room is "convivial", though "noisy", and even if prices run "high", the "incredible" flavor "combinations" have most everyone exclaiming that "more restaurants should be like this."

La Crémaillère ☒ *French*   27 | 26 | 25 | $75

Bedford | 46 Bedford-Banksville Rd. (Round House Rd.) | 914-234-9647 | www.cremaillere.com

Feel like a "European noble" and experience "old-world elegance" at this "romantic" Bedford French located in an "undeniably beautiful" 1750 converted farmhouse where "scrumptious" meals are served by a "knowledgeable", "gracious" staff; a few detractors declare it "overwrought" and "stuffy" (jackets are required), but they're drowned out by the majority that maintains it's "earned its reputation" as one of "the best" "splurges" "every season" of "every year."

La Panetière *French*   27 | 27 | 26 | $78

Rye | 530 Milton Rd. (Oakland Beach Ave.) | 914-967-8140 | www.lapanetiere.com

"When you can't get to Paris", a "remarkable meal" awaits at this Rye "grandmother of elegant French restaurants" that's "beautifully furnished" to resemble a Provençal country inn; owner Jacques Loupiac "oversees every detail", from the staff that "caters to every whim" to the "superb" fare and "voluminous" wine list; N.B. jacket required.

Le Pavillon ☒☒ *French*   27 | 23 | 24 | $45

Poughkeepsie | 230 Salt Point Tpke./Rte. 115 (bet. Bedell Rd. & N. Grand Ave.) | 845-473-2525 | www.lepavillonrestaurant.com

For the "best coq au vin", the "crispest, most succulent duck this side of Normandy" and other "perfect" "classic French fare of the *grandmère* variety", Poughkeepsie denizens head out to chef-owner Claude Guermont's tucked away "longtime favorite"; the "romantic" "country house" setting is "still elegant after all these years" and the staff "lovely", making this "genuine" experience "worth a drive", no matter how "long."

Mulino's of Westchester ☒☒ *Italian*   24 | 24 | 24 | $60

White Plains | 99 Court St. (Quarropas St.) | 914-761-1818 | www.mulinos.us

"If you want to be pampered" "in a *Godfather* setting", book a reservation at this "gorgeous" "old-time" Italian in White Plains known for "generous portions" of "superb" food, "excellent" wines and "top-notch" service that "makes you feel special" (the "gratis antipasto" is a "great touch"); in all, it sets "the standard" "for special-occasion" dining – just "make sure someone else is picking up the check"; N.B. the Christmas decor in the garden is legendary.

Ocean House ☒☒ *New England/Seafood*   27 | 17 | 23 | $41

Croton-on-Hudson | 49 N. Riverside Ave. (Rte. 9A) | 914-271-0702

The "cozy" "Cape Cod" setting suits this "boutique" New England-style seafooder set in a "nautical-themed" renovated diner in Croton-on-Hudson where chef-owner Brian Galvin and his wife, Paula, "couldn't be friendlier" and their "lovingly prepared" cuisine is "consistently" "enjoyable"; it's "worth the wait" "again and again", but be advised there are "no reservations" and it's "BYOB", so "arrive early" with bottle in hand.

One *American* ▽ 27 | 24 | 24 | $58

Irvington | 1 Bridge St. (bet. N. Buckhout & River Sts.) | 914-591-2233
The owners of River City Grille up the street have warmed up the roomy bar and "pretty" dining room of the former Solera space for this expensive Irvington newcomer catering to "Westchester foodies" with New American and raw-bar selections; while few surveyors have found it so far, those who have seem smitten with this "welcome addition" to the "Hudson River scene."

Plates Ⓜ *American* 24 | 20 | 19 | $56

Larchmont | 121 Myrtle Blvd. (Maple St.) | 914-834-1244 | www.platesonthepark.com
"Amiable chef-owner" Matthew Karp serves up "absolutely fantastic" "unusual" fare with a "personal touch" at this Larchmont New American "yuppie hangout" set in a converted landmark building that has "all the style of a city restaurant" while retaining the "charm" of a small town; despite "flawed" service and "small portions" that are deemed "expensive", it remains a "cute, bright spot" in the local dining scene and one that's certainly "different for Westchester."

Relish Ⓜ *American/Eclectic* 25 | 16 | 21 | $50

Sparkill | 4 Depot Sq. (Main St.) | 845-398-2747 | www.relishsparkill.com
Once you discover this "amazing" American-Eclectic in not-yet-chic Sparkill, "you'll go back again and again" declare devotees, citing the "care taken with each course" on the "novel" menu, the "excellent" wine list and "effective team of staffers"; colorful recycled school chairs and plywood banquettes in the "tiny" onetime grocery store add up to a "cool", "downtown" setting that "doesn't have the flash" of some famous neighbors, but not many mind because it's all "super"; N.B. the Food score may not reflect a post-Survey chef change.

Ⓩ Restaurant X & 27 | 26 | 26 | $58
Bully Boy Bar Ⓜ *American*

Congers | 117 Rte. 303 (bet. Lake Rd. & Rte. 9W) | 845-268-6555 | www.xaviars.com
"More casual" than his flagship Xaviar's, this Congers New American is still just "what you'd expect from Peter Kelly": "lovingly prepared", "top-rate" dishes, a "well-trained", "highly professional" staff and "tastefully decorated" rooms in a "picturesque setting"; "while a bit pricey", all the "extra touches" mean "you really don't feel it", especially if you "indulge in glorious excess" at the "magnifico", "all-you-can-eat" Sunday brunch or go for the $20.07 prix fixe lunch; it's all "consistently superior" "and then some."

Sabroso *Nuevo Latino/Spanish* ▽ 26 | 22 | 23 | $45

Rhinebeck | 22 Garden St. (W. Market St./Rte. 308) | 845-876-8688 | www.sabrosoplatos.com
"Perfectly delicious", "spot-on" Spanish and "imaginative" Nuevo Latino dishes come "beautifully presented" (like "the fish standing up") at this Rhinebeck two-year-old set "a wee bit off the main street"; the "food is exciting" for sure, but the vibe in the "very attractive" room is "soothing" and "calm" even when the crowd's indulging in

"awesome margaritas", leading local sophisticates to "linger for hours" attended by the "welcoming" staff.

Serevan *Mediterranean*

25 | 20 | 23 | $47

Amenia | 6 Autumn Ln. (Rte. 44, west of Rte. 22) | 845-373-9800 | www.serevan.com

"A master at flavor and texture", "ambitious" chef Serge Madikians honed his skills at swank NYC spots like Jean Georges and Bouley, then headed to Amenia to open this "great addition to the area"; a simple sage-and-slate-blue "farmhouse setting" forms a backdrop for "imaginative", "delicious" Mediterranean dishes that reflect his Armenian heritage, all served by "an expert staff."

Sonora *Nuevo Latino*

25 | 22 | 21 | $47

Port Chester | 179 Rectory St. (Willett Ave.) | 914-933-0200 | www.sonorany.com

"Brilliant", "well-presented" Nuevo Latino fare and "killer cocktails" make dinner at "fantastically creative" chef Rafael Palomino's "off-the-beaten-path" Port Chester restaurant (sister to Pacifico) like a "sophisticated" "vacation in South America"; it's a "festive" "new favorite" for "special occasions", and if the dining room is occasionally "too noisy", "start with the biggest mojito you can get" and you may not care.

Sushi Nanase *Japanese*

▽ 28 | 14 | 20 | $65

White Plains | 522 Mamaroneck Ave. (DeKalb Ave.) | 914-285-5351 | www.sushinanase.com

The chef-owner at this "tiny" "no-frills" Japanese "inn" in White Plains may strike some as "fussy", but come here for "nothing else" but "exquisite" sushi "delicately" prepared with "special touches" and you'll be in "heaven"; many find it "exorbitantly overpriced" with a $30 minimum per person, but keep in mind "your dinner was in Japan 18 hours earlier", so if "it feels like you're paying to fly in your meals, you are!"

Swoon Kitchenbar *American*

24 | 20 | 20 | $40

Hudson | 340 Warren St. (bet. 3rd & 4th Sts.) | 518-822-8938 | www.swoonkitchenbar.com

"Sounds like a silly name" until you taste the "sumptuous" fare coo Columbia County's "'in' crowd", "swooning" over chef-owner Jeffrey Gimmel's "first-class" New American food and spouse Nina's desserts "beyond your wildest dreams"; there's plenty of "studied elegance" and "arty flair" in the "fabulously lit", flower-bedecked Hudson space, so the one flaw is sometimes "haphazard service" from a "staff that could stand some coaching."

Terrapin *American*

24 | 23 | 20 | $43

Rhinebeck | 6426 Montgomery St./Rte. 9 (Livingston St.) | 845-876-3330 | www.terrapinrestaurant.com

"Once a church, now a sanctuary for gourmands", chef Josh Kroner's "delightful" Rhinebeck two-fer packs in "hip locals and touristas" for "heavenly" New American on the "lovely" "tablecloth side" or "snazzy choices" like "inventive tapas" and "choose-your-own sandwiches" in the "terrific", "bargain" bistro; though service is "hit-or-miss", the "staff looks good" and so does the food: "you can almost hear the hosannas when the beautiful dishes arrive."

Twist 🏷️Ⓜ *American*

25 | 18 | 23 | $42

Hyde Park | 4290 Albany Post Rd. (Pine Woods Rd.) | 845-229-7094 | www.letstwist.com

It can be "tough to snag a table" at this "fabulous" Hyde Park New American, where "talented" chef-owner Benjamin Mauk "lives up to" his reputation with "original presentations" of "superb" food; an "unusual menu format" lets you "choose sides" and meat portion size, pleasing "large or small appetites", so add "marvelous service" and a colorful space that offsets the "dubious strip-mall" locale, and no wonder this is a "favorite new-ish" spot.

Wasabi *Japanese*

27 | 24 | 22 | $51

Nyack | 110 Main St. (Park St.) | 845-358-7977 | www.wasabinyack.com

"All the beautiful people of Nyack go to be seen" at this "upscale", "jumping Japanese" dubbed "Nobu north", where chef-owner Doug Nguyen is "a master artist" proffering "perfectly sculpted" "pristine sushi" and sashimi, "phenomenal ceviche" and such "unusual" dishes that the "entire menu is a treasure"; "chic" modern decor sets a "cool" vibe, but "Manhattan prices" can "sting", so it's even more enjoyable "if someone else is paying."

🏅 Xaviar's at Piermont Ⓜ *American*

29 | 25 | 27 | $79

Piermont | 506 Piermont Ave. (Ash St.) | 845-359-7007 | www.xaviars.com

It's "the epitome of excellence" swoon smitten surveyors voting "brilliant" chef Peter Kelly's Piermont New American No. 1 for Food and Service in Westchester/Hudson Valley; "glorious" cuisine, "magnificent presentation", a "thoroughly professional staff" and "marked attention to detail" including "impeccable tableware" in the "teensy", "pretty" room add up to something "memorable", so never mind the "hefty price tag" ($70 prix fixe, $38 for lunch), "put on your best" duds, and "be a king or queen for an evening"; even with the cash-only (or Amex) policy and "parking hassle", "it's worth it all."

X2O Xaviars on the Hudson Ⓜ *American/Seafood*

- | - | - | E

Yonkers | Historic Yonkers Pier | 71 Water Grant St. (Buena Vista Ave.) | 914-965-1111 | www.xaviars.com

Iron Chef winner Peter X. Kelly (whose three other restaurants are among the top five for Food in Westchester) has opened this New American situated on the historic pier in the burgeoning Yonkers waterfront district, where the chef offers two distinct dining options: table seating in the main dining area, with a 25-ft. vaulted ceiling and three walls of glass, and a more casual lounge featuring a sushi bar and a small-plates menu; panoramic views of the Hudson River and Palisades give sightseers plenty to cheer about.

CUISINES BY AREA
INDEX

Cuisines by Area

Includes restaurant names and Food ratings. ⊠ indicates places with the highest ratings, popularity and importance.

ATLANTA

AMERICAN (NEW)
⊠ Aria	27
⊠ Bacchanalia	29
BluePointe	24
Canoe	25
French Am. Brasserie	–
Muss & Turner's	25
ONE. midtown	21
Park 75	27
⊠ Quinones	28
⊠ Rathbun's	28
Restaurant Eugene	26
Shaun's	–
TAP	–

ASIAN
Sia's	26

CALIFORNIAN
Woodfire Grill	24

CONTINENTAL
Ecco	–

DELIS
Muss & Turner's	25

DESSERT
⊠ Aria	27

FRENCH
Floataway	26
JOËL	26

FRENCH (BRASSERIE)
French Am. Brasserie	–

FRENCH (NEW)
⊠ Ritz/Buckhead Din. Rm.	28
Trois	–

GASTROPUB
TAP	Amer.	–

GREEK
Kyma	25

INDIAN
Madras Saravana	26

ITALIAN
(N=Northern)
Antica Posta	N	24
di Paolo	N	27
Floataway	26
La Grotta	N	26
Sotto Sotto	N	26

JAPANESE
(* sushi specialist)
MF Sushibar*	26
Taka*	26

MEDITERRANEAN
⊠ Ritz/Buckhead Din. Rm.	28

PAN-ASIAN
Eurasia Bistro	25

PAN-LATIN
Tierra	25

SEAFOOD
Atlanta Fish	23
⊠ Chops/Lobster	26
Kyma	25

SMALL PLATES
Ecco	Continental	–
Muss & Turner's	Amer.	25

SOUTHERN
South City	24
Watershed	25

SOUTHWESTERN
Georgia Grille	24
Sia's	26

STEAKHOUSES
⊠ Bone's	27
⊠ Chops/Lobster	26
McKendrick's	26
New York Prime	26

THAI
Nan Thai · 26
Tamarind Seed · 27

VEGETARIAN
Madras Saravana · 26

ATLANTIC CITY

AMERICAN (NEW)
Wolfgang Puck/Grille · 23

CHINESE
☒ P.F. Chang's · 21

ITALIAN
☒ Chef Vola's · 26
☒ Mia · 26
Ombra · 25
Specchio · 25

SANDWICHES
☒ White House · 27

SEAFOOD
☒ Dock's Oyster · 26
☒ SeaBlue · 27

STEAKHOUSES
☒ Old Homestead · 25

AUSTIN

AMERICAN (NEW)
Driskill Grill · 27
☒ Hudson's · 28
Jasper's · -
☒ Jeffrey's · 27
Mirabelle · 27
Starlite · 25
☒ Wink · 28
Zoot · 26

BARBECUE
☒ Salt Lick · 25

ECLECTIC
Bess · -

FRENCH
Aquarelle · 27

ITALIAN
Cibo · -
☒ Vespaio · 28

JAPANESE
(* sushi specialist)
☒ Musashino Sushi* · 27
☒ Uchi* · 26

MEDITERRANEAN
Fino · 23

MEXICAN
Fonda San Miguel · 27

SEAFOOD
☒ Eddie V's · 25
TRIO · -

SMALL PLATES
Fino | Med. · 23

STEAKHOUSES
☒ Eddie V's · 25
TRIO · -

TEX-MEX
☒ Chuy's · 21

BALTIMORE/ANNAPOLIS

AFGHAN
Helmand · 26

AMERICAN (NEW)
Chameleon Cafe · 26
☒ Charleston · 27
Corks · 25
Linwoods · 26
☒ Peter's Inn · 27

AMERICAN (TRADITIONAL)
☒ Clyde's · 18

CRAB HOUSES
Mr. Bill's Terrace Inn · 24

ECLECTIC
Bicycle, The · -

FRENCH
Tersiguel's · 27

GREEK
☒ Samos · 27

HAMBURGERS
☒ Clyde's · 18

ITALIAN
(N=Northern)

Boccaccio | N	25
Pazza Luna | N	–

JAPANESE
(* sushi specialist)

☒ Joss Cafe/Sushi*	28
☒ Sushi Sono*	28

MEXICAN

Mari Luna	27

PUB FOOD

☒ Clyde's	18

SEAFOOD

☒ McCormick & Schmick's	21
Mr. Bill's Terrace Inn	24
O'Learys	26

SMALL PLATES

☒ Charleston | Amer.	27

STEAKHOUSES

☒ Prime Rib	27
☒ Ruth's Chris	24

THAI

Lemongrass	27

BOSTON

AFGHAN

Helmand	27

AMERICAN (NEW)

Franklin Café	24
Locke-Ober	24
Meritage	26
Sage	26
Salts	26
Ten Tables	26

AMERICAN (TRADITIONAL)

Eastern Standard	21
Oak Room	24

ASIAN FUSION

☒ Blue Ginger	27

BARBECUE

East Coast Grill	26

CONTINENTAL

Locke-Ober	24

EUROPEAN

Eastern Standard	21
Ten Tables	26

FRENCH

Butcher Shop	24
Mistral	27
☒ No. 9 Park	27
Salts	26

FRENCH (BISTRO)

Coriander Bistro	27
Craigie Street Bistrot	27
☒ Hamersley's Bistro	26
Petit Robert Bistro	23
Pigalle	25

FRENCH (NEW)

☒ Aujourd'hui	27
☒ Clio/Uni	28
☒ L'Espalier	28
Lumière	27

ITALIAN
(N=Northern; S=Southern)

Butcher Shop	24
Il Capriccio | N	26
La Campania	27
☒ No. 9 Park	27
Rialto	26
Sage	26
Saporito's | N	27
Sorellina	25
Sweet Basil	27
Taranta | S	25
Zabaglione	27

JAPANESE
(* sushi specialist)

☒ Oishii*	28
o ya*	–

MEDITERRANEAN

Mistral	27
Oleana	27
Rendezvous	26

NORTH AFRICAN	
Baraka Cafe	24
PERUVIAN	
Taranta	25
SEAFOOD	
East Coast Grill	26
☑ Legal Sea Foods	22
Neptune Oyster	26
SMALL PLATES	
Meritage | Amer.	26
SPANISH	
(* tapas specialist)	
Taberna de Haro*	25
Toro*	25
STEAKHOUSES	
Oak Room	24

CHARLOTTE

AMERICAN (NEW)	
☑ Barrington's	29
☑ Bonterra	25
Carpe Diem	26
Customshop	–
Sonoma	24
ASIAN FUSION	
Restaurant i	–
ECLECTIC	
Noble's	26
FRENCH	
Lulu	–
FRENCH (NEW)	
Zebra	25
GREEK	
ilios noche	24
ITALIAN	
(N=Northern)	
Fiamma | N	–
ilios noche	24
Luce	26
Toscana | N	26
☑ Volare	28
JAPANESE	
(* sushi specialist)	
☑ Nikko*	26

MEDITERRANEAN	
Lulu	–
SEAFOOD	
☑ McIntosh's	27
☑ Upstream	26
STEAKHOUSES	
☑ McIntosh's	27
☑ Mickey & Mooch	23
☑ Palm	24
☑ Sullivan's	27

CHICAGO

AMERICAN (NEW)	
Aigre Doux	–
☑ Alinea	28
Blackbird	27
BOKA	23
☑ Charlie Trotter's	27
Courtright's	26
Gage	–
mk	26
Naha	26
Niche	–
North Pond	25
Sepia	–
Spring	27
Vie	27
AMERICAN (TRADITIONAL)	
☑ Wildfire	23
FRENCH (BISTRO)	
Barrington Country	27
FRENCH (NEW)	
Avenues	26
☑ Carlos'	29
Everest	27
☑ Les Nomades	28
NoMI	26
Oceanique	27
one sixtyblue	25
☑ Tallgrass	28
☑ Tru	28
ITALIAN	
Osteria di Tramonto	–
Spiaggia	26

CUISINES

SOUTHWESTERN
Telluride 24

SPANISH
(* tapas specialist)
Ⓩ Barcelona* 22
Ⓩ Ibiza 28
Meigas* 26

STEAKHOUSES
Max Downtown 27
Morton's 24

DALLAS/FT. WORTH

AMERICAN (NEW)
Ⓩ Aurora 28
Cafe Aspen 22
Craft Dallas -
Goodhues 26
Grape, The 25
Local 27
Ⓩ Lola 28
Ⓩ Mansion/Turtle Creek 26
Mercury Grill 26
Nana 27
62 Main 23
Ⓩ York St. 28

AMERICAN (TRADITIONAL)
Babe's Chicken 26
Ⓩ French Room 29

BAKERIES
La Duni Latin 25

BARBECUE
Angelo's BBQ 24

CONTINENTAL
Hôtel St. Germain 26

ECLECTIC
Ⓩ Abacus 28

FRENCH
Ⓩ French Room 29
Hôtel St. Germain 26
Lavendou 24
Saint-Emilion 28

FRENCH (NEW)
Bijoux -

ITALIAN
Bice -

JAPANESE
(* sushi specialist)
Nobu Dallas* 25
Tei Tei Robata* 27
Teppo* 27

PAN-ASIAN
Steel 24

PAN-LATIN
La Duni Latin 25

SEAFOOD
Ⓩ Café Pacific 27
Oceanaire 26

SOUTHWESTERN
Bonnell's 27
Fearing's -
Lonesome Dove 27
Reata 23
Stephan Pyles -

STEAKHOUSES
Al Biernat's 26
Capital Grille 25
Ⓩ Del Frisco's 27
Pappas Bros. 27

TEX-MEX
Joe T. Garcia's 20
Ⓩ Mi Cocina 21

THAI
Chow Thai 23

DENVER AREA & MOUNTAIN RESORTS

AMERICAN (NEW)
Duo 24
Flagstaff House 26
Ⓩ Fruition 28
Highland's Garden 25
Juniper 26
Keystone Ranch 27
Ⓩ Mizuna 28
Montagna 26
Palace Arms 25
Potager 25

subscribe to zagat.com

Gravitas	22
☑ Mark's American	28
Mockingbird Bistro	24
Remington	26
17	25
Shade	25
t'afia	24

BRAZILIAN
Fogo de Chão	26

CONTINENTAL
Tony's	26

CREOLE
☑ Brennan's	27

ECLECTIC
Shade	25

FRENCH
☑ Bistro Moderne	27
Chez Nous	27

INDIAN
Indika	26
Kiran's	25

ITALIAN
Amici	-
Arcodoro	23
☑ Carrabba's	23
☑ Da Marco	27
Dolce Vita	-
Frenchie's	26
Quattro	25

MEDITERRANEAN
Ibiza	24

MEXICAN
Hugo's	23

PAN-LATIN
Red Onion	24

PIZZA
Dolce Vita	-

SEAFOOD
Goode Co.	23
Oceanaire	26
Pesce	23
Red Onion	24

Reef	-
Tony Mandola's	24

SMALL PLATES
Catalan | Amer.
	-

SOUTH AMERICAN
Américas	25
Churrascos	26

SOUTHERN
Backstreet Café	24

SOUTHWESTERN
☑ Brennan's	27
☑ Cafe Annie	26

SPANISH
(* tapas specialist)
Ibiza*	24

STEAKHOUSES
Capital Grille	25
Churrascos	26
Fogo de Chão	26
☑ Pappas Bros.	27
Strip House	25
Vic & Anthony's	26

KANSAS CITY

AMERICAN (NEW)
American Restaurant	26
☑ Bluestem	27
Café Sebastienne	24
☑ 40 Sardines	26
MelBee's	26
1924 Main	24
Starker's Reserve	25
Swizzle	23

AMERICAN (TRADITIONAL)
☑ Fiorella's Jack Stack	25
Room 39	26

BARBECUE
Danny Edwards'	25
☑ Fiorella's Jack Stack	25
☑ Oklahoma Joe's	26

ECLECTIC
Grand St. Cafe	24

FRENCH

PotPie	25
☑ Tatsu's	26

FRENCH (BISTRO)

☑ Le Fou Frog	26

ITALIAN
(N=Northern)

☑ Lidia's | N	23
Trezo Mare	24

SEAFOOD

☑ McCormick & Schmick's	23
Trezo Mare	24

SMALL PLATES

MelBee's | Amer.	26

STEAKHOUSES

☑ Plaza III	26

LAS VEGAS

AMERICAN (NEW)

☑ Aureole	25
Bradley Ogden	26
David Burke/American	–
Medici Café	26
Mix	23
☑ Rosemary's	28
Spago	23
Tableau	26

AMERICAN (TRADITIONAL)

Sterling Brunch	26

CAJUN

Emeril's	23

CALIFORNIAN

Nobhill	26

CHINESE
(* dim sum specialist)

Ping Pang Pong*	23

CREOLE

Emeril's	23

ECLECTIC

☑ Bellagio Buffet	24
Todd's Unique Dining	26

FRENCH

Alex	26
André's	27
Eiffel Tower	22
Pamplemousse	26

FRENCH (BISTRO)

Bouchon	24
Le Provençal	21

FRENCH (NEW)

Fleur de Lys	26
Guy Savoy	–
Joël Robuchon	–
L'Atelier/Robuchon	–
Le Cirque	26
Mix	23
☑ Picasso	27

ITALIAN
(S=Southern)

Bartolotta	26
Le Provençal	21
Rao's | S	–

JAPANESE
(* sushi specialist)

☑ Nobu*	27
Okada*	26

MEDITERRANEAN

Alex	26

PIZZA

Le Provençal	21
Spago	23

SEAFOOD

Bartolotta	26
Craftsteak	25
Emeril's	23
Joe's Sea/Steak	24
☑ Michael Mina	27

SMALL PLATES

☑ Rosemary's | Amer.	28

SOUTHWESTERN

Mesa Grill	24

STEAKHOUSES

Craftsteak	25
☑ Delmonico Steak	26

Joe's Sea/Steak 24
☑ Prime Steak 27
Pullman Grille 20
Steak House 26
SW Steak 26

THAI
☑ Lotus of Siam 28

LONG ISLAND

AMERICAN (NEW)
Barney's 25
Chachama Grill 27
Della Femina 25
Fifth Season 27
F.O.O.D. 27
☑ Jedediah's 27
Mill River Inn 27
☑ North Fork Table 27
Panama Hatties 27
Piccolo 27
Plaza Cafe 27
Polo 27
Starr Boggs 26
☑ West End Cafe 25

AMERICAN (TRADITIONAL)
☑ Cheesecake Factory 20
Vine Street 25

CHINESE
(* dim sum specialist)
Orient* 26

CONTINENTAL
Dave's Grill 26

DESSERT
☑ Cheesecake Factory 20

ECLECTIC
La Plage 27
☑ Maroni Cuisine 28
Mill River Inn 27
Mirko's 26

FRENCH
Barney's 25
F.O.O.D. 27
Le Soir 27

Mirabelle 27
Stone Creek 26

FRENCH (BISTRO)
☑ Kitchen à Bistro 27

FRENCH (NEW)
Louis XVI 25

ITALIAN
(N=Northern; S=Southern)
Bravo Nader! | S 25
Dario's | N 27
Galleria Dominick | N 25
Giulio Cesare | N 26
Harvest on Fort Pond | N 26
Il Mulino NY | N 26
La Piccola Liguria | N 26
☑ Maroni Cuisine 28
Piccolo 27
Rialto | N 26

JAPANESE
(* sushi specialist)
☑ Kotobuki* 28
Nisen* 26

MEDITERRANEAN
Harvest on Fort Pond 26
Stone Creek 26

SEAFOOD
Dave's Grill 26
☑ Kitchen à Bistro 27
Plaza Cafe 27
Starr Boggs 26

STEAKHOUSES
☑ Bryant & Cooper 26
☑ Peter Luger 27
Tellers 25

THAI
Siam Lotus 26

LOS ANGELES

AMERICAN (NEW)
bld 21
Brentwood, The 21
Craft -
Foundry on Melrose -
Grace 25

Hatfield's 27
Josie 27
☑ Mélisse 28
Providence 27

**AMERICAN
(TRADITIONAL)**
Grill on Alley 24

ASIAN
Chaya 23

CALIFORNIAN
☑ A.O.C. 26
☑ Café Bizou 23
Campanile 26
Derek's 27
JiRaffe 26
Leila's 27
Rustic Canyon 21
☑ Spago 27

CONTINENTAL
☑ Brandywine 27

DELIS
Brent's Deli 26

DESSERT
Campanile 26
Grace 25
Providence 27
☑ Spago 27

ECLECTIC
Chaya 23

FRENCH
☑ A.O.C. 26
Derek's 27
☑ Mélisse 28

FRENCH (BISTRO)
☑ Café Bizou 23
Mimosa 22

FRENCH (NEW)
La Cachette 27
Sona 27

ITALIAN
Angelini Osteria 27
Capo 26
Piccolo 27

Pizzeria Mozza 26
Tuscany 27

JAPANESE
(* sushi specialist)
☑ Asanebo* 28
Hamasaku* 27
Katsu-ya* 27
☑ Matsuhisa* 27
Mori Sushi* 26
☑ Nobu Malibu* 28
Sushi Nozawa* 27

JEWISH
Brent's Deli 26

MEDITERRANEAN
Campanile 26
Fraiche _
Rustic Canyon 21

MEXICAN
Babita 27

PIZZA
Pizzeria Mozza 26

SEAFOOD
Providence 27
☑ Water Grill 27

SMALL PLATES
☑ A.O.C. | Calif./French 26
Rustic Canyon | Med. 21

STEAKHOUSES
Cut 26

MIAMI

AMERICAN (NEW)
☑ Barton G. 22
Michael's Genuine 25
☑ Michy's 28
North One 25
Talula 24
Wish 24

**AMERICAN
(TRADITIONAL)**
Cheesecake Factory 20

ARGENTINEAN
Graziano's 24

BRAZILIAN
SushiSamba — 22

CALIFORNIAN
Table 8 — 22

CARIBBEAN
Off the Grille — 26
Ortanique — 25

CHINESE
(* dim sum specialist)
Tropical Chinese* — 26

CUBAN
Versailles — 21

ECLECTIC
Azul — 26
Chef Allen's — 26

FRENCH
Café Pastis — 23
Z Michy's — 28

FRENCH (NEW)
Z Blue Door — 24
Z Palme d'Or — 27
Pascal's — 27

ITALIAN
(N=Northern)
Café Ragazzi — 23
Caffe Vialetto — 26
Casa Tua | N — 24
Escopazzo — 26
Osteria del Teatro | N — 26
Z Romeo's Cafe | N — 27
Timo — 25

JAPANESE
(* sushi specialist)
Hiro's Yakko — 26
Matsuri* — 26
Z Nobu* — 27
SushiSamba* — 22

MEDITERRANEAN
Azul — 26
Timo — 25

NEW WORLD
Chef Allen's — 26
Ortanique — 25

NUEVO LATINO
Cacao — 26
OLA — 24

PERUVIAN
Francesco — 26
Z Nobu — 27
SushiSamba — 22

SEAFOOD
Bonefish Grill — 22
Francesco — 26
Z Joe's Stone Crab — 26
Oceanaire — 26
Z Prime One — 27
Quinn's — 26

SMALL PLATES
Z Michy's | Med. — 28

STEAKHOUSES
Bonefish Grill — 22
Capital Grille — 26
Graziano's — 24
Z Prime One — 27

THAI
Tamarind — 24

VIETNAMESE
Little Saigon — 22

MILWAUKEE

AMERICAN (NEW)
Z Bacchus — 26
Dream Dance — 25
Z Immigrant Room — 26
Z Sanford — 29

AMERICAN (TRADITIONAL)
Riversite, The — 25

CALIFORNIAN
Roots — 25

CHINESE
Z P.F. Chang's — 20

FRENCH
Coquette Cafe — 25
Z Lake Park — 25

FRENCH (BISTRO)
Elliot's Bistro — 20

ITALIAN
(N=Northern)
☒ Maggiano's — 20
Osteria del Mondo | N — 25
Ristorante Bartolotta — 25

JAPANESE
(* sushi specialist)
Sake Tumi* — 25

KOREAN
(* barbecue specialist)
Sake Tumi* — 25

SANDWICHES
☒ Potbelly Sandwich — 20

SEAFOOD
River Lane Inn — 25

STEAKHOUSES
☒ Eddie Martini's — 26
☒ Five O'Clock — 26
Jake's Fine Dining — 25

THAI
Singha Thai — 24

MINNEAPOLIS/ST. PAUL

AMERICAN (NEW)
☒ Alma — 28
B.A.N.K. — 21
☒ Bayport Cookery — 28
Cue — 20
☒ Lucia's — 27
Town Talk — 22
20.21 — 26

AMERICAN (REGIONAL)
Dakota Jazz — 21
Heartland — 26

AMERICAN (TRADITIONAL)
St. Paul Grill — 24
Town Talk — 22

ASIAN FUSION
Chambers Kitchen — 25

ECLECTIC
Cosmos — 24
☒ 112 Eatery — 28

FRENCH (BISTRO)
☒ Vincent — 27

FRENCH (NEW)
Fugaise — 26
☒ La Belle Vie — 28

ITALIAN
(N=Northern)
D'Amico Cucina | N — 27

MEDITERRANEAN
☒ La Belle Vie — 28

SEAFOOD
☒ Oceanaire — 26

SPANISH
(* tapas specialist)
Solera* — 23

STEAKHOUSES
☒ Manny's — 26

NEW JERSEY

AMERICAN (NEW)
☒ Amanda's — 26
André's — 27
Bernards Inn — 26
Blue Bottle — 27
Copeland — 25
CulinAriane — 27
David Burke — 26
David Drake — 27
Dining Room — 26
Ebbitt Room — 27
Frog and the Peach — 26
☒ Nicholas — 29
Pluckemin Inn — 25
Saddle River Inn — 27
Whispers — 27

AMERICAN (TRADITIONAL)
☒ Bay Avenue Trattoria — 28
☒ Cheesecake Factory — 19
Perryville Inn — 26

Jacques-Imo's Café	27
Mandina's	-
Muriel's Jackson Square	23
Napoleon House	19
Upperline	26
Vizard's on the Avenue	27

ECLECTIC

Dick & Jenny's	27

FRENCH

Bistro at Maison de Ville	-
☑ Galatoire's	27
La Provence	27

FRENCH (BISTRO)

☑ Alberta	28
La Petite Grocery	26
Lilette	26
Martinique Bistro	25

FRENCH (NEW)

☑ August	28
Gautreau's	-
Herbsaint	27

ITALIAN
(S=Southern)

Eleven 79	-
Irene's Cuisine | S	26
Mosca's	27

MEDITERRANEAN

Napoleon House	19
Vizard's on the Avenue	27

SEAFOOD

Acme Oyster	22
Arnaud's	26
Mandina's	-
Martinique Bistro	25

SMALL PLATES

Cochon | Cajun	25
Herbsaint | Amer.	27

SOUL FOOD

Jacques-Imo's Café	27

STEAKHOUSES

Dickie Brennan's	26
Rib Room	25

AMERICAN (NEW)

Annisa	27
Aureole	27
BLT Market	-
Blue Hill	26
Gotham B&G	27
☑ Gramercy Tavern	27
Modern, The	26
☑ Per Se	28
River Café	26
Saul	27
Telepan	25
Tocqueville	26
☑ Union Square Cafe	26

AMERICAN (TRADITIONAL)

Tavern on the Green	15
21 Club	22
Waverly Inn	18

ASIAN FUSION

Buddakan	23

AUSTRIAN

Danube	26

BARBECUE

Hill Country	-

CHINESE
(* dim sum specialist)

Oriental Garden*	24
Shun Lee Palace	24
Wakiya	-

CONTINENTAL

Four Seasons	25

DELIS

Carnegie Deli	21

EUROPEAN

Cru	26

FRENCH

Bouley	28
Café Boulud	27
Café des Artistes	22
Chanterelle	27
☑ Daniel	28

Eleven Madison 26
Gordon Ramsay 25
⚏ Jean Georges 28
La Grenouille 27
L'Atelier/Robuchon 27
⚏ Le Bernardin 28
Modern, The 26
⚏ Per Se 28
Picholine 27
Tocqueville 26

FRENCH (BRASSERIE)
Balthazar 23

GREEK
Anthos 25
Milos 26

ITALIAN
(N=Northern; S=Southern)
Alto | N 26
⚏ Babbo 27
Del Posto 25
Il Mulino 27
Rao's | S 22
Roberto 27

JAPANESE
(* sushi specialist)
Masa/Bar Masa* 27
Morimoto 24
Nobu* 27
Sushi Seki* 27
⚏ Sushi Yasuda* 28

JEWISH
Carnegie Deli 21

MEDITERRANEAN
Picholine 27

PIZZA
Di Fara 27

SEAFOOD
⚏ Le Bernardin 28
Milos 26
Oriental Garden 24

SMALL PLATES
L'Atelier/Robuchon | French 27

SOUTHEAST ASIAN
Spice Market 22

STEAKHOUSES
Palm 24
⚏ Peter Luger 28

ORANGE COUNTY, CA

AMERICAN (NEW)
Bayside 25
Ramos House 26
⚏ Sage 24
⚏ Stonehill Tavern 28

ASIAN FUSION
⚏ Roy's 24

CALIFORNIAN
Cafe Zoolu 26
⚏ Napa Rose 27
Studio 27

CARIBBEAN
Golden Truffle 26

CONTINENTAL
⚏ Hobbit, The 27

ECLECTIC
Onotria 24

FRENCH
⚏ Basilic 28
Golden Truffle 26
⚏ Hobbit, The 27
Marché Moderne –
Pinot Provence 25
⚏ Tradition by Pascal 27

FRENCH (BISTRO)
⚏ French 75 21

FRENCH (NEW)
Studio 27

HAWAIIAN
⚏ Roy's 24

JAPANESE
(* sushi specialist)
Bluefin* 25

SEAFOOD
Tabu Grill 26

CUISINES

STEAKHOUSES
⊠ Fleming Prime — 25
Mastro's Steak — 25
Tabu Grill — 26

SWISS
⊠ Basilic — 28

ORLANDO

AFRICAN
Boma — 24
Jiko — 25

AMERICAN (NEW)
Beacon, The — -
Boheme, The — 23
HUE — 24
⊠ Seasons 52 — 25
⊠ Victoria & Albert's — 27

ASIAN
Emeril's Tchoup Chop — 23

CALIFORNIAN
⊠ California Grill — 26
⊠ Wolfgang Puck Café — 21

CHINESE
(* dim sum specialist)
Ming's Bistro* — -

CONTEMPORARY LOUISIANA
⊠ Emeril's Orlando — 24

CONTINENTAL
⊠ Chatham's Place — 27
Venetian Room — 24

ECLECTIC
Blue Bistro & Grill — 24
K Restaurant/Bar — 25

FRENCH
⊠ Le Coq au Vin — 27

FRENCH (BISTRO)
Chez Vincent — 23

HAWAIIAN
Roy's — 25

ITALIAN
(N=Northern)
Antonio's | N — 25
Christini's — 24
Enzo's — 25
Primo — 26

JAPANESE
(* sushi specialist)
Amura* — 26
Shari Sushi* — 22
Wazzabi* — -

MEDITERRANEAN
Fifi's — -

MEXICAN
⊠ Taquitos Jalisco — 27

NEW WORLD
Norman's — 26

POLYNESIAN
Emeril's Tchoup Chop — 23

SEAFOOD
Beluga — -
MoonFish — 23
Todd English's bluezoo — 24

STEAKHOUSES
⊠ Del Frisco's — 27
Fleming's Prime — 23
Kres Chophouse — 22
MoonFish — 23
Palm — 24
Ruth's Chris — 25
Vito's Chop House — 25

THAI
Thai House — 25
Thai Thani — 24

PALM BEACH

AMERICAN (NEW)
Cafe Chardonnay — 26
11 Maple Street — 26
⊠ Four Seasons/Restaurant — 27
⊠ Seasons 52 — 23
32 East — 25

AMERICAN (TRADITIONAL)
Cheesecake Factory — 20
Houston's — 21

CONTINENTAL
Café L'Europe — 25
Kathy's Gazebo — 26

FRENCH	
☒ Café Boulud	26
☒ Chez Jean-Pierre	27

FRENCH (NEW)	
☒ L'Escalier	27

HAMBURGERS	
☒ Café Boulud	26

ITALIAN	
☒ Marcello's	27
Trattoria Romana	25

JAPANESE
(* sushi specialist)

Sushi Jo's*	25

SEAFOOD	
Bonefish Grill	22
Chops Lobster Bar	26
☒ Kee Grill	24
☒ Little Moirs	27

STEAKHOUSES	
☒ Abe & Louie's	25
Chops Lobster Bar	26
☒ New York Prime	25

PHILADELPHIA

AMERICAN (NEW)	
Alison at Blue Bell	26
Gayle	26
Jake's	25
James	-
Mainland Inn	26
Marigold Kitchen	25
Rae	-
Southwark	24
Swann Lounge	26
Twenty Manning	21

ASIAN	
☒ Buddakan	27
Twenty Manning	21

CALIFORNIAN	
Sovalo	25

CHINESE	
Shiao Lan Kung	25
Susanna Foo	25

CONTINENTAL	
☒ Fountain	28

FRENCH	
☒ Birchrunville Store	28
Gilmore's	27
La Bonne Auberge	26
☒ Lacroix	27
Nan	26
Overtures	24
Paloma	26
Savona	27
Susanna Foo	25

FRENCH (BISTRO)	
☒ Le Bar Lyonnais	28

FRENCH (NEW)	
☒ Brasserie Perrier	26
☒ Fountain	28
☒ Le Bec-Fin	28
Swann Lounge	26

GREEK	
Dmitri's	24

ITALIAN
(N=Northern; S=Southern)

☒ Birchrunville Store	28
L'Angolo | S	26
Melograno | N	25
Osteria	-
Savona	27
Sovalo	25
☒ Vetri	28

JAPANESE
(* sushi specialist)

Bluefin*	27
Morimoto	27

MEDITERRANEAN	
Overtures	24

MEXICAN	
Paloma	26
Xochitl	-

PIZZA	
Osteria	-

SEAFOOD	
Blackfish	-
Dmitri's	24
Striped Bass	26

CUISINES

SMALL PLATES
Lacroix | French — 27

SPANISH
(* tapas specialist)
Amada* — 27
Tinto* — –

STEAKHOUSES
Prime Rib — 25

THAI
Nan — 26

VEGETARIAN
Blue Sage — 26

PHOENIX/SCOTTSDALE

AMERICAN (NEW)
Binkley's — 27
elements — 25
Lon's — 24
Rancho Pinot — 25

ASIAN
Asia de Cuba — –

CHINESE
P.F. Chang's — 21

CUBAN
Asia de Cuba — –

FRENCH (BISTRO)
Christopher's Fermier — 24

FRENCH (NEW)
Mary Elaine's — 27
Vincent's/Camelback — 26

HAWAIIAN
Roy's — 24

ITALIAN
Postino — 24

JAPANESE
(* sushi specialist)
Sea Saw* — 28

MEDITERRANEAN
T. Cook's — 27

MEXICAN
Barrio Cafe — 27

PIZZA
Pizzeria Bianco — 28

SEAFOOD
Eddie V's — 26

SPANISH
(* tapas specialist)
Sol y Sombra* — –

STEAKHOUSES
Eddie V's — 26
Mastro's City/Steak — 27
Mastro's Steak — 26

VIETNAMESE
Cyclo — 26

PORTLAND, OR

AMERICAN (NEW)
Bluehour — 23
Hurley's — 25
Park Kitchen — 25

FRENCH
Heathman — 26
Hurley's — 25
Le Pigeon — –
Paley's Place — 27

ITALIAN
(N=Northern)
Alba Osteria | N — 24
Caffe Mingo — 26
Genoa — 27

JAPANESE
(* sushi specialist)
Hiroshi* — –

MEDITERRANEAN
Bluehour — 23
Tabla — 26

MEXICAN
Nuestra Cocina — 26

PACIFIC NORTHWEST
Alberta St. Oyster — 26
Heathman — 26
Higgins — 26
Joel Palmer — 26
Paley's Place — 27
Park Kitchen — 25
Wildwood — 25

PERUVIAN
Andina — 25

PIZZA
🅉 Apizza Scholls — 27

SOUTHEAST ASIAN
Pok Pok — _

SPANISH
(* tapas specialist)
Toro Bravo* — _

THAI
Pok Pok — _

SALT LAKE CITY & MOUNTAIN RESORTS

AMERICAN (NEW)
🅉 Bambara — 24
Glitretind — 25
Log Haven — 24
🅉 Mariposa, The — 27
Metropolitan — 25

AMERICAN (REGIONAL)
Tree Room — 25

AMERICAN (TRADITIONAL)
Chez Betty — 25
Franck's — 24
🅉 New Yorker Club — 24

ASIAN
🅉 Shabu — 26

ASIAN FUSION
Wahso — 25

CONTINENTAL
Chez Betty — 25

ECLECTIC
Jean Louis — 21

FRENCH
Franck's — 24

ITALIAN
(N=Northern)
🅉 Cucina Toscana | N — 26
Lugano | N — 24

JAPANESE
(* sushi specialist)
🅉 Takashi* — 27

LEBANESE
🅉 Mazza — 26

MEDITERRANEAN
Martine — 25

MEXICAN
🅉 Red Iguana — 26

SEAFOOD
🅉 Market Street — 23
Seafood Buffet — 25

SMALL PLATES
Martine | Med. — 25
🅉 Takashi | Jap. — 27

STEAKHOUSES
🅉 New Yorker Club — 24

SAN ANTONIO

AMERICAN (NEW)
🅉 Biga on the Banks — 26
Bin 555 — _
🅉 Lodge/Castle Hills — 27
Silo — 25

ASIAN FUSION
Frederick's — 25

BELGIAN
La Frite — _

CHINESE
🅉 P.F. Chang's — 22

ECLECTIC
Grill at Leon Springs — _
Liberty Bar — 23

FRENCH
🅉 Bistro Vatel — 26
Frederick's — 25
Las Canarias — 25
L'Etoile — 26

FRENCH (NEW)
🅉 Le Rêve — 28

ITALIAN
🅉 Paesanos — 22

KOREAN
(* barbecue specialist)
🅉 Korean B.B.Q. House* — 26

CUISINES

MEDITERRANEAN
Grill at Leon Springs — -
Las Canarias — 25

PAN-LATIN
Cafe Paladar — -

SEAFOOD
Boudro's/Riverwalk — 24
L'Etoile — 26
Pesca on the River — 22

SOUTHWESTERN
Francesca's — 25

SPANISH
(* tapas specialist)
Cafe Paladar* — -

STEAKHOUSES
Boudro's/Riverwalk — 24
Fleming's Prime — 25

TEX-MEX
Ácenar — 22

SAN DIEGO

AMERICAN (NEW)
Arterra — 27
Pamplemousse Grille — 27

ASIAN FUSION
Roppongi — 24

CALIFORNIAN
A.R. Valentien — 27
George's Cal. Modern — 25
Grant Grill — -
Quarter Kitchen — -

ECLECTIC
Marine Room — 24

FRENCH
El Bizcocho — 26
Laurel — 24
Marine Room — 24
Pamplemousse Grille — 27

FRENCH (BRASSERIE)
WineSellar — 27

FRENCH (NEW)
Mille Fleurs — 25
Tapenade — 26

JAPANESE
(* sushi specialist)
Sushi Ota* — 27

MEDITERRANEAN
Laurel — 24

MEXICAN
Ortega's — 24

SEAFOOD
Blue Coral — -
Oceanaire — 26

STEAKHOUSES
Donovan's — 26
Ruth's Chris — 25

THAI
Rama — 26

SAN FRANCISCO BAY AREA

AMERICAN (NEW)
Ame — 26
Boulevard — 27
French Laundry — 29
Gary Danko — 29
Manresa — 27
Michael Mina — 28
Myth — 26
Range — 26

AMERICAN (TRADITIONAL)
ad hoc — 26
Lark Creek Inn — 23

CALIFORNIAN
Aqua — 26
Canteen — 25
Chez Panisse — 27
Chez Panisse Café — 27
Coi — 25
Erna's Elderberry — 28
Farmhouse Inn — 27
Fleur de Lys — 28
Jardinière — 26
NoPa — 23
Redd — 26
Rivoli — 27

subscribe to zagat.com

FRENCH
Aqua	26
Coi	25
Z French Laundry	29
Jardinière	26
La Folie	27
La Toque	26

FRENCH (BISTRO)
Bistro Jeanty	25
Chapeau!	27

FRENCH (NEW)
Z Cyrus	28
Z Erna's Elderberry	28
Z Fleur de Lys	28
Le Papillon	27
Masa's	27
Quince	26
Ritz/Din. Rm.	27

ITALIAN
(N=Northern)
Acquerello	27
Delfina | N	26
Oliveto	25
Perbacco	24
Quince	26

JAPANESE
(* sushi specialist)
Kaygetsu*	28
Sushi Ran*	28

MEDITERRANEAN
Chez Panisse	27
Chez Panisse Café	27
Rivoli	27
Zuni Café	25

SEAFOOD
Aqua	26

VEGETARIAN
Greens	24

VIETNAMESE
Z Slanted Door	26

SEATTLE

AMERICAN (NEW)
Cascadia	25
Crush	25
Earth & Ocean	22
Z Lampreia	28
Lark	28
Z Mistral	28
Nell's	26
Union	25

BAKERIES
Bakery Nouveau	-
Macrina	25

CARIBBEAN
Paseo	28

DESSERT
Macrina	25

ECLECTIC
Sitka & Spruce	-

FRENCH
Bakery Nouveau	-
Campagne	26
Georgian, The	26

FRENCH (BISTRO)
Boat Street Cafe	26

FRENCH (CLASSIC)
Le Gourmand	27

FRENCH (NEW)
Z Mistral	28
Z Rover's	28

ITALIAN
(N=Northern)
Armandino's Salumi	28
Boat Street Cafe	26
Z Cafe Juanita | N	28
Il Terrazzo Carmine	26
Tavolàta	-
Volterra | N	26

JAPANESE
(* sushi specialist)
Chiso*	27
Z Nishino*	28
Shiro's Sushi*	27
Toyoda Sushi*	27

MEDITERRANEAN
Carmelita	25

MEXICAN
La Carta de Oaxaca | 26

PACIFIC NORTHWEST
🔳 Canlis | 27
🔳 Dahlia Lounge | 26
Georgian, The | 26
🔳 Herbfarm, The | 28
Inn at Langley | 27
🔳 Lampreia | 28
Nell's | 26

PACIFIC RIM
🔳 Wild Ginger | 25

SANDWICHES
Armandino's Salumi | 28
🔳 Cafe Juanita | 28

SEAFOOD
🔳 Canlis | 27
Seastar | 26

SPANISH
(* tapas specialist)
Harvest Vine* | 27

STEAKHOUSES
El Gaucho | 25
JaK's Grill | 26
🔳 Metropolitan Grill | 26

VEGETARIAN
Carmelita | 25

VIETNAMESE
Green Leaf | 24
Monsoon | 25

ST. LOUIS

AMERICAN (NEW)
Cardwell's at the Plaza | 25
Crossing | 26
Frazer's | 24
Harvest | 25
🔳 Niche | 27
Pomme | 27
🔳 Sidney Street Cafe | 28
Truffles | 23
Zinnia | 24

AMERICAN (TRADITIONAL)
American Place | 25
🔳 Annie Gunn's | 26

CALIFORNIAN
🔳 1111 Mississippi | 25

FRENCH
Atlas | 26

FRENCH (BISTRO)
Chez Leon | 26

FRENCH (NEW)
Pomme | 27

ITALIAN
(N=Northern; S=Southern)
Acero | –
Atlas | 26
Dominic's | 27
🔳 1111 Mississippi | N | 25
🔳 Paul Manno's | S | 28
🔳 Tony's | 27
🔳 Trattoria Marcella | 27

SEAFOOD
Al's Restaurant | 27

STEAKHOUSES
Al's Restaurant | 27

TAMPA/SARASOTA

AMERICAN (NEW)
Black Pearl | 26
🔳 Cafe Ponte | 28
Michael's On East | 24
🔳 Mise en Place | 26
🔳 SideBern's | 27

AMERICAN (TRADITIONAL)
Americano | –
Marlin Darlin' Grill | –

BAKERIES
Pane Rustica | 26

CARIBBEAN
🔳 Columbia | 20

CONTINENTAL
🔳 Bijou Café | 25

ECLECTIC

Euphemia Haye	26
Fly Bar & Restaurant	–
Pane Rustica	26
Savant	–

FLORIDIAN

☑ Beach Bistro	27

FRENCH

☑ Restaurant B.T.	27

HAWAIIAN

☑ Roy's	26

ITALIAN
(N=Northern)

Americano	–
Armani's | N	26

MEDITERRANEAN

Marchand's B&G	24

PIZZA

Pane Rustica	26

SANDWICHES

Pane Rustica	26

SEAFOOD

☑ Roy's	26
Table, The	–

STEAKHOUSES

☑ Bern's	26

VIETNAMESE

☑ Restaurant B.T.	27

TUCSON

AMERICAN (NEW)

☑ Dish, The	28
☑ Grill/Hacienda del Sol	26
Kingfisher B&G	22
Montana Avenue	–
Ventana Room	25
Vintabla	–
☑ Wildflower	24

AMERICAN (REGIONAL)

Montana Avenue	–

BAKERIES

Beyond Bread	24

ECLECTIC

Cuvée World Bistro	23
Feast	25

FRENCH

☑ Le Rendez-Vous	26

ITALIAN
(N=Northern)

Tavolino | N	25
☑ Vivace | N	26

MALAYSIAN

Neo of Melaka	–

MEXICAN

Blanco Tacos	–
☑ Cafe Poca Cosa	26

NUEVO LATINO

J Bar	23

SANDWICHES

Beyond Bread	24

SEAFOOD

Kingfisher B&G	22

SMALL PLATES

Vintabla | Amer.	–

SOUTHWESTERN

☑ Janos	25
☑ Terra Cotta	22

STEAKHOUSES

McMahon's Prime	23

WASHINGTON, DC

AMERICAN (NEW)

BlackSalt	26
Black's Bar/Kitchen	23
Blue Duck	26
Central Michel Richard	26
CityZen	26
Equinox	25
☑ Eve	27
Farrah Olivia	–
Hook	–
☑ Inn/Little Washington	29
Johnny's Half Shell	–
Komi	26
Palena	26

CUISINES

ALPHABETICAL
PAGE INDEX

Ⓩ indicates places with the highest ratings, popularity and importance.

ALPHA INDEX

ALPHA INDEX

ALPHA INDEX

ALPHA INDEX

ALPHA INDEX

ALPHA INDEX

Wine Vintage Chart

This chart, based on our 0 to 30 scale, is designed to help you select wine. The ratings (by **Howard Stravitz,** a law professor at the University of South Carolina) reflect the vintage quality and the wine's readiness to drink. We exclude the 1991–1993 vintages because they are not that good. A dash indicates the wine is either past its peak or too young to rate. Loire ratings are for dry white wines.

Whites

	88	89	90	94	95	96	97	98	99	00	01	02	03	04	05	06
French:																
Alsace	-	25	25	24	23	23	22	25	23	25	27	25	22	24	25	-
Burgundy	-	23	22	-	28	27	24	22	26	25	24	27	23	27	26	24
Loire Valley	-	-	-	-	-	-	-	-	-	24	25	26	23	24	27	24
Champagne	24	26	29	-	26	27	24	23	24	24	22	26	-	-	-	-
Sauternes	29	25	28	-	21	23	25	23	24	24	28	25	26	21	26	23
California:																
Chardonnay	-	-	-	-	-	-	-	-	24	23	26	26	25	27	29	25
Sauvignon Blanc	-	-	-	-	-	-	-	-	-	-	27	28	26	27	26	27
Austrian:																
Grüner Velt./Riesling	-	-	-	-	25	21	26	26	25	22	23	25	26	25	26	-
German:	25	26	27	24	23	26	25	26	23	21	29	27	24	26	28	-

Reds

	88	89	90	94	95	96	97	98	99	00	01	02	03	04	05	06
French:																
Bordeaux	23	25	29	22	26	25	23	25	24	29	26	24	25	24	27	25
Burgundy	-	24	26	-	26	27	25	22	27	22	24	27	25	25	27	25
Rhône	26	28	28	24	26	22	25	27	26	27	26	-	25	24	25	-
Beaujolais	-	-	-	-	-	-	-	-	-	24	-	23	25	22	28	26
California:																
Cab./Merlot	-	-	28	29	27	25	28	23	26	22	27	26	25	24	24	23
Pinot Noir	-	-	-	-	-	-	24	23	24	23	27	28	26	25	24	-
Zinfandel	-	-	-	-	-	-	-	-	-	-	25	23	27	24	23	-
Oregon:																
Pinot Noir	-	-	-	-	-	-	-	-	-	-	-	27	25	26	27	-
Italian:																
Tuscany	-	-	25	22	24	20	29	24	27	24	27	20	25	25	22	24
Piedmont	-	27	27	-	23	26	27	26	25	28	27	20	24	25	26	-
Spanish:																
Rioja	-	-	-	26	26	24	25	22	25	24	27	20	24	25	26	24
Ribera del Duero/Priorat	-	-	-	26	26	27	25	24	25	24	27	20	24	26	26	24
Australian:																
Shiraz/Cab.	-	-	-	24	26	23	26	28	24	24	27	27	25	26	24	-
Chilean:	-	-	-	-	-	-	24	-	25	23	26	24	25	24	26	-

subscribe to zagat.com

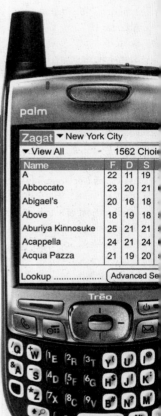

Zagat Products

RESTAURANTS & MAPS

America's Top Restaurants
Atlanta
Boston
Brooklyn (best of)
California Wine Country
Cape Cod & The Islands
Chicago (guide & map)
Connecticut
Downtown NYC
Europe's Top Restaurants
Hamptons (incl. wineries)
Las Vegas (incl. nightlife)
London
London (best of)
Long Island (incl. wineries)
Los Angeles I So. California
(guide & map)
Miami Beach
Miami I So. Florida
Montréal (best of)
New Jersey
New Jersey Shore
New Orleans (best of)
New York City (guide & map)
Palm Beach
Paris
Philadelphia
San Francisco (guide & map)
Seattle
St. Louis
Texas
Tokyo
Toronto (best of)
Vancouver (best of)
Washington, DC I Baltimore
Westchester I Hudson Valley

LIFESTYLE GUIDES

America's Top Golf Courses
Movie Guide
Music Guide
NYC Gour. Shopping/Ent
NYC Shopping

NIGHTLIFE GUIDES

Las Vegas (incl. restaurants)
London
Los Angeles
New Orleans (best of)
New York City
San Francisco

HOTEL & TRAVEL GUIDES

Top U.S. Hotels, Resorts & Spas
U.S. Family Travel
Walt Disney World Insider's Guide
World's Top Hotels, Resorts & Spas

WEB & WIRELESS SERVICES

ZAGAT TO GO℠ for handhelds
Subscribe to ZAGAT.com
ZAGAT.mobi